THE MATURING MARKETPLACE

THE MATURING MARKETPLACE

Buying Habits of Baby Boomers and Their Parents

George P. Moschis,
Euehun Lee, Anil Mathur,
and Jennifer Strautman

QUORUM BOOKS
Westport, Connecticut • London

Library of Congress Cataloging-in-Publication Data

The maturing marketplace : buying habits of baby boomers and their
    parents / George P. Moschis . . . [et al.].
        p. cm.
    Includes bibliographical references and index.
    ISBN 1–56720–344–2 (alk. paper)
    1. Consumer behavior—United States.   2. Baby boom generation—
United States—Attitudes.   3. Middle aged consumers—United States—
Attitudes.   4. Aged consumers—United States—Attitudes.   5. Market
segmentation—United States.   I. Moschis, George P., 1944– .
HF5415.33.U6M36   2000
658.8'34'0844–dc21   99–36602

British Library Cataloguing in Publication Data is available.

Library of Congress Catalog Card Number: 99–36602
ISBN: 1–56720–344–2

First published in 2000

Quorum Books, 88 Post Road West, Westport, CT 06881
An imprint of Greenwood Publishing Group, Inc.
www.quorumbooks.com

Printed in the United States of America

The paper used in this book complies with the
Permanent Paper Standard issued by the National
Information Standards Organization (Z39.48–1984).

10 9 8 7 6 5 4 3 2 1

Contents

Tables

Acknowledgments

The authors wish to thank Annie Dillard for her assistance with the preparation of this book.

1

Overview

If you are a baby boomer, you may remember Anne Roberts, who appeared in television commercials for Charlie fragrance and National Airlines in the mid-1970s. You may even remember her in the late 1960s, when she appeared in a magazine ad for *Playboy* dressed as an astronaut, or perhaps in her first commercial urging women to use Johnson & Johnson Baby Shampoo with the slogan "Don't wait to have a baby to try it." What is interesting about Roberts' career as a commercial spokeswoman is that, after losing a soft drink commercial part to a younger model at age 25, she believed her career would end because of her age. Roberts has not only survived the "age scare" in the past three decades, but she is in greater demand today at age 51 than even before. In early 1998, she signed a six-figure TV and print ad deal with Procter & Gamble for Oil of Olay ProVital, a new product line for women over 50.

What has helped insulate Roberts' career is exactly the same thing she was afraid would end it: her *age*. An increasing number of advertisers and marketers use older models and spokespersons. Today there are more spokespersons in their 50s, 60s, and even 70s than ever before, and the familiar faces of older models continue to appear in commercials. For example, actress Jaclyn Smith, in her 50s, is appearing in ads for Rembrandt's first mouthwash and toothpaste for older consumers. At 64, Joan Collins is appearing in advertisements for Old Navy, and Jack Palance, well into his 70s, has been doing television commercials for Brut cologne.

The main factor that has been fueling the trend toward spokespersons with a few wrinkles is a major demographic trend that has been creating dramatic changes in the composition of the consumer market. We call this trend "the aging of America." Never before in the history of our planet have its nations and their people faced the issues, challenges, and opportunities that are being created today by the enormous gains in life expectancies and the aging of the largest age cohort, the baby boomers. In 1900, for example, the life expectancy in the United States was just 47 years. In just less than 100 years, life expectancy has increased to nearly 76 years.

THE MATURING MARKETPLACE

This "aging" trend is a global phenomenon with increasing relevance. In the United States, the number of people age 65 and over is expected to double in just 30 years. In China, this age bracket will nearly triple. While policy makers are concerned with issues of generational equity and federal entitlement programs like Social Security, families must address issues of long-term care. The term "sandwich generation" has recently emerged to describe family members who must spend time and money on elderly relatives and growing children.

While such public and social concerns are becoming widespread, businesses regard the changing demographics as opportunities for satisfying new and emerging needs of the aging consumers and their younger family members. Labels for "new" market segments such as "mature market" and "care givers" of older relatives have been devised to communicate information about the growing subsegments of the consumer market. And as business interest and efforts to tap these segments have grown, so has the concern of various consumer groups that attempt to protect vulnerable consumers from persuasive and unethical business practices.

Businesses and nonprofit organizations that attempt to serve the growing segments of baby boomers and their older relatives need to better understand these aging segments' needs and buying motives, for two important reasons. First, there is little accurate information on older consumers, since the older consumer market had not justified attention on the part of businesses. For example, until very recently the A. C. Nielsen Company would only gather information on consumers under age 50. Not only has the youth orientation in marketing left a broad gap in our knowledge about how to market to older consumers, but the information on younger age groups is of questionable value, since age cohorts differ. For example, by the time the present middle-aged cohort of baby boomers, who were brought up with television, reach the age of 65, they would have spent an average of eleven years of their lives in front of the tube, something that is very different from what older generations have experienced. Age cohorts also differ due to the differences in their experiences with respect to opportunities for education amount and quality, exposure to technology, and so on. Thus, age groups must be understood for their specific needs and situations as consumers. What was learned about certain age groups yesterday may not be relevant to today's consumers in the same age brackets.

During the past 20 years, the authors have done several dozen studies of aging segments of the population. Most of these studies were done through Georgia State University's Center for Mature Consumer Studies. As we spoke to hundreds of business executives who inquired about our research findings, we became cognizant of the information needs of many institutions that try to serve the aging population. We also learned that many of these business executives were basing their business decisions on stereotypes about older consumers, since reliable and relevant data were not readily available. In order to better serve the needs for information that were suggested from our interactions with practitioners in various types of industries, it was necessary to gather information tailored to specific questions of these business decision makers.

THE FOCUS OF OUR STUDIES

To better understand the buying and consumption habits of aging Americans, we sent out 20,000 questionnaires to people from all walks of life in all 50 states. This exhaustive effort ensured that our participant pool would represent the average American in various demographic brackets. Because of the large number of questions we wanted to ask, we used two surveys, each mailed to approximately 10,000 adults. These surveys included questions about a wide variety of topics ranging from main day-to-day concerns to buying habits and purchasing preferences. However, the majority of questions focused on buying and consumption habits and preferences with respect to the following products and services:

- Health-care products and services
- Insurance
- Housing
- Financial services
- Travel and leisure
- Pharmaceutical products
- High-tech products and telecommunication services
- Apparel and footwear
- Food and beverages

Because we were interested in studying the buying habits of older adults, we focused on the consumer behavior of individuals older than the median age (approximately 35 years). Thus, we included in our investigation baby boomers as well as older age groups.

We wanted to learn about aging consumers' preferences for various products and services in these categories, why they choose specific brands or service providers, and other details about their purchasing habits, including the following:

- Product or service ownership and use
- Buying motives
- Sources of purchasing influence
- Patronage reasons
- Methods of purchasing
- Methods of payment

Finally, we wanted to know the extent to which aging Americans from different backgrounds behave differently as consumers of these products and services. In order to do this, we analyzed the responses given to the two surveys by select background characteristics such as demographics and lifestyles. Approximately 3,700 adults completed surveys and provided the basis for our investigation. Some of our findings are highlighted in this section, while detailed findings on buying and consumption habits of aging Americans are presented in the sections that follow. We use the terms "older" and "mature" to refer to individuals age 55 and over; "baby boomers" are those born between 1946 and 1964; "elderly" or "seniors" are those age 65 and older; and "parents" of baby boomers are individuals age 55 and over, since the young baby boomers can have parents as young as 55 years of age.

THE BUYING HABITS OF BABY BOOMERS AND SENIORS

We were interested in the buying and consumption habits of baby boomers as well as older age cohorts. Consequently, our surveys included nearly 1,000 baby boomers from all states, and we compared their responses to the same questions given by older age groups (age 55 and over) and by seniors (age 65 and over). Some findings concerning baby boomers and seniors:

- Although baby boomers have fewer children than seniors, they are ten times more likely to count on their offspring for care in their old age.
- Baby boomers have become more knowledgeable about nutrition during the past ten to fifteen years, in comparison to seniors. However, they have not

changed their eating habits significantly. By contrast, seniors have changed their eating habits in response to their increased knowledge about nutrition.

- *Health-membership programs* that focus almost exclusively on seniors may be missing a huge market, since a larger percentage of baby boomers (68%) than seniors (43%) prefer these programs.
- Generally, in comparison to baby boomers, seniors prefer to receive a wider variety of *nontraditional financial services*, such as insurance products from traditional financial institutions such as banks.
- Home-equity loans and various reverse-mortgage plans are of much greater appeal to baby boomers. Motives for other types of investments also differ between the two groups.
- Twice as many baby boomers (42%) as seniors (19%) plan to move into or stay in a single-family house. About three out of ten in both age groups plan to live in a *retirement community* at some point later in life.
- When it comes to preferences for *investment instruments*, baby boomers are as conservative investors as their elderly counterparts, while the latter group has substantially higher balances in liquid assets and securities.
- Baby boomers are generally more sensitive to price and sales promotions than their elderly counterparts when it comes to choosing an *airline*, a *cruise line*, or a *hotel/motel*.
- Location of a *pharmacy* is more important to baby boomers than to elderly shoppers; the latter group values product/brand availability and personal assistance more than their younger counterparts.
- Baby boomers are three times more likely than the elderly to own a *telephone-answering machine*, but the latter group is twice as likely to own a *home-security* system.
- The most important reasons for both age groups in deciding whether to buy apparel and footwear products from mail-order sources are price and return/ cancellation policy.
- Baby boomers are more price conscious than the elderly when shopping for *grocery products*, with three-fourths of them (in comparison with 62 percent of the seniors) indicating they consider price reduction or special sales in their brand selection.
- Seniors are nearly twice as likely as baby boomers to read the *newspaper* on a daily basis (85% vs. 47%).
- Baby boomers are equally as likely as seniors to show interest in long-term care insurance, with slightly over seven out of ten from each group indicating ownership or desire for ownership of such a policy, but the two cohorts differ with respect to preferences for benefits (i.e., long-term care services) for which they want coverage.

OLDER CONSUMERS ARE VERY HETEROGENEOUS

Perhaps the single most important general finding that emerged from examining responses given by baby boomers and older adults (age 55 and over) was the great heterogeneity in the buying habits among the older age cohorts. While the buying habits of baby boomers differ relatively little across characteristics of this cohort, we found large differences among older Americans in regard to the ways they acquire consumer products and services. Therefore, we focus our reporting on those consumers age 55 and older by breaking down their responses according to a variety of demographic and lifestyle characteristics. In contrast, the buying habits of baby boomers are merely reported on an aggregate basis when compared to those of older Americans.

OLDER CONSUMERS' HABITS

Following are some findings regarding the concerns and buying habits of Americans age 55 and older:

Main Concerns

Fear of failing health and loss of physical and economic independence surfaced as the main concerns among older Americans. Generally, older women are more concerned with a wider variety of areas than their male counterparts. People from various backgrounds express different concerns. Some detailed findings:

- Women are more concerned than men with being able to take care of themselves when they get older (59% vs. 51%) and about their dependence on others for routine daily tasks (39% vs. 29%).

- Maintaining economic independence was reported as a concern almost as frequently as issues of failing health.

- Women are more likely than men to be concerned with the effects of aging on their appearance. Thirty-one percent of them (vs. 16% of men) express concern with the changes in their hair and skin, and with the shape of their body (24% vs. 14%, respectively). However, a smaller percentage of the two groups is concerned with looking a lot younger than they actually are (11% vs. 6%, respectively).

- The desire for post-retirement employment is linked more to the "need" for maintaining financial independence than to a general "want."

- Concern with crime and fraud is also a relatively important preoccupation among aged Americans; women are somewhat more concerned than men (39% vs. 34%), especially among those in lowest income brackets living in urban areas.

- Nearly half of those over 55, especially those with income over $50,000 (52%) and empty nesters (49%), are looking for ways to indulge themselves.

- Concern with maintaining their physical well-being is reflected in the daily activities of older Americans. Three in five make an effort to maintain or improve their health condition through exercise and diet.

- Many older people have the need for intellectual stimulation. The desire to learn new things is greater among older women than among older men (33% vs. 21%).

Health-Care Products and Services

Mature consumers prefer to receive medical-care services at their homes. Thirty-six percent of Americans age 55 and over prefer receiving medical-care services at home, but only 6 percent actually do. The fact that there are so many more people (about 20 million) who have preference for but no access to (or ability to pay for) at-home health-care services signifies an unmet need and an opportunity for health-care providers.

There appears to be a great demand for preventive health-care services, such as health-membership programs and fitness programs, especially among younger mature Americans. The majority of mature consumers, regardless of age, would like to have access to such programs, but a rather small percentage of them actually use them. Again, this discrepancy may suggest unavailability (low supply) or poor marketing.

Contrary to conventional wisdom, perceived need for health care is not related to age, but to a number of socioeconomic factors. More than half of mature Americans (55+) have a chronic condition for which they take medication, and one in six must use products with (or without) certain ingredients as a result of health-related restrictions. About one in six has diagnostic medical equipment, and four in ten have exercise equipment at home. When it comes to choosing hospitals, older adults consider accessibility to the hospital and ability to receive a wide array of health-care services at the same place. They place equal importance on the way a hospital's personnel/staff treat them. Older patients consider assistance with filling out forms and explanation of various services by staff/personnel in their patronage decision. The same reasons are important in choosing physicians and surgeons.

Insurance

The demand for long-term care insurance is growing as the population ages. One-third of those age 55 and over own a long-term care insurance policy, and an additional 40 percent prefer this type of insurance. Older Americans' desire for long-term care and home-health care insurance is an indication of their preference to remain independent and have the freedom to choose the type and place of care should they need it later in life. Regardless of age, the people with one or both of their parents alive are interested in long-term care insurance that would enable their parents to maintain their independence, with nearly half of adults expressing willingness to purchase such insurance for their parents. Two factors stand out as the main reasons for deciding to buy insurance policies from a specific company: price (premiums) and ease of doing business (by phone or mail).

Housing

When noninstitutionalized Americans age 55 and older were questioned about their future housing plans, only 23 percent expressed a preference for living in a single-family house; nearly 30 percent plan to live in a retirement community, and another 16 percent plan to live in an apartment, townhouse, or condominium. A small percentage (7%) plans to live in a nursing home at some point, and one in four had not made any housing plans for later life. These statistics dispel the myth that older people do not plan to move into other types of housing, since 84 percent of those responding already live in a single-family home.

Mature Americans cited home or personal security and location near shopping centers as important reasons for choosing a house, apartment, townhouse, or condominium. Access to medical care and planned social activities were mentioned as important factors in the selection of a retirement community. Similarly, the availability of medical-care services and distance from friends and relatives are the most important reasons for choosing a specific nursing home. The "new" older consumer appears to be receptive to a wider variety of housing options than previously thought, creating opportunities for developing a diversity of such products to satisfy consumer needs.

Financial Services

Demand for free financial services or "perks" that reward customers for maintaining large balances outpaces the availability of such benefits. Nearly three times as many older Americans would factor such offerings in their patronage decision rather than special deals through group or membership programs, which are widely promoted by many financial institutions. Today's older Americans do not simply prefer safe investments; about half are likely to own or prefer average-risk investments (like balanced mutual funds).

Older adults are also willing to purchase stocks from commercial banks, while the majority are willing to purchase services such as insurance policies from traditional and nontraditional financial institutions such as banks and the American Association of Retired Persons (AARP).

When questioned about reasons for patronizing specific financial institutions, older respondents mentioned the financial-service provider's
staff, and specifically the personnel's ability/willingness to explain various financial services. Three other reasons were of nearly equal importance: convenience, ease of doing business by phone or mail, and ease
of getting related services at the same place. The widely marketed senior
membership or discount programs were not found to be very important
reasons why older Americans patronize financial institutions.

Travel and Leisure

Age does not appear to affect people's desire to travel, but their inability to pay often keeps them at home. When older travelers stay at a
specific hotel or motel it is likely they selected it because of a certain rate
or a special discount. About two-thirds of older travelers decide where
to stay based on rates lodging facilities charge, and another 60 percent
decide on the basis of the facility's discount program. These same reasons are cited for choosing a specific airline or cruise line.

Among other things, our findings suggest the need for developing a
wide range of travel-related offerings that meet the budgets of older
Americans. Direct mail is an important information source for travel
services among older adults. Four in ten prefer to receive news in the
mail, and about one-third prefer to be informed via advertisements.
When asked about their preferences for methods of purchasing vacation
packages, nearly 60 percent of mature Americans indicated preference
for buying travel-related services at vendor's facilities, while slightly
more than 40 percent said they would buy through the mail or by phone.

Pharmaceutical Products

If older consumers cannot read or understand information about over-
the-counter (OTC) pharmaceutical products they need, chances are they
will not bother buying them. Ease of reading information on labels is the
main reason older consumers decide to buy specific brands of OTC drugs
and health aids. Also, ease of understanding and following usage directions provided with the product is important.

When asked about reasons for choosing sp   and pharmacies, older Americans said they value p   ity of familiar brands or products, and ease of locat   the main
reasons for patronizing these stores. Two a   e important to more than half of the mature consun   her retail
facilities and ability of store personnel to a   ked why
they decide to buy or not buy prescripti   aids by
phone or mail, more than half mentioned   40 per-

cent mentioning availability of toll-free (800) number, the number of days they have to wait before receiving the merchandise, and convenience. About half of older Americans prefer paying for prescription drugs with a check or cash, and many use senior discounts.

High-Tech Products and Telecommunication Services

Use of high-tech products and telecommunication services relates to the older person's lifestyle and stage in life rather than age. Products and services which provide an obvious benefit appear to be used, while those which are not important to the person's lifestyle or stage in life are not as likely to be used. Regardless of age, older people with high incomes tend to use a variety of high-tech products and telecommunication services. Older Americans age 55 and over are about as likely to own a recent model of automobile as those under 55. Older adults use telecommunication services less frequently than their younger counterparts. Approximately half of the mature consumers prefer to learn about new electronic products and telecommunication services from TV or print ads. While older consumers prefer to purchase a variety of products through the mail, only one in ten is likely to buy electronic products direct.

Apparel and Footwear

Mature Americans, especially females, are as fashionable nowadays as their younger counterparts. Those with highest levels of income and education are the most fashion conscious. One in five prefers buying clothes through the mail.

Reasons that help most older Americans decide whether to buy apparel and footwear products directly from the source include: price (67.2%), return/cancellation and refund policy (65.8%), days to wait before receiving (56.9%), selection of products (55.3%), and availability of toll-free (800) number (53.4%). When it comes to choosing a specific department store, older Americans' patronage decisions are influenced by sales (66.7%), ease of locating merchandise (60.5%), and availability of personnel who could assist them (59.5%). Price ("sales") is by far the most important reason in deciding which brand(s) of apparel and footwear products to buy.

Food and Beverages

Older people are becoming more health conscious than their younger counterparts. Although younger consumers admit they know more about nutrition today than they did ten to fifteen years ago, they are not as likely as older consumers to sacrifice good taste for good nutrition.

Younger people are more knowledgeable about nutrition, but this is not very likely to influence their eating habits.

When choosing specific food stores, older shoppers value economic factors (such as "specials" and senior discounts), special-assistance services (such as package carry-out), and personnel assistance more than younger shoppers. About half of the respondents age 55 and over mentioned three reasons for choosing specific restaurants: senior discounts, comfortable place for socializing, and location.

BUYING HABITS OF UPSCALE OLDER ADULTS

The buying and consumption habits of older Americans differ according to demographic factors. Even those mature consumers who are in the same demographic group display marked differences in the ways they behave in the marketplace. For example, mature Americans in different income classes (lower-, middle-, and upper-income) have different buying habits; and those in different income levels *within* each income class also tend to behave differently. In order to illustrate this heterogeneity, we are presenting findings regarding the consumption behavior of upscale older adults (age 55 and over) with an annual household income over $50,000.

Several aspects of consumer behavior exhibited by those with incomes between $50,000 and $75,000 were compared with behaviors of older people with incomes greater than $75,000. Some findings:

- In deciding whether to buy *insurance* from a company, the lower-income group ($50,000–$75,000) is five times as likely as the higher-income older adults (income over $75,000) to be influenced by the types of credit card they can use to pay for their premiums.

- In deciding on a *retirement community*, the $75,000-plus income group is more likely to consider the facility's location in relation to the residence of their friends, while the lower-income group is more concerned with their home or personal security in the community.

- When deciding which *financial institutions* to do business with, the upper-income group places more emphasis on personnel/staff assistance in explaining the various services, and ease of doing business by phone or through the mail. The lower-income group is more preoccupied with the institution's policies such as billing and payment options.

- Half (49.2%) of older adults with income over $75,000, in comparison to their lower-income counterparts (24.2%), prefer buying *vacation packages* by phone; but compared to the more affluent group, the less affluent consumers prefer to visit the travel vendor's facilities and pay cash for airline tickets.

- More older people in the lower-income group than in the higher-income bracket indicate preference for using direct mail when purchasing *apparel and footwear* (26.3% vs. 15.6%).

• When considering which department stores to patronize, the lower-income group is influenced more by the availability of billing/payment methods than the higher-income group.

• The less affluent group is nearly twice as likely than the more affluent group (27.8% vs. 15.5%) to read *Readers' Digest* on a regular basis.

MATURE CONSUMER SEGMENTS

As people age, they tend to become more dissimilar with respect to their needs, lifestyles, and consumption habits. Although we estimated responses to our questions for the mature market, we were aware of the great heterogeneity of this group. Besides reporting responses by standard demographic factors such as gender and income, evaluating the mature market on the basis of such objective characteristics is not always adequate because demographic and lifestyle factors by themselves offer weak explanations of consumer behavior.

To better understand and break down the complex mature market, we must understand the factors that contribute to its complexity and that cause individuals to respond differently to market offerings. What makes people behave differently as consumers is not just one factor such as need, but several, including available income and lifestyles. Specifically, the factors that make older consumers more or less responsive to marketing offerings are directly related to their needs, attitudes, demographics, and lifestyles, which are in turn influenced by changing life conditions. As people go through life, they experience major life events or circumstances. Some of these events or life changes are biological, such as menopause and the onset of chronic conditions. Others are social and psychological, reflecting adjustments a person must make to circumstances such as losing a spouse or becoming a grandparent.

When people experience major life events, they often change their outlook on life as they re-evaluate their goals, wants, and roles on both personal and consumer levels. As they confront these changes, older consumers' needs obviously change, but so do their perceptions of, and needs for, specific products or services. We use the term "gerontographics" to refer to life-changing events and circumstances in later life that shape the individual's attitudes and behaviors. Because people differ with respect to their life experiences and biological, social, and psychological circumstances, they also differ when it comes to their behavior as consumers. On the other hand, older people who experience similar circumstances in late life are likely to exhibit similar patterns of consumer behavior. Based on this premise, we classify mature consumers into segments. Individuals in each segment are relatively similar, while consumers in each segment as a group differ from those in other segments. Using sophisticated statistical techniques (factor analysis, cluster analysis), we were able to conclude that older consumers best fit into one of the following four segments of life stages.

Healthy Indulgers (18 percent of the 55-plus population) have experienced the fewest life events such as retirement, widowhood, and chronic conditions that contribute to people's psychological and social aging. As a result, they are the group most likely to behave like younger consumers. The major difference between indulgers and middle-aged baby boomers is that the former group is financially better off and more settled in their careers. Their main focus is on enjoying life rather than trying to "make it."

Healthy Hermits (36 percent) are likely to have experienced life events that have affected their self-concept and self-worth, such as the death of a spouse. They tend to respond to these events with psychological and social withdrawal. Many resent the isolation and the fact that they are expected to behave like old people.

Ailing Outgoers (29 percent), on the other hand, maintain positive self-esteem and self-concept despite life events, including the onset of chronic health problems. Unlike hermits, outgoers accept their "old-age" status and acknowledge their limitations, but are still interested in getting the most out of life.

Frail Recluses, who make up 17 percent of today's mature population, is the fourth group. Like outgoers, they are likely to have accepted their old-age status and have adjusted their lifestyles to reflect physical declines and changes in social roles. In contrast to outgoers, they have chosen to cope with detrimental changes in later life by becoming spiritually stronger. Frail recluses may have been healthy indulgers in the past. They may also have been healthy hermits or ailing outgoers at an intermediate stage, although probably not both. Thus, people in late life can move from one stage to another.

Some changes occur slowly. Full-time workers who wind down to part-time hours may spend years in semi-retirement and become accustomed to a gradual increase in leisure time, as well as a reduced income. A woman whose husband suffers through a long illness before death may experience widowhood in a series of stages. Sometimes changes are abrupt, such as when a stroke hits. Regardless of the time span, the processes or "flows" of aging are _____ ___se they may happen at any poin__ events at all. Many men never exp_ they die first; some people never bec_ people work until the day they die.

Selling Products. Our studies show that the _____ __lder people largely depends on the experiences they _____ the way they adapt to them. Differences in consumer responses to marketing offerings can form the basis for selecting targets, positioning products and services, and developing marketing programs. They vary by industry within groups, too. The strategy that appears to be effective for one product or service may not be effective for another.

Although everyone eats, ailing outgoers deserve special mention when it comes to food, because they are most likely to respond to special attention from grocers and restaurateurs. This is because most ailing outgoers have health problems that may require a special diet. Marketers or establishments who appeal to such needs will get the outgoers' business. Offering and promoting convenient restaurant locations will help bring in ailing outgoers who enjoy outings yet appreciate ease of access. So will special services that minimize the walking they have to do, such as valet parking.

Ailing outgoers like the feeling of independence that eating out provides, but they have to watch their pennies. This group is attracted to restaurants such as International King's Table. Besides offering a healthy menu that changes daily, consisting of eight entrees, several hot vegetables, a salad bar, and a variety of desserts, the Eugene, Oregon–based chain offers many money-saving incentives, such as coupons. Many restaurants in retirement areas have discovered how to pack the house with "early bird" specials. Ailing outgoers appreciate the discount on the meal, and don't mind eating earlier in the day. In turn, restaurants add an extra seating or two to their dinner hours, and can fit in more younger customers later in the evening.

Because they are sociable, ailing outgoers are interested in appearing socially acceptable. But they also want functional clothing that suits their particular needs, such as easy-to-manage fastenings and openings. Ailing outgoers appear to be the prime segment for retailers who put out catalogs designed specifically for older women, many of whom have arthritis. For example, J. C. Penney's Easy Dressing catalog markets fashionable apparel featuring velcro fasteners instead of zippers or buttons, roomier armholes for easier access, large tabs on front zippers, partially elasticized waist bands, and other features that make it easier for women to dress.

Direct-mail catalogs are a good way to promote specialty clothing, especially when they feature sale prices and conveniences like no-fuss return policies. Although healthy hermits are less sociable in general, or perhaps because of this trait, it is best to emphasize conformity when selling clothing to them. They don't want to stand out in a crowd, and they want to know that their appearance is socially acceptable to other seniors. They tend to feel comfortable with well-known brands, and don't mind paying more for them.

Ailing outgoers and healthy indulgers are the two segments most likely to move later in life. Ailing outgoers are more likely than other mature people to be attracted by housing that promotes their independence even as their physical limitations increase. They can benefit from the medical support available in retirement communities and nursing homes, and they like the idea of having a built-in social network. But they also want reassurance that they will have as much independence as possible within such a structured environment. Consequently, access and transportation to shopping and other activities is important to them.

Healthy indulgers, on the other hand, are looking for truly independent living on a reduced scale from their child-raising years. They are the ones who sell their large single-family homes and buy apartments, townhouses, and condo units, preferably near shopping centers. This relatively upscale group often has money invested in furnishings and other possessions, so they are potential customers for home-security systems, as well as discretionary home-care services, such as carpet cleaning. They are also the mature group most likely to be interested in high-tech, home-oriented devices, such as telephone-answering machines.

Healthy hermits and frail recluses prefer to stay put in the single-family home where they raised their families. Among mature consumers, they offer the greatest potential for the remodeling industry. Since these two groups make up more than half of the mature market, it is not surprising that they constitute a large customer base for hardware stores. Home Depot makes a point of addressing their needs by hiring older employees who can better relate to mature customers. Healthy hermits may want to do home improvements themselves, so hardware stores and other retailers would do well to sell tools and materials directly to this group. Frail recluses may do some of their own minor repairs, but they also need help maintaining homes and yards, so affordable home-care services such as weekly lawn mowing appeal to them.

Selling Services. As their names suggest, ailing outgoers and frail recluses are the more important mature market segments for health-care products and services. Outgoers are interested in health-club memberships, especially those that offer senior discounts. Recluses are better bets for home exercise equipment, as well as self-diagnosing kits to monitor blood pressure, blood-sugar level, and cholesterol in the privacy of their homes. Emergency-response systems are also in demand by recluses. The Baptist Medical Centers of Birmingham, Alabama, provide an immediate communications link between a person at home and a central monitor location at the centers.

Recluses can't take care of all their health-care needs on their own, of course, and they value convenience, so health-care clinics should emphasize location when talking to recluses. However, those who can't be close to customers can still bring in business. The LaFayette Eye Center in LaFayette, Indiana, offers its senior clientele free transportation to appointments via its Eye-Van. The mini-van will pick up seniors who live within an hour's drive. Outgoers, on the other hand, value social networks, so clinics should focus on the direct contact seniors will have with providers when appealing to this group.

Outgoers have to think about their health, but they do so in an upbeat and security-conscious fashion. Their willingness to face age head-on and accept the health problems it brings makes them an ideal market for long-term care medical insurance and medigap coverage. They may also be open to learning abut different types of insurance plans, so cross-selling by agents and efficient telemarketing could work for this group. So can a variety of payment systems and liberal cancellation/refund policies that mean customer convenience.

When it comes to money, healthy indulgers value both convenience and personal service. This group is a good market for low- to moderate-risk investments, as well as overdraft protection on checking accounts. They will also sign up for free banking services in exchange for maintaining large account balances. Frail recluses are potential IRA/Keogh account owners. They value the security of overdraft protection on checking accounts and the financial independence that reverse mortgages offer. Both indulgers and recluses appreciate staff trained to explain forms, accounts, and other banking procedures. Many banks have realized the importance of helping their older clientele understand and use various services, and have special training programs for customer-service personnel who interact with older customers. Customer representatives at Penn Central National Bank in Huntingdon, Pennsylvania, taped up their knuckles to simulate arthritis so they could appreciate firsthand the difficulties many elderly people have with counting money and filling out deposit slips.

Travel-service providers have mixed feelings about the potential for travel and other leisure spending among mature Americans. On one hand, they believe that people want to enjoy themselves after they retire and the kids have left home. On the other hand, they worry that seniors don't have the money or energy to travel. The reality is that different mature segments want and need different things, but everyone wants to have fun.

Healthy indulgers can afford to take more expensive trips by air and cruise ship, although they won't complain about special group rates and senior discounts. They enjoy the convenience that packaged travel services provide and are comfortable with signing up by phone or mail. To sell trips to them, marketers should solicit testimonials from satisfied senior customers. Ailing outgoers like to belong to clubs, so national chains of hotels and motels can capture their loyalty with membership programs that provide value wherever they go. And they don't mind

being old, so marketing messages that properly portray elderly people won't be wasted.

Because mature Americans can and do move from one life-stage segment to another in a somewhat predictable fashion as they experience and react to life changes, it is possible to identify those who are "at risk" for moving into a given life stage. Retailers, health-care providers, and banks armed with this information can then be proactive about targeting people even before they enter the next life stage. Those who track the progress of mature consumers will stay ahead of the competition.

ABOUT THE FINDINGS OF OUR SURVEYS

In subsequent sections, we present the results of our surveys by type of product or service. This format was deemed desirable for two reasons. First, consumer buying habits and product preferences vary from one product to another—the way one goes about purchasing a home is different from the process of buying groceries. Second, this format is most helpful for the busy executive who is usually interested in one general product category.

Besides reporting the average response from all survey participants, we also report responses by specific sociodemographic and gerontographic subgroups. For example, responses are reported for the "55-plus," as well as for the 55–64, 65–74, and 75-plus age segments; and we compared responses given by those age 55 and over to those of under 55, as well as those of baby boomers (born between 1946 and 1964) and those of seniors (age 65+).

To further help the reader or potential user of our research, the main findings are summarized and recommendations are offered on the basis of these findings to help decision makers effectively reach the aging consumer market. Only statistically significant findings are presented.

2

Food and Beverages, Food Stores, and Restaurants

One area of focus of our studies was the buying habits of various age groups with respect to food products. Specifically, we asked questions about food products and beverages, patronage of food stores, and patronage of restaurants. One of our interests was in investigating changes in preferences for food products. Another focus of our research was on factors that motivate people to choose specific brands of foods and alcoholic beverages. We also investigated the reasons people choose specific grocery stores and restaurants. Finally, we examined how people pay for food products they consume at restaurants, and tried to identify and profile adults who consume dietary products.

PRESENT VS. PAST TASTES AND PREFERENCES FOR FOOD

A major objective of this research was to assess how consumer preferences for food products have changed over the years. Of course, changes in tastes and preferences may reflect both changes in individual internal factors such as ability to taste and smell chemical substances as well as changes in food products. While a decline in the older person's ability to taste may be attributed to age, changes in food ingredients would also alter taste. Thus, a comparison between younger and older adults should reveal changes in individual abilities, while assessment of perceptions of food changes in both age groups would suggest changes in food ingredients. Finally, there may be variations in perceptions across people of various ages as to what constitutes "food," since younger and older adults may have different lifestyles and, therefore, may think of food differently. As a result, one needs to obtain responses on specific types of foods or food items.

In this research, respondents were asked to indicate their agreement or disagreement with six statements regarding food preferences. Specifically, for each statement they were asked to either agree, disagree, or they are not sure regarding their opinions and preferences for food today, in comparison to their tastes 15 to 20 years ago—response categories were: "I tend to agree," "I tend to disagree," and "not sure." First, we examined "tend to agree" responses to the six statements by those age 55 and over.

In comparison to tastes and preferences for food 15 to 20 years ago, nearly half (46.9%) of the mature Americans seem to sacrifice good taste for good nutrition. More than eight in ten (83.7%) think they are more knowledgeable about nutrition today than they were in the past. More than one in three (36.6%) find meals in restaurants spicier, but only one in four thinks that frozen dinners are not as spicy. Only 18.1 percent think that cookies do not taste as sweet, and only 15.1 percent of older Americans are of the opinion that the same brands of coffee have more aroma.

In order to assess these responses, a comparison with responses of younger adults was necessary. While younger people perceive they have learned more about nutrition, with about nine in ten (91.1%) expressing this opinion, they are less likely than their older counterparts to admit they sacrifice good taste for good nutrition. One may conclude that older people have become more health conscious than their younger counterparts. Finally, a slightly larger percentage of older than younger Americans agreed with the statement: "Cookies do not taste as sweet" (18.0% vs. 14.5%). There were no other differences in opinions about food between younger and older adults.

Baby Boomers vs. Seniors

Changes in Tastes and Preferences. One of the objectives of this research was to determine how tastes and preferences of baby boomers and seniors (65+) may have changed in recent years. As Table 2.1 shows, about nine in ten baby boomers said they are more knowledgeable about nutrition today than they were 15 to 20 years ago. This figure compares with eight in ten of the seniors sample, suggesting that baby boomers have become *relatively* more knowledgeable about nutrition in recent years. Similarly, a higher percentage of baby boomers (37.5%) feels that meals at restaurants are spicier today than they were in the 15 to 20 years prior to the survey, in comparison with 32.9 percent of the 65-plus sample. These differences in taste perception may reflect declines in ability to smell in later life. Finally, a little over one-third (34.8%) of the baby

Table 2.1
Tastes and Preferences for Food Today in Comparison to Tastes 15–20 Years
Ago among Baby Boomers and Seniors (65+) (Percent Who Tend to Agree)

	Baby Boomers (%)	Seniors (%)
Compared to 15-20 years ago, today		
I sacrifice good taste for good nutrition	34.81	48.37
Cookies do not taste as sweet	15.52	18.89
Same brands of frozen dinners are not as spicy	20.69	25.06
Same brands of instant coffee have more aroma	14.13	15.68
Same meals at restaurants are more spicy	37.55	32.93
I am more knowledgeable about nutrition	91.26	81.28
Base:	(N = 883)	(N = 366)

boomers tend to agree with the statement, "I sacrifice good taste for good
nutrition today, in comparison to 15 to 20 years ago." This figure compares with about half (48.4%) of the elderly sample.

Dietary Products. Respondents were also asked to indicate whether they
were using any dietary meal prescription or products for people with
certain health/physical requirements. Only 6.3 percent of baby boomers
and 15.3 percent of seniors said they were using such products.

Differences among Older Adults

Are changes in tastes and preferences for food a matter of sociodemographic characteristics? In order to address this question, responses
to the six statements given by older adults were analyzed by selected
socioeconomic and demographic factors.

Age. Responses given by older adults in the three age groups (55–64,
65–74, 75+) differed only for two statements. With age, mature Americans appear to be less likely to agree with the statement that the same
meals at restaurants are "more spicy," suggesting a decline in ability to
taste after age 55. Second, knowledge about nutrition, although higher
in relation to that of 15 to 20 years ago, shows a gradual decline with
age. Thus, it appears that throughout late life younger age groups acquire greater knowledge about nutrition than older age groups.

Socioeconomic. With increasing household income, older adults tend to
admit they sacrifice good taste for good nutrition, although the pattern
is not very strong. While 44.3 percent of those with incomes less than
$20,000 said they sacrifice taste for nutrition, more than half (51.4%) of
those with incomes $50,000 or higher said the same. Sweet sensation is

related to income in a different fashion; those with less than $20,000 say that cookies do not taste as sweet compared with those with middle incomes ($20,000–$49,999) (21.1% vs. 15.6%). On the other hand, the higher the older person's income the lower the chances that he or she agrees that the same brands of frozen dinners are as spicy, suggesting that older adults with higher incomes perceive greater declines in taste of frozen food over a 15- to 20-year period.

While frozen foods are perceived to have become less spicy, those with incomes in excess of $50,000 gave more affirmative responses to the statement: "Same brands of instant coffee have more aroma." The percentage of "agree" responses given by the three income groups were 13.3 percent, 13.8 percent, and 22.7 percent, respectively. Similarly, with increasing income, there was an increasing tendency among older consumers to agree with the statement: "Same meals at restaurants are more spicy," and to indicate they are more knowledgeable about nutrition now than they were 15 to 20 years ago.

The relationships between education and responses to the six statements given are fairly similar to those observed with respect to income. While there is no clear pattern that the more educated older adults indicate a greater tendency to sacrifice good taste for good nutrition, in comparison to their previous eating habits, they are less likely to indicate that cookies do not taste as sweet (20.3% for the least educated—high school or less—vs. 15.8% for those with college education).

Geographic. There are no differences in responses due to location (urban vs. rural) but there are interesting geographic differences in food perceptions and nutrition knowledge and habits. A larger percentage of southerners indicated changes in eating habits at the expense of good taste, with over half (51.1%) of them saying that they now sacrifice good taste for good nutrition, in comparison to their westerner counterparts (36.7%). Easterners, on the other hand, were the group least likely to agree that same meals at restaurants today are more spicy than they were 15 to 20 years ago, with three in ten (30.5%) of them expressing this view, in comparison with 39.0 percent of westerners and 38.9 percent of southerners. Finally, northerners indicated the lowest gain in nutrition knowledge over the previous 15 to 20 years, with about eight in ten (79.2%) agreeing that they are more knowledgeable now, compared with 87.9 percent of older adults who live in the West and 85.3 of those who live in the South.

Other Demographics. The remaining demographic factors were relatively poor predictors of the older person's self-reported preferences for food, in relation to tastes 15 to 20 years ago. A larger percentage of older adults from families with at least one working person, in comparison to those from families with no working persons, indicated that same meals at restaurants today are more spicy than they were 15 to 20 years ago

(38.8% vs. 31.4%). A larger percentage of older adults who live near their children (42.3%), in comparison to those who do not live near their children (30.4%), indicated that meals at restaurants are more spicy today they were 15 to 20 years ago.

Gerontographics. Gerontographics appear to be very strong predictors of older adults' changes in tastes and preferences over the previous 15 to 20 years. Responses to all six statements showed variation across gerontographic groups. While more than half (53.8%) of ailing outgoers now sacrifice good taste for good nutrition in comparison to their past eating habits, only four in ten (41.0%) of healthy hermits indicated they do the same. Ailing outgoers were also more likely to agree that the taste of cookies is not as sweet today (21.9%) in comparison to 14.0 percent of frail recluses who noticed that the taste of cookies was not as sweet as before.

Ailing outgoers also expressed a greater agreement with the statement: "Same brands of frozen dinners are not as spicy," with one in three (32.2%) of them agreeing, in comparison with less than one in five (19.0%) of frail recluses. Twice as many healthy indulgers as healthy hermits (20.8% vs. 10.6%) agreed that same brands of instant coffee have more aroma today than they did 15 to 20 years ago. Also, a greater number of healthy indulgers (41.4%) and frail recluses (40.9%) than healthy hermits (32.7%) think that meals at restaurants today are more spicy. Finally, healthy indulgers are the group most likely to have learned about nutrition over the previous 15 to 20 years, with nearly one in nine (89.0%) of them expressing knowledge gain, in comparison with healthy hermits (80.5%) and ailing outgoers (83.4%).

REASONS FOR CHOOSING BRANDS OF FOODS AND ALCOHOLIC BEVERAGES

While taste would appear to be a major determinant of brand choice, it shows a wide variability across consumers, due to differences in taste perception. Thus, while some consumers may prefer certain ingredients in food and alcoholic beverages, others may not purchase the same products because they have no preference for the same ingredients. It is, therefore, logical that the large majority of older consumers are not likely to buy food items whose taste they do not like. However, a host of other attributes might determine the brand(s) they would select among those they find acceptable. In our research, we identified twelve possible reasons older people may choose specific brands of food items and alcoholic beverages. Many of these factors were based on results of surveys while others were based on focus groups. Respondents were asked to indicate whether each of the twelve reasons was important in their decision to choose or switch brands.

Table 2.2
Reasons for Choosing Specific Brands of Foods and Alcoholic Beverages among Baby Boomers and Seniors (65+) (Percent Who Feel Reason Is Important)

Reasons	Baby Boomers (%)	Seniors (%)
Price reduction or special sale	76.18	62.79
Ease of reading information on labels or brochures	35.47	36.82
Ease of using the product	25.93	21.26
Ease of understanding and following directions provided with the product	20.38	23.07
Availability of products for people with certain health requirements	23.66	22.34
Availability of coupons	72.02	68.88
Availability of manufacturer rebates	36.16	40.38
Advice of other people your age	38.54	23.81
What others think of people who use certain brands	19.30	19.70
Their ads properly stereotype people your age	10.67	12.94
Advice/request of spouse or other relatives	49.30	28.66
Recommendation of salesperson	8.28	10.45
Base:	(N = 883)	(N = 366)

Baby Boomers vs. Seniors

Many of the factors indicated by older adults are of equal importance to younger adults. Economic reasons are of greater importance to younger adults, while product functionality is of equal importance to both groups. Older adults find two reasons to be more important in their brand selection. Proper age stereotyping is more important to older adults. Similarly, the recommendation of the salesperson is of greater importance to older Americans.

Responses for baby boomers and seniors are presented in Table 2.2. As the table shows, responses given by baby boomers differ from those given by the elderly sample in four cases, with the baby boomers placing greater emphasis on these factors than their elderly counterparts. Three-fourths (76.2%) of the baby boomers indicated they consider price reduction or special sale in their brand selection, in comparison with 62.8 percent of the elderly sample. One in four (25.9%) considers the ease of using the product (vs. 21.3% of the elderly), and 38.5 percent consider the advice of same-age peers (vs. 23.8%). Finally, nearly half of the baby boomers (49.3%) (in comparison with 28.7% percent of the elderly) take the advice or request of a relative into consideration in choosing specific brands. The findings of greater influence of informal sources on baby boomers' decisions, in comparison to their older counterparts, may reflect the latter group's greater social isolation.

Differences among Older Adults

Price. Two-thirds of older Americans indicate economic reasons for choosing specific brands of food products and alcoholic beverages, either in terms of price reduction or special sale (65.9%), or in terms of availability of coupons (67.9%). Third in importance is availability of manufacturer rebates (40.6%), which are also related to economic motives.

The perceived importance of economic factors changes with age in late life. Price reductions or special sales become less of a concern. A larger percentage of mature males considers price reduction or special sale in deciding which brand to purchase, with seven in ten of them indicating this reason, compared with 62.6 percent of older females.

A larger percentage of older women than older men considers the availability of coupons (71.3% vs. 63.8%). Price reduction or special sale is of greater importance to middle-income ($20,000-$49,999) older adults, with about seven in ten (71.7%) of them indicating importance, compared with 58.8 of those with annual household incomes less than $20,000, and 66.1 percent of the high-income bracket. Older people who live with others, in comparison to those living alone, tend to respond to price reduction or special sales, with 68.9 percent and 58.8 percent, respectively, indicating that this factor is important.

Nearly three-fourths (73.4%) of older adults who live in the West consider price reduction or special sale, about 10 percent more than do adults who live in other parts of the country. Availability of coupons is considered by a larger percentage of those who live in the North (72.1%) and East (71.5%) than by those who live in the West (60.2%) and South (66.1%). The importance of availability of manufacturer rebates shows geographic differences similar to those shown for price or special sales, with 47.2 percent of easterners and 46.0 percent of the northerners, in comparison with 36.8 percent and 31.4 percent of southerners and westerners, respectively, attaching importance to rebates in evaluating food products and alcoholic beverages.

Based on the older person's gerontographic profile, we can predict how important each of the factors is to brand-choice behavior concerning food products. A larger percentage of healthy indulgers (69.4%) and frail recluses (70.8%) than of healthy hermits (64.2%) and ailing outgoers (63.1%) considers price reduction or special sale in their brand evaluations. Although ailing outgoers are not as sensitive to price reductions as other gerontographic groups, they are more likely to be concerned with the availability of coupons. More than three-fourths (77.7%) of them indicated availability of coupons is important, in comparison with 59.7 percent of frail recluses, 60.6 percent of healthy indulgers, and 67.2 percent of healthy hermits. Also, the perceived importance of manufacturer rebates is higher among ailing outgoers and healthy hermits, with 43.8 percent and 42.7 percent, respectively, expressing this view, in comparison with just under one-third (32.7%) of healthy indulgers.

Coupons. Coupons are important among older adults with incomes under $50,000, with about seven in ten indicating that coupons influence their brand choice. Among those with annual household incomes of $50,000 or more, a smaller percentage (56.3%) considers coupons important determinants of their brand choice. Similarly, manufacturer rebates are of greater significance to the lower- and middle-income groups, with 43.9 percent and 42.0 percent, respectively, perceiving them to be important in their decision making, in comparison with 29.4 percent of older adults with incomes of $50,000 or more. Coupons tend to be used less frequently by the more educated mature Americans and so are manufacturer rebates. Coupons are more important to older Americans who live with others than to those who live alone, with 69.5 percent and 64.0 percent, respectively, expressing interest.

Product Information. Besides economic reasons, next in importance is ease of reading information on labels, with 37.0 percent of the older Americans indicating this reason to be important. Ease of reading information on labels is of greater importance to ailing outgoers, with four in ten expressing this opinion, in comparison with 31.9 percent of frail recluses and 34.5 percent of healthy hermits.

Spouse/Family Influence. The studies indicated that the importance of advice/request of spouse or other relatives declines with age in late life. One-third of older adults (32.7%) buy specific brands of foods and alcoholic beverages because of request/advice of spouse or other relatives. Nearly one in four (24.3%) is influenced by same-age peers. Among the sexes, males are more likely than females to consider the advice/request of their spouse or other relatives in choosing brands of groceries (36.4% vs. 29.9%). Living arrangements also surfaced as an indicator of an older person's reliance on the advice of a spouse or relative when making food purchase decisions, with a larger percentage of older adults who live alone (37.1%) considering advice, compared to those who live with others (21.8%).

Advice/request of spouse or other relatives is of less concern to older adults who live in the West than those who live in the East and South, with 27.9 percent of the westerners indicating this factor is important, in comparison with 35.5 percent and 36.1 percent for the two other groups, respectively. Older adults who live in rural areas perceive the advice of same-age peers to be more important than those who live in urban areas (28.0% vs. 22.9%).

Healthy indulgers is the gerontographic group most likely to consider the opinion of family while they contemplate the purchase of various food products. A larger percentage of them (38.5%) takes into account the advice/request of spouse or other relatives, in comparison with 31.3% of ailing outgoers and 30.1 percent of healthy hermits.

Peer Influence. Advice of same-age peers increases with income as a factor in decision making. About one in four westerners (26.9%) and northerners (25.2%), in comparison with one in five easterners (20.0%), is influenced by the advice of same-age peers.

Gerontographic groups were also shown to place varying values of peer input when selecting groceries. The percentage of healthy indulgers (29.3%) that takes into account the advice of same-age peers is higher (along with that of ailing outgoers—28.8%) than the percentages of healthy hermits (21.1%) and frail recluses (18.5%) who do the same.

Availability of Products for People with Certain Requirements. Availability of products for people with certain physical/health requirements was mentioned by 23.5 percent of older Americans. Older adults who live in rural areas perceive the availability of products for people with certain physical/health requirements to be more important than those who live in urban areas (29.7% vs. 21.2%). A larger percentage of the older adults who live near their children (28.2%), in comparison to those who do not live near their children (16.7%), decide on brands based on availability of products useful to people with certain physical/health requirements. Ailing outgoers and healthy hermits also show a greater propensity to consider availability of products for people with certain health requirements, again with one-fourth of the first two groups expressing this orientation, compared with one-fifth (20.2%) of healthy indulgers and 17.3 percent of frail recluses.

Product Directions/Use. Ease of understanding and following directions provided with the product was cited as a reason by 22.7 percent of older adults. Ease of using the product is a factor among 22.4 percent of older adults. In general, the more educated older adults have less difficulty using the product as well as understanding and following directions provided with it. Similarly, with age, ease of using food products declines as a motive for brand selection. The perceived importance of ease of using the product, and ease of understanding and following directions decline with income. A larger percentage of ailing outgoers (27.3%) than of healthy hermits (22.2%), healthy indulgers (18.2%), or frail recluses (18.7%) is concerned with ease of using food products they buy. A larger percentage of older women than older men cited ease of understanding and following directions (25.9% vs. 18.9%) and ease of using the product

(25.4% vs. 18.9%). Older adults who live in rural areas perceive the ease of understanding and following directions provided with the product to be more important than those who live in urban areas (27.3% vs. 21.0%).

Ease of reading information on labels is of greater importance to westerners than to southerners, with 40.8 percent and 34.7 percent of older adults in the respective geographic groups expressing concern with this factor. One-fourth of ailing outgoers (25.9%) and healthy hermits (25.1%), compared with a smaller percentage of healthy indulgers (16.6%) and frail recluses (18.4%), is concerned with ease of understanding and following directions provided with the product.

Group Norms. Only one in six (18.4%) of older Americans is influenced by perceptions of how others may respond to them because of their brand preferences. Ailing outgoers are the gerontographic group most sensitive to group norms, with 26.7 percent of them expressing concern about other people's evaluation of their consumer behavior, in relation to 13.1 percent of frail recluses and 14.2 percent of healthy hermits.

Portrayal of Older People in Food/Alcohol Advertisements. One in eight older Americans would buy certain brands because their ads properly stereotype people their age. A larger percentage of older women than older men is concerned with whether the product's advertisements properly depict people their age (14.4% vs. 10.9%). Older people with higher income are less concerned with old-age stereotyping in ads, while higher-educated older adults are less sensitive such stereotyping.

Finally, more mature adults who live in the North, in comparison with those who live in the West (15.5% vs. 9.2%), are concerned with proper age stereotypes of advertisements by food and alcoholic beverage manufacturers. Ailing outgoers are twice as likely as healthy indulgers and frail recluses to express concern with the way older people are portrayed in food advertisements, with 18.0 percent vis-à-vis 7.4 percent and 8.8 percent, respectively, expressing this concern.

Salesperson Recommendations. Less than one in ten (9.4%) would buy as a result of a salesperson's recommendation. Of the different gerontographic groups, ailing outgoers are nearly twice as likely as frail recluses (11.3% vs. 6.5%) to take into account the recommendation of sales personnel in buying brands of food products and alcoholic beverages.

REASONS FOR PATRONIZING FOOD AND GROCERY STORES

Consumers may patronize food stores for a number of reasons. While the listing of all possible reasons can be difficult, there are certain reasons that have been identified through previous research to be significant in grocery store selection. On the bases of previous surveys and focus group interviews, fourteen factors were identified as possible reasons for store selection in the case of grocery products. Respondents were asked to indicate whether each of the fourteen reasons applies to their decision to start or continue to patronize food and grocery stores.

Nearly nine in ten (88.0%) mature Americans indicated that ease of locating merchandise/items applies to their decision to start or continue to patronize food stores. Location near the respondent's residence was named by 84.6 percent of older adults, while eight in ten mature Americans indicated that their patronage was due to the availability of familiar brands or items (80.9%) and fast check-out registers (80.3%). Price reduction was mentioned by three-fourths (76.3%) of older Americans as a reason they consider in their decision to start or continue to patronize food and grocery stores.

Nearly two-thirds (64.1%) of older Americans consider the food store's location in relation to other places they patronize, suggesting that older adults' selection of convenience type of stores (such as food stores) is a multiple-store selection rather than an independent-store choice. Grocery stores provide older adults the opportunity to socialize. More than half (54.7%) of the older respondents indicated that they patronize a grocery store because they find it a comfortable place to shop or socialize. About four in ten patronize food stores because they can find products suitable to their health needs (40.8%), and because the store's personnel can assist them (40.8%). Of equal importance is the ease in returning products or getting refunds (39.8%), and availability of special-assistance services (38.9%). Fewer than one in three (28.5%) considers senior discounts in a store-selection decision concerning the purchase of food items. Nearly one in five (18.0%) relies on same-age peers in selecting grocery stores and only one in ten (10.3%) considers payment methods available by food stores.

Many of these factors considered in the selection of food stores are equally important to those under age 55. However, six factors are valued more by older food shoppers than by their younger counterparts. Specifically, older adults are more likely than their younger counterparts to consider special deals or sales, senior discounts, assistance provided by store personnel, special-assistance services, recommendation of same-age peers, and location near several other places they patronize. Younger adults are somewhat more likely than older adults to consider the food store's location in relation to their residence or place of work, which may be in part due to the fact that many older adults do not work.

Baby Boomers vs. Seniors

One objective of this research was to examine food/grocery store patronage reasons among baby boomers and how these differ from the reasons today's seniors give for patronizing these stores. Table 2.3 shows

Table 2.3
Reasons for Patronizing Specific Food and Grocery Stores among Baby
Boomers and Seniors (65+) (Percent Who Feel Reason Is Applicable)

	Baby Boomers (%)	Seniors (%)
Reasons		
Ease of locating merchandise/items	85.07	87.30
Ease of returning products or getting refunds	39.28	40.39
Location near the place you live or work	91.32	82.79
Frequently have items on sale or special deals	66.91	77.40
Offer special discounts to customers over a certain age	6.80	31.04
Have products suitable to your health needs	34.62	39.16
Have personnel who can assist you	27.43	40.72
Preference for payment method	10.96	10.85
Have fast check-out registers	77.88	80.66
Offer special-assistance services (like wrapping, home delivery, package carry-out) to those who need them	23.22	40.53
Recommended by other people your age	12.46	19.43
Carry familiar brands/items	79.31	80.99
Location near several other places you patronize	61.35	63.89
Comfortable place to shop or socialize	48.61	52.95
Base:	(N = 883)	(N = 366)

responses to fourteen pre-selected patronage reasons commonly revealed
in store patronage studies. As the table shows, there is a wide variability
in perceived importance of the reasons, with location and ease of locating
merchandise on the top of the list.

Baby boomers' perceptions differ from those of their elderly counterparts on nearly half of the attributes/reasons examined. Specifically, a
larger percentage of baby boomers than elderly respondents patronizes
food/grocery stores as a result of locational convenience (91.3% vs.
82.8%). However, a smaller percentage of baby boomers considers items
on sale (66.9% vs. 77.4%), personal assistance (27.4% vs. 40.7%), special-
assistance services (23.2% vs. 40.5%), recommendation of same-age peer
groups (12.5% vs. 19.4%), and, as expected, special discounts to customers over a certain age (6.8% vs. 31.0%).

Differences among Older Adults

The perception of the importance of the fourteen factors in selecting food stores changes very little with age in late life. Only three factors show significant change with age. In the meantime, the higher the older person's household income the lower the importance he or she attaches to most of the factors examined. Only three factors show no decline in importance with income: location near the place one lives or works, availability of products suitable to one's health needs, and availability of fast check-out registers. The relationships between education and perceived importance of patronage factors are similar to those between income and reasons for patronizing food stores. However, in addition to the three factors which show no decline with income, two other factors do not relate to education: ease of locating merchandise/items and recommendation by same-age peers. The older person's gerontographic profile also predicts the importance he or she attaches to all fourteen attributes examined. Ailing outgoers perceive the majority of the factors examined to be more important than other gerontographic groups.

Ease of Locating Items. A larger percentage of older Americans who live alone than those who live with others values more ease of locating merchandise/items (90.9% vs. 86.7%). A larger percentage of ailing outgoers (91.4%) considers ease of locating merchandise/items, in comparison with healthy indulgers (84.3%) and frail recluses (84.9%).

Store Location. Studies showed store location in relation to one's home and place of work as an important factor in selecting food stores for all seniors, though this declines somewhat as people get older. The food store's location near the older person's home or place of work is more important to older adults who live in the West (87.3%) than to those who live in the South (82.6%). In the meantime, a larger percentage of older adults who live in urban areas, in relation to their rural counterparts (86.9% vs. 79.0%), considers location near home or place of work to be important in their patronage decision regarding food stores. While location near one's home or place of work is an important patronage reason for food stores, it is more important to healthy indulgers and frail recluses than to healthy hermits.

Older adults from families where at least one person works are more likely than those from families where nobody works to be concerned with whether a store is located near their home or place of work (86.3% vs. 80.5%). Females are also more likely than their male counterparts to look for food outlets that are near other stores they patronize (67.4% vs. 59.6%). This factor is important to a larger percentage of easterners (69.5%) than northerners (60.7%). Location in relation to other stores is far more important to ailing outgoers than it is to frail recluses (73.1% vs. 53.2%).

Brand/Item Familiarity. A larger percentage of ailing outgoers (85.1%) than frail recluses (76.6%) values their familiarity with brands or food items when selecting grocery stores.

Check-Out Lines. Older adults who live in western states are more concerned with getting through check-out lines quickly than their northerner counterparts, with 86.5 percent and 77.0 percent, respectively, placing emphasis on this patronage factor in selecting food stores. A larger percentage of healthy indulgers (83.2%) and ailing outgoers (84.0%) values fast check-out registers than frail recluses (75.4%).

Sales/Special Deals. Females are the bigger bargain hunters of the sexes. They are more likely to consider items "on sale" or special deals (79.3% vs. 72.4% for men) when selecting food stores. Southerners are less concerned with finding items on sale or special deals (71.8%), in comparison with 78.5 percent of older adults who live in other geographic regions.

Store Environment. Females are more likely than men to consider whether the grocery store is a comfortable place to shop and socialize (57.2% vs. 51.4%). A smaller percentage of older adults who live near their children (44.8%), in relation to those who do not live near their children (61.9%), is looking at food stores for shopping comfort and as places to socialize. Six in ten ailing outgoers, in comparison with just half of healthy indulgers, indicated that they patronize food stores because they are comfortable places to shop or socialize.

Availability of Products Suitable to Health Needs. The perceived importance of available products suitable to their health needs shows only a marginal decline as people age. In the meantime, a larger percentage of older adults who live in the South (43.8%) than those who live in the North (38.3%) considers food stores which have products suitable to their health requirements. A larger percentage (46.7%) of ailing outgoers, in comparison with 34.4 percent of frail recluses and 39.0 percent of healthy hermits, patronizes stores because they have products suitable to their health needs.

Return/Refund Policies. Females are more likely than their male counterparts to consider the ease of returning products or getting refunds (42.0% vs. 37.0%. This factor is more important to easterners than it is to northerners, with 42.3 percent and 36.5 percent of the older adults from these regions expressing this view, respectively. Nearly half (46.0%) of the ailing outgoers also consider the convenience of returning products or getting refunds important in their patronage decision of grocery stores, in comparison with three in ten (30.8%) of healthy indulgers and 36.0 percent of frail recluses.

Sales Personnel/Personal Assistance. When selecting food stores, females are more concerned than males with the availability of personnel to assist them (43.3% vs. 37.9%), and the availability of special-assistance services (44.8% vs. 31.9%). While only three in ten older adults in eastern states consider the availability of store personnel for assistance, nearly 45 percent (44.8%) of northerners do the same and 52 percent of older adults in other geographic areas consider this factor in their food-store patronage decision. In the meantime, older adults who live in the North value special-assistance services more than mature Americans who live in the South, with 42.5 percent and 35.7 percent of the older respondents from these regions, respectively, reporting this attitude. A larger percentage of older Americans who live in rural areas than those who live in urban areas considers the availability of store personnel for assistance (46.4% vs. 38.8%) and special-assistance services (43.4% vs. 37.3%) when assessing food stores.

A larger percentage of older Americans who live alone (46.3%) values assistance provided by store personnel in their food-store patronage decision, compared with 38.6 percent for older adults who live with others. Healthy hermits and ailing outgoers consider whether the grocery store's personnel can assist them, with 44.7 percent and 45.0 percent, respectively, indicating this factor, compared with 32.0 percent of healthy indulgers and 34.6 percent of frail recluses. Special-assistance services are of greater importance to ailing outgoers and healthy hermits, with 46.1 percent and 41.5 percent, respectively, reporting this reason to be a relevant patronage motive in their food-store patronage decision (in comparison with 29.7 percent and 30.2 percent of healthy indulgers and frail recluses, respectively).

Senior Discounts. Senior discounts become increasingly important with age in late life, indicating availability and acceptance by older consumers. Mature Americans who live in rural areas consider senior discounts to be of greater importance in their grocery-store patronage decision than their urban counterparts, with 33.0 percent and 26.9 percent, respectively, expressing this opinion. Senior discounts are twice as important to mature Americans who live in northern states as to those who live in the West (36.6% vs. 18.8%).

A smaller percentage of older adults who live near their children, relative to their counterparts who do not live near their children (23.6% vs. 32.9%), patronizes food stores because they offer senior discounts.

Ailing outgoers, and to a lesser extent healthy hermits, are more likely to patronize food stores because of their prices or special deals than other groups. The percentage of ailing outgoers who would patronize stores because they offer senior discounts is nearly double that of healthy indulgers (36.5% vs. 19.3%).

Same-Age Peer Recommendations. The influence of same-age peers increases with age in late life. Same-age peer recommendation is less important to older adults who live in the West (12.7%) than to those who live in other geographic regions, with nearly one in five of older adults in the latter category expressing preference. Word-of-mouth recommendation from same-age peers is far more important to ailing outgoers than to other gerontographic groups, with frail recluses being influenced the least.

Payment Methods. The availability of various methods for paying for grocery products is important to a larger percentage of westerners than southerners, with 13.9 percent and 8.8 percent, respectively, expressing concern. Twice as many ailing outgoers as frail recluses (13.6% vs. 6.1%) consider payment alternatives available in selecting food stores.

REASONS FOR PATRONIZING RESTAURANTS

The present research was not only concerned with the aging person's consumer behavior regarding food products and food shopping for at-home consumption, but also food-consumption behavior away from home. In order to investigate the latter, the research focused on restaurant patronage behavior, using the same fourteen factors which were applied to the selection of food stores. While some of these factors may be more relevant in the case of food-store selection or restaurant selection, they were selected because they may apply to both cases. Respondents were asked to indicate whether each of the specific reasons applied to their decision to start or continue to patronize restaurants.

More than half of older Americans cited three patronage reasons. Senior discounts were mentioned as a factor they consider in their restaurant selection process, with 55.5 percent of them indicating this reason. Nearly as many (54.8%) patronize restaurants because they are comfortable places to socialize, and 50.3 percent choose restaurants because of their proximity to their homes or places of work. Same-age peer recommendation is also a very important patronage reason, with 44.4 percent of mature Americans expressing this view. Over one-third (35.7%) of them indicated location near other places they patronize as a reason in their restaurant patronage behavior, and nearly three in ten (29.3%) cited the restaurant's personnel as a reason.

Ease of locating items (entrees) to order was cited as a reason by 22.1 percent of older respondents, and one in six patronizes restaurants because of special deals. One in seven (14.9%) patronizes those restaurants which have products suitable to their health needs, and as many (14.1%) are concerned with waiting in lines to pay their bills. Payment methods are not a major factor in restaurant patronage decisions and the same appears to be the case with respect to special-assistance services such as package carry-out.

Many restaurant patronage reasons of older adults differ from those of their younger counterparts. The importance of many reasons for pa-

Table 2.4
Reasons for Patronizing Specific Restaurants among Baby Boomers and Seniors (65+) (Percent Who Feel Reason Is Applicable)

	Baby Boomers (%)	Seniors (%)
Reasons		
Ease of locating merchandise/items	20.78	21.62
Ease of returning products or getting refunds	7.39	3.37
Location near the place you live or work	70.08	47.68
Frequently have items on sale or special deals	24.62	17.56
Offer special discounts to customers over a certain age	13.60	56.99
Have products suitable to your health needs	11.16	13.29
Have personnel who can assist you	34.28	24.66
Preference for payment method	12.65	6.98
Have fast check-out registers	14.59	14.91
Offer special-assistance services (like wrapping, home delivery, package carry-out) to those who need them	10.81	5.43
Recommended by other people your age	61.76	42.56
Carry familiar brands/items	7.49	4.78
Location near several other places you patronize	51.53	33.87
Comfortable place to socialize	70.44	49.36
Base:	(N = 883)	(N = 366)

tronizing restaurants (expressed as percentages) is lower among those age 55 and over than among adults under 55. However, the following reasons for patronizing restaurants are as important to younger as they are to older adults: ease of locating items (on the menu), availability of items suitable to their health needs, fast check-out registers, special-assistance services, and familiar items on the menu.

Baby Boomers vs. Seniors

Baby boomers spend a significant portion of their food budget on food prepared/served away from home—that is, restaurants. Consequently, our interest in this research was also in the reasons baby boomers choose specific restaurants in comparison to seniors.

As Table 2.4 shows, responses by the two groups differ in eleven cases. Three factors stand out. First, seven in ten (70.4%) baby boomers consider the restaurant's comfort for socializing, compared with about half (49.4%) of the elderly Americans. Seven in ten (70.1%) baby boomers also consider the restaurant's proximity to their homes or places of work, compared with nearly half of the elderly (47.7%). Finally, recommendation of same-age peers is valued by six in ten (61.8%) baby boomers, compared with four in ten (42.6%) older Americans.

Half (51.5%) of the baby boomers consider the restaurant's location in relation to other types of retail outlets patronized, compared with one-third (33.9%) of the elderly sample. Personnel assistance is more important to baby boomers (34.3% vs. 24.7%). As expected, senior/member discounts are more attractive to older adults because senior discounts are available only to the aged.

Differences among Older Adults

Special Deals/Incentives. Special deals or price incentives become less important with age, especially after age 75. Similarly, discounts offered to people over a certain age become less important with increasing income. Senior discounts are more important to a large number of older Americans from nonworking families (61.0%), in comparison with those from working families (53.1%). A larger percentage of older adults who live with others, relative to those who live alone, responds to special deals (20.8% vs. 12.9%). Also, mature adults who live with others are more likely to consider senior discounts important when selecting restaurants (58.0% vs. 49.5%).

While over half of older adults who live in the North (60.3%) and West (62.4%) respond to senior discounts offered by restaurants, only half of easterners (51.3%) and southerners (49.2%) do the same. In the meantime, older adults who live in urban areas evaluate and choose restaurants based on available special deals, with 20.4 percent of them indicating this reason to be an important patronage motive, in comparison with 13.9 percent of adults who live in rural areas. Ailing outgoers are by far the group most likely to consider senior discounts in their restaurant selection process, with nearly two-thirds of them indicating this attribute to be an important consideration. By contrast, less than half (45.9%) of frail recluses consider senior discounts for the same reason.

Environment. As people age, they are less likely to patronize restaurants because they are comfortable places for socializing. Older adults' perceptions of restaurants as places for socializing is greater among older adults from working families, with 57.8 percent of them expressing preference, in comparison with 47.7 percent of their nonworking counterparts.

Older patrons of restaurants in northern states are more likely to choose restaurants as places for socializing, in comparison with their counterparts from eastern and southern states, with 59.4 percent vis-à-vis 50.9 percent and 51.4 percent, respectively, indicating this patronage reason to be important.

Location. Location becomes less important with age, suggesting that working people may value location near their work in their restaurant choice. Also, the older people get the less likely they are to choose restaurants because of their proximity to other establishments they patronize. Location of restaurants near the older person's home or work is of greater importance to those from families where at least one person works than to those from nonworking families (52.6% vs. 44.8%). In the meantime, older adults in rural areas are more likely than their urban counterparts to patronize restaurants because of their proximity to other retail establishments patronized (40.4% vs. 34.0%).

Similarly, older adults who have no children near them tend to choose restaurants which are in close proximity to other retail establishments, with 43.3 percent of them indicating preference, in comparison with 31.7 percent of their counterparts who have children in close proximity. A larger percentage of healthy indulgers and frail recluses (55.2%) consider location to be important in their patronage decision, in comparison with the remaining gerontographic groups. Finally, four in ten ailing outgoers, in comparison with one in four frail recluses, consider restaurant location near other retail establishments they patronize an important factor in their restaurant patronage decision.

Personnel Assistance/Special Services. Assistance from personnel also becomes decreasingly important as one ages. The importance of personnel in patronage decisions of older Americans also varies between the two groups, with those from working families showing greater appreciation for personnel assistance than their counterparts from nonworking homes (31.3% vs. 24.4%).

Personnel assistance is important to a larger percentage of southerners (31.4%) and westerners (32.4%) than to easterners (24.2%). And while special services, such as package carry-out, is not an important factor, it is valued even less by easterners than older adults who live in other geographic areas, with only 2.7 percent of them mentioning this patronage reason. About one-third of healthy indulgers, in comparison with one-fourth of healthy hermits, value personnel assistance in choosing restaurants. Ailing outgoers are twice as likely as older adults in other groups to value special-assistance services at restaurants.

Same-Age Peer Recommendations. As one ages, same-age peer recommendation becomes decreasingly important. Older Americans who live with others are more likely than those living alone to choose restaurants based on same-age peer recommendations, with nearly half (46.6%) reporting that this type of recommendation is important in their decision to patronize specific restaurants (compared with 39.2 percent for those who live alone). Half of ailing outgoers, in comparison with four in ten of healthy hermits and frail recluses, choose restaurants on the basis of same-age peer recommendation.

Meal/Menu Familiarity. Overall, familiarity with meals on the menu becomes decreasingly important with increasing age in late life. One-fourth (25.5%) of older females, in comparison with 18.2 percent of older males, consider ease of locating menu items important in their patronage decision. Familiarity of items on restaurant menus is twice as important to older adults with incomes $50,000 or more (11.0%) than to those with lower annual household incomes.

Ease of locating items on the menu becomes less important with increasing income. This tendency is reflected in the fact that nearly 28.0 percent (27.6%) of those with high school or less education, in comparison with just over 18.0 percent of those with higher education, place importance on ease of locating items on the menu. This factor is more important to northerners and westerners, with 25.2 percent and 23.5 percent of older adults who live in these areas, respectively, expressing this opinion, in comparison with 16.7 percent of easterners. Familiarity with items on a restaurant's menu is of greater importance to those who live with others than to those who live alone (7.3% vs. 4.2%). More than one in four (27.6%) of ailing outgoers are concerned with ease of locating menu items, in comparison with about one in five of healthy hermits (21.2%), healthy indulgers (18.4%), and frail recluses (18.7%).

Meals Suitable to Senior Health Needs. A larger percentage of older Americans living with others, relative to the proportion of those living alone, is more likely to consider whether a restaurant has meals suitable to their health needs (16.5% vs. 11.2%).

Payment Methods. Preference for method of payment for meals differs between older adults with incomes between $20,000 and $50,000 and those with incomes $50,000 or more, with a larger percentage (12.1%) of the latter group, in comparison with the former group (5.7%), placing importance on this factor. Waiting in lines to pay for one's bill is twice as important to mature Americans with incomes less than $50,000 than those with higher incomes, suggesting that lower-income older adults may also patronize lower-priced restaurants where payment of bill takes place at the cash register. Lines at cash registers become less important with increasing education, again reflecting preferences for different types of restaurants.

Older adults who live in the East are twice as likely as those who live in the North to be concerned with payment methods available in restaurants they consider patronizing (11.5% vs. 5.0%). Northerners, however, along with their older counterparts who live in the South (16.6 percent and 16.0 percent, respectively) value fast check-out more than those who live in the East (10.3%) and West (10.5%). Older adults who have no children in close proximity are more likely than those who do to be concerned with method of meal payment at restaurants, with 11.6 percent and 3.8 percent, respectively, expressing this opinion. Healthy indulgers are the group most likely to be concerned with available methods for payment of meals at restaurants. Ailing outgoers and frail recluses, on the other hand, are the gerontographic groups most likely to be concerned with lines at the cash register.

PREFERENCES FOR METHODS OF PAYMENT

Consumers have a number of methods or choices of payment for meals at restaurants. Besides the three basic options of cash, credit, and check, consumers may use coupons and discounts given to members of certain groups (e.g., senior citizens) as supplements to the three major payment systems. In our research, we asked our respondents to indicate all the methods they would prefer to use to pay for meals at moderately priced restaurants. Response alternatives were: cash, check, credit card, coupon, and senior/member discount. Thus, respondents could check *all* preferred methods.

Cash is the most preferred methods of payment for meals at restaurants, with four in five (80.4%) of older adults expressing preference for this method. Of the three main methods of payment, one in five (24.1%) prefers credit card, which is far less preferred than cash. Check is only preferred by one in ten of older Americans. Of the two supplemental methods, senior/member discount is the preferred method of payment, five times as much preferred over coupons.

Older adults' preferences for payment for meals at restaurants generally differ from those of younger adults. While preference for cash as a method of payment is fairly similar among younger and older adults, younger adults prefer to pay by check, credit card, and use coupons more than their older counterparts. Since senior discounts are available only to older adults, they also are more likely to be preferred by them. However, besides senior/member discounts, younger adults prefer a larger number of payment methods than their older counterparts.

Baby Boomers vs. Seniors

Responses given by baby boomers were also compared to those given by the senior sample. Cash is the most popular method of payment, equally preferred among baby boomers and elderly, with about four in five expressing preference. Credit is preferred by 28.8 percent of baby boomers, in comparison with 22.6 percent of the elderly, while check is preferred three times more by the younger than the older group. Baby boomers are also more likely than their elderly counterparts to use cou-

pons, with 11.0 percent and 7.0 percent, respectively, expressing preference. Availability of senior discounts may have affected responses in
favor of the elderly sample.

Differences among Older Adults

Cash. Use of cash remains fairly stable with age in late life, though the
more money a person earns, the less likely he or she is to use cash for
payment of meals at moderately priced restaurants. Older women are
somewhat more likely than older men to prefer use of cash for payment
of meals at restaurants, with 82.5 percent and 78.3 percent, respectively,
expressing preference. A relatively larger percentage of older Americans
who live in the North (83.3%) and East (83.0%) than those who live in
the South (77.5%) prefer using cash. A larger percentage of healthy hermits (81.8%) than ailing outgoers (77.4%) prefer using cash to pay for
their meals at restaurants.

Coupons. Use of coupons remains fairly stable with age in late life
(Table 2.2). Females are more likely to prefer use of coupons, with 9.6
percent of them expressing preference, in comparison with 6.5 percent
of their male counterparts.

Use of coupons with meals is far less popular among older restaurant
patrons who live in eastern states, with only 3.5 percent expressing preference, in comparison to those who live in the North (8.5%), South (9.0%)
and West (9.9%). Ailing outgoers are also twice as likely as healthy indulgers to use coupons with their payment.

Credit. The use of credit declines as Americans age. Credit cards are
preferred more by older males than older females (31.1% vs. 17.9%).
Preference for credit sharply rises with income, with a larger percentage
of older adults whose family earns $50,000 or more annually expressing
preference than their counterparts with annual family incomes under
$20,000 (46.9% vs. 11.8%). Similarly, the more educated the mature per-
son, the more likely he or she is to use credit as the chosen form of
payment. Older adults who live with others prefer using credit to pay
for meals at moderately priced restaurants. In comparison with older
adults who live alone, a larger percentage of those who live with others
prefer using credit (26.6% vs. 18.1%). Older adults who live in urban
areas prefer making use of their credit card for meal payment, more so
than their rural counterparts (26.0% vs. 17.5%).

Use of credit card is preferred twice as much by mature Americans
who live in the West than in the North, with 33.1 percent and 16.6 percent, respectively, expressing preference. Mature Americans who live
near their children are more likely than those who do not have children
near them to prefer using a credit card to pay for meals at restaurants,
with 22.9 percent and 12.8 percent, respectively, expressing preference.

While ailing outgoers are less likely than any of the remaining gerontographic groups to prefer making use of a credit card, they are more
likely than healthy hermits and healthy indulgers to write a check for
the amount of their meal.

Check. Use of check declines as Americans age. Paying by check appears to be three times less popular among older adults who live in the
East (3.5%) than in other geographic regions. In the meantime, older
adults who live in rural areas are nearly twice as likely as their urban
counterparts to prefer payment by check for meals at restaurants, with
15.2 percent of the former group (in comparison with 8.6 percent of the
latter) indicating preference.

Senior/Member Discounts. The relationship between age and preference
for senior/member discounts is curvilinear, with more mature Americans between the ages of 65 and 74 likely to favor their use than any
other group. Older adults who live with others prefer using senior/mem-
ber discounts to pay for meals at moderately priced restaurants. In comparison with older adults who live alone, a larger percentage of those
who live with others prefer using senior/member discounts (45.4% vs.
35.4%).

There are geographic variations in preferences for using senior/mem-
ber discounts at restaurants. A larger percentage of northerners (46.1%)
and westerners (46.2%) prefer this method of supplementing one of the
three main forms of payment, in comparison with their counterparts who
live in the East (36.2%) and South (39.7%). About half (48.2%) of older
adults in families that have no working person prefer using senior/mem-
ber discounts, in comparison with older adults in families where at least
one person works (39.9%). Along with frail recluses, ailing outgoers are
heavier users of senior/member discounts than their counterparts in the
two remaining gerontographic segments.

MEDIA USE PROFILES

Media consumption patterns were analyzed among older adults who
prefer (or have need for) certain dietary food products, in comparison
with older adults who do not. Media preferences were analyzed with
regard to both general and specific consumption patterns. Respondents
were asked to indicate how often they watch certain programs on television, read the newspaper, listen to the radio, and use a VCR.

They were also asked to write down the names of magazines they read
on a regular basis.

Older people in need of dietary meals or products for people with
certain health requirements tend to be heavier users of premium TV
cable channels; they are also heavier viewers of TV comedy and variety
shows, TV adventure and drama shows, and TV news and documenta-

ries. Preferences for dietary meals were also analyzed by specific type of magazines read by older adults. Older adults who use or would like to have/use dietary products, or products for people with certain health requirements, in comparison to older adults who do not need such products, tend to read the following magazines:

- *Ladies' Home Journal* (7.2% vs. 4.5%)
- Homes/decorating magazines (13.1% vs. 9.5%)
- Magazines on religion (6.2% vs. 3.7%)

Thus, magazine readership does not differentiate between older adults who are heavy users of dietary products and those who are not.

3

Apparel and Footwear

Clothes and shoes are necessity items, but the consumption of these products also has a symbolic meaning. Preferences for clothes are often dictated by social norms, and many of us use such products to project a desired self-image to others. Consequently, we were interested in learning about people's motivations for purchasing and consumption habits with respect to apparel and footwear.

PURCHASE OF NEW APPAREL AND FOOTWEAR

Consumption of apparel products was examined in the context of consumers' propensity to buy new styles of clothes or shoes. While variations in product use were expected to exist, it was felt that preferences for new styles would be more indicative of their interest in apparel, in comparison to assessing ownership/use of apparel or date acquired, since people vary with respect to the length of time they keep apparel, usage rate, and the like. Respondents in our study were asked to indicate whether they "currently have," "would like to have," "not interested in having," or "don't know" a new style of clothes or shoes ("new" was defined as a style available in the past two years).

In examining ownership among the older group, nearly half (48.6%) of older Americans age 55 and over indicated they own at least one new style of clothes or shoes. This figure is lower than that for younger adults (57.9%). In another comparison of ownership figures between baby boomers and seniors, 61 percent of the former group and 45.7 percent of their elders indicated ownership. While percentage figures are generally lower for the older groups, ownership of new styles of clothes or shoes shows only a minor decline with age, with 51.8 percent of those age 55 to 64 indicating ownership, in comparison with 45.9 percent and 45.7 percent of those age 65 to 74, and 75 or older, respectively.

Ownership of new style of clothes or shoes is higher among older females than older males (55.3% vs. 40.2%) and increases with income and education. Older adults from families where at least one person works (inclusive of themselves) are more likely to have a new style of clothes or shoes, in comparison to older adults from nonworking families (50.3% vs. 43.9%). A larger percentage of mature Americans who live in the East (52.4%), in comparison to those who live in northern states (44.3%), indicated ownership of a new style of clothes or shoes. Finally, a larger percentage of healthy indulgers (54.2%) and ailing outgoers (53.5%), in comparison with healthy hermits (42.4%) and frail recluses (46.8%), indicated ownership of a new style of clothes or shoes.

INFORMATION SOURCES FOR NEW APPAREL

What sources of information are the older consumer groups likely to find most useful regarding apparel? In order to answer this question we examined responses to new clothing and fashion, since consumers have different amounts of information stored in their memory about existing products. Specifically, respondents were asked to indicate the source of information they prefer to learn about new clothing and fashion, whether they prefer to see a TV or print ad, receive news in the mail, be contacted by phone, be visited by an agent, or learn in group meetings or seminars.

Preferences for information sources among the different groups of older consumers we studied are fairly similar. More than half (57.6%) of older Americans prefer to learn about new clothing and fashion from TV or print advertisements. One in three (30.7%) prefers to receive news in the mail. Only 2.6 percent indicated preference for learning about these products in group meetings. Only 1.1 percent would like to be visited by a salesperson about clothing or fashion matters, and virtually none prefer to be contacted by phone. Preferences for information sources among older adults are fairly similar to those of adults under 55 years of age, although the older group is somewhat less likely than their younger counterparts to prefer TV or print ads (57.1% vs. 61.9%).

Baby Boomers vs. Seniors

Comparisons of preferences for information sources between baby boomers and seniors show rather similar patterns. Nearly two-thirds of baby boomers (65.7%) prefer to learn about what is new in fashion from TV or print ads. This percentage is somewhat higher than that for seniors (61.1%). Direct mail is equally preferred by the two groups, with nearly one-third of them (32.7%) preferring this source. Learning in group meeting is not a very popular source of information, although this method is somewhat more popular among senior consumers (0.9% vs. 4.0%).

Differences among Older Adults

The following sections outline how sociodemographic and gerontographic characteristics of older Americans predict their preferences for information sources regarding clothing products.

TV and Print Ads. TV and print ads as sources of information declines in importance with increasing age. It is not clear, however, whether this decline represents a lower interest in these sources or whether the sources do not contain relevant information (e.g., styles and fashion) for older people. The higher the older person's household income the stronger his/her preference for TV and print ads. A larger percentage of older adults who live in the West (64.6%) prefer to receive such information from TV or print ads, in comparison with those who live in the North (54.6%) and South (56.6%). While two-thirds (66.3%) of healthy indulgers prefer to see TV or print ads, only half (49.6%) of ailing outgoers prefer the same sources.

Direct Mail. Preference for direct mail declines with age, especially after age 75, but as in the case of TV and print ads, the reason is not clear. Older people who live in rural areas are more likely than their urban counterparts to prefer learning about new clothing styles and fashion from mail they receive from direct marketers, with 35.9 percent and 29.2 percent, respectively, expressing preferences. Ailing outgoers are nearly twice as likely as healthy indulgers (37.9% vs. 20.9%) to prefer receiving information in the mail.

Personal Sources. Preferences for personal sources of information in the context of group meetings or seminars increases with age. The higher a mature American's income, the lower his/her preference for direct mail and group meetings or seminars as sources of information regarding new clothing styles and fashion. While relatively few older Americans prefer to learn about new clothing styles and fashion in group meetings or seminars, a larger percentage of northerners (5.1%) than easterners (0.5%), southerners (1.8%) or westerners (1.1%) prefers this alternative. A larger percentage of older adults who live near their children prefers to hear clothing or fashion news from an agent at their home, in comparison with those mature Americans who do not live near their children (5.9% vs. 1.0%). Finally, ailing outgoers are more likely than healthy hermits to prefer learning about new clothing and fashion in group meetings or seminars, with 3.9 percent and 1.5 percent, respectively, indicating preference.

PREFERENCES FOR METHODS OF PURCHASING
APPAREL AND FOOTWEAR

Consumers have a number of options available to them in purchasing apparel. Besides buying such products at vendors' facilities, they may also buy through the mail or by phone, and some of them may have the option to buy at their residence. In order to determine preference for purchasing methods, respondents were asked to indicate how they prefer to buy clothes and shoes. (Respondents were asked to indicate as many ways as they prefer.)

Older Americans' preferences for methods of purchasing apparel are fairly similar to those of younger adults with the exception of preferences for direct mail. Nearly one in three (31.7%) of adults under 55, in comparison with one in five of older adults, indicated preference for direct mail. These figures do not change much when comparisons are made between baby boomers and seniors. However, preferences for purchasing methods vary by selected sociodemographic and gerontographic characteristics.

Retail. The vast majority (94.9%) of older Americans prefer buying apparel products at retail outlets. Preferences for buying apparel at retail facilities increase with income, and are stronger among older adults who live with others than those who live alone (95.8% vs. 92.8%). Urban dwellers prefer buying at retail facilities slightly more than older Americans living in rural areas. Healthy hermits are relatively less likely than healthy indulgers and frail recluses to prefer buying apparel at stores.

Buying Direct. One in five (20.2%) of older adults prefers to buy through the mail. A larger percentage of those who live in rural areas (24.5%), in comparison with those who live in urban areas (19.3%), prefers buying apparel through the mail. A larger percentage of frail recluses (23.2%) and healthy hermits (22.6%), in comparison with healthy indulgers (14.0%), prefers buying through the mail. Only a very small percentage (2.3%) prefers to purchase by phone. Healthy hermits are more likely than healthy indulgers (3.9% vs. .6%) to buy by phone. Preference for door-to-door buying is negligible (less than 1 percent).

REASONS FOR PATRONIZING DEPARTMENT STORES

Buying apparel at retail facilities is the most preferred way of buying such products among older Americans. While specialty stores carry specific lines of apparel (e.g., shoes, clothes), department stores were investigated because these outlets tend to carry nearly every type of apparel product and they tend to be preferred by older shoppers. Thus, our survey sought to determine reasons for patronizing specific department stores. Respondents in our survey were presented with a list of patronage reasons and were asked to indicate whether each reason applied to their decision to start or continue to patronize a specific department store.

Ease of returning products or getting refunds is the most important factor among those presented to older Americans, with 78 percent of them indicating this factor applies to their decision to patronize a department store. Other factors, in order of importance, include: "sales" (66.7%), ease of locating merchandise (60.5%), availability of personnel who could assist them (59.5%), availability of familiar brands/items (58.2%); and half of older customers value the store's location near other places they patronize, and the store's comfort for shopping and socializing. Other factors are of lesser importance to older shoppers. Location near one's residence or place of work is valued by 47.7 percent of them, while 42.6 percent consider the store's payment or billing methods. Four in ten (39.1%) value the availability of special-assistance services, and nearly one in three (31.2%) appreciates fast check-out registers. Only one in four (27.5%) considers the availability of senior discounts in their patronage decision, and one in six is influenced by same-age peer recommendations and the availability of products suitable to their physical/health needs.

Despite the older Americans' concerns with these patronage factors, these concerns are not unique to this age group. Rather, younger people are more concerned about the majority of these factors. Only special-assistance services, billing/payment methods, and product suitability to one's physical/health needs are valued equally by both younger and older Americans.

Baby Boomers vs. Seniors

Based on previous research on patronage behavior, a list of fourteen patronage reasons commonly considered important to various age groups was developed. Table 3.1 shows responses given by baby boomers and seniors to each of these fourteen reasons.

Ease of returning products or getting refunds is considered important by the largest majority (86.3%) of baby boomers, compared with two-thirds (74.6%) of the senior sample. Nearly four-fifths (78.5%) patronize specific department stores because of sales or special deals, while senior consumers are less conscious of, and are less concerned with such sales promotions (63.7%). Two-thirds of baby boomers patronize department stores because items can be located with considerable ease (69.6%), availability of familiar brands/items (66.8%), helpful personnel (67.6%), and store location (66.6%). All these factors are of lesser importance to the seniors. In fact, the elderly value nearly all fourteen attributes less than baby boomers. Only availability of products suitable to specific physical/

Table 3.1
Reasons for Patronizing Department Stores among Baby Boomers and
Seniors (65+) (Percent Who Feel Reason Is Applicable)

	Baby Boomers (%)	Seniors (%)
Reasons		
Ease of locating merchandise/items	69.64	58.00
Ease of returning products or getting refunds	86.35	74.59
Location near the place you live or work	66.85	44.22
Frequently have items on sale or special deals	78.47	63.72
Offer special discounts to customers over a certain age	8.14	28.06
Have products suitable to your physical/health needs	14.83	13.63
Have personnel who can assist you	67.62	56.52
Preference for billing/payment method	40.63	41.26
Have fast check-out registers	45.63	29.98
Offer special-assistance services (like wrapping, home delivery, package carry-out) to those who need them	35.82	37.88
Recommended by other people your age	23.91	16.21
Carry familiar brands/items	66.81	54.73
Location near several other places you patronize	62.05	47.66
Comfortable place to shop or socialize	59.32	45.22
Base:	(N = 883)	(N = 366)

health needs is equally valued by both groups; and age-based discounts
are considered more by the elderly due to their availability.

Differences among Older Adults

The importance of most of these patronage factors declines in late life.
Nine of the fourteen factors examined decline with age. Only ease of
locating merchandise, senior discounts, billing/payment methods, fast
check-out registers, and recommendation by same-age peers do not
change in importance with age.

Return/Refund Policies. Ease of returning products or getting refunds is
the most important factor among those presented to older Americans,
with 78 percent of them indicating this factor applies to their decision to
patronize a department store. A larger percentage of older adults who

live with others than those who live alone considers ease of returning products or getting refunds (80.2% vs. 72.8%).

Older adults with children who live more than one hour's drive away place more emphasis on return and refund policies, in comparison with those with children within one hour's drive (77.5% vs. 69.1%). A larger percentage of northerners (82.4%) than easterners (72.2%) considers ease of returning products or getting refunds. Finally, ailing outgoers and healthy indulgers consider ease of returning products or getting refunds more than the other gerontographic groups.

Sales/Special Deals. Well over half of mature Americans—66.7 percent— indicated that "sales" were important in the determination of what department stores they would patronize. However, this becomes less of a factor as an older person's household income increases. Older people who live with others are more likely than their counterparts who live alone to consider sales or special deals (68.6% vs. 62.4%) when choosing a store. Urban-dwelling older Americans are more likely than those in rural areas to place importance on this element (68.8% vs. 61.4%) when choosing department stores. A larger percentage of ailing outgoers (71.6%) than healthy hermits (63.3%) or frail recluses (64.8%) considers "sales" and special deals in patronizing department stores.

Merchandise. The ease with which they could locate merchandise was cited as a factor in their store selection by 60.5 percent of older Americans surveyed. Older females place a greater emphasis on ease of locating merchandise, with 64.9 percent of them indicating this to be an important factor, in comparison with 55 percent of their male counterparts. A larger percentage of older adults from families where at least one person works than adults from nonworking families considers ease of locating merchandise (64.0% vs. 52.1%). Ease of locating merchandise is more important to ailing outgoers and healthy indulgers than to the other gerontographic groups.

Personal Assistance. A majority of older adults (59.5%) indicated that the availability of personnel who could assist them influences their store decisions. Mature Americans living with others are more concerned with this factor than are their counterparts who live alone (61.1% vs. 55.6%). While only half (50.7%) of those who live in eastern states consider availability of personnel assistance, more than six in ten of the older Americans who live in the remaining parts of the country consider this factor in their patronage decision.

Brand/Item Availability. Availability of familiar brands/items was cited by 58.2 percent of mature Americans as a factor in their decision to patronize a store. With increasing household income, older people place more emphasis on the availability of familiar (well-known) brands. In the meantime, this factor is more important to older adults with some college education than to their counterparts who are better or less educated.

The availability of familiar brands/items is more important to older people who live with others than it is to older Americans who live alone (60.0% vs. 53.9%). Familiar brands are more important to older adults with children who live more than one hour's drive away than they are to those mature Americans who live within an hour's drive of their children (60.5% vs. 49.6%). A larger percentage of ailing outgoers (62.5%) and healthy indulgers (61.5%) than healthy hermits (53.8%) considers brand-name familiarity of items carried by department stores.

Location. Half of older customers value the store's location near other places they patronize, and the store's comfort for shopping and socializing. Location near one's residence or place of work is valued by 47.7 percent of them.

The higher older Americans' household income and educational attainment, the less likely they are to be concerned with whether a store is located near other places they patronize. Adults from families where at least one person works are more likely than their counterparts from nonworking families to consider in their patronage decision whether a store is located near their home or place of work (49.8% vs. 42.9%) and near other places they patronize (52.1% vs. 46.2%). In comparison with older adults who live in rural areas, older adults who live in large cities place more emphasis on location near the place they live or work (49.7% vs. 42.8%) in deciding which department stores to patronize. Store proximity to other places patronized is more important to ailing outgoers and healthy hermits than to the other two gerontographic groups.

Payment Methods. Less than half of older Americans—42.6 percent— consider the store's payment or billing methods when choosing a department store. Older females consider billing or payment methods to a greater extent than their male counterparts, with 47.2 percent and 37.3 percent, respectively, indicating this factor to be important in their decision to patronize department stores.

With increasing education, mature Americans are less concerned with billing or payment methods. Relative to mature Americans with children living within one hour's drive, older adults with children who live more than one hour's drive away place more emphasis on billing/payment methods (48.9% vs. 36.3%). A larger percentage of easterners (48.7%) than northerners (40.5%) and southerners (40.9%) considers payment/ billing methods.

There is a wide variability among gerontographic groups regarding their preferences for billing/payment methods, with more than half (52.4%) of ailing outgoers considering this factor in their patronage decision, in comparison with just a little over one-third of frail recluses (34.9%) and healthy indulgers (35.9%).

Special-Assistance Services. Four in ten (39.1%) value the availability of special-assistance services. Compared to mature Americans with children who live within an hour's drive, older adults with children who live more than one hour's drive away place more emphasis on this factor (43.9% vs. 32.6%). A larger percentage of ailing outgoers (45.7%) and healthy indulgers (42.4%), in comparison with frail recluses (31.2%) and healthy hermits (36.3%), considers the availability of special-assistance services in patronizing department stores.

Check-Out Lines. Nearly one in three (31.2%) appreciates fast check-out registers. However, the higher a person's household income and level of educational attainment, the less likely he or she is to consider this factor. Older people who live with others are more likely than those living alone to consider check-out lines (33.7% vs. 25.2%).

Older people with children who live more than one hour's drive away are more likely than their counterparts with children who live within an hour away to place more emphasis on check-out lines (32.8% vs. 18.0%). A larger percentage of northerners (35.0%) than southerners (28.0%) and westerners (28.2%) considers this factor in their patronage decision. Fast check-out registers are more important to ailing outgoers and healthy hermits than to healthy indulgers and frail recluses.

Senior Discounts. Only one in four (27.5%) considers the availability of senior discounts in their patronage decision. The higher older Americans' income and level of education, the less likely they are to be concerned with this element. A larger percentage of those from nonworking families (32.4%) considers senior discounts, in comparison with those from families where at least one person works (25.5%). Senior discounts appeal to a larger percentage of older adults who live in the East (31.7%) and North (30.8%) than to those who live in the South (25.1%) and West (22.1%). Senior discounts are more important to ailing outgoers and healthy hermits than to frail recluses and healthy indulgers.

Peer Influences. Only one in six is influenced by same-age peer recommendations and the availability of products suitable to their physical/health needs. As a mature person's income increases, he or she tends to place less importance on the recommendation of same-age peers when choosing a store.

Those mature Americans from families where at least one person works are more likely than those from nonworking families to consider special-assistance services (40.6% vs. 35.7%). Personal recommendation of department stores by same-age peers is more important to older people who live in the South than among those who live in the West, with 18.8 percent and 12.8 percent, respectively, indicating this factor. When choosing a department store, mature Americans who live in urban areas are more concerned with the recommendation of same-age peers than those who live in rural areas (18.6% vs. 13.6%).

Reliance on word-of-mouth communications in choosing department stores depends on the older person's gerontographic profile as well. One in four of ailing outgoers relies on recommendations given by same-age peers, in comparison with just one in ten of frail recluses and healthy indulgers.

Store Environment. More educated older people are less likely than their less educated counterparts to consider a store's comfort as a place for shopping or socializing. Whether or not a store provides comfort of shopping and socializing is more important to older people from families where at least one person works, compared to those from nonworking families (52.0% vs. 45.5%). Among gerontographic groups, ailing out-goers are more likely than frail recluses to consider a department store's comfort as a place to shop and socialize.

Special Products. Only one in six older Americans indicated that they are influenced by the availability of products suitable to their physical/health needs.

REASONS CONSIDERED BEFORE BUYING APPAREL BY PHONE OR MAIL

Consumers may consider several factors in deciding whether or not to buy direct. Based on previous research, respondents in our study were presented with a list of eight factors and were asked to indicate whether they would consider each before buying clothes and shoes by phone or through the mail.

Again, we found significant differences in responses of consumers in different age groups. Approximately two-thirds of older adults indicated price (67.2%) and return/cancellation and refund policy (65.8%) as reasons. Four other factors were indicated by the majority of older Americans: days to wait before receiving (56.9%), selection of products (55.3%), availability of toll-free (800) number (53.4%), and convenience (53.3%). Also of importance are acceptance of credit cards and availability of pick-up service for returns, with 42 percent of older respondents indicating these factors.

While the eight factors appear to be important considerations in the minds of older Americans, they are even more so among younger consumers. When responses were compared to those given by younger age groups, younger adults mentioned these factors a lot more frequently than their older counterparts.

Baby Boomers vs. Seniors

Each of the eight factors is perceived to be of greater importance to baby boomers than to seniors (see Table 3.2). The most important ones

Table 3.2

Reasons Considered before Buying Clothes and Shoes by Phone or through the Mail among Baby Boomers and Seniors (65+)

Reasons	Baby Boomers (%)	Seniors (%)
Price (including shipping charges)	73.78	66.48
Type of credit card accepted	55.58	40.61
Return/cancellation and refund policy	77.98	62.66
Convenience, in comparison to other ways of buying the same product	66.45	50.13
Free pick-up service for returns	56.59	36.83
Availability of toll-free (800) number	62.21	46.79
Selection of products	67.62	50.72
Days to wait before receiving	65.88	52.64
Base:	(N = 555)	(N = 214)

are: return/cancellation, and refund policy with 78 percent of baby boomers and 62.9 percent of seniors indicating importance, respectively; and price (73.8% vs. 66.5%). All of the factors examined are perceived to be important by the majority of baby boomers.

Differences among Older Adults

The factors considered by older persons in buying apparel by phone or mail differ by select background, sociodemographic, and gerontographic characteristics. In general, with age, older adults place less emphasis on the eight factors examined.

Price. Older Americans age 75 and over are less likely than those age 65 to 74 to consider price. In comparison to their male counterparts, a larger percentage of older female shoppers considers this factor (72.3% vs. 61.1%). Also, a larger percentage of westerners (70.7%) and northerners (70.2%) than southerners (62.9%) considers price before buying by phone or mail. A larger percentage of frail recluses (71.5%) than ailing outgoers (64.8%) considers price.

Return/Cancellation Policies. Return/cancellation and refund policy is more important to the youngest than the oldest group of older adults. More older females than males consider these policies before buying via phone or mail (68.4% vs. 62.8%). With increasing household income, older adults place a greater emphasis on return/cancellation and refund policies. Similarly, the more educated an older American, the more emphasis he or she is likely to place on this element.

A larger percentage of older Americans who live with others (67.6%), in comparison with those who live alone (61.3%), considers return or cancellation policies. Older adults who live in the East are also more likely than their counterparts who live in the West to value this service (47.6% vs. 36.5%).

Selection. Selection is more important to those age 55 to 64 than it is to older groups. Mature Americans with higher household incomes are more likely than their lower-income counterparts to consider selection of products before buying clothes and shoes by phone or through the mail. The more educated an older American is, the more likely he or she is to consider this factor. Also, a larger percentage of healthy indulgers (60.2%) than ailing outgoers (52.4%) considers product selection.

When buying via mail or telephone, mature Americans living with others place more emphasis on the available selection of products than their counterparts who live alone (57.3% vs. 50.2%). Southerners are more likely than easterners to consider this factor (58.8% vs. 51.9%).

Wait Time. The number of days to wait before receiving an order is more important to those age 55 to 64 than it is to the older groups. Relative to men, women place more importance on this lag time (62.0% vs. 50.8%). Finally, both ailing outgoers and healthy hermits are more likely than healthy indulgers to consider days one must wait before receiving apparel ordered direct.

Convenience. Convenience is more important to those under age 75 than to their older counterparts. Overall, older females are more likely than older males to consider convenience (56.2% vs. 49.8%). Convenience becomes more important to older Americans as their household income and level of educational attainment increase. A larger percentage of easterners (59.3%) than southerners (49.2%) and westerners (50.8%) considers the convenience aspect of direct buying.

Availability of Toll-Free Numbers. The importance of the availability of a toll-free number declines with age. This is more important to older women than it is to older men (59.6% vs. 45.3%). Also, the higher an older person's household income, the more likely he or she is to be concerned with the availability of a toll-free number.

Older people who live with others are more likely to be concerned with this element than are those mature Americans who live alone (55.6% vs. 47.7%). Older easterners are also more likely than older northerners to consider whether or not they can make a free call (58.7% vs. 49.3%).

Credit Cards Accepted. Also, the oldest age group is less likely than younger groups to be concerned with type of credit card accepted in the process of buying clothes and shoes direct. This factor is more important to older adults with "some college" education than to those with more or less education, with 47.4 percent (vs. 39.1% and 40.5%, respectively) considering this reason. Among older adults who live alone, those who live away from their children tend to be more likely than those with children nearby to consider type of credit card accepted in buying direct, with 48.4 percent and 36.1 percent, respectively, indicating they consider this factor.

Return Pick-Up Service. Free pick-up service for returns is valued most by the 55-to-64 age group. Mature females are more concerned than their male counterparts with this factor (46.0% vs. 37.0%). Ailing outgoers are more likely than frail recluses and healthy hermits to consider the availability of free pick-up service for returns.

REASONS FOR CHOOSING BRANDS OF APPAREL AND FOOTWEAR

There are several reasons why consumers may choose certain brands of apparel and footwear. Respondents in our survey were presented with a list of reasons for choosing clothes and shoes and were asked to indicate whether or not each reason applies to their decision to choose or switch brands. The sections below highlight the most important reasons.

It should be noted that the reasons for choosing specific brands are not important just to a certain group of people. In fact, most of the reasons are of greater importance to younger than to older Americans, but many others are of greater importance to older adults. For example, factors such as same-age peer advice is twice more important to younger than to older shoppers of apparel.

Baby Boomers vs. Seniors

Why do baby boomers select specific brands of apparel products, and how do their brand-choice motives differ from those of the seniors? A larger percentage of baby boomers, compared to their senior counterparts, considers price (93.7% vs. 76.0%), advice/request of spouse or other relatives (39.1% vs. 25.9%), advice of same-age peers (31.1% vs. 25.6%), how others might perceive them because of the brands of apparel they wear (21.6% vs. 10.4%), how ads of apparel manufacturers stereotype people their age (22.1% vs. 14.9%), and availability of coupons (15.5% vs. 9.8%). On the other hand, baby boomers are less likely than seniors to rely on recommendations of salespersons (21.2% vs. 26.7%) and to mention that ease of reading information on apparel products is an important consideration (8.7% vs. 12.3%).

Differences among Older Adults

The older person's reasons for choosing specific brands of clothes and shoes vary, depending on his or her sociodemographic and geronto-graphic characteristics. The importance of only three reasons for choosing specific brands of apparel remains fairly similar across different age groups—availability of coupons, advice of same-age peers, and proper age-stereotyping of ads are of equal magnitude among older people in the three age groups.

Sales and Coupons. Price is more important to older females than older males, with 81.9 percent and 77.8 percent, respectively, indicating this reason for choosing specific brands of clothes and shoes. Price or sale is more important to the middle-income group ($20,000–$50,000) than to the two extreme groups.

Nearly four in five (79.8%) of older Americans consider "sales" as a reason for switching brands of apparel and shoes. The more educated an older American, the less likely he or she is to be concerned with the availability of coupons and rebates. A larger percentage of older adults who live in families where at least one person works (81.6%) than those from nonworking families (75.4%) considers price reductions or special sales in deciding which brand of apparel to choose.

A larger percentage of those whose children live away, relative to those with children within an hour's drive, places greater emphasis on coupons (13.5% vs. 5.8%) and rebates (14.6% vs. 8.1%). Price reductions or special sales are important to a larger percentage of mature adults who live in the West (84.9%) than to those who live in the East (75.0%) or North (78.2%). Ailing outgoers are more likely than healthy indulgers and frail recluses to consider using coupons with their purchases. Also, a larger percentage of ailing outgoers (15.6%) than frail recluses (9.3%) would consider rebates.

Family Influences. Nearly three in ten (28.6%) of older people rely on advice of relatives when considering brands of clothing and shoes. Older males are more likely than their female counterparts to be influenced by family (34.8% vs. 23.7%). The higher the person's income the more he or she relies on advice of spouse or other relatives.

The advice of spouse or other relatives is important to those who have access to it; it is more important to people who live with others than it is to those older Americans who live alone (32.5% vs. 18.9%). Older people who live farther away from their children are more likely than those whose children are within an hour's drive to rely on the advice of other relatives when considering different brands (28.2% vs. 10.8%). Advice of a spouse is more important to older shoppers who live in the North and West, with 32.0 percent and 30.6 percent, respectively, indicating this reason, in comparison to older Americans who live in the East (24.8%)

and South (26.1%). Healthy indulgers rely on a spouse's advice more than any other group, with healthy hermits being the gerontographic group least likely to rely on a spouse.

Peer Influences and Evaluation. When considering brands, the advice of same-age peers is more important to people whose children live far away than it is to those older consumers who live within an hour's drive of their children (19.6% vs. 12.6%). Advice of same-age peers is more important to healthy indulgers and ailing outgoers than to frail recluses.

Older men are more likely than older women to be concerned with what others might think of them because of the brands of apparel they buy or wear (14.2% vs. 10.5%). The more educated an older person is, the less concerned he or she is with other people's opinions of those who use certain brands of clothing or shoes. Nearly twice as many older adults who live in families where at least one person works (13.9%) as those from nonworking families (7.8%) are concerned with other people's impressions of those who use certain brands. Ailing outgoers are twice as likely as healthy indulgers to be concerned with what others think of people who use certain brands.

Salesperson's Recommendations. Only one in four relies on a salesperson's recommendation when considering a switch to another brand. However, this becomes more important after the age of 75 as more older Americans become widowed and isolated from relatives. Recommendation of salespersons was mentioned more frequently by people who live alone than by older Americans who live with others (28.3% vs. 22.9%). Older people who live in the West are far less likely than their eastern counterparts (18.5% vs. 29.4%) to rely on the word of a salesperson. Finally, salesperson opinion is most important to ailing outgoers and least important to healthy hermits.

Age-Stereotyping in Advertisements. Fewer than one in six older Americans mentions proper age-stereotyping in ads as important when considering a switch to another brand. As older persons' levels of education attainment rises, they are less concerned with this factor. A larger percentage of older people who live with others, in comparison with those who live alone, mentioned proper age-stereotyping in ads (17.5% vs. 11.6%) as a factor when considering brands. A smaller percentage of westerners (10.8%) than southerners (19.1%) and northerners (16.4%) cited this element as a reason for buying specific brands of apparel. Ailing outgoers along with healthy hermits are more concerned with proper age-stereotyping in ads of apparel brand makers, in comparison with their counterparts in the remaining two gerontographic groups.

Ease of Product Use/Reading and Understanding Information and Instructions. Fewer than one in six older people consider the ease of reading information on labels, and ease of understanding and following instructions provided with the product when contemplating a brand change.

Understanding and following directions provided with the product is of greater importance to women than it is to men (13.2% vs. 8.7%).

Ease of using the product and of understanding and following directions declines in importance with increasing levels of education. Westerners are twice as likely as easterners to indicate that ease of reading information on labels is an important factor influencing their brand choice, with 17.9 percent and 8.5 percent, respectively, indicating this reason for buying. Similarly, westerners are more concerned than easterners regarding the ease of using the product (20.7% vs. 10.8%). A larger percentage of ailing outgoers than frail recluses (16.3% vs. 11.3%) cited ease of reading information on labels.

Special Products. Those who live within an hour's drive from their children are more likely than their counterparts living farther away to consider availability of products for people with certain physical/health requirements (14.6% vs. 7.4%). Also, westerners are more likely than any other geographic group to be concerned with product availability for people with certain physical requirements. Healthy hermits and ailing outgoers are twice as likely as their counterparts in the other gerontographic groups to be concerned with the availability of products for people with certain physical requirements.

MEDIA USE PROFILES

Media preferences were analyzed among older adults (age 55 and over) who expressed interest in new styles of clothes and shoes and those who did not. Specifically, older adults were asked to indicate how often they watch certain cable channels and TV programs, read the newspaper, listen to the radio, and use a VCR to record or play movies; and they were asked to write down the names of magazines they frequently read.

Older adults who prefer new styles of apparel products are heavier users of cable channels, with 38 percent of them indicating viewership of such channels once or more frequently a week, in comparison with 32.7 percent of older adults who are not interested in these products. Also, a larger percentage of the former group, in comparison to those with less interest, watch adventure and drama TV shows several times a week (62.5% vs. 54.8%), watch TV news and documentaries every day (81.5% vs. 76.0%), and use a VCR to record or play movies at least once a week (36.5% vs. 29.6%).

Magazine readership patterns also differ among older adults who prefer new styles of apparel and those who do not. A significantly (statistically) larger percentage of the former group, in comparison to the latter group, reads the following magazines on a frequent basis:

- *Family Circle* (6.7% vs. 2.4%)
- *Ladies' Home Journal* (7.0% vs. 2.4%)

- *Modern Maturity* (12.4% vs. 9.9%)
- *People* (5.7% vs. 2.7%)
- General interest magazines to women only (12.1% vs. 5.4%)
- General interest magazines to both men and women (18.2% vs. 13.7)

4

Pharmaceutical Products

Pharmaceutical products were also the focus of our investigation. In this area, we examined the consumption behavior of younger and older Americans with respect to both prescription and over-the-counter (OTC) drugs and cosmetics. Specifically, we were interested in particular product use and how people acquire these products. We investigated sources of information regarding new products of drugs and cosmetics, as well as preferences for various methods of purchasing these products. We also examined reasons for purchasing specific brands, reasons for patronizing specific drug stores and pharmacies, as well as reasons for buying (or not buying) direct. Finally, we examined preferences for payment methods, and investigated characteristics of users and nonusers of drugs and cosmetics.

The older consumer's behavior in the marketplace with respect to pharmaceutical products was examined by questioning respondents in three broad product categories: drugs, health aids, and cosmetic products. With respect to drugs, both prescription and nonprescription categories were examined. Cosmetics, on the other hand, are not as well defined a product category and tend to be perceived as products used exclusively by females. Health aids is a gender-neutral product category. For each of the major aspects of consumer behavior examined (product use, information source utilization, methods of purchasing, etc.) the category studied was that which best lends itself to investigation. For example, in studying information source utilization for new products, the focus was on nonprescription drugs, since decisions for prescription drugs are most likely beyond the individual's choice.

USE OF DRUGS AND COSMETIC PRODUCTS

Respondents were asked to indicate whether they currently use (a) a prescription drug for chronic condition, and (b) hair-care or face-care products (the latter were used to represent the cosmetics category). Responses were analyzed by selected variables.

Prescription Drugs

More than half (53.7%) of older (55+) Americans use at least one prescription drug for a chronic condition. In comparison to their younger counterparts, older adults are nearly twice as likely to use prescription drugs, with 29.7 percent of the former group indicating usage of prescription drugs. Use of drugs for a chronic condition increases with age in late life. While half (50.9%) of older Americans age 55 to 64 use these products, usage slightly increases to 52.7 percent among those age 65 to 74, and to 60.6 percent among the 75-plus age group.

Although there are no differences between older males and older females in usage of prescription drugs, there are interesting variations in usage patterns by income level. Older adults who are the heaviest users of prescription drugs tend to have annual household incomes between $20,000 and $50,000, with nearly six in ten (59.1%) of them indicating use, compared with 52.0 percent for the lower-income and 42.9 for the upper-income brackets. A fairly similar pattern of prescription drug use was observed for education level, with those with some college education being the heaviest users (58.4%) and those with college education being the lightest users (49.8%) of prescription drugs. Older adults from families where no person works use more prescription drugs, in comparison with families where at least one person works (61.1% vs. 50.6%).

Older people who live with others are more likely to report usage of prescription drugs for a chronic condition, in comparison to those who live alone (55.6% vs. 49.1%). Similarly, older adults who live near their children are more likely to report usage of prescription drugs for a chronic condition, in comparison to those whose children do not live near them (54.4% vs. 42.3%). While older adults who live in rural areas are likely to report similar frequency of use of prescription drugs to those who live in urban areas, a larger percentage of those who live in the South (57.9%) than those who live in the East (48.5%) is likely to report use of prescription drugs for a chronic condition.

Finally, the older person's gerontographic profile predicts usage of prescription drugs. Six in ten (61.0%) of ailing outgoers use one or more prescription drugs, compared with 52.3 percent of healthy hermits and 47.3 percent of healthy indulgers.

Cosmetics

Two products were used as representative of the cosmetics category which are not as sensitive to the older person's gender characteristic: hair-care or face-care products. Fifty-eight percent of older Americans age 55 and over use face-care or hair-care products. However, a larger percentage of younger Americans (71.6%) use these types of cosmetics. Use of face-care and hair-care products remains fairly stable in late life, with those age 75 and over as likely to use them as those age 55 to 64. However, while two-thirds (68.1%) of older women use face-care and hair-care products, less than half (45.8%) of older men do the same.

While the percentage of older Americans in the middle-income bracket who use cosmetics (61.2%) does not differ much from that of their upper-income counterparts (58.9%), those in the lower-income category use fewer hair-care and face-care products (53.7%). The same pattern of product use holds for education, with 62.3 percent, 59.0 percent, and 53.9 percent, respectively, using these products. Work status, living arrangements, proximity to one's children and location (urban vs. rural) makes no difference with respect to cosmetic usage patterns. However, a lot more older adults who live in the West (65.6%) and South (64.4%) than those who live in the East (47.5%) and North (52.9%) use hair-care and face-care products.

Finally, the older person's gerontographic characteristic can predict his or her likelihood of using hair-care and face-care products. Ailing outgoers and healthy indulgers use the most, with 65.0 percent and 61.6 percent of them, respectively, reporting usage; frail recluses use the least (51.8%), while healthy hermits also show a relatively low usage (53.8%).

Baby Boomers vs. Seniors

One in five (20.2%) baby boomers, compared with more than half (55.6%) of the senior respondents, said they were using a drug product. Respondents were also asked if they were using any hair-care or face-care products. Three-fourths (75.1%) of baby boomers and 54.4 percent of seniors gave affirmative responses.

PREFERENCES FOR SOURCES OF INFORMATION FOR NEW DRUGS AND COSMETICS

Consumers may learn about new products from a variety of sources. In our research, respondents were asked to indicate whether they prefer to find out about new drug and cosmetic products from TV or print ads, direct mail, be contacted by phone, be visited by an agent, or learn in group meetings or seminars.

Slightly more than half (52.4%) of older adults (55+) prefer to find out about new drugs and cosmetics by seeing information in TV or print ads. Nearly one in three (28.2%) of older Americans prefers to be informed by mail, while only a small percentage of them prefers to be visited by agents (3.3%) or learn in group meetings or seminars (3.1%). Nearly 1 percent prefer to be contacted by phone.

Older adult preferences for sources of information for new drugs and cosmetic products are not very different from those under 55 years of age. A larger percentage of younger adults (60.5 %), compared with older adults (51.8%), prefers to rely on television but both groups are as likely to use the remaining sources of information.

Baby Boomers vs. Seniors

TV and print ads were preferred by the majority of baby boomers (62.7%), while direct mail was preferred by three in ten of them (30.3%). The percentage of baby boomers who prefer the remaining sources (phone contact, agent visit, learning in group meetings or seminars) is negligible. When responses given by baby boomers are compared to those given by seniors, no significant differences are found.

Differences among Older Adults

Sociodemographic characteristics of older adults are generally weak predictors of the older person's preference for sources of information about new drug and cosmetic products. In the meantime, the older person's gerontographic profile is a fairly good predictor of his or her preference for certain types of information sources regarding new drug and cosmetic products.

TV and Print Advertisements. Preference for TV and print ads declines with age while preferences for the remaining sources remain fairly stable in late life. Urban mature Americans are more likely than their rural counterparts to prefer seeing the news on TV or print media, with 54.4 percent and 47.7 percent, respectively, expressing preference. Finally, a larger percentage of healthy indulgers (56.4%) and frail recluses (55.6%) than ailing outgoers (47.1%) prefers receiving the new information via TV and print ads.

Group Meetings or Seminars. The desire to learn about such products in group meetings or seminars declines with increasing income. Mature Americans who live near their children are also more likely than those whose children live far away to prefer learning in these kinds of settings (7.9% vs. 3.0%). Northerners are twice more likely than southerners (7.0% vs. 3.3%) to express preference for learning about new drugs and cosmetics in group meetings.

Agents. Older adults who live with others are more likely than those who live alone to prefer hearing about new drugs and cosmetics from sales representatives at their home, with 4.0 percent and 1.6 percent, respectively, expressing preference. Also, a relatively larger percentage of ailing outgoers than healthy hermits (4.3% vs. 2.0%) prefers to hear about new products from sales representatives who would visit them. Finally, more than twice as many ailing outgoers as frail recluses (6.6% vs. 3.0%) prefer hearing the news in group meetings or seminars.

Mail. Older adults who live near their children are more likely to prefer receiving news in the mail, with more than one-third (34.9%) of them expressing preference for this source, compared with one-fourth (24.0%) of those who do not live near their children. A larger percentage of rural than urban older adults prefers receiving news in the mail (33.4% vs. 26.6%). Finally, ailing outgoers are more likely than their counterparts in other gerontographic segments to prefer receiving news in the mail, with more than one-third of them (34.0%), in comparison with 22.0 percent of healthy indulgers, 26.7 percent of ailing outgoers, and 28.1 percent of frail recluses, expressing preference for this source.

Telephone. Older people who live in rural areas are more likely than their urban-dwelling counterparts to prefer getting such information via telephone contact (2.2% vs. 5%).

PREFERENCES FOR METHODS OF PURCHASING PRESCRIPTION DRUGS

Users of prescription drugs may purchase such products through various channels. The survey asked respondents to indicate the ways they prefer to buy prescription drugs, whether they prefer to buy them at the store (vendors' facilities), from door-to-door sales representatives, through the mail, or by phone. Respondents could indicate more than one preferred method.

Retail establishments are the most preferred channels for purchasing prescription drugs, with 92.3 percent of older Americans expressing preference for this distribution mode. Preference for purchasing prescription drugs by phone and by mail are preferred by 8.5 percent and 7.8 percent of mature adults, respectively, while the percentage of older Americans who prefer buying prescription drugs from door-to-door representatives is insignificant (.6%).

Older adult preferences for methods of purchasing prescription drugs are not very different from those of younger adults. Older adults are more likely than their younger counterparts to prefer purchasing these products through the mail, with 7.7 percent and 4.7 percent of them, respectively, expressing preference for this mode of distribution. Younger adults, however, are somewhat more likely than their older counterparts to prefer purchasing drugs at retail facilities (94.7% vs. 92.4%).

Baby Boomers vs. Seniors

While purchasing such products at the store is the most preferred method among baby boomers, such preferences are stronger among baby boomers than among the seniors, with 94.8 percent and 90.9 percent, respectively, expressing preferences. Purchasing prescription drugs by phone is only preferred by 6.7 percent of the baby boomers (vs. 9.8% of seniors). Although only 5.7 percent of baby boomers would purchase drugs through the mail, a much higher percentage (13.7%) would buy cosmetics and health aids via this channel (vs. 9.0% of seniors); and 9.4 percent would buy door-to-door (vs. 3.5% of seniors). The most preferred method of purchasing cosmetics and health aids is at retail outlets, with 91.4 percent of baby boomers expressing preference (vs. 87.8% of seniors).

Differences among Older Adults

Preferences for methods of purchasing prescription drugs among older Americans can be predicted by selected demographic characteristics. Also, the older person's gerontographic profile is a fairly good predictor of his or her preference for the various methods of purchasing prescription drugs.

Door-to-Door. While the percentage of older adults who favor purchasing these products from door-to-door salespeople is very small, preference for this purchasing mode increases with age. Older adults who live alone are more likely than those who live with others to prefer buying prescription drugs from door-to-door salespeople, despite small percentages of such preferences (1.3% vs. 0.3%, respectively). Finally, although only a small percentage of older adults would buy from door-to-door salespeople, those most likely to buy are the healthy indulgers.

Mail. Older adults from families where no person works are nearly twice as likely as their counterparts from families with working persons to prefer purchasing prescription drugs through the mail, with 11.4 percent and 6.3 percent, respectively, expressing preference for this purchasing mode. Also, ailing outgoers are more likely than healthy hermits to buy through the mail, with 10.2 percent and 6.1 percent, respectively, expressing preference for this purchasing mode.

Telephone. While one in ten older Americans who live in the South and West, and one in twelve of those who live in the North, prefer buying prescription drugs by phone, the percentage of those living in the East who would do the same is much lower (2.7%).

Retail. A larger percentage of older adults who live in the East (95.0%) than of those who live in the South (90.3%) prefers buying prescription drugs at retail establishments. In addition, frail recluses are more likely to prefer retail establishments as sources of prescription drugs.

PREFERENCES FOR METHODS OF PURCHASING COSMETICS AND HEALTH AIDS

Respondents in our survey were also asked to indicate how they prefer to purchase cosmetics and health aids—whether they prefer to buy them from door-to-door salespeople, through the mail, by phone, or at vendors' facilities (retail establishments). (Respondents could indicate more than one method.)

Nine in ten older Americans prefer purchasing cosmetics and health aids at retail outlets. Nearly one in ten (9.9%) prefers buying these products through the mail, and only a small percentage of them prefers purchasing cosmetics and health aids from door-to-door salespeople (3.8%) and by phone (2.8%). These preferences expressed by older Americans differ somewhat from younger adults. A larger percentage of younger people prefer buying cosmetics and health aids from door-to-door salespeople and at vendors' facilities. Among baby boomers, the most preferred method of purchasing cosmetics and health aids is at retail outlets, with 91.4 percent of baby boomers (vs. 87.8% of seniors) expressing preference. Thus, both younger and older Americans prefer purchasing cosmetics and health aids at retail outlets.

Differences among Older Adults

Certain socioeconomic and demographic factors predict the older person's preferences for methods of purchasing cosmetics and health aids. Also, gerontographics predict preferences for three of the four methods of distribution of cosmetics and health aids.

Retail. Preferences for purchasing these products at retail establishments decline with age, especially after age 75. Mature Americans with lower household incomes are more likely than those with relatively higher incomes to prefer purchasing these products at retail establishments. Also, older adults who live with others are more likely than those who live alone to prefer these establishments for cosmetics and health aids, with 91.7 percent and 87.0 percent, respectively, preferring these types of outlets.

Also, older adults who live in urban areas are more likely than their rural counterparts to prefer purchasing cosmetics and health aids at retail outlets, with 91.3 percent and 86.9 percent, respectively, expressing preference. A larger percentage of easterners (93.9%) and westerners (93.0%)

than of southerners (88.7%) prefers buying cosmetics and health aids from retail establishments.

Finally, older adults who buy by phone are more likely to be healthy hermits than frail recluses, but a larger percentage of frail recluses (95.2%) than healthy hermits (88.7%), or ailing outgoers (88.7%), and healthy indulgers (91.0%) prefers purchasing cosmetics and health aids at retail establishments.

Door-to-Door. The higher the older person's income the lower his or her preference for door-to-door salespeople of cosmetics and health aids. A larger percentage of mature Americans who live in rural areas (6.3%), in comparison with those who live in urban locations (3.2%), prefers to buy these products via this channel. Also, more older adults who live in eastern states (4.1%) and northern states (5.2%) than of those who live in western states (1.4%) prefer buying door-to-door.

Mail. Buying cosmetics and health aids through the mail is least common among older adults who live in the East, with 4.6 percent of them expressing preference for this purchasing method, in comparison with their counterparts from the West (11.0%), North (10.7%) and South (9.9%). Also, a larger percentage of ailing outgoers (11.7%) and frail recluses (11.3%) than healthy indulgers (7.0%) prefers buying these products through the mail.

Telephone. Although buying cosmetics and health aids by phone is not a preferred method, those most likely to express preference for this method are likely to live in the South and North rather than in the East.

REASONS FOR PATRONIZING SPECIFIC DRUG STORES/ PHARMACIES

Consumers patronize specific stores or pharmacies for various reasons. In this research, fourteen reasons were identified on the basis of previous research on patronage behavior. Respondents were presented with a list of these reasons and asked to indicate whether each applied to their decision to begin or continue to patronize specific drug stores or pharmacies.

The main reason older Americans patronize specific drug stores or pharmacies appears to be location, with two-thirds (67.4%) of them indicating that they patronize these outlets because they are near the place they live or work. Almost as important is the availability of products suitable to their physical or health needs, with 65.5 percent of the older adults surveyed indicating this reason for their patronage. Approximately six in ten (59.1%) patronize specific outlets because they carry familiar brands or products, and 57.2 percent do so due to ease of locating merchandise in these outlets. Two other patronage reasons appear important among more than half of older Americans: store location near other places they patronize (53.5%), and ability of personnel to assist them (51.4%). Other reasons ranked by frequency mentioned include: senior discounts (44.6%), items on sale or special deals (38.9%), fast check-out registers (34.0%), and comfortable place to shop or socialize (30.7%). One in four (24.6%) of older Americans patronizes specific pharmacies and drug stores because it is easy to return products or get refunds. Other reasons such as availability of special-assistance services, same-age peer recommendation, and billing/payment methods available are of lesser importance.

While many of the reasons for patronizing specific pharmacies and drug stores are considered to be equally important by older and younger Americans, many reasons are of greater importance to either of these age groups. Besides senior discounts which are relevant to older adults, in comparison with their younger counterparts, older people are more likely to value availability of products suitable to their physical/health needs (65.2% vs. 54.8%), helpful personnel (51.2% vs. 42.4%), and recommendation of same-age peers (16.2% vs. 10.3%). On the other hand, younger adults are more likely than their older counterparts to patronize these outlets because of their location near the places they live or work (74.9% vs. 67.0%), and ease of returning products or getting refunds (29.5% vs. 24.6%).

Baby Boomers vs. Seniors

Do baby boomers' patronage motives differ from those of the seniors in choosing drug stores or pharmacies? In order to answer this question, responses given by baby boomers to the list of the fourteen patronage factors were compared to those given by seniors. Table 4.1 shows the percentage of baby boomers who perceive each of the factors to be important in patronizing drug stores or pharmacies.

Location is important to eight in ten baby boomers, but this factor is not as important to the seniors; nearly two-thirds of the latter group consider location in their patronage decisions. Location near other places one patronizes is more important to baby boomers than to seniors (57.1% vs. 52.8%). The last factor important to baby boomers (but of lesser importance to the seniors) is ease of locating merchandise/items, with 30.6 percent and 21.4 percent, respectively, mentioning this patronage motive. On the other hand, several factors important to baby boomers are of even greater importance to the seniors. Availability of products suitable to their health needs (51.3% vs. 64.0%), availability of familiar brands (55.0% vs. 59.4%), and helpful personnel (40.6% vs. 49.7%) are examples of factors in this category.

Table 4.1
Reasons for Patronizing Specific Drug Stores/Pharmacies among Baby
Boomers and Seniors (65+) (Percent Who Feel Reason Is Applicable)

	Baby Boomers (%)	Seniors (%)
Reasons		
Ease of locating merchandise/items	56.34	57.35
Ease of returning products or getting refunds	30.59	21.42
Location near the place you live or work	80.65	65.64
Frequently have items on sale or special deals	35.81	39.43
Offer special discounts to customers over a certain age	14.39	46.99
Have products suitable to your physical/health needs	51.28	64.01
Have personnel who can assist you	40.63	49.68
Preference for billing/payment method	16.87	14.46
Have fast check-out registers	36.36	32.65
Offer special-assistance services (like wrapping, home delivery, package carry-out) to those who need them	13.60	16.94
Recommended by other people your age	6.70	17.08
Carry familiar brands/items	54.96	59.41
Location near several other places you patronize	57.13	52.82
Comfortable place to shop or socialize	27.58	27.11
Base:	(N = 883)	(N = 366)

Differences among Older Adults

A large number of socioeconomic and demographic characteristics predict the older person's perceptions of the importance of the fourteen patronage factors examined. Also, gerontographic characteristics are very strong predictors of the older person's perceptions of the importance of nearly all fourteen patronage factors examined. These differences are as folows.

Location Near Home or Work. A drug store's (or pharmacy's) location near the older person's home or place of work is more important to those who live in urban than in rural areas, with 70.9 percent and 58.8 percent, respectively, indicating this attribute to be important in their patronage decisions. This is more important to easterners and southerners, with seven in ten of them indicating this reason to be important, in comparison with approximately 64 percent of their counterparts in other areas of the country.

Healthy hermits are least likely to be concerned about location of drug stores or pharmacies, with 62.9 percent of them indicating this factor to be important (in comparison with 73.2% of healthy indulgers, 68.9% of frail recluses, and 68.7% of ailing outgoers).

Availability of Products Suitable to Certain Physical or Health Needs. Relative to their less-educated counterparts, mature Americans with more education place less emphasis on whether a pharmacy or drug store makes available products suitable to certain physical or health needs. A larger percentage of older adults who live in rural areas (70.5%) than of those who live in urban locations (63.9%) perceive this factor as important in their drug store or pharmacy patronage decisions.

Seven in ten (69.4%) of older Americans who live in northern states, in comparison with six in ten (60.4%) of their counterparts who live in the West, prefer patronizing drug stores and pharmacies where they can find products suitable to their physical or health needs. Finally, ailing outgoers are the more demanding of the gerontographic groups, with 71.3 percent of them indicating product suitability to their physical/health needs to be an important patronage factor. Six in ten of frail recluses are (59.4%) indicate product suitability to be an important patronage factor.

Familiar Brands. The more education an older person has, the less likely they are to be concerned with whether a pharmacy or drug store carries familiar brands. Mature women are more concerned than their male peers with this factor (63.3% vs. 55.5%). Finally, the availability of familiar brands is a more important factor to ailing outgoers, with nearly two-thirds (65.0%) of them indicating importance, compared with just over half (52.6%) of the frail recluses, 58.2 percent of healthy hermits, and 57.5 percent of healthy indulgers.

Ease of Merchandise Location. A larger percentage of older Americans who live in western states (61.2%) and eastern states (60.7%), than of those who live in the North (53.3%), values ease of locating merchandise in pharmacies or drug stores as a patronage reason. A larger percentage of females than males values this factor (62.5% vs. 50.6%). Finally, while only half (49.3%) of frail recluses think that ease of locating merchandise is important, approximately six in ten of older Americans in the remaining gerontographic groups are of the same opinion.

Location Near Other Stores. A pharmacy's or drug store's location near other places they patronize is more important to older females than it is to older men (55.3% vs. 51.4%). Older adults from families where at least one person works report a greater inclination than their counterparts from nonworking families to value location of drug stores or pharmacies near other places they patronize, with 70.9 percent and 64.8 percent, respectively, reporting preference. Finally, such proximity to other places they patronize is more valuable to ailing outgoers than it is to frail recluses (56.5% vs. 49.6%).

Personnel Assistance. The higher older persons' household incomes, the less likely they are to be concerned with personnel assistance at pharmacies and drug stores. Also, the more educated they are, the less likely they are to place importance on the availability of such services. Older adults whose children do not live near them perceive this to be of greater importance in their patronage decision, with more than half (54.8%) of them indicating this factor, in comparison with 42.4 percent of older adults with children in close proximity. Personnel assistance is also more important to ailing outgoers than to healthy indulgers or frail recluses, with 57.4 percent (compared with 46.3 percent and 46.8 percent, respectively), indicating the importance of this attribute.

Senior Discounts. The higher older persons' incomes, the less likely they are to value senior discounts offered by pharmacies and drug stores. Relative to those with higher education, older people with less education place more importance on such special deals. Also, while nearly half of older adults who live in the East (48.3%) and South (48.7%), and 43.8 percent of northerners cite senior discounts as a patronage reason, only 35.3 percent of older adults who live in the West indicate this patronage motive. Additionally, mature Americans from families where at least one person works are less likely than those from nonworking families to patronize pharmacies or drug stores because of such discounts (40.5% vs. 47.7%).

Senior discounts are by far a more important patronage motive for ailing outgoers than older adults in the remaining gerontographic groups. More than half (51.4%) of ailing outgoers mentioned this reason to be important in their drug store or pharmacy patronage decision, in comparison with 38.7 percent of healthy indulgers, 40.2 percent of frail recluses, and 44.1 percent of healthy hermits.

Money-Saving Incentives. Money-saving incentives offered by pharmacies and drug stores are less important to older people with higher incomes than they are to their counterparts with relatively lower household incomes. Similarly, mature Americans with more education are less likely than their counterparts with less education to be concerned with this factor. Also, special "sales" or deals are more important to older females than they are to older males (43.0% vs. 33.6%). Also, special deals or sales tend to be of greater appeal to ailing outgoers and healthy hermits, with 44.0 percent and 40.3 percent, respectively, citing this patronage reason (in comparison with 33.8 percent of frail recluses and 32.3 percent of healthy indulgers).

Check-Out Registers. Older people who live in the West are more likely than those in the East to place importance on fast check-out registers available in drug stores or pharmacies (38.7% vs. 28.7%). This is more important to ailing outgoers than it is to frail recluses (36.0% vs. 30.9%).

Environment. As older people age in late life, their perception of pharmacies and drug stores as comfortable places to shop or socialize becomes a less important consideration when evaluating pharmacies and drug stores. Drug stores are more important places for socializing among lower-income than upper-income older adults. Along the same lines, mature Americans with less education are more likely than their more educated counterparts to value this characteristic in a pharmacy or drug store. Mature Americans in the western part of the country value whether a pharmacy or drug store is a comfortable place to shop or socialize more than those who live in the East (34.2% vs. 27.0%). Finally, healthy hermits, ailing outgoers, and frail recluses are more likely to consider drug stores and pharmacies as places for socializing, with at least three in ten of older adults in these groups indicating importance, in comparison with 21.9 percent of healthy indulgers.

Return and Refund Policies. The ease of returning products or getting refunds becomes a less important factor as mature Americans get older. Older people with higher household incomes and with higher levels of education are also likely than those with relatively lower incomes and levels of educational attainment to be concerned with these policies. Ease of returning products or getting refunds is an important patronage motive to a larger percentage of older adults who live in the South (29.1%) than to those who live in the East (23.3%), West (22.3%), or North (22.1%). Finally, return/refund policies are important to a larger percentage of ailing outgoers (28.6%) than healthy indulgers (21.8%) or healthy hermits (22.9%).

Special-Assistance Services. Special-assistance services are more important to mature Americans with lower incomes than they are to those with relatively higher household incomes. Older people who live in the West are more likely than their eastern counterparts to value such services (19.8% vs. 14.8%). Also, older women are more likely than their male counterparts to place emphasis on special-assistance services (18.5% vs. 15.2%). Special-assistance services are important to one in four (24.8%) of ailing outgoers, in comparison with one in ten (10.2%) frail recluses, and healthy indulgers (11.7%) and one in six of healthy hermits (16.5%).

Billing and Payment Methods. The more money the older person has, the lower the importance he or she places on billing or payment methods. Similarly, the more educated an older person is, the less likely he or she is to be concerned with this factor. Preference for billing or payment methods at these stores is an important patronage factor to a larger percentage of older Americans who live in the West (17.6%) than to their counterparts who live in the East (10.8%). In addition, relative to frail recluses, ailing outgoers are more likely to be concerned with the billing/

payment methods available at a pharmacy or drug store (17.6% vs. 12.5%)

Peer Recommendations. The higher an older person's household income, the less likely he or she is to value the recommendations of same-age peers in patronizing drug stores and pharmacies. Also, this factor is at least three times more important to ailing outgoers than to older adults in other gerontographic groups.

REASONS FOR CHOOSING BRANDS OF DRUGS AND HEALTH AIDS

While consumers have little say in choosing brands of prescribed drugs, they have freedom in selecting brands of nonprescribed or over-the-counter drugs. There are several reasons buyers of drugs and health aids may purchase specific brands, but based on previous research and analysis of qualitative data, twelve major reasons were identified and formulated into a structured question-response format. Respondents in our survey were asked to indicate whether each of the twelve reasons applied to their decision to choose or switch brands of drugs and health aids.

About six in ten (59.9%) older adults (age 55 and over) indicated that ease of reading information on labels or brochures is the main reason they buy specific brands of drugs and health aids. Product characteristics, rather than brand attributes, are of nearly equal importance, with 58.1 percent of older Americans indicating availability of products for people with certain physical or health requirements. That is, products designed for people with special needs are an equally important factor in brand-choice behavior. Also an important brand-choice criterion is ease of understanding and following directions provided with the product, with 54.1 percent of older adults mentioning this factor. Price reduction or special sale was mentioned by 51.4 percent of older respondents, suggesting price sensitivity in this product category.

Of lesser importance is the recommendation of same-age peers, which was mentioned by 39.0 percent of the older respondents. Nearly as many (37.9%) value the ease with which the product can be used. Slightly more than one in three mentioned availability of coupons (35.0%) and advice/request of spouse or other relatives (34.9%). Last on the list of frequency of factors mentioned were: proper age-stereotyping in ads of products (27.7%), availability of manufacturer rebates (26.3%), recommendation of salesperson (21.4%), and what others think of people who use certain brands (19.6%).

Older people choose specific brands of drugs and health aids for different reasons than younger adults. While ease of reading information on labels or brochures is as important to younger as it is to older Amer-

Table 4.2

Reasons for Choosing Specific Brands of Drugs and Health Aids among Baby Boomers and Seniors (65+) (Percent Who Feel Reason Is Applicable)

	Baby Boomers (%)	Seniors (%)
Reasons		
Price reduction or special sale	53.77	49.82
Ease of reading information on labels or brochures	58.33	57.43
Ease of using the product	45.43	37.60
Ease of understanding and following directions provided with the product	51.44	54.67
Availability of products for people with certain physical/health requirements	49.95	54.75
Availability of coupons	40.76	35.35
Availability of manufacturer rebates	24.60	25.57
Advice of other people your age	34.91	37.97
What others think of people who use certain brands	13.14	19.76
Their ads properly stereotype people your age	6.69	27.74
Advice/request of spouse or other relatives	41.47	30.67
Recommendation of salesperson	20.98	21.64
Base:	(N = 883)	(N = 366)

icans, ease of understanding and following directions provided with the product is important to a larger percentage of older adults than to younger adults (53.6% vs. 48.0%). Similarly, in relation to their younger counterparts, older adults are more likely to choose specific brands of drugs and health aids on the basis of their suitability to their physical or health requirements (57.7% vs. 51.3%), need to conform to expectations (what others think of them because of the kinds of brands they use) (19.4% vs. 13.2%), and proper age-stereotyping shown in ads of these products (27.4% vs. 9.6%). On the other hand, a larger percentage of younger than older adults mentioned coupons (40.5% vs. 35.0%) and advice/request of spouse or other relatives (42.0% vs. 34.3%).

Baby Boomers vs. Seniors

Table 4.2 shows the percentage of baby boomers who consider each factor important; it also shows the percentage of seniors (age 65 and over) who do the same. Two factors are considered important by the majority of baby boomers: price or special sale (53.8%) and ease of reading information on labels or brochures (58.3%). The first factor is of lesser importance to the seniors, with 49.8 percent of these respondents in our sample indicating its importance. Availability of products is important to nearly half of the baby boomers (49.9%), but the elderly find this attribute of greater importance (54.7%). On the other hand, ease of using the product is important to 45.4 percent of baby boomers, in comparison with a smaller percentage (37.6%) of the seniors who consider this factor in their brand decision concerning pharmaceutical products.

Other factors such as availability of coupons and advice/request of spouse or other relatives are important to four of ten baby boomers; these factors are somewhat less important to the seniors. Surprisingly, baby boomers are less conscious of the impressions others may form of them because of the brand of drugs and health aids they use, in comparison to senior consumers.

Differences among Older Adults

A number of socioeconomic and demographic factors relate to the older person's perception of the importance of the twelve factors in the selection of specific brands. For example, the higher the older person's income the lower the likelihood he or she will consider all the factors except advice/request of spouse or other relatives and same-age peers, which show no significantly different levels of sensitivity with respect to income. A very similar pattern emerges in examining the perceived importance of the various factors examined regarding the selection of specific brands of drugs and health aids. Only advice/request of spouse or other relatives is unrelated to increasing levels of the older person's education. Also, older persons differ most on the basis of their gerontographic profile when it comes to choosing brands of drugs and health aids. The importance of each one of the specific factors differs on the basis of the older person's sociodemographic and gerontographic characteristics as indicated in the paragraphs that follow.

Ease of Reading Information. As mature Americans get older, they tend to place less importance on the ease of reading information on labels or brochures. This is important to a larger percentage of females than males (64.0% vs. 55.2%). Also, a larger percentage of healthy hermits (61.4%) and ailing outgoers (62.6%) than healthy indulgers (54.5%) reports that ease of reading information on labels and brochures is important in their brand decisions concerning drugs and health aids.

Products for Certain Health or Physical Requirements. Older adults age 55 to 64 are more likely than those between the ages of 65 and 74 to buy brands on the basis of availability of products for certain health or physical requirements, with 62.1 percent and 53.2 percent, respectively, indicating the importance of this factor (Table 4.2). Availability of such specific products is a more important factor in choosing brands among those who live with others than among those who live alone, with 60.3 percent and 52.6 percent, respectively, expressing preference. Also, this is more important to older adults with children who do not live close to them than it is to their counterparts who live near their children (59.0% vs. 47.8%). Finally, availability of products for people with certain health/physical requirements is most important to ailing outgoers and least important to frail recluses.

Directions. Relative to their male peers, older women are more likely to place emphasis on the ease of understanding and following directions provided with the product (57.6% vs. 50.2%). Compared to the proportion of those living close to their children, a larger percentage of the older adults with children who do not live close to them is concerned with this factor (58.7% vs. 48.4%).

In addition, older persons from families with no working persons are more likely than their counterparts from families where at least one person works (56.5% vs. 50.8%) to indicate that ease of understanding and following product directions is an important factor in choosing brands of drug products and health aids. Finally, this is more important to ailing outgoers and health hermits than it is to the remaining gerontographic groups.

Price and Special Sales. With age, older adults place less emphasis on price. Price reductions or special sales are important factors to a larger percentage of healthy hermits (55.8%) and ailing outgoers (56.5%) than to healthy indulgers (45.0%) and frail recluses (39.9%).

Peer Influences. Advice of same-age peers becomes more important when one's children do not live in close proximity, with 43.4 percent and 34.2 percent, respectively, indicating that they consider such advice in choosing brands of drug items and health aids. This influence is greater on older adults who live in northern states (43.7%) and western states (40.8%) than on those who live in the East (32.4%). In the meantime, advice of same-age peers is much more important to ailing outgoers than to the remaining gerontographic groups, with nearly half (48.6%) of them admitting to social influence, in comparison with roughly two-thirds of the older adults in the remaining gerontographic groups.

Ease of Product Use. Females are more concerned than men with the ease of using the drugs and health aids (42.6% vs. 32.2%). This is more important to ailing outgoers and least important to frail recluses, with 47.5 percent and 28.2 percent, respectively, indicating this factor.

Coupons. Mature females are more likely than older males to place importance on the availability of coupons (39.9% vs. 28.9%). This factor is more important among those who live in urban areas, with 37.0 percent of urban dwellers, in comparison with 29.2 percent of their rural counterparts, expressing preference for coupons. Availability of coupons is also of greater importance to those who live in certain geographic locations, with a larger percentage of older adults who live in the East (40.8%), in comparison to those who live in the West (28.2%) or South (34.2%), indicating this factor to be important in their brand decisions. Also, nearly twice as many ailing outgoers as frail recluses (43.2% vs. 22.6%) are concerned with coupons in choosing specific brands of drugs and health aids.

Family Influences. The advice/request of a spouse or other relatives becomes less important in choosing specific brands of drugs and health aids as people get older. Older males are more likely than their female counterparts to be influenced by such advice or requests, with 38.5 percent and 32.2 percent, respectively, expressing concern. Also, a larger percentage of older adults who live with others (38.7%) than of those who live alone (25.8%) considers this element. Finally, while about one in three of healthy hermits, healthy indulgers, and frail recluses responds to advice/request of a spouse or other relatives, four in ten of the ailing outgoers do the same.

Age-Stereotypes. Older females are more likely than their male counterparts to be influenced by age stereotypes of spokespersons in advertisements of drugs and health aids, with 31.1 percent and 23.7 percent, respectively, expressing concern with proper age-stereotyping in commercials. Also, older adults who live in the North are more sensitive to proper age-stereotypes in ads than those who live in the West, with 31.0 percent and 24.4 percent, respectively, indicating this to be an important factor in choosing brands of drugs and health aids. Of the four gerontographic groups, this is of greatest concern to ailing outgoers and of least concern to healthy indulgers (37.4% vs. 18.0%).

Manufacturer Rebates. Manufacturer rebates are more important to older women than they are to older men (29.8% vs. 22.0%). They are more important to older people who live far away from their children than they are to their counterparts who live close to their children (31.4% vs. 22.1%). Also, the availability of manufacturer rebates is of greater importance to older people who live in the East (30.1%) and North (29.4%) than to those who live in the West (22.6%) or South (23.3%). Of the four gerontographic groups, these rebates are most important to ailing outgoers and least important to frail recluses, with 32.4 percent and 16.8 percent, respectively, reporting interest.

Salesperson Recommendation. The recommendations of salespersons is more important to ailing outgoers, with one in four of them admitting to this influence, in comparison with one in seven of the healthy indulgers.

Peer Evaluation of Brand Choice. Also, with respect to social influence, what others think of the older person's brand choice is more important to ailing outgoers and least important to healthy indulgers, with 27.8 percent and 11.7 percent, respectively, expressing concern with others' evaluation of their brand preferences.

REASONS CONSIDERED BEFORE BUYING DIRECT

Consumers may purchase health aids and prescription drugs by phone or by mail. Because little is known about the characteristics of those who buy direct, our survey attempted to uncover the factors which are considered important in the decision to buy such products direct. Based on qualitative research and previous surveys on direct buying behavior, eight factors were identified and cast into a question-response format. Respondents were presented with these factors as "reasons for buying or not buying" by phone or through the mail, and they were asked to indicate whether they would consider each before buying health aids and drugs by phone or by mail.

The majority of older respondents age 55 and over (55.1%) consider price. Four in ten consider availability of toll-free (800) number (40.7%), days to wait before receiving (39.9%), and convenience in buying through the mail or by phone (in comparison to other ways of buying the same product) (39.5%). Also, of equal importance is product selection, with 37.2 percent of the older respondents indicating they would consider this factor before buying direct. Return or cancellation and refund policy is less important on the list, with 27.7 percent of the respondents indicating concern. Type of credit card accepted and availability of free pick-up service for returns by the service provider are last on the list of eight factors, yet important considerations in buying direct, with 22.6 percent and 18.5 percent of the older Americans, respectively, estimated to consider these two factors.

The factors older Americans consider in buying direct are of equal importance to younger adults who contemplate purchases by phone or by mail. When responses of older adults are compared to those of their younger counterparts, only price and return/cancellation policy are perceived differently by the two groups. Specifically, a larger percentage of older Americans (54.9%) would consider price of drugs and health aids before buying these products direct, compared with 46.4 percent of younger adults. On the other hand, younger adults are more likely than their older counterparts to consider return or cancellation policy of the company from which they contemplate purchasing such products, with 32.7 percent and 27.2 percent, respectively, expressing preference.

Table 4.3

Reasons Considered before Buying Health Aids and Drugs by Phone or through the Mail among Baby Boomers and Seniors (65+)

Reasons Considered	Baby Boomers (%)	Seniors (%)
Price (including shipping charges)	44.96	50.97
Type of credit card accepted	20.48	20.04
Return/cancellation and refund policy	21.37	30.79
Convenience, in comparison to other ways of buying the same product	39.69	36.54
Free pick-up service for returns	19.45	12.72
Availability of toll-free (800) number	36.96	36.22
Selection of products	36.85	33.56
Days to wait before receiving	43.82	35.69
Base:	(N = 555)	(N = 214)

Baby Boomers vs. Seniors

There are significant differences in the perceived importance of some of these factors among baby boomers and the seniors (see Table 4.3). Price appears to be among the most important considerations to baby boomers, with 45.0 percent of them mentioning this reason. This factor is even more important to senior consumers (51.0%). Days to wait before receiving the product is of greater importance to baby boomers, with 43.8 percent of them indicating this reason (compared with 35.7% of seniors). The least important factor among those presented to respondents is free pick-up service for returns, a factor that is of even lesser importance to elderly consumers (19.4% vs. 12.7%). The remaining factors were found to be important by a little over one-third of the baby boomers, and they were also perceived as of equal importance by the seniors.

Differences among Older Adults

The older person's socioeconomic and demographic characteristics are fairly good predictors of the reasons he or she buys (or does not buy) direct. Age, income, and living status in particular make a difference in the factors considered by mature Americans. For example, while older adults do not differ significantly from their younger counterparts with respect to most of the eight factors examined, older adults' perceptions of these factors change with age. Specifically, with age, there is a decline in the importance older people attach to these factors. Also, the importance of each of the eight reasons examined before buying direct depends on the older person's gerontographic profile, with ailing outgoers being the group most likely to consider the largest number of factors.

Price. Older Americans whose annual household income is between $20,000 and $50,000 tend to consider a larger number of factors before buying health aids and drugs direct, in comparison with older adults with higher or lower household incomes. Specifically, a larger percentage of this middle-income group (58.9%), in comparison with 52.6 percent and 50.7 percent for the lower- and upper-income groups, respectively, would consider price. Finally, a larger percentage of ailing outgoers (62.5%) than of healthy hermits (49.6%) and frail recluses (53.6%) would consider price.

Toll-Free Number. More older adults who live with others than those who live alone consider the availability of toll-free (800) numbers before buying direct (43.9% vs. 32.6%). This is more important to older adults who live in rural areas than to those who live in urban areas, with 45.6 percent and 38.7 percent, respectively, indicating they would consider this factor before buying direct.

Availability of toll-free (800) numbers is of greater interest to older adults who live in northern states than to those who live in the East, with 44.5 percent and 31.1 percent, respectively, indicating consideration. The percentages of older residents of the South and West who would consider this factor before buying are 42.4 and 38.2 percent, respectively. Finally, ailing outgoers are also more likely than older adults in the remaining gerontographic groups to consider this element.

Wait Time. About half (46.1 percent) of older people in middle-income households would consider the number of days they would have to wait before receiving their order, compared to 32.7 percent of those from upper-income households and 38.2 percent of those from lower-income households. Compared to their counterparts who live alone, older people who live with others are more concerned with this factor (43.0% vs. 32.1%).

Furthermore, mature adults who live in northern states consider number of days they must wait before receiving these products to be more important than their counterparts from eastern and western states (44.8% vs. 35.0% and 35.7%, respectively). Finally, this is more important to ailing outgoers than it is to healthy hermits and frail recluses, with 45.1 percent of the former group mentioning this factor, compared with 35.9 percent and 36.8 percent of the latter two groups, respectively.

Convenience. A larger percentage of older adults who live with others, in comparison to those who live alone, buys direct for convenience reasons (41.4% vs. 34.9%). A larger percentage of northerners (43.3%), in comparison with their easterner counterparts (33.9%) and those older adults who live in the West (35.7%), is likely to perceive convenience in direct buying (in comparison to other ways of buying health aids and drugs). Also, a larger percentage of ailing outgoers (44.2%) than frail recluses (34.9%) and healthy indulgers (37.2%) mentions convenience for buying direct.

Product Selection. Mature Americans who live with others are more likely than their counterparts who live alone to consider the selection of products before buying direct (39.0% vs. 32.4%). This factor is far more important to older Americans who live in the South (41.4%) than those who live in the West (32.0%) or East (34.4%). Also, of the four geronto-graphic groups, ailing outgoers are the most likely to be concerned with product selection.

Return/Cancellation Policies. Older adults with incomes in excess of $20,000 are more likely than their lower-income counterparts to consider return/cancellation policy and convenience in buying direct. College-educated mature Americans are more likely than their counterparts with less education to be concerned with these policies. In the meantime, older adults from families where at least one person works are more likely than their nonworking counterparts to consider return or cancellation policy before buying direct, with 29.6 percent and 23.5 percent, respec-tively, considering this factor. Also, almost one-third (32.0%) of older southerners, in comparison to their counterparts who live in the East (23.5%) and West (25.1%), consider return/cancellation and refund pol-icy. Finally, a larger percentage of ailing outgoers (31.9%) than healthy indulgers (24.6%) considers the seller's return/cancellation and refund policy.

Credit Cards Accepted. A larger percentage of older adults who live in the West (25.9%) than of those who live in North (20.0%) or East (20.2%) considers the type of credit card accepted by the company that sells direct. Also, this factor is more important to ailing outgoers than it is to older adults in the remaining gerontographic groups.

Free Pick-Up Service. Just under one-quarter—22.2 percent—of mature Americans from middle-income households are more likely than their upper- and lower-income counterparts to consider free pick-up service before buying health aids and drugs direct (15.3% and 15.5, respectively). Mature Americans from families where at least one person works are more likely than those from nonworking households to consider the availability of such service (20.0% vs. 15.0%). Additionally, the availa-bility of free pick-up service for returns is more important to older people who live with others than it is to those who live alone (19.9% vs. 14.9%). More southerners than easterners place emphasis on this factor when making a decision about direct purchasing, with 20.8 percent and 13.1 percent, respectively, expressing interest.

PAYMENT METHODS

Preferences for payment methods were also examined. Older consumers have three traditional methods of paying for drugs—cash, check, and credit card. In addition, they may use coupons and senior/member discounts along with one of the major forms of payment. Respondents in our survey were asked to indicate the methods they would prefer to use to pay for prescription drugs; they could indicate more than one method of payment.

About half (49.2%) of older Americans age 55 and older prefer cash as a form of payment for prescription drugs, and nearly as many (47.1%) prefer to pay by check. Credit card is far behind on the list of main forms of payment, with 17.7 percent of older respondents indicating preference. Nearly half (46.6%) of older Americans are estimated to prefer making use of senior/member discounts when paying for prescription drugs, while the percentage of those who would use coupons is very small (3.0%).

Payment-method preferences of older adults differ from those of their younger counterparts. Generally, younger people prefer using a larger number of methods of payment for prescription drugs. They prefer using more cash, checks, and coupons. Preference for credit among older Americans is similar to that of their younger counterparts, while (as expected) older adults prefer using senior/membership discounts.

Baby Boomers vs. Seniors

Cash is by far the payment method preferred by baby boomers, with nearly two-thirds (63.0% of them (in comparison with 46.9% of the seniors) expressing preference. Check is the second most preferred method (56.2% vs. 45.4%), while credit card is equally preferred as a method of payment by the two groups. Although the incidence of coupon use was relatively small, this method had greater appeal to baby boomers than to senior consumers (6.5% vs. 2.5%). Finally, senior/member discount differences are likely to reflect the availability of such offerings.

Differences among Older Adults

Several socioeconomic and demographic factors predict preferences for methods of payment for prescription drugs. Also, the older person's gerontographic characteristic predicts rather well his or her preference for payment methods concerning prescription drugs. These differences are discussed in detail in the sections that follow.

Cash. The older the mature American, the less likely he or she is to prefer paying cash. Preference for cash as a method of paying for prescription drugs is the same regardless of the older person's income. Also, older adults who have children in close proximity are more likely than those whose children live far away to prefer this payment method for prescription drugs, with 56.5 percent and 41.0 percent, respectively, expressing preference for this method.

Sixty-one percent of older adults who live in the East indicated preference for cash, in comparison with slightly less than half of older Americans in other geographic areas. Finally, healthy hermits are more likely to prefer cash than ailing outgoers, with 54.2 percent and 43.8 percent, respectively, indicating preference.

Check. As mature Americans age, their preference for paying with a check declines. Half (50.9%) of those with incomes between $20,000 and $50,000, in comparison with 41.6 percent of those with higher incomes, indicated preference for paying this way. In addition, a larger percentage (51.7%) of older adults who do not have children in close proximity, in comparison to those who do (41.1%), prefers writing a check for payment of prescription drugs.

Check writing for prescription drugs is more common among older Americans who live in rural than in urban areas, with 56.5 percent and 44.8 percent, respectively, expressing preference. While only 28.9 percent of easterners prefer paying by check, about half of older adults who live in other states do the same. Also, ailing outgoers are more likely than healthy indulgers to prefer this payment method, with 51.9 percent and 44.5 percent, respectively, indicating preference.

Credit Card. The preference for paying with a credit card declines with age in late life. However, older adults with income in excess of $50,000 are three times as likely as those with incomes under $20,000 to indicate preference for using credit cards (32.1% vs. 10.2%). Preference for credit also increases with education.

A larger percentage of older males (21.8%) than older females (14.2%) prefers using credit to pay for prescription drugs. Older adults who live with others are more likely than those who live alone to prefer doing so, with 19.3 percent and 14.1 percent, respectively, indicating preference. Credit use for prescription drugs is more common among urban than rural older consumers (19.3% vs. 11.6%). Also, use of credit card is favored by twice as many older westerners (24.6%) as easterners (11.2%) or northerners (15.3%). Finally, a larger percentage of frail recluses (21.9%) than ailing outgoers (14.3%) and healthy indulgers (16.8%) prefers paying by credit card.

Senior/Member Discounts. Preference for senior/member discounts is higher among those age 65 to 74 than among those age 55 to 64 or 75 and older. These discounts are equally preferred by older adults, regardless of income. A larger percentage of older adults who live with others (49.3%) than of those who live alone (40.1%) prefers taking advantage of senior/membership discounts.

Older adults from households with nonworking members prefer senior/membership discounts to a greater degree than older adults in households with at least one working member (54.6% vs. 43.1%). Finally, senior/member discounts are more likely to be preferred by frail recluses and ailing outgoers, with about half of them (53.7% and 51.6%, respectively), expressing preference, in comparison with 39.8 percent of healthy indulgers and 42.2 percent of healthy hermits.

Coupons. Finally, preference for coupons remains fairly constant with age. Also, coupons are equally preferred by older adults in various income groups. Use of coupons is highest among southerners, with 4.5 percent of them expressing preference, in comparison with less than 1 percent of older adults who live in the East. While use of coupons is very low, ailing outgoers prefer using coupons twice as much as healthy indulgers (4.2% vs. 1.6%).

MEDIA USE PROFILES

Media use profiles were analyzed among users and nonusers of prescription drugs and selected cosmetics. Media consumption was examined with regard to both general and specific preferences. Respondents were asked to indicate how often they watch TV cable channels, read the newspaper, listen to the radio, watch comedy and variety TV shows, watch adventure and drama TV shows, watch TV news and documentaries, and use a VCR to record or play movies. In addition, respondents were asked to name the magazines they read on a frequent basis. Responses to less popular magazines (based on Simmons statistics) were grouped into broader categories representing different types of magazines.

Users vs. Nonusers of Prescription Drugs

Users of prescription drugs are more likely than nonusers to watch premium TV channels; and they are also more likely to watch comedy and variety TV shows, adventure and drama TV shows, and TV news and documentaries. However, users of prescription drugs are less likely to listen to the radio on a daily basis. With respect to magazine readership habits, older adults who are likely to use prescription drugs differ in many ways from their nonuser counterparts with respect to specific and general types of magazines they read on a regular basis. Specifically, a larger percentage of users than nonusers reports readership of the following magazines:

- *Good Housekeeping* (10.3% vs. 7.1%)
- *Ladies' Home Journal* (7.2% vs. 2.6%)
- *TV Guide* (4.0% vs. 2.0%)
- Travel/leisure, geographic, and history (9.3% vs. 6.5%)
- Business (professional) (10.9% vs. 7.8%)
- General interest (women) (10.9% vs. 7.9%)

Users vs. Nonusers of Cosmetics

Users of cosmetic (face-care and hair-care) products are heavier users of TV than their nonuser counterparts. A larger percentage of users, in comparison to nonusers of these products, watch comedy and variety TV shows (58.7% vs. 53.2%), adventure and drama TV shows (63.5% vs. 51.6%), and TV news and documentaries (81.0% vs. 75.5%); and they report heavier use of a VCR (36.7% vs. 27.8%).

Users of the selected cosmetic products are heavier readers of the following magazines, in comparison to nonusers.

- *Family Circle* (6.0% vs. 3.5%)
- *Good Housekeeping* (10.3% vs. 6.1%)
- *Ladies' Home Journal* (6.9% vs. 1.9%)
- *McCall's* (5.7% vs. 2.6%)
- *Modern Maturity* (12.8% vs. 8.6%)
- *People* (6.0% vs. 1.6%)
- *Reader's Digest* (36.7% vs. 29.1%)
- *Woman's Day* (3.5% vs. 1.3%)
- General interest—women (11.5% vs. 5.8%)

5

Housing

Another focus of our research was on housing preferences. Housing is a broad area that includes single-family houses, townhouses or condominiums, various types of retirement communities, and nursing homes. While people may occupy one specific type of housing facility at a given point in time, our interest was also in their perceptions of, and experiences with, other types of facilities. Consequently, we asked questions about past, present, and future housing preferences. Also, we wanted to know why people move from one type of housing facility into another, and the reasons they choose one specific type of home, such as in a retirement community, over another. Specifically, we wanted to know what factors appeal to present and future consumers of specific housing facilities, and how their choices might be influenced by specific marketing and social factors.

HOUSING PREFERENCES

It has been found in previous studies that older Americans prefer living in single-family homes. The intent of this research was not to address the same question but rather to examine individual differences in preferences for alternative types of housing. Because our samples included noninstitutionalized older adults, our studies are limited in that they overrepresent older adults who live in independent housing alternatives (single homes, apartments, condominiums/townhouses).

Rather than relying upon present housing arrangements to determine their preferences for types of homes, our respondents were asked to indicate, in addition to the present type of home they live in, their past type of home arrangement and their plans for the future. They were asked to respond to five types of housing: (1) single-family house, (2) apartment, townhouse, or condominium, (3) retirement community without health-care services, (4) retirement community with health-care services, and (5) nursing home.

Type of Housing

Among those age 55 and older, 84.1 percent indicated they live in a single-family house, 15.6 percent in an apartment, townhouse, or condominium, and 4.6 percent in a retirement community (with or without health-care services). Less than 1 percent of the older respondents indicated living in a nursing home. Given that respondents were noninstitutionalized these figures underrepresent older adults who live retirement communities and nursing homes. Because the total percentage exceeds 100.0, we can assume that about 5 percent of the respondents gave multiple responses because they were not sure of the type of housing they presently live in.

Single-Family Houses. Among older Americans age 55 and over, there is a decreasing likelihood an older person will be living in a single-family house with increasing age. A larger percentage of older males than older females (88.3% vs. 80.9%) lives in such a house. Additionally, a larger percentage of older adults (in families where at least one person works) lives in single-family houses than their counterparts in nonworking households (89.5% vs. 81.9%).

If the older person lives with others, chances are he or she lives in a single-family house. Nine in ten (90.8%) of older Americans who live with others live in a house, in comparison with 68.0 percent of their counterparts who live alone. When older people live alone, the extent to which they are likely to live in a house depends on their proximity to their children. A larger percentage of those who do not live near their children than those who live near them (74.6% vs. 62.6%) lives in single-family houses. Also, older adults who live in rural areas are more likely than their urban counterparts to live in a single-family house, with 91.0 percent and 82.0 percent, respectively, indicating this type of housing arrangement.

Apartment, Townhouse, or Condominium. As people age in late life, it becomes increasingly likely that they live in an apartment, a townhouse, or a condominium. Older women are more likely than older men to live in one of these kinds of residences (18.8% vs. 11.4%). Also, a smaller percentage of older people in families with at least one working person compared to those in nonworking families lives in apartments, townhouses, or condominiums (17.4% vs. 11.2%).

Upscale older Americans are more likely to live in these multi-family developments than their lower-income counterparts. Older people who live alone are three times as likely as their counterparts who live with others to live in an apartment, townhouse, or condominium, with 29.6 percent and 9.8 percent, respectively, indicating such housing arrangements. Additionally, one-third of older people who live near their children (in comparison with one-fourth of those who live farther away from their children) live in an apartment, townhouse, or condominium. City-dwelling older people are more likely than their rural counterparts to prefer living in multi-family housing, with 18.2 percent and 8.1 percent reporting living in these types of facilities, respectively. A larger percentage of older adults who live in the east (18.8%) than those who live in the west (13.8%) reports living in apartments, townhouses, or condominiums.

Retirement Community without Health-Care Services. As mature Americans become older, they are increasingly likely to live in a retirement community without health-care services. Mature females are more likely to reside in these kinds of communities (4.3% vs. 1.3%). Relative to those with relatively lower incomes, upscale mature Americans are less likely to live in a retirement community without health-care services, although they do not necessarily live in a retirement community with health-care services. One in twenty (5.6%) of those who live alone lives in this type of retirement community. A larger percentage of westerners (4.5%) than northerners (1.3%) lives in retirement communities without health-care services.

Retirement Community with Health-Care Services. As people's age increases in late life, so does the likelihood that they will reside in a retirement community with health-care services. Older males are less likely than their female peers to reside in this type of community (0.6% vs. 2.6%). Nearly one in five (19.3%) healthy indulgers, compared with 13.4 percent of healthy hermits and frail recluses, lives in apartments, townhouses, or condominiums. Finally, a larger percentage of ailing outgoers (4.5%) than frail recluses (0.2%) lives in retirement communities with health-care services.

Present vs. Past Type of Housing. About four in ten older adults presently living in a single-family house have lived in another single-family home in the past; another 15.1 percent indicated they had lived in an apartment, townhouse, or condominium, but the largest majority (44.6%) gave no response, suggesting they may have lived in the same house. Of interest, however, is the relatively large percentage of those older adults that presently lives in an apartment, townhouse, or condominium who have previously lived in a single-family house (61.8%), suggesting that a relatively large percentage of older renters or townhouse/condominium owners has moved out of single-family houses. The percentage of the present apartment, condominium, or townhouse dwellers who have lived in similar types of housing facilities in the past (15.9%) is similar to that of present single-family home dwellers. These figures indicate that the move into apartments, townhouses, or condominiums is from single-family houses rather than from similar types of housing facilities.

While a small percentage of older respondents had lived in a retirement community (with or without health-care services), the largest percentages of older residents who had moved into these housing facilities had previously lived in a single-family house.

Plans for Future Housing

Respondents were also asked to indicate their future housing plans. Almost 23 percent of older adults (22.9%) plan to live in a single-family house. Another 21.4 percent plan to live in a retirement community with health-care services. Sixteen percent plan to live in an apartment, townhouse, or condominium, 8.5 percent in a retirement community without health-care services, and 6.9 percent in a nursing home. One in four older adults indicated no housing plans.

Single-Family House. Only 22 percent of older adults have made plans to live in a single-family house in the future, a figure much lower than that of those under age 55 (38.6%). With age, older people become decreasingly likely to report plans to live in a single-family house in the future. Older males are more likely than their female counterparts to report plans to live in a single-family house, with 27.8 percent and 19.1 percent, respectively, expressing preference.

With increasing income and education older adults tend to report plans to live in a single-family house. In the meantime, a larger percentage of older adults who live with others (26.5%), in comparison with those who live alone (14.3%), plans to live in a single-family house. Also, one-third of westerners, in comparison with approximately one-fifth of older adults who live in other parts of the country, plan to live in a single-family house. Interestingly, nearly twice as many frail recluses as ailing outgoers (31.6% vs. 17.2%) prefer to live in a single-family home.

Apartment, Townhouse, or Condominium. The higher an older person's annual household income and level of education attainment, the higher his or her likelihood to have plans to live in an apartment, townhouse, or condominium. Among older adults who live alone, those who plan to live in an apartment, townhouse, or condominium are more likely to live near their children. Twenty-one percent of those who live within one hour's drive, in comparison with 13.2 percent of those who live farther away, indicated plans to live in these housing facilities. Plans to live in an apartment, townhouse, or condominium were mentioned by nearly 20 percent (19.7%) of older adults who live in the South and 17.5 percent of those who live in the North, figures much higher than 12.4 percent of southerners.

Retirement Community with Health-Care Services. A larger percentage of college graduates reports plans to move into a retirement community with health-care services, with 28.2 percent of college graduates indicating such a plan, in comparison to no more than 19 percent of their counterparts with less education. A larger percentage of those who presently live alone (24.9%) than those who live with others (20.0%) plans to move into this kind of community. Over one-quarter—27.7 percent—of older people who live near their children (vs. 21.5% of those who live further away from their children) plan to move into a retirement community with health-care services. Additionally, nearly one-fourth (24.8%) of ailing outgoers plan to move into a retirement community with health-care services, in comparison with 19.0 percent of healthy hermits.

Retirement Community without Health-Care Services. A larger percentage of those who live near their children, compared to those who live farther away from their children, plans to move into a retirement community without health-care services (8.0% vs. 3.9%).

Nursing Homes. College graduates report a stronger preference for living in a nursing home in the future, with almost one in ten (9.7%) of them expressing preference, compared with about 5 percent for those with less education. In the meantime, a larger percentage of southerners (8.8%) than easterners (4.4%) and westerners (5.6%) plans to move into such a facility. Finally, nearly twice as many healthy indulgers and ailing outgoers as healthy hermits (5.0%) and frail recluses (4.4%) plan to move into a nursing home.

Baby Boomers vs. Seniors

We were also interested in finding out if future housing plans of baby boomers differ from those of seniors. Table 5.1 shows future housing plans of the two generations. While about three in ten older Americans indicated no future housing plans, of interest are the differences between the two generations. While 42.8 percent of baby boomers plan to move into or stay in a single-family house, less than one in five (18.3%) of those age 65 and over plans to do the same. A slightly larger percentage of elderly (15.0%) than baby boomers (11.0%) plans to live in an apartment, townhouse, or condominium in the future. A larger percentage of baby boomers (10.1%) than elderly (7.2%) plans to live in a retirement community without health-care services; however, nearly as many baby boomers (10.4%) as seniors (23.2%) plan to live in a retirement community with health-care services. Nearly one in twenty (4.9%) baby boomers plans to live in a nursing home at some future time, compared with 7.1 percent of those age 65 and over. There are wide variations in

Table 5.1
Future Housing Plans of Baby Boomers and Seniors (65+)

Future Housing	Baby Boomers (%)	Seniors (%)
Single-family house	42.77	18.34
Apartment/townhouse/condominium	10.96	15.04
Retirement community without health-care services	10.12	7.24
Retirement community with health-care services	20.43	23.25
Nursing home	4.91	7.13
Base:	(N = 853)	(N = 337)

future plans for housing among older adults based on sociodemographic and lifestyle factors.

Present vs. Future Preferences

Older adults' future housing plans were analyzed by present type of housing arrangement. Only a little over one-quarter (26.3%) of the respondents who presently live in a single-family house have made plans to stay in a single-family house. Another 15.5 percent who presently live in this type of housing facility plan to move into an apartment, townhouse, or condominium in the future. Nearly three in ten (29.8%) plan to move into a retirement community, primarily into one with health-care services (21.5%), while only 7.1 percent of the older respondents who presently live in a single-family house plan to move into a nursing home. The remaining older respondents (21.3%) had made no plans at the time of this survey.

Among those who live in an apartment home, townhouse, or condominium, about one in twenty (5.9%) has plans to move into a single-family house. One in five (20.6%) plans to stay in the same type of housing, and about as many of them (20.7%) plan to move into a retirement community with health-care services. The percentage of those who presently live in an apartment home, townhouse, or condominium who plan to move into a retirement community without health-care services is only 8.7 percent, while only 4.8 percent plan to move into a nursing home. Almost 40 percent (39.3%) had made no plans. However, the largest percent of "no planners" for future type of housing were those older adults who at the time of the survey were living in a retirement community without health-care services.

REASONS FOR MOVING INTO AN APARTMENT, TOWNHOUSE, OR CONDOMINIUM

Given that the large majority of Americans live in a single-family house, this research sought to uncover reasons for moving into alternate housing. One type of alternative housing was apartments, townhouses, or condominiums. Based on previous research, eight main reasons were presented to respondents, who were asked to indicate if they think each of them applies to their decision to move into these alternate housing options. (Respondents could indicate more than one reason.)

Two factors seem to stand out as major reasons for moving into an apartment, townhouse, or condominium among older respondents (55+): to have freedom and independence, and loss of spouse, with 71.7 percent and 69.8 percent, respectively, mentioning these reasons. Two other reasons were mentioned by the majority of older adults: to reduce housing costs and to be closer to relatives, with 55.1 percent and 53.6 percent, respectively, mentioning these reasons. About one in three older Americans (34.0%) mentioned that the reason for moving into these housing facilities is unwillingness or inability to do house chores. One in ten (31.5%) said that access to social contacts and activities is a reason. Personal care and health-related reasons were mentioned by a smaller percentage (13.3 percent and 7.5 percent, respectively).

Responses were also analyzed only among those older Americans who had lived in an apartment, townhouse, or condominium. While the percentage figures change, somewhat, the relative importance of the eight factors remains the same.

In order to examine the extent to which older adults (55+) view these factors differently than their younger counterparts, responses given by older Americans were compared to those given by younger adults. A larger percentage of younger adults mentioned the majority of these factors; only need for continuous health-care and access to personal-care services were mentioned by a larger percentage of older adults. Unwillingness or inability to do house chores was mentioned by nearly as many younger as older respondents.

Baby Boomers vs. Seniors

Table 5.2 shows reasons given by baby boomers and seniors. There are significant differences in perceptions of reasons people move from a single-family house into each of these types of homes. A larger percentage of baby boomers than seniors thinks that people move into an apartment, townhouse, or condominium because of loss of spouse (81.0% vs. 65.1%), to have freedom and independence (83.9% vs. 68.3%), to reduce housing costs (74.9% vs. 48.5%), and to be closer to relatives (49.8%); and

Table 5.2
Reasons for Moving into an Apartment, Townhouse, or Condominium
among Baby Boomers and Seniors (65+) (Percent Who think Reason Is
Important)

Reasons	Baby Boomers (%)	Seniors (%)
Loss of spouse	81.00	65.09
Unwilling or unable to do house chores	36.01	34.43
To reduce housing costs	74.88	48.52
To be closer to relatives	71.54	49.82
Need for continuous health-care assistance	5.60	9.02
To have access to personal-care services	8.33	12.22
To have more social contacts and activities	40.53	28.20
To have freedom and independence	83.93	68.30
Base:	(N = 853)	(N = 336)

a smaller percentage of them feels they do so to have more social contacts
(40.5% vs. 28.2%), while the two age groups equally think that unwillingness or inability to do house chores is a reason (36.0% vs. 34.4%).
While the two remaining attributes are not of importance, boomers are
less likely than seniors to perceive the need for continuous health-care
assistance (5.6% vs. 9.0%) and access to personal-care services (8.3% vs.
12.2%) as important reasons for moving out of a single-family house into
an apartment, townhouse, or condominium.

Differences among Older Adults

The reasons older Americans give for moving into an apartment,
townhouse, or condominium relate to a number of sociodemographic
characteristics. The older person's gerontographic characteristics are also
strong predictors of the types of reasons he or she gives for moving into
an apartment, townhouse, or condominium.

Greater Freedom and Independence. Older adults with higher incomes are
also more likely to say that people move into these types of housing for
greater freedom and independence. Approximately three out of four of
older adults who live in northern and western states are likely to see this
as a reason why people move into an apartment, townhouse, or condominium, compared with two-thirds of southerners who think the same
way. Also, older adults from households with at least one person working were more likely than their counterparts from nonworking house-

holds to mention that people move into these housing facilities to reduce housing costs.

Finally, frail recluses are more likely to indicate that freedom and independence are important reasons why people move into an apartment, townhouse, or condominium, with 79.5 percent of them expressing this opinion, in comparison with 66.6 percent of ailing outgoers, 70.7 percent of healthy hermits, and 74.5 percent of healthy indulgers.

Loss of Spouse. The larger the older person's household income the greater the chances he or she will mention "loss of spouse" as a reason for moving into an apartment, townhouse, or condominium. Older adults who live alone and have children who live in close proximity are less likely than those who do not have children within one hour's drive to say people move into an apartment, townhouse, or condominium for this reason (61.6% vs. 74.4%). Finally, eight in ten healthy indulgers, in comparison with two-thirds of older adults in other gerontographic groups, indicated loss of spouse as the main reason for moving.

Reduced Housing Costs. Older Americans who say that people move into these housing facilities in order to reduce housing costs are more likely to have higher than lower household incomes. A larger percentage of healthy indulgers (64.5%) than healthy hermits (51.7%) and ailing outgoers (51.3%) said people move into these types of housing facilities for this reason.

Proximity to Family. The proportion of older adults in the four gerontographic groups who said people move into these facilities in order to be closer to relatives is lower for healthy indulgers (47.3%) than for any of the remaining three groups.

Unwillingness or Inability to Do Household Chores. Unwillingness or inability to do house chores is a reason cited by seniors regardless of their age. Older adults living in various parts of the country are also likely to interpret one's decision to move into an apartment, townhouse, or condominium differently. For example, a larger percentage of easterners (36.6%) and northerners (38.5%) than southerners (30.5%) and westerners (29.7%) said people move into these types of housing facilities because they are unwilling or unable to do house chores.

A larger percentage of male respondents, in comparison with their female counterparts (37.5% vs. 31.3%), indicated unwillingness or inability to do house chores as a reason for moving into such housing facilities. Finally, a much larger percentage of frail recluses (42.6%) than older adults in other gerontographic groups mentioned unwillingness or inability to do house chores as a reason for moving.

Increased Social Interaction. Apparently, children serve as substitutes for nonfamily social contacts and activities, since a smaller percent of those with children in close proximity (24.7%), in comparison to those without children near by (36.8%), say that people move into an apartment, townhouse, or condominium to increase their social interaction and activities. In the meantime, a larger percentage of westerners (38.2%) sees such a decision to move into a multi-family housing development as a way to increase one's social contacts, compared to their older counterparts who live in the North (28.6%) and South (29.1%).

Need for Health-Care/Personal Assistance. Mature Americans cited the need for health-care assistance as a reason for moving into an apartment, townhouse, or condominium, regardless of age. However, the more money a person has, the lower the likelihood he or she will say that people move into these facilities because they need continuous health-care or personal assistance. Also, ailing outgoers are more likely than healthy indulgers and frail recluses to mention that need for continuous health-care or personal assistance as a reason for moving into a multi-family housing unit.

REASONS FOR MOVING INTO A RETIREMENT COMMUNITY

Older adults perceive retirement communities as vehicles to continue their active lifestyles. When asked to indicate the reasons people move from a single-family house into a retirement community, 71.5 percent of older respondents (age 55 +) mentioned: "To have more social contacts and activities." This compares with 51 percent of the older Americans who said the reason is to have access to personal-care services, 49.1 percent who said it is because of unwillingness or inability to do house chores, and 47.1 percent due to loss of spouse. Of interest is the large percentage of respondents who mentioned the various reasons, suggesting that differences exist in the images of retirement communities as housing alternatives.

Reasons for moving into a retirement community were also examined separately for those relatively few respondents (N = 63) who had lived in a retirement community. In comparison to the responses given by all adults age 55 and older, older adults who had lived in this type of housing facility place a significantly greater importance on freedom and independence, with 59.8 percent of them indicating this reason for moving. These respondents de-emphasize the importance of access to personal-care services as a reason for moving into a retirement community, with 39.7 percent of them expressing this opinion. They also downplay the person's unwillingness or inability to do house chores as reasons for moving, with 39.7 percent of them indicating this to be a major reason.

Next, the research investigated perceptions of reasons for moving into a retirement community among younger and older adults. Several significant differences in perceptions appear to exist, suggesting that retirement communities have different images in the eyes of the two large age

Table 5.3
Reasons for Moving into a Retirement Community among Baby Boomers
and Seniors (65+) (Percent Who Think Reason Is Important)

	Baby Boomers (%)	Seniors (%)
Reasons		
Loss of spouse	61.11	46.52
Unwilling or unable to do house chores	60.40	47.77
To reduce housing costs	36.87	40.35
To be closer to relatives	32.24	22.14
Need for continuous health-care assistance	40.53	29.71
To have access to personal-care services	72.62	48.58
To have more social contacts and activities	83.36	67.45
To have freedom and independence	46.11	39.65
Base:	(N = 853)	(N = 336)

groups. Older adults downplay almost all the reasons presented to them, except reduction of housing costs, and freedom and independence; alternatively, younger adults perceive the important of these factors to be stereotypical of the older people who move into a retirement community.

Baby Boomers vs. Seniors

What are the reasons people move out of a single-family house into a retirement community? Baby boomers and seniors placed different value on the eight reasons they were presented (see Table 5.3). Generally speaking, baby boomers perceive each of the eight reasons to be of greater importance than their senior counterparts, with social reasons topping the list (83.4% vs. 67.4%). Six in ten boomers (compared with slightly under half of seniors) feel that people move into a retirement community because of loss of spouse and unwillingness or inability to do house chores. "Freedom and independence" are lower on the list of reasons given by the two groups, with 46.1 percent of baby boomers and 39.6 percent of seniors expressing this opinion. Need for continuous health-care assistance is perceived to be a reason by four in ten baby boomers, compared with two in three seniors, while one-third (32.2%) of the former group (vs. 22.1% of seniors) feel that people move into a retirement community to be closer to relatives.

Differences among Older Adults

Differences in responses varied across various demographic and gerontographic groups of the older population.

Social Contacts and Activities. The older mature Americans become, the
more likely they are to minimize social contacts and activities as a reason
for living in a retirement community. The higher a mature American's
household income and level of educational attainment, the more likely
he or she is to mention this as a reason for moving into a retirement
community. Also, a larger percentage of healthy indulgers (75.6%) than
frail recluses (69.3%) indicates social contacts and activities as reasons
for moving. A larger percentage of older adults who live in western
states than those who live in eastern states (75.8% vs. 68.1%) mentioned
increasing social contacts and activities as reasons for making a move to
such a facility.

Access to Personal-Care Services. As people age in late life, they tend to
downplay access to personal-care services as a reason for moving into a
retirement community. In the meantime, older people with higher levels
of education attainment, compared to those with less formal schooling,
are more likely to say access to personal-care services prompts seniors
to move to these kinds of facilities.

A smaller percentage of easterners than older adults who live in other
parts of the country is likely to mention access to personal-care services.
Finally, a larger percentage of healthy indulgers (56.5%) than healthy
hermits (49.7%) and frail recluses (46.9%) reports access to personal-care
services as a reason for moving into a retirement community.

Unwillingness or Inability to Do House Chores. Generally, with age, older
people downplay their unwillingness or inability to do house chores. The
higher their level of education the more likely older people are to mention these as reasons for moving into this kind of housing. Westerners
were more likely than easterners to indicate unwillingness or inability to
do house chores as a reason for such a move, with 51.7 percent and 44.5
percent, respectively, mentioning this factor. Finally, this is a reason most
likely to be given by frail recluses; it is more likely to be cited by this
group than by ailing outgoers or healthy hermits, with 56.3 percent, 44.4
percent, and 47.8 percent of older adults in these three groups expressing
this opinion, respectively.

Loss of Spouse. Older adults who live in western states are more likely
than their counterparts who live in other parts of the country to indicate
that loss of spouse is a reason for moving. Older adults who live with
others are more likely than those who live alone to indicate that this is
a major reason, with 49.1 percent and 42.2 percent, respectively, expressing this opinion. Also, older adults in households where at least one
person works are somewhat more likely than those from nonworking

households to say that loss of spouse is an important reason for moving into a retirement community, with 49.1 percent and 42.2 percent, respectively, expressing this view.

Finally, older adults feel that loss of spouse is an important reason why older people move into a retirement community, regardless of gerontographic profile.

Freedom and Independence. As older people age, they cite less emphasis on freedom and independence as a reason for moving to a retirement community. A larger percentage of easterners (45.6%) and westerners (45.1%) than northerners (38.7%) indicated that freedom and independence are reasons for making such a move. Finally, frail recluses is the gerontographic group least likely to mention freedom and independence as a reason for moving into a retirement community.

Reduced Housing Costs. The more money an older person has the less likely he or she is to say people move into this type of housing facility in order to reduce housing costs. A larger percentage of older adults who live in rural areas (45.2%) than their urban counterparts (37.8%) said that this is an important reason for moving into a retirement community. Also, older adults who live in the East and North are more likely than those who live in the South and West to mention housing costs as a reason for such a move. A larger percentage of older adults who do not have children living in close proximity (43.7%), in comparison to those with children living nearby (29.1%), mentioned that people move into a retirement community to reduce housing costs. Additionally, lower housing costs is an important reason for moving into this type of housing among ailing outgoers, much more so than among healthy indulgers, with 44.9 percent and 30.4 percent, respectively, mentioning this reason for moving. Frail recluses are also less likely than ailing outgoers to mention this reason.

Access to Continuous Health Care. Southerners are more likely than easterners (34.2% vs. 27.9%) to mention that need for continuous health-care assistance is a reason for moving to a retirement community. Also, a larger percentage of healthy indulgers (35.0%) and ailing outgoers (33.8%) than frail recluses (29.0%) and healthy hermits (29.5%) gave this as a reason why people make such a move.

Proximity to Family. Being close to relatives was mentioned as a reason why people move to retirement communities more frequently by those who live in rural areas than by those who live in urban areas (28.8% vs. 22.0%). Westerners are more likely than older adults who live in other parts of the country to mention this as a reason why people move into a retirement community.

Female older adults are more likely than their male counterparts to indicate that proximity to relatives is an important reason, with 26.1 percent and 21.4 percent, respectively, expressing this opinion. Finally, ailing outgoers are more likely than older adults in other gerontographic groups to say that being close to relatives is a reason for moving into a retirement community.

REASONS FOR MOVING INTO A NURSING HOME

Respondents were asked to indicate the reasons for which an older person might decide to move into a nursing home from a single-family home. Two-thirds of older Americans think that need for continuous health-care assistance would make an older person move into a nursing home. More than two in five (43.4%) indicated that access to personal-care services is a reason why older people would be willing to move into a nursing home. Nearly as many (38.4%) indicated that unwilling-ness or inability to do house chores could lead them to moving into a nursing home, and nearly 15 percent move due to loss of spouse. The remaining reasons given were not nearly as important, as indicated by the percentage of older respondents (less than 10%) who mentioned them.

Reasons for moving from a single-family house into a nursing home differ between younger (under 55) and older adults. Younger adults per-ceive each of the reasons presented to be significantly more important than older adults. For example, twice as many younger as older adults indicated that loss of spouse is a reason why older people move into a nursing home. Only freedom and independence associated with the life-style in a nursing home did not differ in perceptions of the two age groups. These findings suggest that younger people's perceptions of the reasons for which older adults move into a nursing home reflect stere-otypes of the older population as unhealthy, dependent, and isolated, in relation to the perceptions held by older adults.

Baby Boomers vs. Seniors

The study also sought to determine the perceptions of reasons for moving into a nursing home held by the two generations. Table 5.4 shows responses to the same eight reasons which were also evaluated with respect to the other types of homes. While the results are not sur-prising, of interest are the differences in perceptions held by baby boom-ers and seniors. The latter group consistently downplayed the importance of nearly every reason. These findings suggest that the ster-eotypes of the people who move, and the reason for moving into a nurs-ing home are more prevalent among the younger population. Alternatively, seniors view these factors to be of lower importance as a defense mechanism, since they are likely to identify more with those who move into nursing homes.

Table 5.4
Reasons for Moving into a Nursing Home among Baby Boomers and Seniors
(65+) (Percent Who Think Reason Is Important)

	Baby Boomers (%)	Seniors (%)
Reasons		
Loss of spouse	30.66	11.72
Unwilling or unable to do house chores	60.50	32.40
To reduce housing costs	10.48	4.12
To be closer to relatives	13.76	6.28
Need for continuous health-care assistance	92.06	60.19
To have access to personal-care services	68.27	38.85
To have more social contacts and activities	22.35	7.14
To have freedom and independence	2.98	3.08
Base:	(N = 853)	(N = 337)

Differences among Older Adults

The stereotypes of those who move into a nursing home held by older adults are more obvious when responses are compared across selected sociodemographic characteristics. With age, older adults are likely to downplay the importance of most of the factors presented to them as reasons why people move into a nursing home. Only two reasons do not show drastic decline with age: reduced housing costs and freedom and independence. The perceptions of these factors are not only insignificant as reasons for moving into a nursing home, but also change little with age in late life. Again, the decline in perceptions of the factors that make older people move into a nursing home suggests stereotypic perceptions among younger age groups which fail to live up to reality when they are compared to perceptions held by the very old (who are most likely to move into a nursing home).

Need for Continuous Health Care. Older adults with higher incomes are more likely to mention need for continuous health-care assistance as a reason for moving into a nursing home. People who live with others are more likely than those who live alone to say that the need for these kinds of services is a reason for making such a move (73.8% vs. 53.1%). A larger percentage of older females (72.2%) than their male counterparts (64.4%) mentioned need for continuous health-care assistance as reasons why people move into a nursing home. Additionally, approximately three-fourths of healthy indulgers and frail recluses, in comparison with a little over 60 percent of older adults in other groups, think that older people move into a nursing home because they need continuous health-care assistance.

Need for Personal-Care Assistance. The higher an older person's household income, the more likely he or she is to mention the need for personal-care assistance as a reason for moving to a nursing home. Older Americans who live with others are more likely than their counterparts who live alone to mention access to these services as a reason for moving to such a home (47.3% vs. 33.8%). Access to personal-care services was mentioned by a larger percentage of females than males (48.9% vs. 39.0%). Finally, more than half (52.4%) of frail recluses are of the opinion that people move out of a single-family house into a nursing home in order to have access to personal-care services, in comparison with 37.3 percent of ailing outgoers and 42.2 percent of healthy hermits.

Unwillingness or Inability to Do House Chores. With increasing household income, older adults are more likely to mention unwillingness or inability to do house chores as a reason for moving into a nursing home. A larger percentage of those who live with others (42.3%) than those who live alone (28.9%) said this is a reason for moving into a nursing home. Unwillingness or inability to do house chores was mentioned by a smaller percentage of older people living in eastern states (32.1%) than by older respondents living in other states.

Loss of Spouse. Older adults who live with others are more likely than their counterparts who live alone to indicate that loss of spouse is a common reason why older people move from a single family home into a nursing home, with 16.9 percent and 10.7 percent, respectively, expressing this opinion. Finally, a larger percentage of frail recluses (18.9%) than healthy hermits (13.5%) than ailing outgoers (13.1%) indicated loss of spouse to be a reason for moving into a nursing home.

Social Contacts. A higher proportion of older people who live with others, compared to that of people who live alone, mentioned more social contacts as a reason for moving to a nursing home (10.2% vs. 5.3%). This was given as a reason by a larger percentage of older females than by older males (11.0% vs. 7.0%).

Freedom and Independence. The more income the older person has, the lower the likelihood he or she will mention freedom and independence as a reason for moving into this type of housing facility.

REASONS FOR CHOOSING A SINGLE-FAMILY HOUSE

Important attributes found to influence home buyers' selection of single-family homes were conceptualized and translated into nine major attributes dealing with accessibility to a number of services, home or personal security, and influence of others (relatives). Attributes dealing with the home's physical structure such as the number of rooms and amenities were not examined, since extensive research has already dealt with these issues and they tend to be specifically related to the type of house under consideration.

Percentage distribution of responses in each attribute category examined among older Americans revealed home or personal security and location near shopping centers lead the list in importance, with 59.6 percent and 58.5 percent of older respondents, respectively, mentioning these reasons to be important in choosing a single-family house. Distance from friends and relatives and access to medical services were also mentioned by slightly more than half of the older respondents. Location near hospitals and access to public transportation are of lesser importance to older Americans in buying a house, with approximately 44 percent of them giving these reasons. About one in three mentioned access to personal and home-care services, 27 percent said access to planned social activities is important, while advice of relatives was mentioned by fewer than 20 percent (18.1%) of the older respondents.

Responses were further analyzed only among those older respondents who had been involved in a buying experience concerning a single-family house. Because nearly nine out of ten had such an experience, the results were fairly similar to those obtained for the entire older sample.

Our interest was also in examining the extent to which responses given by older Americans differ from those given by the younger population. Therefore, we compared the responses given by the two groups. The results of these comparisons are rather interesting in that the two age groups value some attributes differently, and these differences in perceptions of attribute importance are significantly different between the two groups. Location near shopping centers is more important to those age 55 and over, with 58.1 percent of the older respondents mentioning this reason, in comparison with 49.3 percent of younger adults. Other factors considered more important by older adults in choosing a single-family house, in comparison to their younger counterparts, are: access to medical services (51.0% vs. 43.3%), access to personal and home-care services (36.6% vs. 27.2%), access to planned to social activities (30.0% vs. 26.1%), location near hospitals (44.2% vs. 38.9%), and access to public transportation (44.1% vs. 37.9%).

Younger adults, on the other hand, are more likely than their older counterparts to perceive the following attributes to be important in choosing a single-family house: distance from friends and relatives (58.5% vs. 52.6%), home or personal security (75.8% vs. 59.0%), and advice of relatives (26.0% vs. 17.9%). While the latter finding appears to contradict conventional wisdom that older people, with age, rely increasingly more on younger relatives (children in particular), one must keep

Table 5.5
Reasons for Choosing a Single-Family House among Baby Boomers and
Seniors (65+) (Percent Who Think Reason Is Important)

Reasons	Baby Boomers (%)	Seniors (%)
Location near shopping centers	51.82	57.49
Distance from friends and relatives	57.53	51.48
Access to medical services	45.37	51.62
Access to personal and home-care services	23.82	35.36
Access to planned social activities	27.17	29.30
Home or personal security	79.93	54.41
Location near hospitals	40.77	41.80
Access to public transportation	35.61	43.04
Advice of relatives	31.32	18.78
Base:	(N = 876)	(N = 353)

in mind that a larger percentage of younger adults lives with a spouse, who is considered in their responses.

Baby Boomers vs. Seniors

Perceptions of the reasons for choosing a single-family home differ among baby boomers and seniors (see Table 5.5). A larger percentage of baby boomers, in comparison to their senior counterparts, perceives the following factors to be important in choosing a single-family house: security (79.9% vs. 54.4%), distance from friends or relatives (57.5% vs. 51.5%), and advice of relatives (31.3% vs. 18.8%). On the other hand, seniors place greater value on location near shopping centers (51.8% vs. 57.5%), access to medical services (45.4% vs. 51.6%), access to public transportation (35.6% vs. 43.0%), and access to personal and home-care services (23.8% vs. 29.3%).

Differences among Older Adults

A large number of sociodemographic characteristics of older respondents relate to the perceived importance of the attributes examined regarding selection of a single-family house. Also, older adults differ with regard to the reasons they cite for choosing a single-family house based on their gerontographic profiles.

Home or Personal Security. Home or personal security as a reason for choosing a single-family home shows constant decline with age in late life. Older males are more likely than older women to mention this as a reason for such a decision (66.2% vs. 54.5%). Also, home or personal security is valued mostly by those with annual household incomes in the range of $20,000 to $50,000, with nearly two-thirds of mature individuals in this category responding affirmatively to this attribute, in comparison with just over half (53.5%) of those with incomes under $20,000. Additionally, mature Americans who live with others are more likely than their counterparts who live alone to put importance on home or personal security (64.0% vs. 49.2%). In comparison with about half of those who live in eastern states, slightly over 60 percent of those who live in other states value home or personal security.

Proximity to Shopping Centers. A larger percentage of older males than females believes that location near shopping centers is an important factor in (62.8% vs. 55.1%) in choosing a single-family home. Older adults who live in urban areas place greater emphasis on this factor, in comparison to those who live in rural areas (60.5% vs. 54.0%). In the meantime, older adults who live in western states are more likely than their counterparts who live in other parts of the county to think that proximity to shopping centers is an important factor in selecting a single-family house, with nearly two-thirds of them (65.5%) expressing this view.

Proximity to Family and Friends. With increasing age, older adults perceive distance from friends and relatives to be of decreasing importance, especially after age 75. A larger percentage of older adults with annual incomes under $20,000 than those with annual incomes between $20,000 and $50,000 (57.1% vs. 49.9%) considers this to be an important attribute. In the meantime, older adults who do not have children in close proximity (within one hour's drive), in comparison to older adults who do, place greater emphasis on distance from friends and relatives (56.7% vs. 45.4%). Finally, healthy hermits and ailing outgoers differ from healthy indulgers with respect to the emphasis they place on the distance of the house from friends and relatives, with the former groups placing more emphasis on this factor than the latter group.

Access to Medical Services. Older males are more likely than their female counterparts to mention access to medical services (54.3% vs. 48.9%) as a reason for choosing to live in a single-family house. In the meantime, about half of mature adults with annual household incomes under $50,000, in comparison with about four out of five of those with higher incomes, are likely to place greater importance on this factor. A larger percentage of people in nonworking families, in comparison to their counterparts from households where at least one person works, perceives access to medical services to be of greater importance in choosing a single-family house (55.9% vs. 49.3%). Those older people who live with others are more likely than those who live alone to be concerned with this factor (53.6% vs. 45.7%). Finally, access to medical services is of greater concern to ailing outgoers and frail recluses than to healthy indulgers.

Proximity to Hospitals. The older the mature person is the lower the likelihood he or she will say location near hospitals is important in choosing a single-family house. Also, older men are more likely than their female counterparts to mention this as an important factor (49.1% vs. 40.9%). The importance of location near hospitals declines with increasing levels of education. Mature Americans in nonworking families are slightly more likely than their counterparts in families where at least one person works to put importance on this factor when choosing a single-family house (48.8% vs. 42.7%). Also, location near hospitals is more important to older people who live with others than it is to those who live alone (48.8% vs. 34.4%). This is a less significant factor among healthy indulgers than among other gerontographic groups. More than 60 percent (61.7%) of those who live with others, in comparison with just half (50.6%) of those who live alone, think location is important when choosing a single-family house. This consideration is more important to healthy hermits and ailing outgoers, with six in ten of people in these groups citing this reason, in comparison with a little over half (53.0%) of healthy indulgers.

Public Transportation. Access to public transportation is of greater importance to those with incomes under $50,000, with nearly half of older adults in the two lower-income groups, in comparison with about one-third of those with higher incomes, expressing this view. This is more important to people who live with others than it is to their peers who live alone (46.1% vs. 40.1%).

About half of the northerners (50.2%) and westerners (52.0%), in comparison with 37.7 percent of older adults who live in eastern states and 38.2 percent of those who live in the South, think that access to public transportation is an important factor to consider in choosing a single-family house. Finally, the house's access to public transportation is valued by a larger percentage of ailing outgoers (48.7%) and healthy hermits (46.4%) than by healthy indulgers (38.6%) and frail recluses (38.6%).

Access to Personal and Home-Care Services. Mature men are more likely than older females to mention access to personal and home-care services (40.0% vs. 34.1%). This factor is more important to older people in families where nobody works than it is to their counterparts in families with at least one working member (40.6% vs. 35.1%). Also, access to personal and home-care services is more important to older people who live far away from their children (more than an hour's drive) than it is to those who live closer to their children (39.2% vs. 29.2%).

Older Americans in rural areas are more likely than their urban-dwelling counterparts to value access to these kinds of services (42.1% vs. 34.8%). Additionally, of the gerontographic groups, healthy indulgers are the least concerned with accessibility to personal and home-care services.

Planned Social Services. The importance of having access to planned social services declines with increasing household income, with more than one-third (35.6%) of those with incomes under $20,000, in comparison with 20.2 percent of those with incomes greater than $50,000, perceiving this factor to be important. Mature Americans who do not live close to their children are more likely than their counterparts who do to indicate that access to planned social activities is important when choosing a single-family home (37.6% vs. 23.1%). Regarding the gerontographic groups, this factor is valued by nearly twice as many healthy hermits as healthy indulgers and frail recluses, with 37.7 percent and 21.0 percent, respectively, reporting preference.

Family Influences. With increasing income, older adults place less importance on the advice of relatives in choosing a single-family house. Similarly, the importance of this input declines with increasing education. Older people who live more than an hour's drive from their children are more likely than their counterparts who live closer to their children to consider the advice of relatives when deciding whether to live in a single-family residence (22.2% vs. 12.8%). Advice of relatives is valued more by older adults who live in the East (21.8%) and North (20.0%) than older Americans who live in the South (15.6%) and West (15.4%). Twice as many ailing outgoers and healthy indulgers as frail recluses are likely to consider this advice in choosing a single-family house, although this factor is not cited as important in this type of housing selection.

REASONS FOR CHOOSING AN APARTMENT, TOWNHOUSE, OR CONDOMINIUM

Respondents were presented with a list of factors that are likely to be considered in choosing an apartment, townhouse, or condominium. They were asked to check those they think are important reasons for choosing these types of housing facilities.

Nearly half (48.5%) of older Americans think that location near shopping centers is an important reason for choosing these types of housing facilities. Nearly as many (47.8%) feel that home or personal security is an important reason, while 42.8 percent think that access to public transportation is an important consideration. Roughly one in three older Americans feels that access to medical services, distance from friends and relatives, and location near hospitals are important reasons in choosing an apartment, townhouse, or condominium. Access to personal and home-care services is perceived to be important by 28.4 percent of older adults, while 27.2 percent of them feel that access to planned social activities is important in choosing these types of housing facilities. Finally, advice of relatives was indicated as a reason by just 13.9 percent of older Americans.

Responses to the same question were analyzed among those who had lived in an apartment, townhouse, or condominium. A total of 412 older adults had indicated they had lived in one of these housing facilities. In comparison to all older respondents, a larger percentage of those who had lived in an apartment, townhouse, or condominium mentioned the nine reasons to be important in their decision process concerning this type of housing.

Responses given by those age 55 and older were also compared to those in younger age groups. Generally, younger adults are more likely to perceive the various factors to be of greater importance than their older counterparts. Specifically, younger people value a lot more than do older Americans attributes such as location near shopping centers, distance from friends and relatives, access to planned social activities, home or personal security, access to public transportation, and advice of relatives. Thus, contrary to conventional wisdom that older people consider factors such as security and access to commercial and public services, this research does not support this conviction. Instead, it is the younger person who is mostly concerned with these decision criteria in choosing an apartment, townhouse, or condominium.

Baby Boomers vs. Seniors

There are also similar differences in perceptions between the two groups for choosing a specific apartment/townhouse or condominium. A larger percentage of baby boomers than seniors places importance on security (64.9% vs. 42.3%), location near shopping centers (58.0% vs. 44.1%), access to public transportation (46.1% vs. 40.25), distance from friends and relatives (39.5% vs. 30.5%), and advice of relatives (19.3% vs. 14.3%). Baby boomers, however, place less emphasis on access to personal and home-care services, with 21.6 percent of them indicating the importance of this factor, compared with 26.1 percent of the seniors.

Differences among Older Adults

Perceptions of the importance of various criteria are likely to differ on the basis of the older person's sociodemographic characteristics. Specifically, factors such as age, socioeconomic status, living conditions, and geographic location make a difference in how a person perceives the various factors in choosing an apartment, townhouse, or condominium.

Also, gerontographics are very strong predictors of the older person's propensity to consider the nine reasons in choosing an apartment, townhouse, or condominium.

Proximity to Shopping Centers. With increasing age, the older person is less likely to consider location near shopping centers when considering a move to an apartment, townhouse, or condominium. With education, older adults place greater emphasis on this factor. In the meantime, more individuals from working households than those from nonworking families said it is important to consider location near shopping centers (50.4% vs. 44.0%). A larger percentage of older adults who live alone (52.6%), in comparison to their counterparts who live with others (46.7%), thinks that this consideration is important in choosing these types of dwelling facilities. Finally, more than half (56.9%) of the healthy indulgers, in comparison with 40.8 percent of healthy hermits, consider location near shopping centers important in choosing such housing facilities.

Home/Personal Security. As mature Americans age, they become less likely to consider home or personal security important reasons for moving to an apartment, townhouse, or condominium. The higher older people's level of educational attainment, the more likely they are to place emphasis on this factor when considering multi-family housing units. Home or personal security is more important to people from working families than it is to their counterparts from families where nobody works (50.2% vs. 42.1%). Also, older adults who live in urban areas are more preoccupied with this factor than their rural counterparts in choosing such types of housing facilities (49.8% vs. 43.4%). Finally, the differences on home or personal security are striking among the four gerontographic groups. While just more than half of the healthy indulgers and frail recluses consider this factor to be important, only 42.6 percent of healthy hermits and 49.6 percent of ailing outgoers consider it to be important in choosing an apartment, condominium, or townhouse.

Access to Public Transportation. The older a mature person, the less likely he or she is to regard access to public transportation as an important factor in deciding to move to an apartment, townhouse, or condominium. Mature Americans from families where at least one person works are more likely than those from nonworking families to consider this an important factor (44.8% vs. 38.2%).

Access to public transportation is more important to older people who live alone than it is to their counterparts who live with others (47.1% vs. 41.0%). It is of greater importance to older Americans living in most regions of the country except the South, where 38.1 percent of older adults perceive this factor to be important, in comparison with about 45 percent of older adults in other regions. Finally, access to public transportation is of greater importance to ailing outgoers than to healthy hermits and frail recluses, with 46.5 percent vs. 40.2 percent and 40.0 percent, respectively, expressing this opinion.

Access to Medical Services. Compared to their peers with less formal education, access to medical services is more important to those older people with higher levels of educational attainment. A larger percentage of northerners (41.3%), in comparison with one-third of their southern and western counterparts, considers this an important factor. Additionally, four in ten ailing outgoers and 39 percent of frail recluses consider proximity to medical services to be an important reason people choose an apartment, townhouse, or condominium, but a relatively smaller percentage of healthy hermits (31.6%) are of the same opinion.

Proximity to Family/Friends. The more educated the older American, the more likely he or she is to place emphasis on distance from friends and relatives when considering an apartment, townhouse or condominium. Also, a larger percentage of people who live alone, compared to the proportion of those who live with others, considers this to be important (36.9% vs. 31.0%).

Contrary to our expectations, a larger percentage (35.2%) of older Americans who live in urban areas considers distance from friends and relatives important in choosing a multi-family housing facility, in comparison to those who live in rural areas (26.6%). Geographically, older Americans who live in eastern states are more likely than their southern counterparts to consider this important when choosing an apartment, townhouse, or condominium, with 37.3 percent and 28.3 percent, respectively, indicating this factor. Finally, while only 28.8 percent of healthy hermits consider distance from friends and relatives to be important, the percentages for older adults in the remaining gerontographic groups that do the same is over one-third.

Proximity to Hospitals. An apartment's, townhouse's, or condominium's location near hospitals is considered to be of greater importance by easterners (38.7%) than by northerners (32.3%), southerners (32.6%), or westerners (28.0%). Among older adults who live alone, those who live near their children are more likely than those who have no children in close proximity to consider this when choosing one of these multi-family housing units, with 37.2 percent and 27.8 percent, respectively, expressing this opinion. Additionally, location near hospitals is an attribute considered most important by ailing outgoers, with 37.8 percent of them expressing this opinion, in comparison with nearly 30 percent of healthy hermits and healthy indulgers.

Access to Personal and Home-Care Services. The higher a person's education level, the more likely he or she is to consider access to personal and home-care services an important factor in choosing an apartment, townhouse, or condominium. A larger percentage (32.9%) of easterners, in comparison to southerners (24.6%), thinks that this is important in choosing these types of housing facilities. Finally, access to personal and home-care services is valued by one-third of healthy indulgers and by three in ten ailing outgoers and frail recluses; yet, only 23.4 percent of healthy hermits feel the same way.

Access to Social Programs. Older people from families where at least one person works put more emphasis than their counterparts from non-working families on access to planned social activities (28.9% vs. 23.1%). This factor is more important to ailing outgoers than to frail recluses, with 31.4 percent and 15.5 percent, respectively, indicating this factor to be important in choosing these types of homes.

Family Influences. Older adults with more education are less likely to consider advice of relatives to be an important reason for choosing these types of housing facilities. Such input is more important to older people from working families than it is to their counterparts from families where nobody works (15.6% vs. 10.1%).

Older people who live alone are more likely than those who live with others to think that advice of relatives is important when making a decision about an apartment, townhouse, or condominium (17.4% vs. 12.5%). In the meantime, family input is more likely to affect the decision of older adults who live in the East (19.7%) and North (16.3%) than those older Americans who live in the South (10.2%) and West (10.5%). The advice of relatives is of greater importance to older adults who have no children in close proximity (22.5%) than to those who do (12.8%).

Furthermore, ailing outgoers are twice as likely as frail recluses to consider the opinion of relatives in choosing these types of housing facilities, with 19.5 percent and 9.9 percent, respectively, indicating this factor to be an important one. Responses to this factor by older adults in the two remaining gerontographic groups were also lower than those of ailing outgoers.

REASONS FOR CHOOSING A RETIREMENT COMMUNITY

Previous research suggested a number of possible criteria an older person might use to select a retirement community. Our respondents were presented with a list of nine reasons for choosing a retirement community, and were asked to indicate whether *they think* each of these reasons is important in selecting one to move into. Based on the results given by mature respondents, there is no single predominant factor, but several considered to be important in choosing a retirement community. More than half (53.5%) mentioned access to medical services, and nearly as many (48.3%) said access to planned social services. Of equal importance is access to public transportation, with 47.9 percent of the older respondents indicating this reason to be an important one. Forty-seven percent of the older respondents indicated location near shopping centers and near hospitals, while another 44.5 percent mentioned access to personal and home-care services. Of somewhat lesser importance in choosing a retirement community are home or personal security, with 39.7 percent of the respondents mentioning this factor. Distance from friends and relatives was mentioned by 37.5 percent of the older respondents, while about one in five (21.9%) mentioned advice of relatives as a factor in choosing a retirement community.

Responses were also analyzed among those who had lived in a retirement community. Each of the factors was indicated to be important by a larger majority of these respondents. Specifically, access to medical services was mentioned by 64.3 percent of the older respondents who had lived in a retirement home, followed by planned social activities (63.6%). Home or personal security was mentioned by 62.2 percent of the respondents who had experienced this type of housing facility, while location near shopping centers and hospitals is of equal importance, with 61.4 percent and 61.2 percent, respectively, mentioning this reason. Two in three (59.8%) are of the opinion that access to personal and home-care services is important. About half (47.3%) of these selected respondents consider distance from friends and relatives to be a factor in choosing a retirement community. Access to public transportation is an important factor for older adults in general, since only 38 percent of those who have previously lived in a retirement community (compared with 47.9% of the general older population), indicated this reason. Advice of relatives was perceived as important by those who had lived in a retirement community, as it was for those who had not lived in a retirement community, with 23.7 percent of the former group giving an affirmative response to this factor.

In order to determine whether perceptions of those age 55 and older are different from those of their younger counterparts, responses given by the two groups were compared. Responses by the younger age group tend to reflect stereotypes of those who move into a retirement community—such as need for medical services, location near hospitals, and access to public transportation. Advice of relatives was mentioned by a larger percentage of older adults (33.4%) than by either those who had lived in a retirement community (23.7%) or the younger respondents in general (21.4%).

Baby Boomers vs. Seniors

Table 5.6 shows perceptions of the importance of the same nine reasons for choosing a specific retirement home for the two select age groups. As can be seen, the perceived importance of all nine factors is greater among baby boomers than among seniors. Access to medical

Table 5.6
Reasons for Choosing a Retirement Community among Baby Boomers and
Seniors (65+) (Percent Who Think Reason Is Important)

Reasons	Baby Boomers (%)	Seniors (%)
Location near shopping centers	68.22	40.40
Distance from friends and relatives	61.42	33.93
Access to medical services	78.58	46.96
Access to personal and home-care services	69.18	39.75
Access to planned social activities	67.13	44.27
Home or personal security	57.68	33.26
Location near hospitals	74.23	39.66
Access to public transportation	73.98	42.17
Advice of relatives	36.22	18.42
Base:	(N = 876)	(N = 355)

services, hospitals, and public transportation tops the list, with about
three-fourths of baby boomers indicating their importance, compared
with about four in ten seniors. Similarly, approximately two-thirds of
baby boomers think that people choose a retirement home because of
access to personal and home-care services, access to planned social activities, and location near shopping centers, whereas these features are
perceived to be important by only four in ten older adults. Twice as
many baby boomers as elderly think distance from friends and relatives
(61.4% vs. 33.9%), and advice of relatives (36.2% vs. 18.4%) are important
factors, while 57.7 percent of the former group (vs. 33.3% of seniors)
perceive home or personal security to be important.

Differences among Older Adults

The criteria used in choosing a retirement community differ among
older Americans who posses certain demographic and socioeconomic
characteristics. Factors such as age, income, and education are particularly important determinants of perceived important of the selection criteria concerning retirement communities. Gerontographics also are
powerful predictors of older adults' perceptions of the importance of
various factors in choosing a retirement community. Specifically, the perceived importance of the selection criteria for retirement communities
declines with increasing age. This pattern may in part reflect younger

people's stereotypes of older adults' motives for choosing a retirement community. With increasing income, older people tend to consider a larger number of factors to be important in selecting a retirement community. Only advice of relatives did not show variation with household income. The remaining factors were perceived as of greatest importance among those older adults with the highest incomes. The relationships between perceived importance of the criteria used in selecting a retirement community and education were similar to those found for income.

Access to Medical Services. A larger percentage of those who live with others (55.5%), in comparison to those who live alone (48.6%), mentioned access to medical services as an important consideration when choosing a retirement community. Healthy indulgers and frail recluses are more likely than their healthy hermit counterparts to emphasize this factor when making such a decision.

Planned Social Programs. Healthy indulgers are more likely than healthy hermits (54.8% vs. 43.4%) to value access to planned social activities.

Public Transportation. Access to public transportation is more important to mature Americans who live with others than it is to those who live alone (49.9% vs. 43.2%). A larger percentage of older males (51.1%) than older females (45.6%) perceives this to be an important factor. Finally, of the four gerontographic groups, healthy hermits are the least concerned with access to public transportation.

Proximity to Shopping Centers. Location near shopping centers was perceived to be of greater importance among westerners than among older adults living in other geographic areas, with 54.9 percent of the former group expressing such an opinion. Healthy indulgers and frail recluses are those most likely to indicate that this is an important consideration, while healthy hermits are least concerned with this factor.

Proximity to Hospitals. Older people who live with others are more likely than their counterparts who live alone to put emphasis on location near hospitals when considering a retirement community (49.2% vs. 41.5%). About half of older adults who live in the South and West, in comparison with 40.6 percent of those who live in the East, think that this is an important factor in choosing among retirement communities. In the meantime, older males are more likely than their female counterparts to indicate location near hospitals to be an important factor, with 51.1 percent and 43.9 percent, respectively, mentioning this factor.

Access to Personal and Home-Care Services. Access to personal and home-care services is least important among healthy hermits; it is of nearly equal importance among the remaining gerontographic groups.

Home or Personal Security. A larger percentage of westerners (48.4%) than older adults who live in other parts of the country perceives home or personal security to be important in choosing a retirement community.

Of the four gerontographic groups, this factor matters the least to healthy hermits.

Proximity to Family/Friends. Distance from friends and relatives is most important to healthy indulgers and frail recluses, while healthy hermits are less concerned with this factor when considering a retirement community.

Family Influence. Older people who live with others are more likely than their counterparts who live alone to consider the advice of relatives when making a decision about retirement communities (23.6% vs. 17.8%). Ailing outgoers are more likely than healthy hermits and frail recluses (28.3% vs. 17.1% and 19.4%, respectively) to perceive this input as important when selecting a retirement community.

REASONS FOR CHOOSING A NURSING HOME

What factors do older adults feel are important in choosing a nursing home? In order to answer this question, respondents were asked to give us their opinion on the nine preselected factors representing different reasons for choosing a nursing home. Of those 55 and older, access to medical services and distance from friends and relatives are almost of equal importance, with roughly one-third of them expressing the view. Location near hospitals was also mentioned by nearly three in ten (28.7%) of older Americans. Advice of relatives is important to 21.4 percent of the respondents. About one in five said that access to transportation, access to personal and home-care services, and access to planned social activities are important in choosing a nursing home, while 18.4 percent and 15.4 percent said that home or personal security and access to public transportation are important, respectively. A nursing home's location near shopping centers was considered important by one in ten older Americans.

One of the most interesting findings of our research on factors considered important in choosing a nursing home was the differences in perceptions between younger and older adults. In most cases these factors are perceived to be twice as important by the younger as by the older age group. These findings reflect the misconceptions in reasons for choosing a nursing home on the part of younger adults, and in part the older person's reluctance to admit the attributes are important, since many of them may have considered entering a nursing home at some point in late life.

Baby Boomers vs. Seniors

While perceptions of reasons people choose specific nursing homes differ between the two groups, the pattern is rather similar to that for retirement communities. A much larger percentage of baby boomers than seniors thinks the nine factors are important in choosing a nursing home. In fact, the differences between the two groups are rather striking, reflecting possible misconceptions of reasons for choosing nursing homes on the part of baby boomers, and perhaps a defense mechanism among the elderly.

Differences among Older Adults

There are differences, as well as similarities, in how seniors with different demographic characteristics perceive factors related to the selection of a nursing home. For example, with age, older adults increasingly de-emphasize the importance of the main reasons considered in choosing a nursing home. While much of the decline might be attributed to ability to provide responses to questions, it is not quite so, since older respondents, regardless of age, gave similar responses to reasons for choosing other types of housing facilities. Furthermore, the drop in importance of stereotypical conceptions about those who enter a nursing home suggests the opposite. Also, reasons for choosing such a facility are significantly related to the older person's gerontographic background. Generally, the higher the older person's income the greater his or her likelihood to perceive the various factors to be important in choosing a nursing home. Also, the older person's living arrangement is a very strong predictor of his or her perceptions of the importance of the various reasons in choosing a nursing home, with those who live with others perceiving the various factors to be of greater importance than those who live alone. Exceptions to these generalities are noted in the following profiles.

Access to Medical Services. While 86.1 percent of the under 55 group feel that access to medical services is important in choosing a nursing home, only 17.9 percent of those age 75 and over express the same view. Mature men are more concerned with this factor than are their female counterparts (42.0% vs. 29.5%). Also, the more education an older person has, the more likely he or she is to consider access to medical services important when choosing one of these facilities. This factor is of greater importance to westerners, with nearly four in ten older adults who live in western states mentioning it to be important, in comparison with one in ten older adults who live in the East and one-third of those who live in the North. Finally, access to medical services is more important to healthy indulgers and frail recluses than it is to healthy hermits.

Proximity to Friends/Family. Distance from friends and relatives is important to 53.4 percent of younger adults and 19.4 percent of those 75 and older. This factor is more important to older men than it is to their female counterparts (35.9% vs. 30.1%). In the meantime, the higher a mature American's level of education, the more likely he or she is to be concerned with how far away a nursing home is from friends and relatives. Finally, healthy indulgers and frail recluses are more likely than healthy hermits and ailing outgoers to indicate distance from friends and relatives.

Proximity to Hospitals. Location near hospitals is more important to older men than it is to older women (32.1% vs. 26.2%) when he or she is considering nursing homes. The more education an older person has, the more likely he or she is to consider this to be an important factor. Westerners are more likely than their easterner counterparts to consider location near hospitals, with 33.9 percent and 24.1 percent, respectively, expressing this view. One in four (26.5%) of northerners expressed the same opinion. Also, healthy indulgers and frail recluses are more likely than healthy hermits to emphasize this when choosing a nursing home.

Family Influences. However, a smaller percentage of westerners (18.7%) than southerners (25.4%) would rely on advice of relatives in choosing a nursing home.

Public Transportation. Older men are more likely than older women to be concerned with a facility's access to public transportation (18.6% vs. 13.0%). This factor is perceived to be of equal importance regardless of the older person's level of household income.

Access to Personal and Home-Care Services. Access to personal and home-care services is valued by one-fourth (24.2%) of older Americans who live in western states, in comparison with 18.8 percent of those who live in the South, and 14.8 percent of those who live in the East.

Planned Social Programs. As an older person's level of educational attainment increases, so does the likelihood that he or she will be concerned with access to planned social activities. The availability of these kinds of services is valued by one in eight (12.9%) of older adults who live in eastern states, in comparison with approximately one-fifth of the older adults who live in other parts of the country. Furthermore, a larger percentage of healthy indulgers than older adults in any of the remaining gerontographic groups is likely to mention access to planned social services, with about one-fourth (26.6%) of them expressing this view.

Home or Personal Security. Home or personal security becomes more important to mature Americans as their level of education increases. Westerners are twice as likely as their easterner counterparts (23.5% vs. 11.6%) to perceive these factors as important when choosing a nursing home, while the perceptions of mature Americans who live in North and South were 18.3 percent and 19.4 percent, respectively.

Proximity to Shopping Centers. In comparison to their female counterparts, a larger percentage of older males considers location near shopping centers to be important in choosing a nursing home (12.4% vs. 8.8%). Perceptions of the importance of location of shopping centers does not differ between older adults who live alone and those who live with others. This factor is perceived to be far more important in choosing a nursing home by older adults who have children in close proximity than by older adults who do not have children in close proximity (12.5% vs. 4.7%). Finally, frail recluses are nearly twice as likely as healthy hermits (14.0% vs. 7.4%) to cite location near shopping centers as an important reason for choosing this type of housing facility.

PREFERENCES FOR SOURCES OF INFORMATION

Older consumers may obtain information about new housing alternatives from a variety of sources. In this research we asked our respondents to indicate the most preferred alternative from the following list of company-controlled sources: TV/print ads, direct mail, telemarketing, agent visitation, and group meetings or seminars. About one in four older respondents indicated no preference or no opinion by not checking one of the response alternatives. Among those who responded, however, 44.3 percent of adults age 55 and over indicated preference for seeing a TV or print ad, and three in ten (29.7%) would prefer to receive information in the mail. Agent visitation was lower on the list, with 16.7 percent of older respondents indicating preference. Learning in group meetings was preferred by nearly 8 percent (7.9%) of older respondents, while telephone solicitation was the least preferred alternative (2.4%).

Responses given by older adults were somewhat different from those given by their younger counterparts. A larger percentage of respondents under 55 years of age (37.0%) would prefer to receive news in the mail, compared with 29.8 percent of the older consumers; and they would also prefer to learn about new housing options in group meetings or seminars (7.9% vs. 4.9%).

Differences among Older Adults

Preferences for sources of information regarding new housing alternatives show variations based on the older person's demographic and socioeconomic characteristics. However, gerontographic characteristics of older Americans are the best predictors of the sources of information preferred.

TV/Print Advertising. With increasing household income, older Americans increasingly prefer TV or print ads as sources of information about new homes. About half (48.7%) of older Americans living in the West in comparison with two-fifths (39.6%) of those who live in the North prefer to find out about new housing from these media. Older adults from families where at least one person works are more likely than their counterparts from nonworking families to prefer TV or print ads, with 45.5 percent and 41.6 percent, respectively, expressing preference. Furthermore, half of healthy hermits prefer to find out about new housing options from these ads but fewer ailing outgoers (38.5%) and frail recluses (41.1%) prefer them.

Group Meetings/Seminars. With age, mature Americans prefer to learn about new housing options in group meetings or seminars. However, the higher an older person's household income, the less likely he or she is to prefer getting information via this format. Older females are twice as likely as their male counterparts to prefer learning about new housing products in group meetings or seminars, with 10.3 percent and 5.4 percent, respectively, expressing preference. In terms of geography, a larger percentage of older adults who live in the North (12.6%) prefers to hear news this way, in comparison with their counterparts who live in the East (3.7%), South (5.5%), and West (6.6%). Also, learning in group meetings or seminars is preferred by a larger percentage of healthy indulgers (11.6%) and ailing outgoers (11.1%) than healthy hermits (4.1%) and frail recluses (6.6%).

Agents. As older Americans age, their preference for having an agent explain new housing options at their home increases. The higher an older person's household income, the more likely he or she is to prefer learning about housing options this way. Specifically, nearly one in five (19.6%) of older Americans having annual household incomes in excess of $50,000 prefers to be visited by an agent, in comparison with 13.5 percent of those with incomes between $20,000 and $50,000. Finally, a larger percentage of healthy indulgers (18.8%) and frail recluses (19.7%) than healthy hermits (13.3%) and ailing outgoers (13.9%) prefers to be visited by an agent.

Direct Mail. Preference for receiving information in the mail decreases in late life. Healthy hermits are the group least likely to prefer receiving news in the mail, with 22 percent of older adults in this group expressing preference for this source, compared with over one-third (34.5%) of ailing outgoers and about three in ten of the older adults in the remaining gerontographic groups.

PROFILE OF POTENTIAL RESIDENTS OF RETIREMENT COMMUNITIES

We considered potential residents to be those closest to retirement age, and we confined our analysis to the older population (55+). Although nearly 30 percent of older adults had indicated plans to move into a retirement home with or without health-care facilities, the actual percentage of older adults who plan to live in such facilities is smaller, since many respondents gave multiple responses. Responses of those older adults who indicated plans to move into a retirement community were compared across various background characteristics. With approximately one-fourth of older Americans surveyed indicating plans to move into a retirement community at some point in the future, a profile of those who are more likely to do so can be developed by examining percentages of affirmative responses given by those who have certain characteristics.

Sociodemographic Characteristics

Age. Surprisingly, older and younger Americans gave similar responses to the question concerning future plans to move into a retirement community. While the percentage of the 65-to-74 age bracket who plans to do so is higher than that of those age 55 to 65, age does not seem to be a good predictor of the older person's likelihood of moving into a retirement community.

Socioeconomic. While income is not a good predictor of the older person's propensity to plan to move into a retirement community, education appears to be a rather good indicator of the person's likelihood of having such housing plans. While only one in five (21.5%) of the lower-educated older Americans considers this housing option, the percentage jumps to nearly one-third (31.2%) among those with college education.

Other. A larger percentage of older females (27.0%) than older males (23.1%) plans to move into a retirement community. Also, a higher percentage of older Americans who presently live alone, in comparison to those who live with others, plans to move into a retirement community (27.6% vs. 24.1%). More northerners (26.9%) than westerners (22.7%) plan to move into a retirement facility.

Gerontographics

Gerontographic characteristics of older Americans predict plans to move into a retirement community. Ailing outgoers are more likely than healthy hermits to plan to move into a retirement community, with 27.0 percent and 22.8 percent, respectively, indicating plans.

Mass Media Use

Older Americans who indicated plans to move into a retirement facility can be profiled with respect to their media use habits. A larger percentage of those who have such housing plans, in comparison to those who have alternate plans, reads newspapers daily (86.4% vs. 82.7%), listens to the radio every day (67.9% vs. 61.0%), and watches TV news and documentaries every day (82.5% vs. 77.4%). They also differ in terms of magazine preferences. Specifically, prospective retirement community dwellers are more likely than those who do not plan to move into such facilities to read *Ladies Home Journal* (9.2% vs. 4.0%), *Modern Maturity* (14.5% vs. 10.5%), *Reader's Digest* (38.5% vs. 34.0%), and magazines about news and public affairs (12.9% vs. 8.6%) and arts and sciences (8.7% vs. 5.3%).

PROFILE OF POTENTIAL RESIDENTS OF NURSING HOMES

Again, we confined our analysis to the older sample (55+). As it was indicated earlier, nearly 7 percent (6.9%) of the older respondents in our sample indicated plans to move into a nursing home at some point in the future. Can these individuals be profiled on the basis of sociodemographics, lifestyles, and media use patterns?

Sociodemographics

Sociodemographic characteristics are poor predictors of the older person's likelihood of having plans to move into a nursing home. Age is not a good predictor of future plans, nor is it sex, socioeconomic characteristics, or other demographics. Only geographic location differentiates among older adults who plan to move into a nursing home, with a larger percentage of southerners (8.8%) than easterners planning to move into a nursing home at some point in the future.

Gerontographics

Gerontographics are strong predictors of the older person's intentions to move into a nursing home. Nearly twice as many healthy indulgers and ailing outgoers as frail recluses and healthy hermits plan to move into a nursing home (9.2% and 9.4% vs. 4.4% and 5.0%, respectively).

Media Use

There are few differences in media use habits between older adults who plan to move into a nursing home and those who do not. Specifically, a larger percentage of the former group (83.9%) in comparison with the latter group (78.3%) watches TV and documentaries on a daily basis, and reads arts and science magazines (10.4% vs. 5.9%) and general interest magazines (25.5% vs. 15.9%) on a regular basis.

6

Technology Products and Telecommunication Services

Many questions in our surveys were designed to help us learn how baby boomers and their elders react to high-tech products, large-tag appliances such as cars, and telecommunication services. We designed questions to gather information on preferences for selected products and services, sources of information about electronic products, and telecommunication services. We were also interested in learning how these older consumers prefer to buy such products, including their preferences for buying direct and for methods of payment, and how their consumer behaviors differ from those of their younger counterparts.

Because of the great heterogeneity of the older population, we wanted to analyze how older consumers respond to these products and services according to sociodemographic and gerontographic characteristics. We, therefore, analyzed responses to the questions by factors such as income and education, and we examined the media preferences of those older adults who have or expressed interest in having or receiving the selected products and services in our study.

PREFERENCES FOR HIGH-TECH PRODUCTS AND TELECOMMUNICATION SERVICES

While there is a plethora of high-technology products and technology-based services, many of them are most relevant to people at different stages in life. Products such as personal computers, for example, do not provide the older person with the same benefits as they do to younger adults, who are more likely to be employed or in school. Therefore, it is not surprising to find results of studies which show that older adults are less likely to prefer technology-based products and services than younger adults, but more or equally as likely to prefer those products or services which provide them with an obvious and immediate benefit.

In order to assess respondents' preferences for high-tech and telecommunication products and services, products which are relevant to people at later stages in life or are consistent with their lifestyles were selected from a wide variety of areas. Telephone answering machine, home-security system, and energy-saving appliances or installed devices were selected to represent the high-tech product area. Another three services were selected from the telecommunications field: operator-assisted services (such as directory assistance), discount or "package" long-distance telephone plan, and operator-assisted service that locates people with whom you have lost touch (the latter being a nonexistent service). Respondents were asked whether they currently have/use, would like to have/use, are not interested in having/using, or never heard of or don't know.

Nearly one in four (24.2%) of older adults has or uses an answering machine and one in eight (12.7%) has a home-security system. More than half (55.2%) of older Americans have energy-saving appliances or installed devices. Nearly half (44.4%) of older adults presently use operator-assisted services, and 18.0 percent have/use a discount or "package" long-distance telephone plan. Nearly one in five (17.7%) prefers to have a service that would help locate people with whom they have lost touch.

In order to determine the extent to which the responses given by the older population differ from those of younger adults, preferences for these products and services were compared among younger and older adults. A larger percentage of adults under age 55, in comparison to those age 55 and over, currently has a telephone answering machine (43.8% vs. 23.9%). However, nearly as many younger as older adults (53.2% vs. 55.2%) have energy-saving appliances or installed devices, and a slightly larger percentage of older Americans (12.5%) has a home-security system in comparison with their younger counterparts (9.9%).

A similar analysis was performed for the three telecommunication services, but since one of the three services was not available, "currently use" and "would like to use" responses were combine for this and subsequent analyses. The data clearly show that adults under 55 years of age prefer the three services more than their older counterparts. About four in five (81.4%) of the former group, in comparison with 62.7 percent of the older adults, use operator-assisted services. They are also more likely to subscribe to a discount or "package" long-distance plan than their older counterparts (56.3% vs. 42.6%). The younger group is also twice as likely to prefer the service that locates people one has lost touch with (36.2% vs. 18.5%).

Table 6.1
Preferences for Selected Products and Telecommunication Services among
Baby Boomers and Seniors (65+)

	Baby Boomers (%)	Seniors (%)
Ownership/Use of Selected Products		
Home-security system	7.88	13.59
Telephone answering machine	46.92	16.62
Energy-saving appliances or installed devices	52.78	52.83
Base:	(N = 883)	(N = 368)
Preferences for Selected Services		
Operator-assisted services (such as directory assistance)	82.44	58.60
Operator-assisted service that locates people you have lost touch with	38.18	15.64
Discount or "package" long-distance telephone plan	54.99	38.12
Base:	(N = 597)	(N = 249)

Baby Boomers vs. Seniors

The consumer behavior of the two age groups with respect to these types of technologies was also investigated by comparing responses given by baby boomers to those given by seniors (65+). Baby boomers are three times as likely as seniors to own or use a telephone answering machine, with 46.9 percent and 16.6 percent of them, respectively, indicating ownership/use. On the other hand, the seniors are twice as likely to have a home-security system, while about half of both groups have energy-saving products. Preferences for telecommunication services are stronger for baby boomers than for seniors (see Table 6.1).

Differences among Older Adults

Many sociodemographic factors appear to make a difference in the older person's preference for high-tech and telecommunication products and services. The older person's gerontographic characteristics are strong predictors of his or her preference for high-tech and telecommunication products and services. These elements are reflected in the discussion that follows.

Overall Ownership and Preferences. Older adults are more likely to own or use the various high-tech and telecommunication products and services to the extent they have higher incomes. Only the nonexistent service of locating people one has lost touch with is not sensitive to various levels of income. These findings also apply to the older person's behaviors by education level. The more educated own/prefer more products and services, with the exemption of the hypothetical service. Users of high-tech products are more likely to be urban than rural dwellers.

Ownership of Telephone Answering Machine. Ownership of a telephone answering machine gradually declines with age in late life. A slightly larger percentage of older males than older females (26.4% vs. 22.3%) reported having such a device. A larger percentage of older adults in families where at least one person is employed has a telephone answering machine, in comparison with those from nonworking families (28.5% vs. 13.9%). Older adults who live with others are as likely as their counterparts who live alone to own a telephone answering machine. Older adults who live in urban areas are nearly twice as likely to own a telephone answering machine as their rural counterparts, with 27.7 percent and 15.5 percent, respectively, indicating ownership. A larger percentage of westerners (37.0%) than northerners (16.7%) and easterners (19.5%) owns telephone answering machines, with southerners being near the norm (26.7%). While four in ten (39.6%) of healthy indulgers own a telephone answering machine, only 14.8 percent of healthy hermits do the same, while ownership/use of this product among ailing outgoers and frail recluses is 22.1 percent and 31.8 percent, respectively.

Ownership of Energy-Saving Appliances or Installed Devices. As people age, the likelihood that they own energy-saving appliances remains unchanged. There are no sex differences in ownership of such appliances. Older adults who live with others are more likely than their counterparts who live alone to have this kind of appliance, with 59.5 percent and 44.9 percent, respectively, expressing ownership. Ownership of energy-saving appliances is more prevalent among older people who live in the West and South, with 59.2 percent and 57.1 percent, respectively, indicating ownership, in comparison with about half (49.9%) of easterners. Finally, a significantly larger percentage of frail recluses (63.5%) and healthy indulgers (61.3%) than healthy hermits (52.9%) and ailing outgoers (49.5%) owns energy-saving appliances or installed devices.

Ownership of Home-Security Systems. The prevalence of home-security systems is higher in families where no person works than in those with at least one person working (15.9% vs. 11.3%). Mature urban dwellers are twice as likely as older people in rural areas to have home security installed in their houses (14.9% vs. 6.7%). Nearly one in five (19.9%) of older adults who live in the West has a home-security system, in comparison with only 8.3 percent of older Americans who live in northern states, 12.9 percent and 12.8 percent of easterners and southerners, respectively. Ownership of home-security systems is twice as high among frail recluses and healthy indulgers as it is among healthy hermits, with 17.9 percent of older adults in the former groups (in comparison with 9.5 percent in the latter group, respectively) indicating ownership.

Telecommunication Services. As older people age, there is a decline in their preferences for the three telecommunication services examined. With respect to preferences for telecommunication services, older adults in families with no working members prefer existing services more than those in families where at least one person works, but there are no differences between the two groups for the nonexistent telecommunication service. In the meantime, mature Americans who live with other people express marginally stronger preferences from their counterparts who live alone in their preferences for the three telecommunication services. Urban-dwelling older adults are no more or less likely to prefer the three telecommunication services.

Geographic differences among older adults emerged with regard to two of the three telecommunication services examined. Preference for a discount or "package" long-distance telephone plan is higher among older Americans who live in the North than those who live in the East or South, with 47.1 percent of the former group indicating use, in comparison with 36.3 percent and 40.5 percent for the remaining two groups, respectively. While one in four (24.2%) westerners would use an operator-assisted service that would help them locate certain persons, only one in seven (14.9%) of the easterners and one in six of northerners (16.4%) would do the same. Of the services included in the study, only for operator-assisted services, such as directory assistance, a larger percentage (64.1%) of older adults whose children do not live within one hour's drive, in comparison with those with children in closer proximity (53.0%), prefers using operator-assisted services.

The gerontographic groups differ significantly in their preferences for the three telecommunication services examined. Ailing outgoers, healthy indulgers, and frail recluses prefer operator-assisted services the most, with about two-thirds of mature adults in these groups indicating preference for such services, compared with 56.0 percent of healthy hermits. The same three groups also are likely to be the heaviest users of discount or "package" long-distance telephone plans, with nearly half (49.3%) of ailing outgoers expressing preference, in comparison with 35.3 percent of healthy hermits.

AUTOMOBILES

Automobiles may be considered as large appliances which are becoming increasingly high-tech oriented. Thus, the more recent the model a person drives the greater the number of gadgets one is expected to find on these products. In our survey, respondents were asked to indicate whether or not they owned a recent model of automobile (less than six years old). Nearly two-thirds (63.3%) of the older Americans indicated ownership of a recent model.

Younger Americans were more likely than their older counterparts to own a recent model of automobile, with 68.0% percent of them indicating ownership. With increasing age, older Americans are less likely to be driving a recent model of automobile, suggesting either a low usage of the existing car(s) or increasing repairs rather than replacement. Specifically, while more than two-thirds (69.7%) of older Americans age 55 to 64 own a recent model of automobile, only half (49.8%) of those age 75 and older do the same. Seventy percent (70.1 %) of older males, in comparison with their female counterparts (57.7%), own a recent model of automobile.

Ownership of recent automobile models increases with income. For example, while less than half of older adults with annual household incomes under $20,000 own a recent model, the percentage of ownership jumps to 83.6 percent among those with incomes $50,000 or greater. Also, an independent study found that the higher one's level of education the greater the likelihood of owning a certain type of automobile. For example, nearly 70 percent (69.7%) of older adults with college degrees, in comparison with high school or lower education, indicated ownership of a recent model automobile.

Older adults from families where at least one person works are more likely than those from nonworking families to own a recent model of automobile, with 68.2 percent and 61.2 percent, respectively, expressing ownership of a five-year-old or more recent model. Older Americans who live with others are more likely than their counterparts who live alone to own a recent model automobile, with 70.5 percent and 45.9 percent, respectively, expressing ownership. Westerners are more likely than southerners to hold on to their cars, with 58.3 percent of the former group, in comparison with 66.9 percent of the latter group of older adults, indicating ownership of a recent model.

Gerontographics are very strong predictors of new automobile purchase. Healthy indulgers are the group most likely to report ownership of a five-year-old (or more recent) model, with 81.3 percent of them indicating present ownership, in comparison with 55.3 percent of healthy hermits, 56.6 percent of ailing outgoers, and 73.3 percent of frail recluses.

PREFERENCES FOR SOURCES OF INFORMATION REGARDING NEW ELECTRONIC PRODUCTS

Consumers may use a number of information sources to find out about electronic products before buying one. However, people in general have different amounts of information about products stored in their memory, and asking them to indicate their information-source preference, could produce invalid findings. To more accurately assess their information-source preference, one must measure such preferences when no information is available in the consumer's memory. This can be done by asking respondents to express preference for information sources in the case of a new product.

Respondents in our survey were asked to indicate how they would prefer to find out about new electronic products and services—whether they would prefer to see TV or print ads, receive news in the mail, be contacted by phone, be visited by an agent, or learn in group meetings or seminars. More than half (53.9%) of mature Americans age 55 and over indicated preference for TV or print ads, and 27.6 percent prefer to receive news in the mail. Only a small percentage (4.8%) prefers to learn in group meetings or seminars. Definitely, older people do not like to be approached by a sales agent, over the phone or in person.

The way older Americans prefer to be informed about new electronic products is similar to the way younger people wish to be informed. There are few differences in preferences for information sources expressed by older adults in relation to their younger counterparts. Younger adults are more inclined to indicate they wish to see an ad than their older counterparts, with 59.2 percent and 53.4 percent, respectively, expressing preference for TV or print ads.

Baby Boomers vs. Seniors

Two main sources of information for new electronic products are important to baby boomers and seniors. TV and print ads are preferred by six in ten baby boomers and seniors, while about three in ten prefer to receive news about such products in the mail. Learning in group meetings or seminars is a preferred alternative among just 2.7 percent of baby boomers, compared with 7.0 percent of seniors.

Differences among Older Adults

Preferences for sources of information among older Americans show variation across a number of demographic and social factors, as well as gerontographic characteristics.

TV/Print Ads. Preferences for TV or print ads declines after age 75. A larger percentage of older males than older females prefers to find out about new electronic products from these media (58.3% vs. 50.7%). Older adults from families where no person works are more likely than those from families where at least one person works to prefer seeing TV or print ads about new electronic products (58.9% vs. 51.9%). Nearly two-thirds (63.8%) of frail recluses, in comparison with less than half of ailing outgoers (47.4%), prefer to see TV or print ads of new electronic products.

Direct Mail. There is also a slight decline in preference for direct mail after age 75. Older males are more likely than older females to prefer this vehicle (30.4% vs. 25.8%). Older adults who live with others are more likely than their counterparts who live alone to prefer learning about new electronic products from direct mail they receive, with 29.3 percent and 23.7 percent, respectively, expressing preference. Preference for direct mail as a source of information increases with income. Among older adults who live alone, a larger percentage of those who have children living in close proximity (29.4%), compared with those whose children live farther than one hour's drive (18.5%), prefers to learn about new electronic products by receiving news in the mail. One in three of healthy hermits and ailing outgoers, in comparison with approximately 23 percent of older adults in the other gerontographic groups, prefers to receive news in the mail.

Group Meetings/Seminars. After age 75, older peoples' preference for learning in group meetings or seminars increases. A larger percentage of older females (6.9%) than older males (2.3%) prefers learning about new electronic products this way. Older adults who live alone are more likely to prefer finding out about new electronic products in group settings (3.8% vs. 7.2%). A larger percentage of older adults in northern states (6.8%) than those in western states (2.9%) prefers learning in group meetings or seminars. A larger percentage of ailing outgoers (6.8%) than healthy hermits (3.5%) and frail recluses (3.9%) prefers to hear about new electronic products in group meetings or seminars.

Agent. Older adults who live in rural areas are more likely than their urban counterparts to prefer hearing about new electronics from an agent, with 4.2 percent and 2.0 percent, respectively, expressing preference for agent visitation. Frail recluses are the group most likely to prefer an agent's visit (4.2%), although the incidence of preference for this source is rather low.

SOURCES OF INFORMATION FOR
TELECOMMUNICATION SERVICES

Respondents were also asked to indicate the sources they would prefer to use to learn about new telecommunication services. Fifty percent of older adults said they prefer to see TV or print ads. Three in ten prefer to receive news in the mail, and nearly 7 percent (6.8%) prefer to learn about these services in group meetings or seminars. Sales agent contact by phone or in person was the least preferred method of learning about new telecommunication services.

As in the case of electronic products, younger adults prefer to see TV or print ads more than their older counterparts, with 61.9 percent and 49.5 percent, respectively, expressing preference. On the other hand, a larger percentage of older adults than younger adults (6.9% vs. 2.8%) prefers to learn about new telecommunication services in group meetings or seminars.

Baby Boomers vs. Seniors

A larger percentage of baby boomers (63.8%) than seniors (56.5%) prefers to see TV or print ads about new telecommunication services. Slightly less than 30 percent of both groups prefer to receive news in the mail, while learning in seminars or group meetings is less important to baby boomers than to senior consumers (3.6% vs. 8.9%).

Differences among Older Adults

Older people's preferences for information sources about telecommunication services vary according to several demographic and social characteristics. The older person's gerontographic profile can also predict the type of information source he or she may prefer in relation to older adults having other gerontographic profiles.

TV/Print Advertisements. With age, the older person's preference for impersonal sources of information, including print and TV advertisements, declines. A larger percentage of older adults who live with others (52.3%), in comparison to those who live alone (44.5%), prefers to hear about new telecommunication services from TV and print ads. TV and print ads are preferred by a larger percentage of older adults who live in western states (57.0%) than those who live in eastern states (42.9%) or in northern parts of the country (48.2%). A larger percentage of older adults from families where no person works (55.8%) prefers to see TV or print ads, in comparison to their counterparts from families where at least one person works (47.5%).

Direct Mail. As people age, they are less likely to prefer learning about these services through mail they receive at their homes. On the other hand, preference for hearing about new telecommunication services through the mail increases with increasing household income. A larger percentage of frail recluses (36.3%), in comparison to healthy indulgers (24.5%), prefers receiving news in the mail about telecommunication services.

Agent. Preference for personal sources (visited by agent, learning in group meetings or seminars) increases with age. Older adults who live within one hour's drive from their children, in comparison to those who live farther, prefer to be visited by an agent (4.5% vs. 1.0%). Frail recluses are also more likely than healthy hermits to prefer to be visited by an agent, with 4.7 percent and 1.1 percent, respectively, expressing prefer-ence.

Group Meetings/Seminars. Learning about these services in group meet-ings or seminars is most preferred by the college-educated older adults. Older females are more likely than their male counterparts to prefer learning about new telecommunication services in group meetings or seminars, with 8.9 percent and 4.4 percent, respectively, expressing pref-erence.

Older adults who live alone are twice as likely as their counterparts who live with others (10.3% vs. 5.4%) to prefer learning about new tel-ecommunication services in these settings. Mature Americans who live within an hour's drive from their children are twice as likely as those who live farther away from their children to express preference for hear-ing news in group meetings or seminars (13.0% vs. 6.7%). In the mean-time, older adults who live in urban areas are more likely than their rural counterparts to prefer learning about such services in group meet-ings or seminars, with 7.6 percent and 3.4 percent, respectively, indicat-ing preference. Finally, more ailing outgoers (8.7%) and healthy indulgers (7.7%) than frail recluses (3.9%) prefer hearing information about new telecommunication services in group meetings or seminars.

Telephone. Telephone contacts show no variation with age in late life.

PREFERENCES FOR METHODS OF PURCHASING
ELECTRONIC PRODUCTS

While purchase of electronic products is most likely to take place at vendors' facilities, consumers may also buy such products directly from the source either through the mail, by phone, or even from door-to-door representatives. In our research, respondents were asked to indicate the most preferred method of buying such products. More than nine in ten adults we surveyed prefer the traditional retail establishment as a place at which to buy electronic products. Door-to-door buying is the least preferred method, with approximately 1 percent preferring buying elec-tronic products via this channel.

Do older consumers prefer buying electronic products from different types of outlets than their younger counterparts? In order to answer this question, responses given by adults age 55 and over were compared to those of younger Americans. These comparisons revealed that, in gen-eral, younger adults would buy electronic products from a larger variety of retail outlets. Younger people are twice as likely as mature adults to prefer buying such products through direct mail, with 21.2 percent and 10.2 percent, respectively, expressing preference. Younger adults are also twice as likely to buy by phone, with 4.5 percent and 1.9 percent, re-spectively, indicating preference for this method. There are no significant differences in preferences between the two age groups when it comes to buying electronic products at vendors' facilities or door-to-door.

Differences among Older Adults

Preferences for retail outlets are not uniform among older adults, but they differ based on selected socioeconomic and demographic factors and gerontographic characteristics of older consumers.

Retail Establishments. Preferences for retail establishments decreases slightly as people age. As an older person's household income increases, so does his or her preference for buying electronic products at vendors' facilities. A larger percentage of easterners than westerners prefers retail facilities (96.3% vs. 90.1%). Those older adults who live in urban areas are slightly more likely than their rural counterparts to prefer buying electronic products at vendors' facilities, with 94.3 percent and 91.3 percent, respectively, showing preference for this distribution mode. Older people who live with others prefer purchasing electronic products at retail establishments, in comparison to their counterparts who live alone, with 94.7 percent and 89.7 percent, respectively, expressing preference.

Mail and Telephone. As people get older, their preferences for buying electronic products through the mail decreases. On the other hand, preference for mail purchasing electronic products increases with income and education. Older males are nearly twice as likely as older females to buy via this channel, with 13.4 percent and 7.1 percent, respectively, expressing preference. A larger percentage of mature Americans who live in the West (12.5%) than their counterparts who live in the East (6.7%) prefers buying electronic products this way. Healthy indulgers are less likely than healthy hermits to buy through the mail, with 6.8 percent and 11.2 percent, respectively, expressing preference for this method.

Buying over the telephone is preferred equally by older adults, regardless of income and education. Older adults who live in rural areas are twice as likely as their urban counterparts to prefer buying electronic products by phone, with 3.2 percent and 1.3 percent, respectively, expressing preference.

Door-to-Door. The preference for door-to-door shows a slight increase in late life. This purchase method is preferred equally by older adults, regardless of income and education. While the incidence of purchasing electronic products door-to-door is very small, older Americans who prefer this method are more likely to be healthy indulgers than healthy hermits or frail recluses.

REASONS CONSIDERED BEFORE BUYING DIRECT

Consumers may consider several factors in deciding whether or not to buy electronic products by phone or through the mail. A list of reasons

Table 6.2

Reasons Considered before Buying Electronic Products by Phone or through the Mail among Baby Boomers and Seniors (65+)

Reasons Considered	Baby Boomers (%)	Seniors %
Price (including shipping charges)	72.80	42.56
Type of credit card accepted	47.03	22.65
Return/cancellation and refund policy	73.12	45.32
Convenience, in comparison to other ways of buying the same product	59.04	31.93
Free pick-up service for returns	58.35	30.81
Availability of toll-free (800) number	62.70	36.90
Selection of products	61.93	31.61
Days to wait before receiving	63.75	29.06
Base:	(N = 555)	(N = 214)

people may consider before deciding whether or not to buy products direct was developed based on previous research. Respondents were presented with the list of eight factors they may consider, and they were asked to indicate whether they would consider each reason before buying electronic products by phone or through the mail.

The estimated percentage of Americans who considers each reason before buying electronic products by phone or through the mail varies. Generally, older Americans do not consider these factors to be as important as their younger counterparts. When responses are compared to those of younger adults, older adults are shown as having a lower propensity to consider each of the eight factors before buying electronic products by phone or through the mail. Specifically, about half of them consider return/cancellation policy (51.9%) and price (49.1%). Nearly as many (45.2%) look for the availability of toll-free (800) numbers. A smaller, but still significant, percentage considers product selection (40.1%), convenience in relation to other ways of buying the same product (38.9%), free pick-up service for returns (37.7%), and days to wait before receiving (36.4%). Finally, nearly one in three (29.1%) older Americans considers the type of credit card accepted.

Baby Boomers vs. Seniors

Similarly, baby boomers view all eight factors to be of greater importance than their counterparts (see Table 6.2). Price and return/cancellation and refund policy are considered by nearly three-fourths of the baby boomers, compared with less than half of the senior sample. For the remaining factors, baby boomers are twice as likely as senior consumers to indicate the factors are important in their decision to buy or not buy electronic products by phone or by mail.

Difference among Older Adults

A number of demographic and socioeconomic characteristics predict the older person's likelihood to consider the eight different factors. The older person's likelihood of considering most of the factors examined also appears to be influenced by his/her gerontographic profile.

Overall. The older person's propensity to consider each of these eight factors declines with age. While many of these declines occur throughout life, certain declines occur through approximately age 65 (see below); after this stage the importance of some factors remains the same. Generally, older males are more likely than their female counterparts to consider each factor before buying an electronic product by phone or through the mail. These differences may reflect differences in sex roles concerning the purchase of electronics, with males being more likely to buy such products, and therefore more concerned with the various factors.

The older person's household income predicts his or her likelihood of considering each of these eight factors. The higher mature adults' income the higher their inclination to report they would consider these factors. Similarly, education is associated with one's tendency to take these factors into account in the same fashion. Only price, free pick-up service, and availability of a toll-free number do not increase in importance with the older person's education level. All eight factors are more important to older adults who live with others than to those who live alone. This higher propensity may reflect the older adults' cognizance of the various factors as a result of the discussion with others with whom they live.

Return/Cancellation and Refund Policies. A smaller percentage of easterners (45.7%) considers return/cancellation and refund policy, in comparison with older adults who live in the South (54.5%) and West (54.7%). Older adults who live near their children tend to be more likely to consider a company's return and refund policy before buying electronic products, with half of them (49.8%) expressing this opinion, in relation to older adults whose children do not live near them (37.4%).

Price. Price is most important to the 55-to-64 age group, and of equal importance to older adults in the 65-to-74 and 75-and-over age brackets.

Toll-Free Number. Availability of a toll-free (800) number is important to nearly half of all older Americans who live in the West (50.8%) and South (48.9%), in comparison with four in ten easterners (40.4%) and northerners (41.6%). Older adults from families where at least one person works are somewhat more likely than those who come from families where no person works to consider days one must wait before receiving the product, with 38.1 percent and 32.3 percent, respectively, indicating this factor. Availability of a toll-free number is of greater importance to frail recluses than to healthy hermits, with 49.8 percent and 42.1 percent, respectively, expressing this opinion.

Product Selection. Older adults who live in urban areas are more likely than their rural counterparts to consider the selection of products offered, with 41.5 percent and 34.5 percent, respectively, expressing this attitude. A larger percentage of mature adults who live in the South (42.9%), in comparison to those who live in the East (36.0%), considers this factor before buying electronic products by phone or through the mail.

Free Pick-up Service. Free pick-up service for returns is important to 34.3 percent of healthy hermits, in comparison to the remaining gerontographic groups in which nearly four in ten mature Americans consider this service before buying direct.

Days to Wait. Older adults from families where at least one person works are somewhat more likely than those who come from families where no person works to consider days one must wait before receiving the product, with 38.1 percent and 32.2 percent, respectively, indicating this factor.

Convenience. Fewer older Americans who live in the East (33.3%), in comparison to those who live in the South (41.1%) and West (40.8%), value the convenience of using these direct methods over other methods of buying electronic products. Convenience, in relation to alternative methods of buying electronic products, is of greater importance to healthy indulgers than to any other gerontographic group.

Credit Card Acceptance. Type of credit card accepted is less important to older adults who live in the East than to those who live in other parts of the country. About one-third (34.5%) of frail recluses, in comparison with one in four (26.3%) of healthy hermits, indicated they would consider type of credit card accepted.

PAYMENT METHODS FOR BURGLAR OR FIRE ALARM SYSTEM

Consumers may pay for high-tech products using a variety of methods, including cash, check, and credit cards. Also, coupons and senior/member discounts may be used along with the main methods. In our study, respondents were asked to indicate which method of payment they would prefer to use to pay for burglar or fire alarm system, whether they would use cash, check, credit card, coupon, or senior/member discount (respondents could indicate more than one method). Older adults' preferences for payment methods for a burglar alarm or fire alarm system differ from preferences reported by their younger counterparts. More than half (52.6%) of older Americans age 55 and over are estimated to prefer paying for a burglar or fire alarm system by check. About one in five (20.8%) prefers paying by credit card, and nearly as many (19.4%) prefer to pay cash. Regardless of which major method is used, more than one in four (27.9%) of older adults would take advantage of a senior/ membership discount, but only 3.2 percent would use a coupon. Younger adults, on the other hand, are likely to use a variety of methods to pay for such products. Only senior/membership discounts would be used to a greater extent by older adults, since only older adults are likely to be eligible.

Baby Boomers vs. Seniors

Six in ten baby boomers prefer to use a check to pay for a burglar alarm system, compared with less than half (47.7%) of seniors. One-third would rather use a credit card, compared with only 17.4 percent of the senior respondents. Nearly three in ten (28.4%), compared with 17.5 percent of seniors, prefer to pay cash. Three times as many baby boomers as seniors (7.7% vs. 2.0%) would use coupons.

Differences among Older Adults

Preferences for payment methods in the case of a fire alarm or burglar alarm system vary among older adults who have certain sociodemographic characteristics. Gerontographic characteristics also predict the older person's preference for certain types of payment systems in the case of burglar or fire alarm system purchases. Generally, with age, older people prefer fewer methods. In fact, people age 75 and older checked, on the average, one payment method.

Check. The higher an older person's household income, the more likely he or she is to pay for a fire alarm or burglar system with a check. This payment method is mostly preferred by older adults who live in the South, with six in ten of them (60.7%) expressing preference, in comparison with half (50.5%) of those who live in the North, 47.3 percent of westerners, and 46.3 percent of easterners. Older adults who live with others are more likely than their counterparts who live alone to prefer paying by check for burglar or fire alarm systems, with 56.8 percent and 42.8 percent, respectively, reporting preference. A larger percentage of frail recluses (57.0%) than healthy indulgers (49.0%) prefers checks as a payment method.

Cash. Older people with higher incomes and levels of education attainment are less likely to pay cash than their lower-income and less-educated counterparts. Older adults who live in rural areas are more likely than their urban counterparts to prefer paying cash for a burglar or fire alarm system, with 25.4 percent and 17.8 percent, respectively, expressing such a preference. Cash is predominantly preferred by easterners and northerners, with 22.7 percent and 21.4 percent, respectively, indicating preference, in comparison with 14.2 percent among older adults who live in the West.

No gerontographic group surfaced as being any more or less likely to prefer cash as their selected payment method.

Credit. The higher the older person's income, as well as level of education, the more likely he or she is to use credit as a method for paying for a burglar or fire alarm system. Credit is a more preferred method among urban than rural older Americans (22.6% vs. 15.0%). Credit cards are preferred by a larger percentage of older people who live in the South (23.5%) and West (23.3%) than by those who live in the North (17.7%). One in four (24.4%) of frail recluses, in comparison with less than one in five among healthy indulgers (19.4%) and ailing outgoers (18.4%), would use a credit card.

Senior/Member Discounts. Use of senior/member discounts is highest among older adults reporting household incomes in the range of $20,000 to $50,000. While two in ten of older people who live in eastern states would use senior or membership discounts, a lot more (3 in 10) older consumers who live in other parts of the country prefer this mode of payment. Senior/member discounts are more likely to be used by frail recluses and ailing outgoers than by the remaining gerontographic groups.

Coupons. Coupons are more likely to be preferred by southerners (4.6%) than by easterners (1.7%). Coupons are more likely to be used by ailing outgoers than by healthy indulgers, with 4.2 percent and 1.1 percent, respectively, expressing preference.

PAYMENT METHODS FOR HOME-APPLIANCE SERVICES

Check writing as a form of payment is not only preferred by older adults in buying burglar or fire alarm systems but also in paying for home-appliance repair services. Three-fourths (74.9%) of older adults indicated they prefer to pay for such services by check. Only one in four (23.5%) would pay cash, and one in six (16.8%) would use credit to pay for home-appliance repair services. One in three (29.2%) would be willing to take advantage of senior/membership discounts, and only 3.5 percent would use coupons.

Preferences for payment methods regarding the purchase of home-appliance services are different between older and younger adults. Older Americans use cash, credit, and coupons to a lesser extent than their younger counterparts. Checks are preferred equally by both groups, while older adults prefer senior/member discounts more than younger adults, since the latter group does not have a similar access to these promotional stimuli.

Baby Boomers vs. Seniors

Baby boomers are as likely to use a check to pay for such repairs, with 73.1 percent and 73.3 percent, respectively, expressing preference. One-third (33.8%) of baby boomers (compared with 22.5% of seniors) would use cash.

Differences among Older Adults

Preferences for payment methods concerning home-appliance services are not uniform across older adults. Rather, they tend to differ on the basis of several socioeconomic and demographic characteristics. The older persons' gerontographic characteristics may also predict their preferences for payment methods regarding home-appliance repair services.

Check. Preference for paying by check slightly declines after the age of 75. The higher an older American's household income and level of educational attainment, the higher their propensity to pay by check. A larger percentage of southerners (79.1%) than older adults from other geographic groups, especially easterners (69.6%), prefers this payment method.

Cash. Preference for cash remains constant with age. The higher the person's household income the lower his or her propensity to pay for home-appliance services this way. Generally, one in three (33.9%) of older people who live in the East prefers to pay cash, a figure which is 11 to 13 percent higher than that of older people in other geographic regions. Frail recluses are somewhat more likely than ailing outgoers to prefer using cash, with 26.2 percent and 21.2 percent, respectively, expressing preference.

Credit. Preference for credit declines after the age of 75, and a larger percentage of older males (19.4%) than older females (14.6%) expressed preference for using a credit card to pay for home-appliance repair services. As an older person's household income and education increases, so does the likelihood that a credit card will be his or her selected payment method. Credit is the preferred payment method of urbanites. A larger percentage of older adults who live in urban areas (18.4%) prefers to pay for home-appliance services with plastic, compared with their rural counterparts (11.5%). A larger percentage of westerners (21.9%) and southerners (18.8%) than easterners (12.8%) and northerners (13.9%) is likely to use a credit card to pay for home-appliance repair services.

Nearly one in five of healthy hermits (19.2%) and frail recluses (19.4%), in comparison with 13.2 percent of ailing outgoers, prefers credit cards.

Coupons. Use of coupons shows little variation with age in late life, expressed in terms of preferences. Older adults who live in the South are more likely than their easterner counterparts to use coupons when paying for home-appliance repair services, with 4.6 percent and 1.5 percent, respectively, indicating preference. Coupons are preferred more by those who live with others than by those who live alone (4.2 vs. 1.8%). Healthy indulgers are less likely to use coupons than any other gerontographic group.

Senior/Member Discounts. Preference for senior/member discounts is higher among those between the ages of 65 and 75 than for the other two age groups of older adults (55–64 and 75+). In terms of preferences, using senior/member discounts shows little variation with age in late life. One-third (33.3%) of mature Americans who live in the West in comparison with one in four (24.0%) of those who live in the East expressed preference for using senior/member discounts. Finally, ailing outgoers is the group most likely to prefer senior/member discounts, while healthy indulgers prefer these offerings the least.

MEDIA USE PROFILES

Media consumption patterns of older adults were examined with respect to four types of diverse products: telephone answering machine, home-security system, energy-saving appliances or installed devices, and new model of automobile. For each of these products, older adults' media use habits were compared and contrasted between those who presently have or would like to have the product and those who do not have it or are not interested in it.

Media behavior was analyzed with respect to broad and specific media use patterns. Respondents were asked to indicate how often they read newspapers, listen to the radio, use a VCR to record and play movies, watch premium TV cable channels, watch TV comedy and variety shows, adventure and drama shows, and TV news and documentaries. In addition, respondents were asked to write down the names of magazines they read on a frequent basis. Based on circulation numbers (obtained from Standard Rates and Data), responses were tabulated for the most popular magazines; the less popular magazines were classified into broader categories based on descriptions of their content in Standard Rates and Data.

Telephone Answering Machine. Older adults who are owners of telephone answering machines are also heavier users of other technology-based entertainment innovations. Specifically, a larger percentage of older adults who said they have a telephone answering machine, in comparison to their counterparts who do not use this product, watch premium TV cable channels (42.0% vs. 32.1%) and use a VCR to record or play movies at least once a week; they watch TV news and documentaries less (73.0% vs. 80.5%).

Older adults who prefer telephone answering machines are not heavy users of print media in relation to those who do not want these products. However, a relatively large proportion of the former group reads *Time* (13.5% vs. 10.5%) and various types of business magazines (professional) (12.0% vs. 8.2%). These data, collectively, suggest that users of telephone answering machines do not spend much time at home, or they do not have much time to spend with various forms of mass media.

Home-Security System. Owners of home-security systems differ little from older nonowners with respect to media consumption. A larger percentage of them (42.1%) watches premium TV cable channels once or more frequently a week, in comparison to those who do not have or do not want a home-security system (34.2%). A slightly larger percentage of the former group (13.9% vs. 9.9%) reads *Time* on a frequent basis as well as other magazines about business (professional) (12.1% vs. 7.8%), consumer finances/money (10.1% vs. 7.6%), arts and sciences (8.1% vs. 4.7%), and other general interest magazines (19.2% vs. 14.7%).

Energy-Saving Appliances or Installed Devices. Older adults who have energy-saving appliances or installed devices differ from nonowners of these products with regard to selected media-use habits. A larger percentage of the former than the latter group (37.9% vs. 32.0%) watches premium TV cable channels once or more frequently a week and reads the newspaper on a daily basis (85.0% vs. 81.9%). Similarly, a larger percentage of those who prefer energy-saving appliances, in comparison to those who do not (36.7% vs. 28.1%), uses a VCR to record or play movies once or more a week. Older adults who prefer energy-saving appliances or installed devices are more likely than those who do not to read the following magazines on a regular basis: *Good Housekeeping* (9.6% vs. 6.2%), *Reader's Digest* (36.2% vs. 30.3%), *Woman's Day* (3.3% vs. 0.5%), and several types of magazines, including health/nutrition (5.2% vs. 2.7%), food/cooking (3.7% vs. 1.2%), business (professional) (10.1% vs. 7.4%), and homes/decorating magazines (11.1% vs. 7.9%).

Automobiles. Older adults who own a new model of automobile, in comparison to those who do not, use a VCR to record or play movies at least once a week (34.7% vs. 29.6%). Owners of new car models are more likely than nonowners to read the following:

- *National Geographic* (17.5% vs. 11.8%)
- *People* (5.1% vs. 1.7%)
- *Reader's Digest* (36.5% vs. 27.4%)

- *Time* (12.1% vs. 8.8%)
- Business (professional) magazines (10.2% vs. 6.0%)
- Consumer finances/money magazines (9.1% vs. 6.2%)
- Sports/athletics/fitness (participant) magazines (6.8% vs. 3.1%)
- Wildlife/nature/outdoors magazines (5.0% vs. 1.4%)
- Arts and sciences magazines (6.7% vs. 2.6%)
- General interest magazines (16.9% vs. 12.8)

Reasons for Buying Direct. Another objective of this study was to examine reasons for buying high-tech products direct. Respondents were asked to indicate whether they consider eight reasons before buying electronic products by phone or through the mail.

Payment Methods. Preferences for payment methods were examined in two situations: burglar or fire alarm systems and home-appliance repair services. Respondents were asked to indicate the methods they would prefer to use to pay for each; whether they would use cash, check, or credit card, or coupon or senior/member discount (respondent could check more than one method).

7

Health Care

The provision of health care to the aging population is a major topic of public discussion and debate. Our research focused on several areas related to health care. First, we examined one's need for health-care services and preferences for selected health-care products. Second, we investigated the buying process involving the use of health-care services, including use of sources of consumer information about health-care services, reasons for patronizing specific health-care providers and deciding to use specific services, and preferences for payment for the provision of such services. Third, we analyzed media preferences of those who prefer selected health-care products or utilize selected health-care services. Finally, we examine these preferences, needs, and motives in greater detail to help us gain insights into the behavior of aging consumers.

DEMAND FOR HEALTH-RELATED SERVICES

Unlike many other types of products and services, the demand for health-care services cannot be accurately assessed by asking consumers to indicate their preferences. If given the choice, consumers would "prefer" not to receive *any* health-care services.

While demand for specific health-care services can be assessed by estimating the incidence of various diseases in different age groups, this method appears to yield better measures of potential rather than effective demand. Thus, for example, many older people (according to statistics) experience hearing loss but few are aware of it or interested in using the services of health-care professionals. Given this problem, it was felt that demand for various types of health-care services could be better assessed by obtaining the respondent's attitude toward a health problem he or she may or may not have, since many people engage in preventive health-care behaviors. Thus, the level of expressed concern with the various body systems and general attitude toward health would appear to be a reasonable measure of demand for specific health-care services.

Respondents were asked to indicate whether they were "concerned a lot," "concerned a little," or "not concerned at all" with several health conditions ranging from specific problems concerning a body system (e.g., vision) to overall ability to function independently. Generally, concerns with general health and physical fitness were rated higher among older Americans, as indicated by the percentage of those who gave "concerned a lot" responses. While such general concerns may reflect the effects of a certain disease (e.g., arthritis), they may also be measuring present health problems as well as concerns with one's future health condition. On the other hand, concerns with specific health problems such as kidney or bladder function may reflect problems older people are presently experiencing, since the percentage figure (29.1%) closely reflects the 10 million (mostly older) people who are estimated to have this problem.

Another way of assessing perceived versus actual health problems experienced is to compare responses given by older respondents to those given by their younger counterparts. One would expect that concerns with preventive health care (vs. present health problems) would be greater among younger than among older people. As expected, a larger percentage of younger adults (69.7%), in comparison with their older counterparts (63.2%), are concerned a lot with improving or maintaining their health condition through exercise and diet. However, for the remaining health problems, with the exception of vision and dental, older adults expressed a greater concern than their younger counterparts. Quite likely, younger people may experience vision and dental problems at early stages in life, and, therefore, they may express a concern equal to that expressed by older adults.

Differences among Older Adults

Contrary to conventional wisdom, health problems experienced by older adults (55+) are not age-related. Differences in concern with various health problems can better be predicted by socioeconomic factors than by age alone. Gerontographic characteristics are very strong predictors of the older person's level of concern with various types of health problems. Since gerontographics are based in part on the older person's health status it is not surprising that they predict rather accurately his or her concern with a number of health problems. Generally speaking, ailing outgoers are those most concerned with the various health-related problems; healthy hermits are those least concerned, with the remaining two groups falling in-between. Differences were found for the following health-related concerns. With the exception of health maintenance through diet and exercise, income and education are *inversely* related, suggesting a greater preoccupation with health-related problems among older Americans in lower than in higher socioeconomic classes.)

Memory

Concern with ability to remember to do certain things increases after 65. Mature Americans in households with at least one working member are more likely than their counterparts in nonworking households to be concerned with this (30.4% vs. 20.9%). Older people who live near their children are more likely than those who do not to be concerned with remembering to do certain things (24.6% vs. 19.7%). Also, a larger percentage of southerners (25.7%) than westerners (20.0%) expressed concern with their ability to remember to do certain things—like take medication.

General Mobility. After the age of 65, older people become more concerned with becoming immobile due to physical impairment. This is a bigger concern to those older people who live near their children than it is to those who do not (47.0% vs. 37.8%).

Vision. A larger percentage of older females than older males is concerned with having visual problems (37.3% vs. 29.9%). The prospect of having visual problems that cannot be corrected with glasses is of more concern to older people in households where at least one person works than it is to those in nonworking households (38.6% vs. 32.3%). Older people who live with others are more concerned than their counterparts who live alone with having visual problems that cannot be corrected with glasses (36.0% vs. 29.9%).

Hearing. The ability to hear becomes more of a concern to older people after they reach the age of 65. Older people in families where at least one person works are more concerned about having a hearing problem than those in families where nobody works (34.2% vs. 25.9%). Mature Americans who live with others are more likely than their counterparts who live alone to be worried about this (30.0% vs. 24.7%). Also, compared to their counterparts whose children live far away, older people who live near their children are more concerned with having hearing problems (28.0% vs. 22.5%).

Kidney/Bladder Problems. Concern about kidney or bladder problems intensifies after mature Americans reach the age of 65. Older females are more likely than their male counterparts to be worried about such health problems (30.7% vs. 26.5%). In the meantime, concern with having kidney or bladder problems is greater among older adults who live in the

South than in the West, with 31.9 percent and 25.1 percent, respectively, expressing such a concern.

Self Care. Relative to older men, mature females are more concerned with being unable to take care of themselves physically when they get older (58.2% vs. 50.2%). Mature Americans in households where at least one person works are more likely than those in nonworking households to be concerned with this when they get older (32.9% vs. 27.4%). Mature Americans who live near their children are more worried about being able to take care of themselves when they get older than their counterparts whose children live far away (60.6% vs. 47.6%).

Daily Tasks. Older women are more concerned than older men with having to depend on others for routine daily tasks (38.2% vs. 29.1%). Southerners as well as easterners are also more concerned with this, with 36.7 percent and 35.2 percent, respectively, expressing concern, in comparison to their western counterparts (29.3%).

Chores. Mature American females are more concerned than their male counterparts with being physically fit to do the required daily chores (52.4% vs. 46.6%). Older people whose children live close by are more concerned about this than are those whose children live farther away (53.0% vs. 47.4%).

Gum Disease/Dentures. Mature females are more likely than older males to be concerned with getting gum disease or dentures (25.7% vs. 18.8%). Older people in rural areas are more concerned with these problems than are their urban-dwelling counterparts (27.9% vs. 21.0%). Also, southerners are more concerned with having gum disease or dentures than their counterparts who live in the East (25.2% vs. 18.8%).

Diet/Exercise. Concern with improving or maintaining one's health condition through exercise and diet increases with increasing levels of income and education.

High Blood Pressure. Older people who live in households where at least one person works are more likely than those in nonworking households to report concerns about high blood pressure (49.0% vs. 37.8%). Older adults who live with others are more concerned about this health problem than their counterparts who live alone, with 43.3 percent of them, in comparison with 36.1 percent of the latter group, expressing such a concern. In the meantime, a larger percentage of older adults who live near their children, in comparison to those who live away from them, is concerned with having high blood pressure (39.1% vs. 33.3%). A larger percentage of those who live in rural areas, in comparison with their urban counterparts, has such concern (44.7% vs. 39.7%). Also, a larger percentage of older adults who live in northern states (43.3%) and southern states (42.2%), in comparison with those who live in eastern states (35.3%), is concerned with having high blood pressure.

PREFERENCES FOR NONTRADITIONAL HEALTH-CARE SERVICES

The study also assessed preferences for health-care services in several nontraditional areas. Specifically, respondents were asked to indicate whether they have/use, would like to have/use, not interested, or never heard of, four types of services related to health care: health-club membership, paid at-home assistance with personal needs and chores, health-membership program, and medical-care services provided at the respondent's home.

One in ten older Americans presently has or uses a health-club membership, and at least as many (13.4%) would like to have one. Paid at-home assistance is used by a smaller percentage of older adults (7.8%), but nearly one in five (19.6%) would like to be able to use this service. While about one in eight (13.3%) presently has access to health-membership programs, three times as many (39.3%) would like to use such programs. Similarly, while the percentage of older people who receive medical-care services provided at their own homes is small (6.3%), more than one in three (36.5%) would like to receive such services.

How much do older adults' preferences differ from those of younger Americans? To answer this question, responses given by those age 55 and older were compared to those under 55 years of age. For comparison purposes, those who indicated both actual use and desire for such services were combined to arrive at an overall "preference" figure for each of the two age groups. Younger Americans are twice as likely as their older counterparts to express preference for health-club membership, with nearly half (48.5%) of the first group, in comparison with nearly one-fourth (23.0%) of the latter group, expressing preference. For paid at-home assistance, on the other hand, older Americans are as likely as their younger counterparts to express preference.

While present health-membership programs are targeting the mature market almost exclusively, our survey results suggest a stronger demand among younger Americans. Half of older adults expressed preferences, while 64.5 percent of those under 55 years of age gave similar responses. Older Americans, on the other hand, were more likely than their younger counterparts to indicate preference for medical-care services provided at their homes (40.9% vs. 33.7%).

Baby Boomers vs. Seniors

About half of baby boomers (51.6%), compared with 19.0 percent of seniors, prefer (have/use or would like to have/use) health-club membership, while about three in ten of the respondents in both groups prefer to receive assistance with personal needs and chores. Two-thirds (67.9%)

of baby boomers, compared with 43.2 percent of seniors, prefer health-membership programs. However, a smaller percentage of baby boomers (31.9%) than seniors (42.8%) prefers to have medical services provided at their home.

Differences among Older Adults

Preferences for the four types of health-care services were analyzed by selected sociodemographic characteristics of older Americans. Factors such as age, sex, socioeconomic characteristics, and geographic location were examined for their possible association with preferences for the four types of health-care-related services studied. Some of these factors were stronger than others. Urbanity and geographic location do not influence the older person's preferences for the health-care services examined. While sociodemographic characteristics were rather weak predictors of the older person's preferences for the four types of health-care services examined, gerontographics were very strong determinants of these preferences.

Health Clubs. The person's weaker preferences for health clubs with increasing age continues throughout life. There appears to be a sharp drop in preferences for health clubs after the age of 75. In the meantime, preferences for these facilities and their services increase with income and with level of education. Membership in health clubs is higher among ailing outgoers and healthy indulgers, with 30.9 percent and 27.0 percent of older adults, respectively, in these gerontographic groups indicating use or desire for this service.

At-Home Assistance. Paid at-home assistance with personal needs and chores appears to increase with age in late life, despite lack of differences between adults age 55 and over and those under 55. Thus, it appears that these types of services are of special value to the younger and the very old people, perhaps for different reasons. For example, the younger people might view these services as a way of enabling them to do away with chores they do not want to do, while to older persons these services are valuable because of their inability to engage in such activities. Paid at-home assistance is most valuable to healthy indulgers, with over one-third (34.3%) of older adults in this group expressing preference. Three in ten of ailing outgoers are likely to prefer receiving assistance with personal needs and chores for a fee, in comparison with two in ten of healthy hermits. The higher an older person's level of education, the more likely he or she is to have a preference for paid at-home assistance with chores and personal needs. A larger percentage of female than male mature consumers (30.3% vs. 21.6%) prefers such services, reflecting sex roles and higher female-to-male ratios in late life. Also, a larger percentage of those who live alone (34.7%), in comparison to those who live with others (22.7%), prefers at-home assistance with personal needs and chores for a fee.

Health-Membership Programs. Health-membership programs also continue to decline in popularity in late life. Those who live with others are more receptive to such programs than those who live alone (52.8% vs. 45.3%). Frail recluses are a prime target for health-membership programs, with two in three expressing preference. On the other hand, healthy hermits are least likely to favor these programs, with only four in ten expressing preference. Ailing outgoers are also prime prospects for health-membership programs, with 57.5 percent of individuals in this group expressing preference. Half of the healthy indulgers are likely to express preference for health-membership programs.

At-Home Medical Services. Preference for receiving medical services at home increases in late life, with those age 65 and older being most likely to prefer them. Finally, one in two of frail recluses is likely to indicate preference for receiving medical-care services at home, in comparison with nearly 30 percent (29.4%) of healthy hermits. The two remaining groups are also likely to be prime prospects, with about 45 percent of individuals in these groups likely to express preferences for receiving medical-care services at their homes.

PREFERENCES FOR HEALTH-RELATED PRODUCTS

Besides health-care services, people make use of several health-related products. In our research we examined the responses to a wide range of health-related products: prescription drugs, dietary meal prescriptions or products for people with certain health/physical requirements, self-diagnostic medical equipment, exercise equipment (at-home), and hair-care or face-care products. These products are representative of a number of aspects of health care, including preventive health care. Hair-care or face-care products were included on the list because some of them, such as monoxidil and Retin-A, are prescribed by a physician. Respondents were asked to indicate whether they presently have/use, would like to have/use, are not interested in having/using, or never heard of/don't know of these products.

More than half (53.7%) of mature Americans age 55 and over have a chronic condition for which they take medication. About one in six (15.7%) must use products with certain ingredients as a result of dietary restrictions or due to physical/health requirements. About the same number (16.0%) have self-diagnostic medical equipment at home, and four in ten (40.5%) have exercise equipment at home. Finally, nearly six in ten (58.0%) use one or more hair-care or face-care products.

Older Americans differ from younger adults in the way they use the selected products. Older adults are nearly twice as likely as their younger counterparts to take medication for chronic conditions and more likely to need products due to physical/health needs they may have. However, younger adults are slightly more likely to have/use exercise equipment at home and significantly more likely to use face-care and hair-care products.

Baby Boomers vs. Seniors

A smaller percentage of baby boomers (9.1%), in comparison to seniors (15.1%), reported ownership or use of self-diagnostic medical equipment, but a larger percentage of baby boomers (43.5%) than seniors (36.9%) reported ownership or use of exercise equipment.

Differences among Older Adults

A number of socioeconomic and demographic factors can describe heavy users or owners of the five health-related products examined. While the same factors do not relate to each of the products, they collectively help us profile the heavy users. Gerontographic characteristics also predict ownership/use of all five products examined.

Prescription Drugs. With age, there is an increasing likelihood of use of prescription drugs for chronic conditions. Prescription drug use is heavier among older adults with annual household incomes between $20,000 and $50,000, with nearly 60 percent of older adults in this income group (59.1%) reporting use, compared with 52.0 percent of older adults with incomes under $20,000 and 42.9 percent of those with incomes $50,000 or more. Older adults with college education are less likely than those who didn't finish college to report use of these drugs for chronic conditions, with 49.8 percent and 58.4 percent, respectively, reporting usage.

Also, older adults from families where no person works are more likely than older adults from families with at least one working person to use prescription drugs for chronic conditions, with 61.1 percent and 50.6 percent, respectively, reporting usage. In the meantime, older people who live with others are more likely than those who live alone to use such drugs for these conditions (55.6% vs. 49.1%). A larger percentage of older Americans who live in the South (57.9%) and West (55.8%) than in the East (48.5%) reports use of prescription drugs for chronic conditions. A larger percentage of older adults who report living near their children (54.4%) indicated such usage, compared with 42.3 percent of their counterparts who do not live near their children. Finally, ailing outgoers are more likely than any other gerontographic group to report such use of prescription drugs (61.0%).

Dietary Meal Prescription or Products. Use of products for certain health/physical requirements remains fairly stable in late life. A larger percentage of older people from families where no person works (20.3%), in comparison with those from nonworking families (13.7%), is likely to use these products. Also, mature Americans who live with others are more likely than those who live alone to use products for people with certain health/physical requirements (17.8% vs. 10.4%). A larger percentage of older people in the South and West (17.5%) than in the East (12.9%) use such dietary products. Finally, ailing outgoers are more likely than healthy hermits and healthy indulgers (19.8% vs. 14.1% and 10.3%, respectively) to report usage of products for people with certain health/physical requirements.

Self-Diagnostic Medical Equipment. The use of self-diagnostic medical equipment drops after age 75. A larger percentage of males (20.5%) than females (12.4%) have/use such equipment at home. In the meantime, self-diagnostic medical-equipment ownership is higher among older adults with annual household incomes in excess of $20,000 than among their lower-income counterparts. It is used mostly by older adults who had some college or graduated from college.

Also, mature Americans from nonworking families have/use self-diagnostic medical equipment more than those from working families (22.5% vs. 13.3%). The use of this kind of medical equipment is more common among older people who live with others than it is among those who live alone (19.8% vs. 6.9%). More southerners (18.8%) than easterners (12.9%) have/use self-diagnostic equipment at home. Frail recluses are about twice as likely as older adults in the remaining gerontographic groups to report ownership/use of self-diagnostic medical equipment.

Exercise Equipment (At Home). Use/ownership of exercise equipment steadily declines in late life. Older men are more likely than older women to have/use such equipment at home, with 43.0 percent and 38.5 percent, respectively, indicating ownership/use. The higher an older person's household income, the more likely he or she is to report ownership or use of home exercise equipment.

At-home exercise equipment is more popular among older people who live with others than it is to those who live alone (44.3% vs. 31.4%). Ownership/use of exercise equipment is higher among older adults who live in the West (45.8%), North (41.7%) and South (40.6%) than among those who live in the East (33.0%). Of the four gerontographic groups, frail recluses are the most likely to report use/ownership of exercise equipment, with half of them (in comparison with about one-third of the healthy hermits) reporting ownership/usage.

Hair-Care or Face-Care Products. Use of hair-care and face-care products remains fairly stable with age. Older females are more likely than their male counterparts to use these products, with 68.1 percent and 45.8 percent, respectively, indicating usage. Also, use of hair-care or face-care products is higher among older adults with incomes between $20,000 and \$50,000 than among their lower-income counterparts, with 61.2 percent and 53.7 percent, respectively, reporting use.

These products are more popular among older adults with some college education (62.3%) than they are among those with less education (53.9%). Furthermore, a larger percentage of older adults who live in the South (64.4%) and West (65.6%) than those who live in the North (52.9%) and East (47.5%) reports use of hair-care or face-care products. Finally, healthy indulgers and ailing outgoers make heavier use of hair-care and face-care products than their counterparts in the remaining gerontographic groups.

PREFERENCES FOR SOURCES OF INFORMATION

Preferences for sources of information were assessed by asking respondents to indicate the most preferred source of information about new health-care services. Response alternatives included: see TV/print ad, receive news in the mail, be contacted by phone, be visited by agent, and learn in group meetings or seminars (respondents could only indicate one source).

Direct mail is the most preferred source of information for new health-care services. More than four in ten (42.6%) expressed preference for this source in relation to other sources. One in five (20.8%) would prefer to find out about new health-care services from TV or print media. Learning about new health-care services in group meetings was preferred by one in seven (14.4%) older adults. Other direct methods are less desirable. Only one in ten (10.4%) preferred to be visited by an agent, while telephone contact was the least desirable method, with a negligible 3.4 percent of older Americans expressing preference for this method.

Do preferences for sources of information regarding new health-care services differ between older and younger Americans? To answer this question, answers given by those age 55 and older were compared to those given by the under-55 age group, showing few differences between the two age groups. Younger adults are somewhat more likely than their older counterparts (25.9% vs. 20.7%) to prefer seeing news on TV or print ads. There were no significant age-group differences for the remaining sources of information.

Responses to information sources were also compared between baby boomers and seniors. The percentage of baby boomers who prefer to find out about new health-care services from each of the five sources of information is not different from that of seniors.

Differences among Older Adults

Several sociodemographic characteristics relate to information-source preferences. Each of these factors appears to affect preference for specific sources, but there is no uniform pattern. The older person's level of income does not relate to his or her preference for sources of information regarding new health-care services. Also, not all gerontographic segments prefer to learn about new health-care services from the same sources. The following differences were found for each type of information source.

TV/Print Advertisements. A larger percentage of older adults who live in the South (23.5%) and West (22.3%) than those who live in the North (17.4%) prefers to find out about new health-care services from TV or print ads. Also, a somewhat larger percentage of healthy hermits (22.4%) and health indulgers (22.4%) than of ailing outgoers (18.1%) expressed preference for seeing the information via these media.

Mail. Preference for receiving news in the mail declines with age, possibly reflecting the older person's increasing difficulty with reading print material due to vision problems. Older males expressed a stronger preference for receiving news in the mail about new health-care services than their female counterparts (47.9% vs. 38.1%). Getting news this way is more preferable to older adults who live with others than it is to those who live alone (45.0% vs. 37.2%). Frail recluses are the group most likely to prefer receiving news in the mail, with 47.5 percent of older adults in this group expressing preference; healthy indulgers are least likely to prefer this source, with 36.4 percent of them indicating preference. Ailing outgoers are also likely to prefer this source, with 44.4 percent of them expressing preference for this source.

Agent. Older adults age 65 to 74 are more likely than those age 55 to 64 and age 75 and over to report preference for being visited by an agent, with 13.3 percent, in comparison with 8.9 and 9.1 percent, respectively, expressing preference. A larger percentage of older adults who live in rural areas (15.0%), in comparison to their urban counterparts (9.4%), is likely to prefer this method of information gathering. Furthermore, a larger percentage of those older adults who live in the North (13.2%) prefers to be visited by an agent, in comparison to older adults who live in eastern states (7.8%), the West (9.0%), and the South (9.8%). Finally, ailing outgoers are more likely than healthy hermits (13.0% vs. 8.9%) to prefer an agent's call for information about new health-care services.

Group Meetings/Seminars. Older females were more likely than their male counterparts (17.7% vs. 10.4%) to express preference for hearing the news in group meetings or seminars. The higher an older person's level of education, the more likely he or she is to prefer hearing news about health-care services in such settings. Also, those who live alone are more likely than those who live with others to express preference for learning in group meetings or seminars about new health-care services (17.9% vs. 12.9%). Older adults who live alone and have children living within one hour's drive are twice as likely as those whose children live farther away to prefer learning about new health-care services in group meetings or seminars, with 23.7 percent and 11.5% percent, respectively, expressing preference.

Telephone. With increasing education, older Americans are less likely to prefer telephone contact. Older adults who live in rural areas are more likely than their urban counterparts to prefer hearing about new health-care services this way, with 6.7 percent and 2.3 percent, respectively, expressing preference.

REASONS FOR PATRONIZING SPECIFIC HOSPITALS

Respondents were presented with a list of patronage reasons and were asked to indicate those reasons which were important to them in their decision to start or continue to patronize specific hospitals. The main patronage reason among those age 55 and older appears to be convenience in reaching the hospital, with nearly 60 percent (58.6%) of the respondents indicating this reason to be important. Personnel/staff assistance with filling out forms was a surprising second in importance, with 41.1 percent of the respondents indicating this reason. Other patronage reasons, in order of importance, were: ease of getting related services at the same place (36.3%), explanation of various services by staff/personnel (34.3%), preference for billing/payment methods (24.6%), reasonable fees (22.4%), and referrals/endorsements (20.5%). Other reasons were of lesser significance and included senior discounts (19.1%), advice of people their own age (19.6%), and membership programs (14.9%).

Do older people differ from younger adults with regard to reasons for patronizing specific hospitals? To address this question responses given by those age 55 and older were compared to those given by the younger age group. As expected, discounts were more important to older than to younger people, with 18.9 percent and 14.1 percent, respectively, indicating this patronage motive (reflecting greater availability of senior discounts to older adults). While the way ads portray older people is not an important reason, it is more important to older than to younger adults. Ten percent of the older respondents and just over 5 percent (5.7%) of the younger group indicated approval of the way people their age are portrayed in hospital ads. Also, younger people are twice as likely as older people (25.0% vs. 12.9%) to take the advice of children and close relatives, dispelling the traditionally held belief that the children of older people are a viable vehicle for reaching the elderly population. Younger people are also more likely than older adults (24.5% vs. 19.4%) to rely on advice of nonrelatives close to their age in choosing hospitals; and they also tend to rely on referrals or endorsements (34.3% vs. 20.3%). However, older adults are more likely than their younger

Table 7.1

Reasons for Patronizing Specific Hospitals among Baby Boomers and Seniors
(65+) (Percent Who Feel Reason Is Applicable)

Reasons for Patronizing	Baby Boomers (%)	Seniors (%)
Reasonable prices or fees	20.61	22.17
Convenience in reaching the service provider	59.97	60.47
Ease of getting related services at the same place	40.86	37.36
Explanation of various services by staff/personnel	41.29	31.34
Personnel/staff assistance with filling out forms	44.75	35.52
Discounts to age groups (children, seniors)	11.86	17.76
Preference for billing/payment methods	37.87	21.19
You like the way their ads show people your age	5.06	12.44
Special deals through group or membership programs	10.78	14.16
Advice of children or close relatives	28.14	11.95
Advice of other people your age	25.01	18.68
Referrals/endorsements by firms or professionals	35.04	16.68
Ease of doing business by phone or by mail	7.76	10.44
Base:	(N = 589)	(N = 236)

counterparts to consider ability (ease) of doing business by phone (11.2%
vs. 7.5%) in their patronage decision.

Baby Boomers vs. Seniors

Perceptions of the importance of patronage reasons differ between the
two generations, with baby boomers attaching greater importance on
most of the reasons examined (see Table 7.1). Specifically, while the majority of respondents in both groups think that convenience in reaching
the service provider is important, their perceptions do not differ significantly. Personnel-related reasons also appear to be of importance to both
age groups, with 44.7 percent of baby boomers (compared with 35.5% of
seniors) indicating that assistance with filling out forms is important in
their patronage decisions. Another 41.3 percent of boomers (compared
with 31.3% of seniors) report that staff's willingness to explain various
services is an important patronage motive.

Twice as many baby boomers as seniors (35.0% vs. 16.7%) rely on
referrals by firms or professionals, and 37.9 percent of the former group

(vs. 21.2% of seniors) patronize a specific hospital because of reasons related to billing or payment policies of the hospital. Nearly three in ten (28.1%) of baby boomers compared with 11.9 percent of seniors, consider the advice of children or close relatives, while the advice of same-age peers is of greater importance to baby boomers than to seniors (25.0% vs. 18.7%).

Differences among Older Adults

Several sociodemographic characteristics relate to the older persons' propensity to rely on these reasons in their hospital patronage decision. Again, there is no specific pattern, but different sociodemographic characteristics are associated with different patronage reasons. Patronage reasons do not differ significantly in late life based on the person's age. Rather, they tend to be equally important among the three age groups examined (55–64, 65–74, 75+). Also, the older person's gerontographic profile explains nearly every patronage reason when it comes to choosing among hospitals.

Convenience. Older males, in relation to their female counterparts, tend to place greater importance on convenience in reaching the health-care service provider when considering hospitals (62.8% vs. 55.1%).

Personnel/Staff Assistance Filling Out Forms. As mature Americans age in late life, they are less likely to place importance on personnel/staff assistance with filling out forms when evaluating hospitals. Older people who live with others are more likely than their counterparts who live alone to value such assistance (43.8% vs. 34.8%). Also, relative to their urban-dwelling counterparts, older people who live in rural areas are more likely to place importance on hospital staff/personnel's ability to provide assistance with filling out forms (47.0% vs. 39.5%). Northerners are more likely than their eastern counterparts (44.2% vs. 33.7%) to value this kind of help.

Availability of Related Services. Older adults who live with others, in comparison to their counterparts who live alone, tend to place more emphasis on the ease of getting related services at the same place (39.1% vs. 29.6%). This factor is valued more by older adults who live in western states (40.2%) than by those who live in eastern (32.9%) or southern (33.0%) states. Finally, a larger percentage of healthy indulgers (38.9%) than frail recluses (31.8%) values the importance of getting other health-care services at the same place.

Service Explanations. Getting explanations of various services by hospital staff/doctors is more important to mature Americans who live with others than it is to those who live alone (36.5% vs. 29.3%). A larger percentage of healthy indulgers (40.2%) than frail recluses (31.6%) and healthy hermits (32.2%) would patronize a hospital because of staff/personnel willingness to provide such explanations.

Billing/Payment Methods. The older mature Americans become, the weaker their preferences for certain billing/payment methods at hospitals become. Older men are more likely than older women to place importance on this factor (27.3% vs. 22.1%). Billing and payment methods are less important to older people with higher levels of education and with higher household incomes than they are to their relatively less-educated and lower-income counterparts.

Older people who live with others are more likely than those who live alone to place emphasis on a hospital's methods and options (27.5% vs. 17.6%). Available billing and payment options are more important to older people who live in rural areas than they are to those who live in urban areas (30.2% vs. 23.1%). Also, ailing outgoers and frail recluses are more concerned with the types of payment or billing methods available than older adults in the remaining gerontographic groups.

Prices/Fees. Prices/fees tend to become of lesser importance as the older person's income and education increases. Older adults who live in rural areas are more likely than those who live in urban locations to be concerned with paying reasonable fees for health-care services obtained (28.7% vs. 20.8%). Furthermore, fees are of greater importance to older adults who live in the West and South than among those who live in other parts of the country. With respect to the importance of fees charged for health-care services, ailing outgoers are nearly twice as likely as healthy hermits (30.4% vs. 16.3%) to value low fees/prices charged by hospitals.

Referrals/Endorsements. Referrals/endorsements by firms or professionals become less important to mature Americans as they get older. Older men are more likely than mature women to emphasize this factor when making a decision about hospital patronage (23.4% vs. 18.2%). Also, the importance of referrals and endorsements steadily increases as a patronage reason with increasing household income. Older people who live with others are more likely than those who live alone to consider referrals/endorsements when evaluating hospitals (22.8% vs. 15.3%). Finally, healthy indulgers are more likely than older adults in the remaining gerontographic groups to rely on this factor when making decisions about hospitals.

Peer Advice. When evaluating hospitals, the advice of other people their age is more important to older men than it is to older women (23.5% vs. 16.4%). This is a stronger factor among those in the $20,000-to-$50,000 income bracket than among those having higher or lower incomes. Also, older adults who have children within one hour's drive are three times as likely to rely on advice from people their own age, in comparison with older adults who do not have children in close proximity (26.4%

vs. 8.4%). Older adults who have children living within one hour's drive are three times more likely than those whose children live farther away to follow the advice of their peers when choosing among hospitals, with 26.4 percent and 8.4 percent, respectively, expressing preference.

Price-Saving Incentives. The higher an older person's household income and level of education, the less importance he or she tends to place on price-saving incentives (discounts and membership programs). A larger percentage of older adults who live in the South (21.6%) and West (20.4%) than those who live in eastern states (13.3%) considers senior discounts. Furthermore, older people in western states are twice as likely as those who live in eastern or northern states to consider special deals through group or membership programs (23.3% vs. 11.0% and 11.6%, respectively). Also, ailing outgoers are twice as likely as healthy hermits to consider the availability of senior discounts (27.0% vs. 13.5%). Finally, of the four gerontographic groups, ailing outgoers are more likely than healthy hermits (17.8% vs. 12.3%) to value special deals through group or membership programs.

Age-Stereotypes. With increasing levels of education and income, older people are less likely to admit that the way people their age are portrayed in advertisements for hospitals is a strong patronage reason. In the meantime, ailing outgoers are more likely than other gerontographic groups to patronize hospitals because they like the way hospital ads show people their own age. Furthermore, healthy indulgers are more likely than their healthy hermit counterparts to rely on advice from people their own age, with 23.4 percent and 17.7 percent, respectively, indicating this to be an important patronage reason.

Family Advice. Older adults who live in the South are twice as likely as westerners (16.5% vs. 8.1%) to rely on advice of children or close relatives. While advice of children or close relatives is not reported by older Americans to be a determinant patronage reason, a larger percentage of ailing outgoers (16.5%) is likely to rely on such advice, in comparison with healthy hermits (11.0%).

Ease of Doing Business via Mail or Phone. Older Americans who live in rural areas are more likely than their urban-dwelling counterparts to consider ease of doing business by phone or by mail an important factor when evaluating hospitals (15.2% vs. 10.5%). Ailing outgoers are more likely than frail recluses (14.6% vs. 7.0%) to factor this consideration into their hospital patronage decision.

REASONS FOR CHOOSING SPECIFIC PHYSICIANS AND SURGEONS

One of the relatively unexplored patronage issues is whether hospital patronage affects physician patronage or vice versa. To address this question we examined patronage motives for selecting physicians and surgeons, and we compared these patronage reasons to those for hospitals. As in the case of hospitals, proximity is the major reason for patronizing certain physicians, with 55.5 percent of older Americans indicating convenience in reaching the health-care service provider to be important. Similarly, personnel/staff assistance with filling out forms is second on the list (38.9%), with explanations of various services given by staff or personnel (37.3%), and ease of getting related services at the same place (36.3%) equally as important. About one-third of the older respondents mentioned referrals and advice of other people their age to be important in choosing physicians and surgeons. One in ten mentioned price or fees and 27.1 percent indicated that billing or payment methods were important in their patronage decision concerning health-care professionals. Special deals such as senior discounts and membership programs were lower on the list of factors indicated as important patronage motives.

In order to determine the extent to which these factors are uniquely important to the older population or apply to the entire U.S. population, responses were also analyzed and compared between younger (under 55) and older adults. Differences between younger and older Americans emerged for about half of the patronage reasons. Specifically, convenience in reaching the health-care professionals, preferences for billing/payment methods, advice of children or close relatives and referrals are more important factors for such patronage decisions among younger than among older adults. On the other hand, older adults are more likely to value senior discounts (due to their availability) and ease of doing business with health-care professionals by phone or by mail.

Baby Boomers vs. Seniors

Table 7.2 shows percentage distribution of responses among baby boomers and seniors (age 65+), with baby boomers perceiving most of the thirteen reasons to be of greater importance than the latter group. First, with respect to the factors which are more important to baby boomers, convenience appears to be of greater importance to them than to their senior counterparts, with 61.3 percent and 54.2 percent, respectively, indicating this reason. About half (51.4%) of baby boomers, compared with about three in ten elderly (30.6%), go to a certain physician due to referral or endorsement by firms or other professionals. Nearly as many choose a physician or surgeon because these professionals explain their services (46.9% vs. 36.0%), or because of the advice of children or close relatives (45.3% vs. 31.8%). Four in ten baby boomers (39.1%), compared with about one in three seniors (35.5%), go to certain health-care professionals because they assist them with filing out forms. Pref-

Table 7.2
Reasons for Patronizing Specific Physicians and Surgeons among Baby
Boomers and Seniors (65+) (Percent Who Feel Reason Is Applicable)

Reasons for Patronizing	Baby Boomers (%)	Seniors (%)
Reasonable prices or fees	27.83	34.11
Convenience in reaching the service provider	61.26	54.24
Ease of getting related services at the same place	36.21	37.33
Explanation of various services by staff/personnel	46.90	35.96
Personnel/staff assistance with filling out forms	39.13	35.55
Discounts to age groups (children, seniors)	13.81	19.07
Preference for billing/payment methods	34.95	26.71
You like the way their ads show people your age	4.42	7.32
Special deals through group or membership programs	10.78	10.73
Advice of children or close relatives	35.80	22.96
Advice of other people your age	45.30	31.82
Referrals/endorsements by firms or professionals	51.44	30.64
Ease of doing business by phone or by mail	11.97	16.68
Base:	(N = 588)	(N = 236)

erence for billing/payment policies is important to many more baby
boomers (34.9%) than seniors (26.7%), and so is the advice of a close
relative (35.8% vs. 23.0%).

Other factors are less important to baby boomers than to seniors in
their decision to select a specific physician or surgeon. These factors include: price, with 27.8 percent of baby boomers and 34.1 percent of senior
indicating price as an important patronage motive; ease of doing business by phone or by mail (12.0% vs. 16.7%); discounts to age groups
(13.8% vs. 19.1%); and proper age stereotyping in ads of physicians (4.4%
vs. 7.3%).

Differences among Older Adults

Not all older persons are likely to name the same patronage reasons
for choosing health-care professionals. Rather, the reasons they cite are
likely to be affected by a number of sociodemographic factors. Gerontographic characteristics of older adults are very strong predictors of the

types of criteria mature patients will rely upon in selecting physicians and surgeons.

Convenience. Convenience in reaching the service provider declines in importance after age 75. Older adults with higher levels of education are more likely than their less-educated counterparts to value convenience in reaching the service provider. This is more important to mature Americans in nonworking families than it is to their counterparts in families where at least one person works (60.3% vs. 53.4%).

Older adults who live with others are more likely than those who live alone to feel that convenience is important in selecting health-care professionals (57.9% vs. 49.7%). It is more important to older adults who live in the North than it is to those who live in the South, with 60.2 percent and 51.3 percent, respectively, indicating this factor to be important. Ailing outgoers and healthy hermits are less likely than frail recluses to choose health-care professionals on the basis of convenience.

Assistance with Forms. Mature Americans in families where nobody works are generally more likely to put importance on assistance with filling out forms than those who live in families where at least one person works (43.4% vs. 36.9%). Older people who live with others are more likely to value this help than those who live alone (41.3% vs. 33.2%). In addition, healthy indulgers are more likely than healthy hermits (42.5% vs. 35.8%) to value assistance offered in filling out forms.

Service Explanations. As mature people get older, their need to have the various services explained to them becomes less important to them. Older people with higher levels of education do not have as much need for these explanations as do their counterparts with less education. In the meantime, older adults who live in northern states are more likely than older adults who live in other geographic areas to be influenced by health-care professionals' willingness to explain their services.

Finally, a larger percentage (44.9%) of healthy indulgers than healthy hermits (33.6%) and frail recluses (35.1%) patronizes certain physicians and surgeons because these professionals satisfactorily explain the various health-care services to them.

Related Services. The importance of ease of getting related services at the same place declines with increasing income. This factor is indicated as a patronage motive by a greater percentage of those who live in the West (42.6%) and North (40.8%) than by those who live in the South (30.8%) and East (31.3%).

Referrals/Endorsements. The older person's propensity to rely on referrals or endorsements declines after the age of 75. The higher an older person's household income and level of education, the more he or she tends to value the word of other professionals when making a decision about physicians and surgeons. Also, those who live with others are more likely than those who live alone to rely on referrals and endorsements by other professionals (36.2% vs. 27.6%).

Peer Advice. The advice of others near their own age is of more value to older people who live in families where nobody works than it is to those in families where somebody works (38.8% vs. 29.6%). Older males are somewhat more likely than their female counterparts to report selection of health-care providers due to peer advice (35.2% vs. 29.9%).

Fees. The importance of fees for professional services increases after retirement. Also, the higher an older person's household income and level of education, the less likely he or she is to place importance on the fees charged by health-care professionals. In the meantime, older people in nonworking families are more likely to be concerned about fees than those in families where at least one person works (35.6% vs. 28.0%). Furthermore, a larger percentage of ailing outgoers (42.4%) than older adults in other gerontographic groups is likely to select health-care professionals on the basis of the fees they charge for their services.

Billing/Payment Methods. When considering physicians and surgeons, billing and payment methods are of greater concern to older people with lower household incomes than they are to their counterparts with relatively higher incomes. This factor is more important to older people in nonworking families than it is to their counterparts who live in families where at least one person works (32.7% vs. 24.7%). Furthermore, mature Americans who live with others are more likely than those who live alone to patronize health-care professionals because of their billing methods (29.1% vs. 22.4%). A larger proportion of those who live in northern states (30.8%) and southern states (27.7%) than of those who live in eastern states (21.7%) are likely to base their selection of physicians and surgeons on available billing/payment methods. Finally, ailing outgoers and frail recluses are more likely than older adults in other gerontographic groups to consider the various billing/payment options available to them.

Senior Discounts. Senior discounts are more important to the 65-to-74 age group than to the older and younger groups. This factor is more important to older people with lower household incomes than it is to those with relatively higher incomes. Relative to their counterparts who live alone, older people who live with others are more likely to prefer senior discounts (20.9% vs. 15.8%). Furthermore, these price breaks are more likely to be an important patronage reason among older adults who live in eastern states. Also, senior discounts as patronage incentives are of greatest appeal to ailing outgoers and least appealing to healthy hermits, with 28.6 percent of the former group and just 11.5 percent of the latter group indicating preference.

Membership Programs. The higher an older person's household income, the less likely he or she is to place emphasis on the availability of membership programs. Older adults who live in the West are twice more likely than mature patients who live in other parts of the country to base their selection of health-care professionals on such programs. Finally, membership programs are likely to be of greater appeal to frail recluses than to healthy hermits, with 15.8 percent and 9.2 percent, respectively, expressing preference.

Age-Stereotypes. The higher an older person's household income, the less likely he or she is to consider advertising portrayal of other older people when making decisions about physicians and surgeons. The more educated an older person, the less likely he or she is to be concerned with this factor. Also, ailing outgoers and frail recluses are more likely than healthy hermits to like the way people their age are portrayed in advertisements by health-care professionals.

Family Advice. The patronage decision of older adults who live in eastern states is more likely to be influenced by advice from their children and relatives in comparison with those who live in northern and western states. Also, such family advice is of greater influence on ailing outgoers than on any other gerontographic group, and so is the advice of other people their age.

Direct Contact. Older adults in northern states are more likely to value direct contact with their health-care professionals (by phone or by mail) than those from eastern states. Also, ailing outgoers are more likely to value the convenience of doing business by phone or mail than older adults in other gerontographic groups.

PAYMENT METHODS FOR HEALTH-CARE SERVICES

Another objective of this study was to examine patients' preferences for payment methods for health-care services. As the findings of this study show, about one in four older Americans considers methods of paying for services important in their patronage decisions regarding hospitals and doctors. Respondents were given a list of five different payment methods and were asked to indicate all the methods they would prefer to use to pay for health-care services. Direct billing for medicare/ medicaid recipients was not considered as a "choice." (Since respondents could check more than one method total percentage exceeds 100.0 percent.)

Check is by far the most preferred method of paying for health-care services among older adults. Seven in ten older adults (70.8%) expressed preference for this method. Nearly four in ten (39.2%) indicated they would like to use a senior/member discount in paying for such services. Cash was preferred by approximately one in six (17.8%) of older Americans, while credit card was preferred by 13.6 percent. Coupons were preferred by a negligible 2.4 percent of the older respondents.

Are these preferences unique to older Americans or do they also apply to younger populations? In order to answer this question, responses given by older adults were compared to those given by younger respondents. Significant differences in preferences for payment methods were found between younger and older adults for all but paying by check. For cash, credit card, and coupon, younger respondents expressed stronger preferences than their older counterparts. As expected, older adults expressed stronger preferences for senior/member discounts than their younger counterparts. Thus, it appears that younger adults prefer a larger number of payment methods; with age, older adults prefer using fewer methods—mainly paying by check.

Baby Boomers vs. Seniors

Nearly three-fourths of baby boomers (73.7%) and seniors (73.1%) prefer to pay for health-care services by check, while twice as many seniors as baby boomers (29.1% vs. 14.8%) prefer to use cash. A larger percentage of baby boomers (16.0%) prefers to use credit, compared to seniors (10.4%), while membership/senior discounts are mostly preferred by the latter group (5.8% vs. 40.7%). Coupons are not very popular, with only 4.5 percent and 1.7 percent of baby boomers and seniors, respectively, expressing preference.

Differences among Older Adults

A larger number of sociodemographic characteristics of older adults relate to their preferences for payment methods for health-care services. Also, gerontographics are good predictors of preferences for certain methods of payment for health-care services.

Cash. With increasing age, older adults are less likely to pay cash for health-care services. The higher an older person's household income and level of education, the less likely he or she is to prefer paying for health-care services this way. Finally, older adults who live in southern states are more likely than their counterparts who live in eastern states to prefer paying for health-care services using cash, with 74.2 percent and 65.7 percent, respectively, expressing preference for this method of payment. Finally, frail recluses and healthy hermits are more likely to prefer paying cash for health-care services than ailing outgoers.

Check. Check as a form of payment remains the most preferred method. Older adults with higher incomes and levels of educational attainment are more likely than those with relatively lower incomes and less education to prefer paying with a check. In addition, older people in families where no household member works are more likely than their counterparts in families where at least one person works (74.9% vs.

69.0%) to express preference for this payment method. Also, those who live with others are more likely than those who live alone to express preference for using a check to pay for health-care services (72.7% vs. 66.4%).

Credit. The older a mature American, the less likely he or she is to use credit to pay for health-care services. Older adults with higher incomes and education levels are more likely than those with relatively lower incomes and levels of educational attainment to prefer this payment method. Also, older males have stronger preferences for paying by credit for health-care services, with 16.5 percent of them (in comparison with 11.1 percent of their female counterparts) expressing preference for this method. Finally, frail recluses are more likely than ailing outgoers to prefer paying by credit card.

Presence of children in close proximity increases the likelihood the older person would prefer to use credit to pay for health-care services, with 17.6 percent of the older persons who have children within one hour's driving distance expressing preferences, in comparison with 8.5 percent of older people with no children in close proximity. Older people in urban areas are more likely than their counterparts who live in rural areas to use credit for health-care services (15.6% vs. 6.1%).

Senior/Member Discounts. Senior/member discounts show the highest preference among older adults age 65 to 74 than any other age group. Older people with some college education are more likely than their counterparts with less or more education to prefer taking advantage of senior/member discounts in paying for health-care services, with 44.9 percent of them expressing preference, in comparison with 37.5 percent and 36.0 percent among those with lower and higher education, respectively. Furthermore, both frail recluses and ailing outgoers are more likely than the remaining gerontographic groups to take advantage of senior/member discounts.

PAYMENT METHODS FOR EYEGLASSES

How do consumers prefer paying for health-care products? While one may not be able to generalize across a large variety of such products, since these may range from appliances such as exercise equipment bought at specialty stores to prescription drugs bought at a drug store, we chose to address this question by examining a representative product that we felt best describes the various health-related products—eyeglasses. Eyeglasses may require the input of both an eye doctor and an optometrist, and their value may vary depending on the quality of the material used and place of purchase. Furthermore, eyeglasses are a product most likely to be used by the large majority of older adults, since vision begins to deteriorate around age 40, and one cannot adapt to these changes as easily (for example, one must pass an eye exam for driver's license renewal). Finally, the product lends itself to payment via a number of methods, including senior/ membership discounts and coupons.

Respondents to our survey were asked to indicate the methods they would prefer to use to pay for eyeglasses purchased at optical centers. Response categories were: cash, check, credit card, coupon, and senior/ member discount. Check is by far the most preferred method of payment for such a health-care product, with nearly two-thirds (63.7%) of older Americans reporting preference, in comparison with approximately one-fourth of mature adults who prefer to use the other major methods of cash and credit. Four in ten would take advantage of a senior/membership discount, and only a negligible percentage of them would use a coupon to pay for their eyeglasses.

The way older people prefer to pay for eyeglasses is not similar to preferences among the younger adults. Younger adults generally prefer to use a larger number of payment methods than their older counterparts. Only senior/member discounts are preferred as a form of payment by older adults, since the former group is not eligible for many age-related marketing offerings.

Differences among Older Adults

Several demographic and socioeconomic factors help us describe or profile older adults who prefer to use the various methods of payment for eyeglasses. Gerontographic characteristics also offer additional input into the description of older adults' preferences for payment of eyeglasses.

Cash. Preference for cash as a main method of payment for glasses declines with age in late life. While a little over 27 percent of older adults with incomes less than $50,000 prefer cash, only one in five of those with greater incomes does same. Also, there is a declining preference for cash with increasing level of education. A larger percentage of older people who live with others, compared to the proportion of people who live alone, prefers using cash for eyeglass purchases (28.2% vs. 21.2%). Finally, a larger percentage of frail recluses (31.3%) than ailing outgoers (23.1%) and healthy hermits (25.4%) prefers payment by cash.

Check. With age, older adults prefer to use fewer methods of payment, but generally prefer to pay for eyeglasses with a check. Preference for check-writing is fairly stable regardless of the person's level of annual household income, although middle-income mature Americans show a greater tendency than their upper-income counterparts to prefer to write a check for eyeglasses (66.8% vs. 58.6%).

In the meantime, older adults who live in rural areas are more likely than their urban counterparts to pay for their new eyeglasses with this payment method (71.5% vs. 62.1%). A larger percentage of frail recluses (69.0%) than healthy indulgers (59.4%) and ailing outgoers (62.8%) prefers check as a form of payment for eyeglasses purchased at optical centers.

Credit. As mature Americans get older, their tendency to use credit to pay for eyeglasses declines. Preference for this payment method sharply increases with increasing household income of older Americans. Similarly, with higher levels of education, there is an increasing preference for paying by credit card for eyeglasses.

Furthermore, older people who live with others are more likely than their counterparts who live alone to prefer using a credit card for these purchases (26.5% vs. 19.4%). Urban adults are nearly three times as likely as mature Americans who live in rural areas to use a credit card for these purchases, with 27.9 percent and 11.0, respectively, reporting preference. A larger percentage of older adults who live in the West (29.6%) and South (25.1%) than of those who live in the East (18.6%) prefers using their credit card to pay for their glasses. This method is preferred by a larger percentage of males (28.2%) than females (21.1%) for payment of eyeglasses at optical centers. Finally, credit card preference is higher among healthy indulgers than ailing outgoers, with 26.5 percent and 21.4 percent, respectively, expressing preference.

Senior Discounts. Senior/membership discounts are mostly preferred by older adults between the ages of 65 and 74. Preference for these discounts show no change with income. In the meantime, older people who live with others have a slightly stronger preference for senior/member discounts than those who live alone (42.3% vs. 36.6%). Older adults from families where no person works are more likely than those from families with at least one working person to prefer using senior or membership discounts with their payment for eyeglasses, with 45.9 percent and 38.4 percent, respectively, reporting preference. Finally, these discounts are preferred more by frail recluses and ailing outgoers than by older adults in the remaining gerontographic groups.

Coupons. As mature Americans age in late life, their preference for using coupons for eyeglass purchases declines. Preferences for supplemental methods of payment, including coupons, show no change with income. In addition, relative to their counterparts who live alone, older Americans who live with others are slightly more likely to use coupons (3.8% vs. 1.9%).

MEDIA USE PROFILES

Media consumption was analyzed among older adults who prefer or use (vs. those who do not prefer or use) self-diagnostic medical equipment and exercise equipment. Owners or users of the former product are more likely than their nonowner/nonuser counterparts to be heavier users of TV cable channels, with 43.8 percent of the former group (vs. 33.5% of the latter) expressing viewership at least once a week. The former group is also more likely than the latter to report watching TV news and documentaries on a daily basis (82.0% vs. 78.0%). However, the former group lags behind the latter group in viewership of TV comedy and variety shows (51.0% vs. 57.3%).

Older adults who have preferences for owning/using exercise equipment (at home) also differ from those who do not have such preferences with respect to several media-use variables. A larger percentage of them watches premium TV cable channels once or more frequently a week (41.2% vs. 30.9%), reads the newspaper daily (86.1% vs. 81.9%), listens to the radio daily (65.5% vs. 60.9%), watches TV news and documentaries every day (82.6% vs. 76.0%), and uses a VCR to record or play movies at least once a week (37.0% vs. 29.9%).

Turning to preferences for specific and general types of magazines, there are only few differences in the types of magazines preferred among those older adults who currently have/use and those who do not prefer or use self-diagnostic medical equipment. Specifically, a larger percentage of the former group, in comparison with the latter group, reads the following magazines on a frequent basis:

• Business (professional) (13.7% vs. 7.8%)
• Consumer finances/money (11.5% vs. 7.4%)
• Arts and sciences (8.2% vs. 5.2%)
• Do-it-yourself (5.1% vs. 2.2%)
• General interest (19.8% vs. 15.1%)

On the other hand, older adults who are favorably oriented toward exercise equipment, in comparison with those who are not, read the following types of magazines on a frequent basis:

• Health/nutrition (6.5% vs. 2.3%)
• Business (professional) (11.0% vs. 7.7%)
• Sports/athletics/fitness (participant) (7.4% vs. 4.8%)
• General interest (18.4% vs. 14.0%)

8

Travel and Leisure

Travel is an area of great interest to aging consumers. With increasing age, people's financial situation is likely to improve and they can afford to travel. Retirement and empty nest create free time that allows people to travel for extended periods of time. Marketers of travel and leisure services have long recognized the importance of the aging consumer market and have tried to appeal to this segment with a variety of offerings such as senior discounts. Yet, we know relatively little about the effectiveness of some of the marketing offerings, in part because we do not fully understand the needs and purchasing motives of this diverse consumer market for travel and leisure services.

Our research attempted to fill gaps in existing knowledge about the behavior of baby boomers and older adults as buyers and consumers of travel and leisure services. We sought to answer several questions regarding preferences for selected travel and leisure services. Also of interest were the questions of how these groups of consumers learn about various vacation or travel packages, and what methods of purchasing vacation packages they prefer. We were particularly interested in finding out how the older age segments of the population go about choosing specific airlines, cruise lines, and specific hotels or motels, and how they pay for these services.

PREFERENCES FOR TRAVEL AND LEISURE SERVICES

Travel and leisure services cover several broad areas, including transportation, lodging, entertainment, and to some extent eating and drinking places. Within each category there are specific areas of interest. For example, transportation includes air, surface (e.g., bus, rail), and water (e.g., cruise lines). Furthermore, travel and leisure are often defined differently from the perspective of the consumer, based on his/her motives. For example, travel can be for business, pleasure, or both, and so can various types of entertainment. While it often becomes difficult to separate the motives for travel and leisure, it becomes important to understand the reasons underlying such behaviors, since different motivations and, therefore, different behaviors may be observed as a result of the intent for travel and leisure activities. Rather than trying to uncover the reason(s) for travel and leisure activities for each specific occasion, this research focuses on factors that clearly define them. For example, it can be assumed that in a family where no adult member works, travel and leisure activities are primarily intended for one's own (or other family members') personal gratification. On the other hand, activities which are influenced by company policies or other factors (e.g., company awards) may result in travel and leisure and may not be decided by older family members who are still employed.

In our research we chose four indicators of travel and leisure activities, covering transportation, lodging, eating and drinking places, and foreign travel in general. Specifically, in attempting to assess the older person's orientation toward travel and leisure services, four services were presented to our respondents: (1) airline package (fly anywhere for the same price); (2) travel club or program where one pays $50-$100 to join and gets discounted rates and rebates; (3) valid passport; and (4) restaurant club where one pays about $30 to join and gets discounts at member restaurants.

Respondents in one of our national surveys were asked to indicate whether they currently have/use, would like to have/use, are not interested in having/using, or never heard of or don't know of the four travel-related services. Responses were analyzed only for the first two categories, and collapsed into one category to come up with a "preference" definition. Thus, those who say they prefer a travel/leisure-related service are those who either currently have/use or would like to have/ use that service.

Nearly one in three (31.9%) of mature Americans has a valid passport, and another 16.4 percent of the respondents who do not have one would like to have one. While only 4.1 percent of adults age 55 and over presently use an airline package that enables them to fly anywhere for the same price, another 42.1 percent expressed desire to have or use such a package. While 5.4 percent of older Americans presently use a travel club or program where one pays $50-$100 to join and gets discounted rates and rebates, another 17.3 percent of those who were surveyed would like to have such an arrangement. Finally, nearly one in ten (9.9%) presently uses the services of a restaurant club where they pay to join and get discounts at member restaurants; and as many (9.8%) would like to join such a club.

How do older Americans differ from their younger counterparts when it comes to these travel/leisure-related services? To answer this question, responses of those age 55 and over were compared to those under 55. Older adults show significantly weaker preferences for three of the four services examined. Only in the case of the travel club or program where one pays to join and receives discounted rates and rebates were there no significant differences in preferences between younger and older adults.

Baby Boomers vs. Seniors

We also examined responses to travel/leisure-related questions among baby boomers. In order to gain a perspective on how the responses of this group differ from those of senior Americans, we compared them to the responses given by seniors who were one generation (approximately 25 years) older than the average baby boomer.

More than half of baby boomers (53.7%) use or would like to use airfare packages (unlimited trips for one price), compared with 40.7 percent of seniors. About one in five (22.1%) baby boomers is, or would like to be, a member of a travel club or program where one must pay $50-$100 to join in order to get discounted rates and rebates, compared with about one in six of the senior sample. More than half (56.16%) of baby boomers and 46.1 percent of seniors have or would like to have a valid passport. Finally, about one-third (32.0%) of baby boomers (compared with 15.5% of older adults) are members of a restaurant club where one must pay about $430 to join, in order to get discounts at member restaurants.

Differences among Older Adults

Demand for Travel and Leisure Services. Older adults' preferences for travel and leisure services are expected to differ depending upon their level of need for such services. Older Americans with lifestyles focusing on leisure were expected to show stronger preferences for travel and leisure services. In our study, we asked respondents to indicate their level of concern with "finding ways to enjoy themselves." Older respondents who indicated they were "concerned a lot" were compared with those who said they were "concerned little" or "not concerned at all" with respect to their preferences for specific travel/leisure-related services. Forty-three percent of older Americans (55+) said they were concerned a lot. Older adults who showed a high concern were more likely than their counterparts who showed little or no concern to use these services. Specifically, a larger percentage of the former than of the latter indicated they were using an airline package (5.9% vs. 2.5%), were members of a travel/leisure program (7.3% vs. 3.8%), had valid passports (38.5% vs 25.2%), and were members of a restaurant club (12.9% vs. 7.3%).

Older consumer preferences for travel and leisure services vary by selected socioeconomic and demographic characteristics, as well as by their different gerontographic profiles.

Airline Package. With age, older Americans show decreasing interest in using airline packages. This may reflect a weaker preference for these offerings, not necessarily less desire for travel. Just over one-third of older people with household incomes under $20,000 (36.1%) expressed preference for airline packages, compared to 57.2 percent of those with incomes over $50,000. Preference for packages also increases with an older person's level of educational attainment.

Older adults in households where at least one person still works are more likely to express stronger preferences for airline package "deals," with 47.2 percent of them indicating current use or desire for such an offering, in comparison with 40.7 percent of adults from nonworking families. More than half (52.1%) of older adults who live in western states are likely to express preference for an airline package, a percentage significantly different from that of older adults who live in the East (41.0%), North (44.1%), and South (45.1%). Urban older adults are more likely than their rural counterparts to prefer using a package, with 46.7 percent and 39.4 percent, respectively, expressing preference.

More than half of healthy indulgers (55.4%) and ailing outgoers (50.7%), in comparison with 36.8 percent of healthy hermits, and 44.2 percent of frail recluses, either use or would like to use airline package deals.

Travel Club or Program. As people age in late life, they become less interested in travel clubs or programs. However, as the older person's education and annual household income increases, so does his or her preferences for the various "deals" available through various types of service providers. Specifically, relative to their counterparts with household incomes exceeding $50,000, older people in households where annual income is under $20,000 showed a weaker preference for travel clubs or programs (16.1% and 34.4%).

Nearly 30 percent (29.5%) of ailing outgoers prefer travel clubs or programs, a figure which is nearly twice as high as that for healthy hermits.

Valid Passport. Age has no effect on the older person's desire to have a valid passport. Even among individuals age 75 and over, a large percentage of them prefer to have a valid passport, suggesting that they plan to travel abroad when the opportunity arises. Older males are more likely than their female counterparts to have one (50.4% vs. 44.3%).

The higher the older person's level of education and annual household income the greater his or her likelihood of expressing preferences for foreign travel. While only 30 percent of older Americans with annual household incomes less than $20,000 have a valid passport, nearly three-fourths (73.3%) of those with incomes in excess of $50,000 have one. More than half (51.8%) of older adults who live in urban areas have a valid passport, in comparison with three in ten (30.5%) of older adults who live in rural areas.

Older westerners are more likely to have or want to have a valid passport, with nearly six in ten (58.8%) of them expressing preference. The figure for northerners is below 40 percent (39.9%); for easterners it is 50.6 percent, and for older adults who live in the South the percentage figure is 46.3.

Healthy indulgers is the group most likely to show interest in foreign travel, with 54 percent of them having or expressing desire to have a valid passport, in comparison with 40.7 percent of frail recluses and 44.7 percent of ailing outgoers.

Restaurant Club. Older Americans show decreasing interest in using restaurant clubs as they move throughout late life. Among older people with household incomes under $20,000, the preference for restaurant clubs was less than half of that expressed by mature Americans in households with annual income over $50,000 (11.9% vs. 26.1%). In the meantime, preferences for these kinds of clubs do not significantly relate to the older person's level of education.

More older adults from the nonworking families than those from families where at least one person works expressed preference for a restaurant club where you pay to join and get discounts at member restaurants (22.7% vs. 18.0%).

Older adults who live with others are more likely than those who live alone to prefer to join a travel club or program and get discounted rates and rebates, with nearly one-fourth (24.1%) of them expressing preferences, in comparison with 18.1 percent of those older adults who live alone. Similarly, a larger percentage of people who live with others (21.1%), in comparison with their counterparts who live alone (15.5%), has joined or would join a restaurant club.

One in five (20.7%) of mature Americans who live in larger cities has joined or would like to join a restaurant club, in comparison with 14.9 percent of their rural counterparts. A larger percentage of older adults who live in eastern states (26.6%) than of those who live in northern and southern states (17.0% and 17.3%, respectively) shows preference for these clubs. Finally, a larger percentage (22.7%) of ailing outgoers expressed preference for restaurant clubs, compared with 16.9 percent of healthy hermits and 17.8 percent of frail recluses.

SOURCES OF INFORMATION FOR VACATION/TRAVEL PACKAGES

Consumers may seek information about travel and leisure services from a number of sources. The most reliable source, however, is one's own experience or information stored in memory. Consumers make decisions based on information they receive from their environment, including information they received from various services in the past, or their own experience with the service(s) used.

The intent of the present research was not to determine how people acquire and store information to be used in various purchasing decisions; rather, the concern was primarily with differences in consumer experiences which may affect their use of various sources of information. In order to account for such differences, respondents were asked to indicate their information source preference about *new* vacation and travel packages—that is, products or services for which they had no prior information or experience. They were asked to indicate whether they prefer to see a TV or print ad, receive news in the mail, be contacted by phone, be visited by an agent, or learn about new vacation/travel packages in group meetings or seminars.

About four in ten (41.3%) indicated they prefer to receive news in the mail, and about one-third (34.7%) prefer to see a TV or print advertisement. Less than one in ten (8.8%) said they would prefer to learn about such new offerings in group meetings or seminars. Finally, only a negligible percentage of Americans prefers to be visited by agents or contacted by phone. Thus, it appears that people at later stages in life prefer to learn about travel-related services at their own pace, rather than being approached by a representative.

Do older adults' preferences for such sources of information differ from those of younger adults? In order to answer this question responses given by those age 55 and over were compared to responses given to the same question by adults under 55 years of age. The percentage of older adults who prefer to receive news in the mail is similar to that for their younger counterparts, suggesting that direct mail is an important information source about travel and leisure services throughout the life span. Older adults, however, were less likely than younger adults to indicate preference for TV or print messages, with one-third (34.3%) of the former group, in comparison with 43.8 percent of the younger adults, expressing preference. On the other hand, older adults are more likely to prefer learning about new travel and leisure services in group meetings, in comparison with younger consumers (8.9% vs. 4.9%).

Baby Boomers vs. Seniors

Nearly half of baby boomers (45.1%), compared with 36.6 percent of senior respondents, prefer to see TV or print ads. About four in ten (41.7%) of the younger sample prefer to receive information in the mail, compared with 43 percent of the elderly. Finally, obtaining information in group meetings or seminars is preferred by 6.1 percent of the younger respondents, while twice as many seniors (13.4%) prefer to be informed about new vacation/travel packages through the same channel.

Differences among Older Adults

TV/Print Ads. With age, mature Americans become less likely to express interest in seeing news about vacation/travel services on TV or reading such news in newspapers. TV and print advertisements tend to be preferred more by the lower- than the higher-educated older adults.

A larger percentage of mature Americans who live with others, in comparison with those who live alone, prefers to receive information about travel services from TV and newspaper advertisements (36.7% vs. 30.0%). These vehicles are more likely to be preferred by older adults who live in western than those who live in eastern states, with 37.5 percent and 28.6 percent, respectively, expressing preference.

Of the four gerontographic groups, healthy hermits are the most likely to show preference (37.1%) and ailing outgoers the group least likely to prefer information from ads in these media regarding travel packages.

Direct Mail. Interest in receiving news in the mail declines with age in late life. A larger percentage of older males (44.7%), in comparison with older females (38.2%), is likely to express interest in receiving news in the mail about vacation/travel packages. The higher the older adult's household income and level of education, the stronger the person's preference for receiving news in the mail.

A larger percentage of older adults in eastern states (49.6%) than those from western states (37.6%) is likely to express preference for receiving information about new vacation/travel packages in the mail.

Group Meetings/Seminars. Preference for learning in group meetings or seminars increases with age in late life, with those age 75 and older being three times as likely as those age 55 to 64 to indicate interest in receiving information about new vacation/travel packages through this vehicle. Older females are nearly twice as likely as older males (11.1% vs. 6.1%) to prefer receiving information this way.

Older people with higher incomes are less likely than those with lower incomes to prefer learning about new vacation/travel packages in group meetings and seminars. A larger percentage of mature adults who live alone (12.8%) than those who live with others (7.1%) prefers to hear about new travel-related services via these vehicles. Northerners are four times as likely as their easterner counterparts to prefer receiving such information in group meetings, with 13.6 percent and 3.0 percent, respectively, expressing preference. Preferences for the same information channel were 8.3 percent and 7.0 percent for westerners and southerners, respectively. Finally, healthy hermits is the group least likely to prefer learning about such services in group meetings or seminars, in comparison with ailing outgoers, which is the group most likely to prefer this information source (6.1% vs. 11.3%).

Other Sources. More mature Americans who live with others, in comparison with those who live alone, prefer learning of vacation/travel packages from visiting agents (4.0% vs. 1.8%). Older adults with higher education are likely to prefer learning about such services by being contacted by telephone.

PREFERENCES FOR METHODS OF PURCHASING VACATION PACKAGES

Consumers have a number of methods available to them for purchasing vacation packages. They may purchase them at the travel-service provider's facilities, by phone, through the mail, or they may even be able to purchase them from door-to-door solicitors (at their home or office). One of the objectives of the present research was to examine consumer preferences for purchasing methods concerning vacation packages. Therefore, respondents were asked to indicate the ways they prefer purchasing vacation packages (they were asked to indicate as many of the four methods as they prefer).

Responses to methods of purchasing vacation packages among older adults were fairly similar to those given by their younger counterparts. Nearly 60 percent (58.6%) of older Americans prefer buying these products at vendors' facilities. One in four (24.7%) prefers buying vacation packages by phone, and one in five (19.8%) through the mail. Only a very small percentage (2.7%) would buy from door-to-door vendors.

Baby Boomers vs. Seniors

The majority of the respondents indicated preference for purchasing them at vendors' facilities, with 66.2 percent of baby boomers, compared with 54.5 percent of elderly, respectively, expressing preference. The two groups also differed with respect to their preference for buying vacation packages by phone, with 27.0 percent and 20.5 percent, respectively, expressing preference. About one in five in both groups prefers direct mail, while preference for door-to-door was low (4.5% vs. 2.7%, respectively). (Respondents could indicate preference for more than one method.)

Differences among Older Adults

Preferences for purchasing vacation packages are not uniform among older Americans. They tend to differ on the basis of several demographic and socioeconomic factors. The place of purchase of travel or vacation packages an older person prefers is likely to depend on background characteristics such as age, income, living status, and location. The older person's gerontographic profile also predicted fairly well his or her preference for three of the four methods examined: door-to-door, mail, and at vendors' facilities. Let's see how responses varied by such selected characteristics.

Vendors' Facilities. With age, mature Americans decreasingly prefer purchasing vacation packages at vendors' facilities. However, preference for purchasing vacation packages this way becomes stronger with higher household income. Specifically, while less than half (48.4%) of those with the lowest income prefer buying vacation packages at vendors' facilities, a larger percentage (61.6%) of those in the high-income bracket would do the same.

Older males are more likely than older females to prefer purchasing such services at vendors' facilities, with 62.5 percent and 55.8 percent, respectively, expressing preference. In the meantime, there is a greater likelihood for the higher educated to prefer making vacation purchases via this channel, in relation to lower-educated mature Americans. A larger percentage (62.2%) of those who live with others, in comparison with those who live alone (50.3%), prefers buying vacation packages using this channel. A larger percentage of westerners (62.5%) and southerners (61.1%) than of northerners (55.4%) and easterners (55.3%) prefers buying vacation packages at vendors' facilities. Finally, ailing outgoers are more likely than frail recluses to prefer purchasing travel-related services at vendors' facilities.

Mail. Preference for purchasing those services by mail remains fairly unchanged with age in late life. Nearly one in four (24.5%) of easterners, in relation to less than one in five of northerners (19.2%) and southerners (18.0%), would buy through the mail. A larger percentage of ailing outgoers (24.3%) than of healthy hermits (16.2%) and healthy indulgers (18.0%) prefers buying vacation packages through the mail.

Door-to-Door. As mature Americans age, they do not become any more or less likely to buy these services from a door-to-door solicitor. Mature adults who live with others are more likely to prefer buying such services this way, in relation to those who live alone (3.3% vs. 1.2%). A relatively larger percentage of healthy indulgers (4.1%) and ailing outgoers (3.7%) than of frail recluses (0.83%) expressed preference for door-to-door purchase of vacation packages.

Telephone. As older people age, their preference for purchasing vacation packages by phone declines. Preference for purchasing vacation packages by phone becomes stronger with higher household income. For example, while only 21.2 percent of older Americans with total annual household income under $20,000 would buy such services by phone, one-third of those whose income is $50,000 or more would do the same. Three in ten older Americans (30.1%) who live in northern states would buy by phone, in comparison with one in five (20.8%) of easterners and a smaller percentage of westerners (17.6%).

REASONS FOR PATRONIZING AIRLINES AND CRUISE LINES

Consumers may select a particular carrier or cruise line for a number of reasons. While an exhaustive list of all reasons people use to evaluate and select airlines and cruise lines would be a cumbersome task, based on previous research we can identify at least thirteen reasons that could be considered by users of such services. Respondents were presented with this list of patronage reasons and were asked to indicate whether each would apply to their decision to start or continue to patronize an airline or cruise line.

The main reasons older adults patronize airlines and cruise lines (among those investigated) are economic in nature. About half (51.4%) indicated that prices or fees are important in their decisions to patronize these carriers. Almost as many (45.7%) indicated that discounts to specific age groups is a major consideration. The third reason in terms of importance, as indicated by frequency mentioned, is special deals through group or membership programs, with about one in three (34.8%) older Americans mentioning this reason. About one in three (29.0%) considers convenience of doing business by phone or by mail in evaluating these travel-service providers.

The remaining nine reasons were considerably less significant. About one in five (21.5%) considers whether they like the way ads show people their age, while one in six (16.5%) older adults considers important the explanation of various services by staff/personnel. Convenience in reaching the travel-service provider was mentioned by 14.4 percent of older Americans. About as many (15.3%) mentioned they are influenced by advice of other people their age in their decision to select a specific travel-service provider.

One in ten indicated the importance of billing or payment methods as a factor in choosing a specific airline or cruise line (10.6%), and referrals or endorsements by firms or professionals (10.5%), as well as the advice of children and close relatives (9.7%). Ease of getting related services at the same place and personnel or staff assistance in filling out forms were the last on the list of mentions, with 7.8 percent and 7.3 percent, respectively, mentioning these reasons.

Older adults' responses to these patronage factors generally differ from the responses given by those adults under 55 years of age. Only three factors were rated similarly by the two age groups: discounts to age groups, preference for the way the ads of airlines and cruise lines depict people their own age, and personnel/staff assistance with filling out forms. Discounts to age groups apparently available to both children and mature adults are equally important to both age groups, since those under 55 are likely to have children, while most of those over 55 may qualify for senior discounts. Special deals through membership programs such as frequent-flyer programs are available to all age groups and are considered to be more important by the younger group. The latter finding, along with the higher percentage of younger than older Americans who consider economic factors, suggest that discounts and deals may be more effective if targeted at younger rather than older age groups.

Baby Boomers vs. Seniors

Economic factors appear to motivate the patronage decisions of both age groups with regard to airlines/cruise lines (see Table 8.1). The economic motive is stronger among baby boomers than among elderly as expressed in the form of price (65.7% vs. 46.0%) and special deals through group or membership programs (44.4% vs. 28.5%), while discounts to different age groups are of equal appeal to younger and older travelers (41.0% vs. 43.2%), respectively. Ease of doing business by phone or by mail is important to nearly four in ten (38.3%) baby boomers, while this factor is of lessor importance to elderly travelers (25.1%).

The remaining factors are less important to both groups. Explanation of various services by staff/personnel is twice as important to baby boomers as to elderly (24.3% vs.13.8%). Similarly, advice of same-age peers is more important to the younger than the latter group, with 33.1 percent and 17.8 percent, respectively, expressing preference. The way people of various ages are portrayed in ads of airlines or cruise lines not only is not a very important reason (mentioned by one-fifth of the respondents), but it is also perceived as of equal importance by the two age groups.

Differences among Older Adults

Older Americans differ in the way they value certain patronage factors in choosing airlines and cruise lines. The importance of these factors is different among older adults possessing certain demographic and socio-

Table 8.1
Reasons for Patronizing Airlines/Cruise Lines among Baby Boomers and Seniors (65+) (Percent Who Feel Reason Is Applicable)

Reasons for Patronizing	Baby Boomers (%)	Seniors (%)
Reasonable prices	65.70	45.99
Convenience in reaching the service provider	18.56	13.75
Ease of getting related services at the same place	13.05	7.76
Explanation of various services by staff/personnel	24.26	13.80
Personnel/staff assistance with filling out forms	9.39	6.62
Discounts to age groups (children, seniors)	40.98	43.17
Preference for billing/payment methods	16.07	10.14
You like the way their ads show people your age	19.84	19.17
Special deals through group or membership programs	44.44	28.54
Advice of children or close relatives	16.40	7.64
Advice of other people your age	33.09	17.79
Referrals/endorsements by firms or professionals	17.47	7.74
Ease of doing business by phone or by mail	38.29	25.08
Base:	(N = 589)	(N = 236)

economic characteristics. Factors such as age, income, living status, and location play a role in the way older respondents perceive and report the importance of various factors. Generally, males perceive these factors to be of greater importance in decision making than females. The higher the older person's household income, the greater the importance he or she attaches to various factors in deciding on airlines and cruise lines. Education shows a similar pattern of relationship.

Also, gerontographic characteristics of older Americans are strong predictors of their perceptions of the importance of most of the patronage factors examined concerning the choice of airlines and cruise lines.

Price. Older adults who live with others are more likely than those who live alone to consider prices (53.8% vs. 45.5%). Relative to mature Americans who live in rural areas, a larger percentage of older adults who live in urban areas considers prices and fees (55.4% vs. 39.4%). Additionally, a larger percentage of older adults who live in the West (59.1%) than of those who live in the North (47.6%) or South (50.4%) considers prices charged by airlines or cruise lines.

Prices are of greater concern to healthy indulgers than to ailing out-goers and healthy hermits. Nearly 60 percent (59.1%) of the former group, compared with 47.2 percent and 49.8 percent for the other two groups, respectively, expressed this opinion.

Senior Discounts. Older males are more likely than their female counterparts to consider discounts to specific age groups (50.3% vs. 42.0%). A larger percentage of mature Americans who live with others, relative to their counterparts who live alone, places emphasis on this factor (49.3% vs. 37.2%).

In the meantime, urban-dwelling older people are more likely than their counterparts who reside in rural areas to put emphasis on discounts to specific age groups (49.6% vs. 33.8%). Discounts to age groups (e.g., seniors) are more important to older adults who live in the West, with 55.5 percent of them showing preference, compared with 42.0 percent for older adults who live in the South, 44.4 percent for those who live in the East, and 45.4 percent of northerners. Regarding discounts to age groups (seniors), about half of healthy indulgers (51.1%) and ailing out-goers (50.1%), in comparison with 41.3 percent of healthy hermits and 42.8 percent of frail recluses, indicated this reason for patronage.

Membership Discounts. Older males are more likely than older females to put emphasis on special deals through membership programs (40.5% vs. 29.9%). This factor is more important to older Americans who live with others than it is to those who live alone (37.5% vs. 28.2%). Also, special deals through group or membership programs are more important to older people who live in urban areas than to those who live in rural areas (37.8% vs. 25.7%). Special deals through membership programs are also of interest to healthy hermits, with 42.2 percent of them expressing this opinion in comparison with smaller percentages of older adults in other gerontographic groups.

Business via Telephone or Mail. The ease of doing business by phone shows only a slight decline with age in late life. A larger percentage of older adults from families where at least one person works expressed interest in considering the ease of doing business by phone or by mail, in comparison with their nonworking counterparts (31.1% vs. 24.1%). A little over one in five (22.2%) of frail recluses considers this factor, in comparison with approximately three in ten of older adults in the re-maining gerontographic groups.

Staff/Personnel Explanation. The explanation of various services by staff/personnel is more important to older men than it is to their female counterparts (19.6% vs. 14.1%). Westerners are more likely to appreciate this factor, with 22.1 percent of them indicating importance, compared with 14.0 percent of easterners, 15.0 percent of northerners, and 16.6 percent of southerners. Healthy indulgers are more likely than frail re-cluses to value explanations of various services by staff/personnel in choosing airlines or cruise lines, with 19.3 percent and 14.6 percent, respectively, stating this factor to be important in their patronage decision.

Age-Related Stereotypes. Age-related stereotypes in ads are of equal importance regardless of education level of older adults. Older people who live with others are more likely than those who live alone to consider such stereotypes in ads (23.5% vs. 16.8%). Age-stereotypes in advertisements enjoy wider acceptance among ailing outgoers than other gerontographic groups, with 28.8 percent of them indicating importance of this factor in their patronage decision. A smaller percentage of healthy indulgers (23.5%) expressed a similar view, while healthy hermits and ailing outgoers were the least concerned about age-stereotypes in ads, with only 17.0 percent and 17.6 percent, respectively, saying this factor affects their patronage decision concerning airlines and cruise lines.

Convenience of Reaching Provider. Convenience in reaching the service provider is equally valued by mature adults regardless of their age, with approximately one in seven of them indicating that this factor is important in their decision to patronize airlines or cruise lines.

Payment Methods. Preference for billing or payment methods changes little with age in late life. Education level does not impact how likely it is that an older American will consider this factor. Among gerontographic groups, healthy indulgers are more concerned than ailing outgoers with the billing or payment methods available to them (12.9% vs. 8.8%).

Personnel/Staff Assistance in Filling Out Forms. The travel-service providers' personnel/staff assistance with filling out forms is also equally important to all age groups in late life. This element is of equal importance to older Americans regardless of income. The importance seniors place on personnel/staff assistance with filling out forms is not related to their education level. A larger percentage of healthy indulgers (11.7%) than of other gerontographic groups values personnel/staff assistance with filling out forms.

Ease of Buying Complementary Services. As older people age, they become slightly less concerned with the ease of getting related services at the same place. This factor is more important to older men than it is to older women (11.3% vs. 5.0%). The ease of getting related services at the same place is more important to mature Americans who live with others than it is to their counterparts who live alone (10.0% vs. 2.8%).

A larger percentage of older adults who live in the South (9.5%) and West (9.0%), in comparison with those who live in the East (5.1%), is likely to indicate that ease of getting related services at the same place is important in deciding which airline or cruise line to choose. Finally, this factor is more important to healthy indulgers than to healthy hermits, with 10.0 percent and 5.9 percent, respectively, expressing this opinion.

Referrals/Endorsements. Relative to older women, mature males are more concerned with referrals/endorsements (13.5% vs. 8.1%). Healthy hermits tend to rely more on referrals than frail recluses, with 12.9 percent and 7.3 percent, respectively, indicating the importance of this factor in their patronage decision.

Peer Influence. As older people age in late life, there is little change in the influence of other older people. Older adults with children in close proximity (within one hour's drive) were four times as likely to consider the advice of other people their own age important in choosing airlines and cruise lines, with 19.8 percent and 4.4 percent, respectively, indicating this factor to be important. Finally, relative to ailing outgoers, healthy indulgers are more likely to value the advice they receive from others their age (18.1% vs. 12.1%).

Family Influence. Older males are slightly more likely than older females to prefer the advice of children or close relatives (12.1% vs. 7.8%). Mature Americans place the same importance on this factor, regardless of their level of educational attainment. In the meantime, older people who live with others are more likely than those who live alone to consider the advice of children or close relatives (11.5% vs. 5.4%).

Older adults from families where no person works are twice as likely to consider the advice of children or close relatives important in choosing an airline or cruise line, with 15.3 percent and 7.3 percent, respectively, indicating the importance of this factor. The perceived importance of advice of children or close relatives did not differ among older Americans who have and those who do not have children in close proximity, suggesting that children may only play an informing role—which can take place over the phone, while those who have children nearby may have the need to validate children's suggestions by discussing them with same-age peers.

REASONS FOR PATRONIZING HOTELS/MOTELS

Why do consumers patronize specific hotels or motels? What motivates their choice? Do their patronage motives concerning hotels/motels differ from those of younger adults? How do patronage motives vary by selected characteristics of mature Americans? This section attempts to answer these questions by presenting the results of our survey of older Americans.

First, with respect to patronage factors, a preselected list was used. While this list does not include all possible reasons for patronage, it does include several attributes important in patronage decisions for hotels and motels. Respondents were asked to indicate whether each reason applied to their decision to start or continue patronizing a hotel or motel.

Price is in the minds of two-thirds of older Americans when they contemplate choosing to stay at a particular hotel or motel. Discounts are also important in their patronage decision, with 60.3 percent of older Americans expressing this view. The remaining factors were of much lesser importance. One-third (34.7%) of the older respondents consider special deals through group memberships, and 27.2 percent value the ease of doing business by phone or by mail. Along the same lines, 22 percent may choose a particular hotel or motel because it is convenient to reach this establishment.

One in five older Americans values the advice of other people their age in choosing a hotel or motel. Nearly as many (18.1%) consider the ease of getting related services at the same place, and one in six (16.5%) considers age-stereotyping in advertisements. About one in seven (13.7%) of older Americans considers the explanation of various services by staff/personnel of hotels/motels in their patronage decision. About one in eight pays attention to referrals (12.5%), advice they receive from children or close relatives (12.8%), and the payment methods available to them (12.4%). Assistance with filling out forms by personnel or staff is only valued by one in twenty (4.6%) older Americans.

These patronage reasons are not unique to older Americans. In fact, younger Americans are even more likely to consider most of these factors in their selection of hotels or motels. Two factors, age-stereotyping in ads and special deals through group memberships, are of equal importance to both younger and older groups. Discounts to age groups (e.g., seniors) are more important to older people (as expected), while the remaining factors are more important to younger than to older adults.

Baby Boomers vs. Seniors

About three-fourths (76.6%) of baby boomers consider room rates, compared with 60.9 percent of elderly travelers. Discounts to certain age groups (children, seniors) are of importance to nearly half of baby boomers (46.0%) and six in ten (59.0%) of elderly travelers. Another set of factors is considered by approximately one-third of baby boomers, while the same factors are as important to elderly. These include convenience in doing business by phone (36.3% vs. 21.1%), accessibility of the hotel/motel (36.2% vs. 19.2%), and group or membership programs available (33.1% vs. 17.8%). The remaining factors are less important to both groups, especially to older travelers (see Table 8.2).

Differences among Older Adults

Several demographic and socioeconomic factors may play a role in the way older people perceive the importance of the thirteen patronage factors examined. For example, older mature Americans are less likely to

Table 8.2
Reasons for Patronizing Hotels/Motels among Baby Boomers and Seniors
(65+) (Percent Who Feel Reason Is Applicable)

Reasons for Patronizing	Baby Boomers (%)	Seniors (%)
Reasonable prices	76.69	60.92
Convenience in reaching the service provider	36.24	19.23
Ease of getting related services at the same place	22.54	15.49
Explanation of various services by staff/personnel	20.28	11.29
Personnel/staff assistance with filling out forms	7.66	3.92
Discounts to age groups (children, seniors)	46.04	58.99
Preference for billing/payment methods	16.83	12.18
You like the way their ads show people your age	15.21	16.19
Special deals through group or membership programs	35.49	29.94
Advice of children or close relatives	19.63	11.27
Advice of other people your age	33.09	17.79
Referrals/endorsements by firms or professionals	17.70	9.75
Ease of doing business by phone or by mail	36.35	21.10
Base:	(N = 589)	(N = 236)

consider most of the patronage factors examined in their decision to choose a specific hotel or motel. Similarly, perceived importance of hotel/motel patronage factors is not uniform across older adults possessing different gerontographic profiles.

Price. More older males than older females pay attention to price (74.7% vs. 64.4%). The more educated a mature American, the more likely he or she is to be concerned with this factor. About three-fourths (76.0%) of adults who live with others, in comparison with half (51.9%) of those who live alone, consider price.

Older adults in western states are more preoccupied with paying reasonable prices for hotel/motel accommodations, with 72.7 percent and 65.1 percent, respectively, expressing concern. Finally, of all the gerontographic groups, ailing outgoers is the group least concerned with prices.

Senior Discounts. Older males are more likely than older females to put emphasis on senior discounts (67.8% vs. 54.1%). More educated seniors tend to consider this factor than do their less educated peers. Two-thirds

(67.1%) of older adults who live with others, compared with 44.0 percent of the those who live alone, consider senior discounts.

Older adults from families with no working members, in comparison with those from families where at least one person works, perceive these kinds of price breaks to be important in selecting hotel/motel accommodations (65.9% vs. 57.9%). In terms of gerontographic groups, senior discounts are of greatest importance to frail recluses, with nearly seven in ten of them expressing interest. Healthy hermits and healthy indulgers are the groups least likely to be concerned with senior discounts, with 56.3 percent and 56.7 percent, respectively, indicating this factor to be important.

Membership Discounts. More mature men than women put importance on special deals through membership programs (41.1% vs. 29.2%). More older people with higher levels of education than those with lower levels of educational attainment consider such discounts important. In the meantime, special deals through membership programs are considered by 38.9 percent of those who live with others, compared with 24.7 percent of those who live alone.

A larger percentage of older adults who live in the North (37.6%) and South (36.0%) than of mature Americans living in the East (30.8%) and West (29.7%) considers special deals through group memberships. Also, such deals are of less interest to healthy hermits than to any of the remaining gerontographic groups.

Convenience. Convenience in reaching the specific hotel/motel is more important to older men than it is to their female counterparts (27.9% vs. 17.3%). This element is more important to more educated seniors than it is to less educated older people. In the meantime, mature Americans who live with others are more likely than those who live alone to consider convenience in reaching the service provider (26.4% vs. 11.7%).

Nearly one-fourth of southerners (24.4%) and westerners (24.0%), in comparison with one in six of easterners (16.0%), value convenience in reaching hotels/motels. A larger percentage of older adults who live near their children, in comparison with those who have no children in close proximity, values this kind of accessibility (16.8% vs. 6.3%). Lastly, ailing outgoers is the gerontographic group least likely to consider convenience in reaching the particular hotel/motel.

Complementary Services. Ease of getting related services at the same place as a patronage factor shows a decline only in very late life (75+). This factor is more important to older men than it is to older women (21.3% vs. 15.5%) and is more important to seniors with higher levels of education than it is to those with lower educational attainment. Older people living with others are more concerned with the ease of getting related services at the same place than those who live alone (20.0% vs. 13.4%).

Age-Stereotypes. Preferences for age-stereotypes in ads shows no significant decline in importance with age in late life. Concern with age-stereotypes in ads is independent of the older person's level of education, but a higher percentage of older adults who live with others, relative to the proportion of their peers who live alone, is likely to consider age-stereotypes in ads (19.1% vs. 10.5%) when making a decision in this area. Additionally, mature Americans in families where nobody works, relative to their counterparts in families where at least one person works, put more emphasis on proper age-stereotyping in ads (20.4% vs. 14.9%) when choosing a hotel or motel.

Southerners are more concerned with age-stereotypes in ads in comparison with their northern counterparts, with one in five of the former geographic group (compared with one in eight in the latter group) expressing concern. And of the gerontographic groups, it is the ailing out-goer segment that is the most concerned with the proper age stereotypes in advertisements.

Ease of Doing Business via Telephone or Mail. Relative to older people who live alone, mature adults who live with others are more likely to emphasize the ease of doing business by phone or by mail (31.0% vs. 18.2%).

Payment Method. Preference for billing/payment methods as a patronage factor shows no significant decline in importance with age in late life. Mature males are more likely than older women to consider this element (16.6% vs. 8.9%). Mature Americans of all income and education levels put the same emphasis on billing/payment methods as a patronage factor. Available billing/payment methods is a factor more important to older Americans who live with others than it is to those who live alone (13.6% vs. 9.4%).

Referrals. Referrals are more important to older men than they are to older women (15.9% vs. 9.8%). Older Americans with higher levels of education tend to pay more attention to referrals than their less educated counterparts. Referrals play a more important role in patronage decisions of older adults who live in eastern states (17.1%) than among older Americans who live in the West (10.5%) and North (11.3%).

Personnel/Staff Explanation of Services. As mature people age, they become less likely to put emphasis on this factor when selecting a hotel or motel. Older men are more likely than their female counterparts to emphasize this in their decision-making process (16.2% vs. 11.8%). Preferences for explanation of various services by staff/personnel as a patronage factor are of equal importance among older adults regardless of their educational background and level of household income. Mature Americans who live with others are more likely than those living alone to place importance on the explanation of various services by staff or personnel (15.1% vs. 10.4%).

Personnel/Staff Assistance with Forms. The importance mature Americans place on personnel/staff assistance with filling out forms stays about the same as they age in late life. This assistance is valued at the same rate by seniors, regardless of their household income or their level of education. Healthy indulgers and ailing outgoers are more likely than healthy hermits to consider hotel/motel personnel assistance in filling out forms, with 6.1 percent and 6.6 percent versus 2.4 percent, respectively, expressing interest.

Family Influence. The advice of children or close relatives becomes slightly less important to mature Americans as they get older. However, older men are slightly more likely than older women to consider input from such sources (14.9% vs. 11.1%). The higher an older American's educational level, the more likely he or she is to place importance on advice from family members. Advice of children or close relatives is more important to older people who live with others than it is to those who live alone (15.2% vs. 7.0%). Advice from their families is of greater concern to mature southerners and easterners than to their western counterparts, with 14.9 percent and 13.9 percent vs. 9.6 percent, respectively, expressing preference.

Peer Advice. Advice of same-age peers is more important to older people who live with others than it is to their counterparts who live alone (22.7 vs. 13.4%). Also, older adults who live near their children are more likely than those who live farther away from their children to consider peer advice (20.3% vs. 7.5%).

PREFERENCES FOR PAYMENT FOR AIRLINE TICKETS

How do aging consumers prefer paying for airline tickets? In order to determine payment-method preferences, respondents were asked to indicate all methods they prefer to use to pay for airline tickets—that is, cash, check, credit card, coupon, senior/member discount. While use of coupons and senior/member discounts do not constitute a formal or complete payment for transportation services, they may be used along with the main forms of payment (cash, check, credit).

Preferences for payment methods tend to be unique to older adults, since they differ from those of younger people. The vast majority of older Americans prefer to make use of a credit card for paying for airline tickets, with over half (56.4%) of them expressing preference. Senior/member discounts are of equal preference (57.6%). The second main form of payment preferred is by check, with more than four in ten (41.9%) older adults preferring this method. Cash is a relatively less popular way of paying for airline tickets, with only one in six (17.0%) of older Americans expressing preference, while only 7 percent would use a coupon.

On the other hand, younger adults prefer using multiple methods of payment for airline tickets to a greater extent than their older counter-parts. Specifically, seven in ten prefer use of credit card, one in four (25.9%) prefers cash, and four in ten would write a check. As a main form of payment, check is the only method which is as popular among younger as it is among older travelers. Coupons are preferred by twice as many younger adults (14.2%), while preference for senior/member discounts is substantially lower (9.9%) due to lower availability of these instruments to the younger age group.

Baby Boomers vs. Seniors

A similar pattern exists for airline tickets. Cash is preferred by baby boomers more than their elderly counterparts, with 27.4 percent and 16.0 percent, respectively, expressing preference. Credit is the most popular method of payment among both groups (70.5% vs. 55.4%, respectively). Payment by check is equally preferred (40.4% vs. 43.6%), and coupons are preferred three times more by baby boomers than by elderly (16.3% vs. 5.7%). Again, senior/member discounts are preferred by a little over six in ten seniors, but this is not surprising given the fact that nearly all major carriers offer senior discounts.

Differences among Older Adults

Payment preferences are not uniform across the older population. Rather, the method(s) the older person prefers to use to pay for airline tickets varies considerably by selected demographic and socioeconomic factors, as well as by gerontographic group. While cash as a form of payment for airline tickets shows little variation across gerontographic segments, use of check and credit varies across the four segments.

Credit. Preference for use of credit declines after age 75. Use of credit for payment of airline tickets is higher among older males, with nearly two-thirds (65.2%) of them, in comparison with less than half (48.9%) of their female counterparts, expressing preference. As income rises, older people are increasingly likely to prefer using credit. For example, while a little over one-third (35.6%) of older adults with household incomes under $20,000 would use a credit card to pay for airline tickets, nearly four-fifths (78.8%) of those with incomes $50,000 or more would do the same.

Older adults who live with others are more likely than those who live alone to prefer this payment method (58.6% vs. 51.0%). Those mature Americans who live in urban areas are more likely than their rural coun-terparts to prefer use of credit, with 61.4 percent and 38.5 percent, re-spectively, expressing preference.

Also, nearly two-thirds of westerners (64.2%) prefer making use of a credit card for payment for airline tickets, in comparison with half (50.9%) of those who live in the North, and 56.6 percent and 57.7 percent of those who live in the East and South, respectively. Healthy indulgers prefer using credit to pay for this transportation service, more so than ailing outgoers (63.2% vs. 48.3%).

Senior/Member Discounts. While use of senior/member discounts increases with age in late life, preference for senior/member discounts shows no variation with level of education. Relative to those older people who live alone, people who live with others are somewhat more likely to take advantage of such deals (59.3% vs. 53.9%).

A larger percentage of older adults who live in the West (62.2%) and North (60.4%) than of those who live in the East (48.3%) expressed preference for using senior/member discounts. Also, a larger percentage of older persons from nonworking families, in comparison with those from families with at least one working member (63.5% vs. 55.2%), expressed preference for senior/member discounts.

While only half (51.7%) of healthy hermits prefer using senior/member discounts, about six in ten older adults in the remaining gerontographic groups prefer to use this option.

Cash. Use of cash for payment for airline tickets remains fairly constant with age among many mature Americans. As seniors' household incomes rise, they become slightly less likely to prefer using cash to pay for their airfare. Older adults who have gone to college at least for a few years are less likely than their counterparts with lower levels of education to use cash as a form of payment for this type of transportation service.

Mature Americans living with others are more likely than their counterparts who live alone to prefer using cash (18.7% vs. 13.3%). Nearly half of older adults who live in the West (47.8%) and 46.1 percent of those who live in the North prefer use of cash, compared with just one-third of easterners and 37.9 percent of older adults who live in the South.

Check. Using checks to pay for airline tickets remains a fairly constant practice with age among many mature Americans. More older females than older males tend to prefer paying this way, with 44.3 percent and 39.2 percent, respectively, indicating such a preference. The higher seniors' incomes, the less likely they are to prefer using a check. In the meantime, the preference for this method shows no variation with level of education.

Whether an older person lives alone or with others does not make a difference in his or her preference for use of check in this purchase situation. However, a larger percentage of older Americans who live in rural areas (50.9%), in comparison with those who live in urban areas (39.5%), prefers using a check as a form of payment for airline tickets.

Check is the preferred payment system among frail recluses, with 45.8

percent of them expressing preference. Use of a check is lowest among healthy indulgers, with 38.7 percent of older adults in this group expressing preference for payment of airline tickets by check.

Coupons. As older people age, they tend to continue using coupons when purchasing airline tickets at a consistent rate. However, the use of coupons increases with income, but the tendency to redeem coupons when making these purchases shows no variation with level of education. Westerners are likely to be heavy users of coupons, in comparison with their easterner counterparts, with 10.3 percent and 4.6 percent of the older adults in these regions, respectively, expressing preference.

PREFERENCES FOR PAYMENT FOR HOTEL/MOTEL ACCOMMODATIONS

How do older consumer groups prefer paying for lodging services? In order to answer this question we asked our respondents to indicate the methods they prefer to use in order to pay for hotel/motel accommodations. Response alternatives were: cash, check, credit card, coupon, and senior/member discount. While only the first three are main payment systems, coupons and senior/member discounts can be used along with one of the main forms of payment. Because respondents could choose more than one method, the total percentage exceeds 100.0 because of multiple responses.

Preferences for payment methods vary among age groups. Credit card is the most preferred method for payment for lodging services in all age groups. Approximately three-fourths (74.4%) of younger adults, in comparison with 61.6 percent of their older counterparts, prefer making use of credit. Senior/member discounts are equally preferred by the older age group. Nearly one in three (30.3%) of older Americans prefers paying by check, and 22.4 percent prefer paying cash; a small percentage (5.5%) of older adults would use coupons. Preference for check as a method of payment is not unique to older adults, but applies to younger consumers as well. Use of cash is higher among younger than among older Americans, with 31.3 and 22.3 percent, respectively, preferring payment in cash for hotel/motel accommodations. Use of coupons is 11.5 percent and 5.4 percent, respectively, for the two age groups. Finally, use of senior/member discounts is ten times higher among older than among younger adults, reflecting (in part) greater availability of senior discounts to older Americans.

Baby Boomers vs. Seniors

Of the three major methods of payment for lodging services, cash and credit are more popular among baby boomers than among older adults.

Thirty-one percent (31.1%) of the former group (vs. 20.5% of the latter group) prefer paying cash, while the majority of both groups prefers using credit (73.%% vs. 58.3%, respectively). Payment by check is equally preferred by the two groups (34.1% vs. 30.7%), while coupons are four times more likely to be used by baby boomers than by elderly (12.8% vs. 2.8%). A large percentage (62.0%) of the elderly sample prefers senior/member discounts.

Differences among Older Adults

Preferences for payment methods show wide variations among older Americans possessing various socioeconomic and demographic characteristics. While preference for each specific method does not necessarily differ across similar background factors, each of the selected demographic variables shows marked differences in preference for one or more methods of payment for hotel/motel accommodations.

The older person's gerontographic profile is a good predictor of most of his or her preferences for methods of payment for lodging services, though preferences for cash and coupons as methods of payment show no variation across gerontographic groupings.

Cash. With age, preference for using cash to pay for hotel/motel accommodations remains fairly constant among mature Americans. In the meantime, the higher the older person's annual income and level of educational attainment, the less likely he or she is to use cash. Older Americans who live with others are more likely than their counterparts who live alone to pay this way, with 23.9 percent and 18.9 percent, respectively, reporting preference. Almost one in four (24.2%) of older adults who live in the North, in comparison with less than one in five (19.0%) of those mature Americans who live in the West, prefers using cash for payment for hotel/motel accommodations.

Check. As mature Americans age, their preference for using a check to pay for hotel/motel accommodations remains fairly consistent. A larger percentage of older females (35.6%) than of older males (23.9%) expressed preference for this particular payment method.

The higher the older person's educational level and annual income, the lower the preference for using a check. Older Americans who live with others are less likely than those living alone to prefer this payment method (28.7% vs. 33.8%). A smaller percentage of older people who live in urban areas (28.4%), in comparison with those who live in rural areas (36.1%), prefers using a check to pay for lodging services.

Older adults who live in northern states also tend to prefer use of a check for payment for lodging services, with one-third of the older adults who live in this region expressing preference, compared with 27.6 percent and 27.8 percent, respectively, of older adults who live in the East and South. Finally, writing a check is the most preferred method of payment among ailing outgoers, with 37.3 percent of them expressing preference; it is preferred the least by healthy indulgers (23.9%).

Credit. The preference for using credit for hotels and motels declines with age. Older males expressed a stronger preference for use of a credit card to pay for lodging services than their female counterparts, with 70.8 percent and 54.8 percent, respectively, expressing preference for this payment system.

The higher a mature American's household income, the more likely he or she is to prefer using a credit card to pay for hotel/motel accommodations. An older person whose annual family income is $50,000 or more is twice as likely as an older person with income under $20,000 to prefer use of credit (83.3% vs. 42.4%). Similarly, preference for credit is positively related to the older person's level of education—the more educated have a greater preference for use of credit cards for lodging services.

More older adults who live with others (64.4%) than of those who live alone (56.1%) prefer using credit to pay for lodging services. However, two-thirds (66.5%) of older adults who live in urban areas, in comparison with less than half (47.5%) of their rural counterparts, prefer this method to pay for such services.

Credit card use enjoys the highest preference among older adults who live in the West. Seven in ten of mature Americans from this region expressed preference for paying for lodging services by credit card, in comparison with 56.4 percent of those who live in the North and 63.2 percent of those who live in the South. This way of paying for lodging services is preferred more by older Americans with children in close proximity, with 63.2 percent of older adults who have children within an hour's drive expressing preference, in comparison with 53.2 percent of older adults who do not live near their children. Healthy indulgers show the highest preference for use of credit for payment for lodging services, with 69.4 percent of them indicating preference, compared with just half (52.3%) of ailing outgoers.

Coupons. As older people age, the likelihood that they will redeem coupons when paying hotel/motel bills declines. Coupons are also increasingly preferred with higher income, with 8.3 percent and 4.0 percent of older adults in the extreme income brackets, respectively, preferring use of these instruments.

Coupon use is higher among older adults who live with others, with 7.0 percent of them reporting preference, in relation to 2.3 percent of those who live alone. Easterners are less concerned with use of coupons than older adults from other regions, with only 1.8 percent of the older people who live in eastern states expressing preference (compared with an average of 5 to 6 percent of those who live in other regions of the country).

Senior/Member Discounts. Preference for senior/member discounts is higher among those aged 65 to 74, than among the younger or older age groups, with two-thirds (67.1%) of older adults in the former age group expressing preference. Preference for senior/member discounts shows less variation with income, with those older adults in the middle-income bracket ($20,000-$49,999) being more likely than their lower-income counterparts (62.6% vs. 55.4%) to prefer use of these promotional stimuli. In the meantime, a larger percentage of older Americans (64.7%) who have had some college education, in comparison with their counterparts with lower education (55.7%), prefers use of senior/member discounts. These discounts are preferred more by those who live with others than those who live alone (62.5% vs. 51.8%).

Senior/member discounts are more popular among older Americans in northern states than those from eastern states, with 62.3 percent and 53.7 percent, respectively, expressing preference. They are more popular among older adults from families where no members work than those from families where at least one person works, with 63.6 percent and 57.4 percent of older Americans in the two groups, respectively, expressing preference. Finally, senior/member discounts is the most preferred payment method among frail recluses, with two-thirds of the older adults in this group expressing preference for this payment method, in comparison with 54.4 percent of healthy hermits.

9

Financial Services

Another area of investigation was consumers' responses to financial services. Given that this area is rather broad, our investigation was confined to selected topics and types of financial services. Specifically, we examined use of selected financial services and instruments, including credit cards. We also investigated asset ownership and composition, and attitudes toward home-equity loans and reverse-mortgage plans. Consumer habits for purchasing financial services were also studied in great detail, with focus on preferences for sources of information about new financial services, preferences for methods of purchasing financial services and for providers of specific financial products. Finally, we examined reasons consumers patronize financial institutions, and developed customer profiles of present or potential users of selected financial services.

PREFERENCES FOR FINANCIAL SERVICES

The first objective of our research was to examine preferences for a selected number of financial services. Respondents were asked to indicate whether they currently have or use, would like to have or use, are not interested in having or using, are not aware of or "don't know" of seven different types of services.

Approximately one in four older adults (age 55+) either uses or would like to use financial advice from professionals for a fee; a little over 10 percent (10.8%) are potential users, since they expressed interest in this service. Nearly 60 percent (59.4%) presently use electronic fund transfer (EFT), while only 6 percent (5.9%) said that they were interested in this service. Providing older Americans with free financial services for keeping large balances received the highest positive response among the services examined, with nearly half (45.2%) of the older respondents indicating either present use or interest in this type of service. Apparently, the demand for this service is greater than its availability, suggesting an opportunity for providing such a service. More than one in three (35.7%) older Americans presently uses overdraft privilege or personal line of credit, and a significantly smaller percent (8.8%) are interested in this service.

Respondents were also asked to respond to three different types of investments and were given examples of each. The first type was: "Risky investments that could produce much higher than average income (like stocks and options)." Among older adults, only 7.5 percent indicated present ownership of such investments, with another 4.7 percent expressing interest. The second type of investment was: "Average-risk investments producing an average level of income (like balanced mutual funds and Ginnie Maes)." About half of older Americans said they presently own or would like to own such investments. Among them, almost one in five (18.9%) expressed interest in owning such investments. Finally, our respondents were asked to respond to: "Safe investments that could produce lower than average income (like money market funds and CDs)." Fifty-seven percent of the respondents indicated ownership of such financial instruments, and another 12.5 percent expressed interest.

In order to determine whether these responses are unique to the older population or apply to the adult population in general, comparisons of responses were made between older (55+) and younger adults by combining users/owners of services with those who expressed interest in them. Responses were found to differ for six of the seven services. Specifically, younger adults, in comparison to their older counterparts, were more likely to prefer professional advice on investments for a fee (31.2% vs. 24.2%), overdraft privilege or personal line of credit (63.1% vs. 43.4%), free financial advice for keeping large balances (54.3% vs. 43.2%), risky investments (30.0% vs. 12.2%), and average investments (61.2% vs. 48.0%). Older adults were more likely than their younger counterparts to use EFT (63.9% vs. 51.6%). The two groups equally prefer safe investments.

Baby Boomers vs. Seniors

We also examined preferences for these financial services among baby boomers and compared them to those of senior citizens (age 65+). As Table 9.1 shows, baby boomers prefer a larger number of financial services than senior respondents. Two-thirds of both groups prefer safe investments; and two-thirds of baby boomers prefer average-risk investments, but only 44 percent of the seniors do the same. Risky in-

Table 9.1
Preferences for Financial Services among Baby Boomers and Seniors (65+)
(Percent Who Currently Have/Use or Would Like to Have/Use)

Services	Baby Boomers (%)	Seniors (%)
Professional financial advice on investments for a fee	28.07	22.60
Automatic deposit of your check (EFT)	49.47	73.49
Free financial services for keeping large balances	55.55	38.17
Overdraft privilege or personal line of credit	67.23	35.20
Risky investments that could produce much-higher-than-average income	31.19	9.36
Average-risk investments producing an average level of income	66.27	44.37
Safe investments that could produce lower-than-average-income	68.52	68.86
Base:	(N = 597)	(N = 248)

vestments are preferred by three in ten (31.2%) of baby boomers but only by 9.4 percent of individuals age 65 and over. While two-thirds (67.2%) of baby boomers prefer overdraft privilege or personal line of credit, only half as many (35.2%) seniors prefer this service. Only one service, EFT, is preferred less by baby boomers than by senior citizens, with 49.5 percent and 73.9 percent, respectively, indicating preference.

Differences among Older Adults

Besides sociodemographics and gerontographics, the older person's preferences for the seven financial services were analyzed by value of various types of assets:

- Liquid (cash, CDs, checking and savings accounts owned—under $5,000, $5,000–$49,999, and $50,000 or more);
- Securities (stocks and bonds or mutual funds owned—under $5,000, $5,000–$49,999, and $50,000 or more);
- Real estate (personal and commercial);
- Tangibles and collections (jewelry, cars, artwork, etc.—under $5,000, $5,000–$24,999, and $25,000 or more); and
- Other assets (business owned, insurance value, etc.)

Furthermore, based on the number of services they prefer receiving from the various financial-service providers, respondents were grouped into four general patron groups: bank patrons, brokerage and mutual fund patrons, thrift patrons, and patrons of multiple types of financial institutions. The following differences were found for each of the seven services examined.

Financial Advice. Preference for professional financial advice for a fee tends to decline with age. However, there is no difference in the rate at which older males and females prefer this service. Professional financial guidance is preferred more among older people with higher household income and level of education than it is among relatively lower incomes and less educated segments of the mature market. Older consumers in households with at least one working member, in comparison to their counterparts in nonworking households, were more likely to prefer financial advice on investments for a fee (26.0% vs. 20.7%). In the meantime, older adults who live in urban areas are more likely than those living in rural locations to prefer professional financial advice on investments for a fee (26.0% vs. 19.6%). Healthy indulgers are more likely than any of the remaining groups to express preferences for receiving financial advice. Nearly one-third (32.4%) of older adults in this group, in comparison with 17.2 percent of frail recluses and 20.9 percent of healthy hermits, either use or would like to use professional financial advice on investments for a fee. Ailing outgoers was the second group most likely to express preferences, with 28.7 percent of older adults in this group responding affirmatively.

In the meantime, the higher the value of older persons' securities and real estate holdings, the greater their likelihood to use professional financial advice. Preferences for professional financial advice on investments for a fee showed no variation with tangible/collection asset or "other asset" values. Nearly half (48.6%) of broker or mutual fund patrons currently receive or would like to receive professional financial advice for a fee. This percentage is significantly higher than those in other patron-type groups. Also, patrons of multiple institutions are more likely than patrons of thrift financial providers to prefer professional financial advice on investments for a fee (27.5% vs. 18.2%).

EFT. Electronic funds transfer (EFT) services become more popular among older Americans as they age. In general, men and women prefer EFT at the same rate. Preference for EFT was inversely related to income, with those having incomes in excess of $50,000 being less likely to use EFT. Preference for EFT remains relatively stable with increasing education. Older adults in nonworking households were more likely than their counterparts in families with at least one member working to use EFT (73.5% vs. 59.4%). Also, mature Americans who live in western states are more likely than older adults who live in other parts of the country to prefer EFT. Three-fourths (74.1%) of westerners expressed preferences for EFT, in comparison to older adults who live in the East (59.5%), North (59.4%), and South (64.8%).

In general, EFT is the only service desired/used by older adults independent of the type and value of their assets. Preference for EFT is lower among older adults with liquid assets valued at less than $5,000 (57.0%), in comparison to older adults with assets valued between $5,000-$49,999 (65.8%) and $50,000 or more (64.4%). Preferences for EFT showed no variation with the values of securities, real estate, tangible/ collection, and "other asset" holdings. Finally, customers who patronize thrift institutions, however, are more likely than those who patronize multiple types of financial-service providers to use EFT.

Safe Investments. Preference for safe investments shows no significant change with age in late life. Older American men are more likely than their female counterparts to prefer these kinds of investments (70.6% vs. 65.1%). The higher an older person's household income and level of education, the more likely he or she is to favor safe investments. Mature Americans in nonworking households were more likely than those in families where at least one person works to prefer safe investments (73.3% vs. 65.1%). Older adults who live alone are more likely to have preferences for them than those who live with others (69.4% vs. 63.2%). Healthy indulgers is also the group most likely to have or express interest in having low-risk investments, with 71.1 percent of older adults in this group expressing preference; healthy hermits is the gerontographic cluster least likely to prefer low-risk investments (64.1%).

The higher the value of the person's liquid assets the greater his or her likelihood to prefer safe investments. Specifically, 43.7 percent of those with the lowest value of liquid assets (under $5,000) expressed preference for safe investments, compared with 71.3 percent and 76.4 percent for the middle ($5,000 to $50,000) and high level ($50,000 or more) of liquid asset categories, respectively. The higher the value of the older person's securities and real estate holdings, the greater his or her likelihood to express interest in or involvement with this level of investment activity. Preference for low-risk investments was stronger among older adults with higher tangible/collection assets and "other asset" values than among those with lower values. Older adults who patronize brokerage houses and mutual fund companies are more likely than patrons of other types of financial institutions to prefer safe investments, with 77.8 percent of patrons in this group expressing preference.

Average-Risk Investments. This caliber of investment loses favor among older Americans as they age in late life. Older males are more likely than older females to prefer average-risk investments (54.0% vs. 43.3%). In addition, preference for these investments among older people increases with household income and level of educational attainment. Older consumers in families where at least one person works are slightly more likely than those in nonworking families to favor average-risk investments (49.8% vs. 44.2%). Older adults living with others reported a stronger preference for this level of investment than their counterparts who live alone (50.6% vs. 42.5%). Also, older consumers who live in urban areas are more likely than those in rural areas to prefer average-risk investments producing an average level of income (50.8% vs. 40.8%). While preferences for risky investments are low among older adults in the gerontographic clusters, preferences vary considerably for average-risk investments. Ailing outgoers is the group least likely to have or aspire to have such investments, with 43.9 percent of mature Americans in this group expressing preference, compared with 54.4 percent of healthy indulgers.

The higher the value of the person's liquid assets the greater his or her likelihood to prefer average risk. While only 34.2 percent of those having liquid assets worth under $5,000 prefer average-risk investments, such preferences increase to 51.1 percent among those with assets of $5,000 to $50,000, and to 52.3 percent for those with liquid assets valued at $50,000 or more. The higher the value of the older person's securities and real estate holdings, the greater his or her likelihood to express interest in or involvement with this level of investment activity. Also, preferences for average-risk investments were stronger among older adults with higher tangible/collection asset values, as well as "other asset" values than among those with lower values. Four out of five patrons of brokerage houses or mutual fund companies either have or would like to have average-risk investments producing an average level of income. This compares with 46.3 percent of older adults who tend to patronize banks, and a little less than 40 percent among patrons of thrift institutions and multiple-institution patrons. Bank patrons are somewhat more likely to prefer investments with this level of risk than are older adults who tend to patronize thrift institutions.

Risky Investments. The older mature Americans become, the less likely they are to prefer investments classified as risky. Older women are slightly more risk-averse with more older men than older women preferring risky investments (15.1% vs. 9.2%). Also, the higher a mature American's household income and level of education, the more likely he or she is to prefer this level of investment. Mature Americans in families with at least one working member are slightly more likely than their counterparts in nonworking families to prefer risky investments (13.1% vs. 9.4%).

Although preferences for risky investments are low among the older population, value of liquid assets does not appear to affect the older person's propensity to take high risks in investing. The higher the value of the older person's securities and real estate holdings, the more likely he or she is to express interest in or involvement with this level of investment activity. Also, preference for high-risk investments was stronger among older adults with higher tangible/ collection asset and "other asset" values than among those with lower values. Multiple-institution patrons are more likely to prefer risky investment than patrons of thrift institutions (17.0% vs. 6.6%). Bank patrons are somewhat more likely to prefer high-risk investments than older adults who tend to patronize thrift institutions.

Free Financial Services for Large Balances. Such free financial services become less important to older Americans as they mature in late life. Older males are more likely than their female counterparts to prefer free financial services for keeping large balances (49.0% vs. 37.7%). Also, older people with higher household incomes and levels of educational attainment have a higher tendency than their counterparts with relatively lower levels of education and income to prefer this feature. There were no differences in preferences for free services for keeping large balances based on work status. Also, nearly half (49.8%) of healthy indulgers also prefer free financial services for keeping large balances, in comparison with 39.5 percent of healthy hermits.

The desire to receive free financial services for keeping large balances grows stronger with increasing value of liquid assets, securities, and real estate holdings. Also, preference for these services were stronger among older adults with higher tangible/ collection asset and "other asset" values than among those with relatively lower values. Half of the older broker or mutual fund patrons also expressed preference for receiving free financial services for keeping large balances.

Overdraft Privilege/Personal Line of Credit. The older a mature American, the less likely he or she is to be concerned with overdraft privileges or personal lines of credit. In the meantime, older men are more likely than older women to prefer these financial-service features (48.1% vs. 40.0%). The higher an older person's household income and level of education, the more likely he or she is to value them. Overdraft privilege or personal line of credit are services that are more popular among older people in households where at least one person works than they are among those in nonworking families (47.8% vs. 33.8%). A large percentage of older people who live in western states (49.6%), as well as those living in the South (46.5%), prefers overdraft privilege or personal line of credit, in comparison to those who live in the East (41.3%) and North (38.7%). Also, differences in preferences for overdraft privilege or personal line of credit were found among gerontographic groups. Healthy hermits prefer this service the least (40.6%), while healthy indulgers and frail recluses prefer it the most, with 47.6 percent and 46.7 percent of them, respectively, indicating preference for overdraft privilege or personal line of credit.

Overdraft privilege or personal line of credit is of greater value to those who have liquid assets valued at $5,000 to $50,000 (46.4%) than to those with liquid assets over $50,000 (40.3%). The higher the value of the older person's securities and real estate holdings, the more likely he or she is to express use or desire to use these features. Also, preferences for overdraft privilege or personal line of credit were stronger among older adults with higher tangible/collection asset values, as well as higher "other asset" values, than among those with lower values. Preference for overdraft privilege or personal line of credit among broker or mutual fund patrons is also high, with more than half (52.5%) of this group expressing preference for this service.

PREFERENCES FOR SOURCES OF INFORMATION

Another objective of this study was to investigate preferences for sources of information regarding new financial services. Respondents were asked to indicate how they prefer to find out about new financial products and services, whether they would prefer to see a TV or print ad, receive news in the mail, be contacted by phone, be visited by an agent, or learn in group meetings or seminars. (Respondents could indicate one—the most preferred—source. Some did not indicate preference.)

A little over one-third (35.8%) of the older (55+) respondents indicated preference for receiving news in the mail. This percentage was roughly twice as large as that for the second most preferred type of source—TV/print ad (17.1%). Fifteen percent of those 55 and older indicated they would rather learn about new products from agents at their home or place of work. Nearly as many (14.2%) expressed interest in learning about new financial services in group meetings or seminars. Only 6.3 percent would prefer to be contacted by phone.

Responses of older adults were also compared to those given by younger adults (under 55 years of age) in order to determine the extent to which the responses differed. We found older consumers to have different preferences for sources of information concerning new financial services than their younger counterparts. Older adults are more likely to prefer receiving information by phone and hearing about new financial services in group meetings or seminars. Preferences for the remaining sources were greater among younger adults.

Baby Boomers vs. Seniors

Forty-four percent of baby boomers, compared with 36.0 percent of seniors, prefer to receive news in the mail. About one in five of the younger group would like to be informed through ads or visited by an agent, and nearly as many seniors prefer the same sources. While about one in ten (9.5%) of baby boomers prefers to learn about new financial services in group meetings or seminars, twice as many seniors (18.1%) favor this source. Also, the younger group is less likely than the older group to indicate preference for telephone solicitation (3.8% vs. 0.5%).

Differences among Older Adults

Sociodemographics and gerontographics are fairly good predictors of the older person's preferences for most sources of information regarding new financial services, while preferences for information about new financial services differ little among older adults possessing various types and amounts of assets. However, patrons of different types of institutions are likely to differ with regard to their preferences for information sources concerning new products. These differences are discussed in the sections that follow.

TV/Print Advertisements. Only preferences for TV or print ads appear to be related to income, with those in higher income brackets being less likely to prefer these sources. The more education a person has, the less likely he or she is to prefer receiving financial information from media ads (TV or print). Also, older adults in southern and western states show stronger preferences for TV or print ads than their counterparts who make their homes in other states. However, preferences for TV or print ads do not show variability across gerontographic segments.

Group Meetings or Seminars. Older females indicated a stronger preference for receiving information about new financial services in group meetings or seminars than did mature male consumers (16.2% vs. 11.7%). Learning about financial services in such settings has more appeal among people with less education than it does among their more educated counterparts. Also, urban-dwelling older people are more likely to prefer getting financial service information in group meetings or seminars (15.5% vs. 9.5%). A larger percentage (17.8%) of residents of northern states shows preference for receiving new product information this way, in comparison to those who live in eastern states (9.0%) and western states (11.1%). Those in southern states are also likely to report relatively strong preferences for learning in group meetings or seminars (14.5%).

Healthy hermits are less likely than any other gerontographic group to express preference for learning about new financial services in group meetings or seminars, with only 10.5 percent of them indicating such preferences, in comparison to healthy indulgers (16.4%), ailing outgoers (15.3%), and frail recluses (17.6%). Patrons of thrift institutions are less likely than patrons of other institutions to prefer learning about new financial services in group meetings or seminars.

Agents. The higher an older person's level of educational attainment, the less likely he or she is to prefer visitation by agents. Older urban dwellers are less likely to prefer getting information from these representatives than their rural counterparts (13.4% vs. 21.2%). Mature Americans living in eastern and northern states report stronger preferences for agent visitation than those living in southern states (17.7% and 18.5% vs. 10.3%, respectively). Those who have higher assets in securities are more likely to prefer visits by agents. The more money people have in real estate equity the more likely they are to prefer hearing about new financial services from agents on a person-to-person basis. This is also the case for liquid assets—that is, the higher the value of such assets held the greater the preference for learning about new products from agents. In the meantime, bank and mutual fund patrons are more likely than patrons of thrift institutions to prefer receiving information about new financial services from agents who visit them.

Mail. Among mature consumers, preference for receiving news through the mail significantly declines while preference for phone contact increases with age. Also, among those 55 or older, a large percentage of males (39.2%) prefers to receive information in the mail in comparison to their female counterparts (32.9%). Those who live with others are more likely to prefer receiving information in the mail than those who live alone (38.3% vs. 30.1%). A smaller percentage of healthy indulgers (28.8%) prefers receiving news in the mail, in comparison to healthy hermits (37.0%), ailing outgoing (37.0%), and frail recluses (38.5%).

Patrons of multiple types of institutions appear to be those most likely to prefer finding out about new financial services through direct mail. Nearly half (48.6%) of older adults in this group expressed preference for this source, compared with 38.7 percent of bank patrons, 34.9 percent of patrons of brokerage and mutual fund companies, and 31.7 percent among patrons of thrift institutions.

Telephone. Older people who live in urban areas are somewhat more likely than older adults who live in rural areas to prefer telephone contact (7.2% vs. 3.8%). Older adults in households with no working persons, in comparison to those where at least one person works, report stronger preferences for telephone contact (8.4% vs. 5.4%). In addition, healthy indulgers are more likely to prefer to be contacted by phone than ailing outgoers (8.1% vs. 4.7%). With increasing value of liquid assets and securities there is a corresponding increase in preference to learn about new financial services by telephone contact. Brokerage or mutual fund company patrons have the highest likelihood to prefer phone contact (12.8%).

PREFERENCES FOR METHODS OF PURCHASING
FINANCIAL SERVICES

Older adults have a number of options available to them when buying financial services. In this research four main methods were examined: door-to-door (at home or office), through the mail, by phone, or at vendors' facilities. Respondents were asked to indicate their preferred ways of buying financial services. Purchasing services at vendors' facilities is the most preferred method among those age 55 and older, with 64.6 percent of the respondents indicating preference. Buying financial services by phone is preferred by nearly one-fourth (23.8%) of the older respondents, while door-to-door is the next most preferred method of buying financial services (10.4%). Direct mail is the least preferred method with about one in twenty respondents (5.4%) expressing preference.

Preferences of older adults differ somewhat from those of younger adults. Specifically, those under 55 years of age are more likely than those 55 and older to prefer buying financial services from door-to-door agents (14.0% vs. 10.3%) as well as through the mail (8.6% vs. 5.2%).

Baby Boomers vs. Seniors

Baby boomers and seniors equally prefer purchasing financial services at financial-service providers' facilities, with about six in ten indicating preference; and both groups equally prefer buying financial services by phone, with about one-fourth of them indicating preference. However, baby boomers are more likely than seniors to indicate preference for buying door-to-door (15.3% vs. 9.8%) and through the mail (7.6% vs. 3.7%).

Differences among Older Adults

Preferences for methods of purchasing financial services were analyzed by select sociodemographic characteristics and gerontographic segments. Preferences for each of the four purchasing methods were also tabulated for each of the four major patronage clusters: multiple, banks, broker/mutual fund, and thrift. The results of these analyses are discussed for each purchasing method.

Door-to-Door (at Home or Office). Older people's preferences for buying financial services door-to door do not change with increasing age. There were no sex differences in preferences for door-to-door purchasing of financial services. However, preferences for purchasing financial services from door-to-door agents do not vary with income. Preferences for buying financial services using this channel are fairly similar across older adults with different education background. Preference for door-to-door is four times greater among healthy indulgers than among frail recluses (15.2% vs. 3.8%). Also, a larger percentage of healthy hermits (10.5%) and ailing outgoers (11.3%) than frail recluses prefers to purchase financial services from door-to-door agents.

The size of older adults' liquid assets relates to their propensity to prefer purchasing financial services from door-to-door agents. Those with liquid assets valued between $5,000 and $50,000 are less likely to prefer this method than their counterparts with more or less liquid assets. Patrons of brokerage or mutual fund companies and thrift institutions are more likely to express preferences for purchasing financial services door-to-door than bank patrons.

Mail. Older peoples' preferences for mail channels of purchasing financial services do not change with increasing age. Older males are more likely than their female counterparts to prefer purchasing financial services through the mail (6.9% vs. 4.1%). Preferences for purchasing financial services this way do not vary with income. In the meantime, tendencies for buying financial services using this channel are fairly similar across older adults with different education background.

Older people with $5,000 to $50,000 in liquid assets are nearly twice as likely as those with liquid assets valued under $5,000 (6.8% vs. 3.5%) to prefer direct mail. Finally, those who patronize several types of financial institutions are more likely than any other type of patrons to prefer purchasing financial services through the mail.

Telephone. As older people age in late life, their preference for buying financial services by phone declines. Older females are slightly more likely than older males to prefer buying such services this way (25.8% vs. 21.5%). Also, older adults with higher incomes and levels of educational attainment show stronger preferences than their lower-income and less educated counterparts for purchasing financial services by phone. One in four healthy hermits (25.6%) and frail recluses (26.2%) prefers purchasing financial services by phone, compared with one in five (20.4%) among ailing outgoers.

One-fourth of those with liquid assets in excess of $5,000 are likely to prefer buying financial services by phone, in comparison with a little over 15 percent (15.3%) of those with liquid assets less than $5,000. Also, the older person's propensity to prefer purchasing such services by phone is directly proportional to the size of assets he or she has in securities and the higher one's equity, the more likely he or she is to express preference for purchasing financial services this way. Older people with more tangible and collections assets are more likely to report preferences for buying financial services by phone. In the meantime, older people with greater value of such assets expressed stronger preferences for purchasing financial services via this channel. Finally, more than half

(53.2%) of those who patronize brokers or mutual fund companies are likely to express preferences for buying financial services by phone, in comparison with multiple-institution patrons (20.8%), bank patrons (20.7%), and patrons of thrift institutions (14.1%).

Vendors' Facilities. Purchasing financial services at vendors' facilities becomes somewhat less favored by mature Americans as they age in late life. Mature men are more likely than older women to prefer buying these services via this channel (70.9 vs. 59.3%). Older adults with higher incomes show stronger preferences than their lower-income counterparts for purchasing financial services at vendors' facilities. Preferences for buying financial services using this channel are fairly similar across older adults with different educational background. Older Americans who live with others are more likely than those who live alone to prefer purchasing financial services at vendors' facilities (66.5% vs. 60.1%). Frail recluses are more likely to prefer purchasing financial services at vendors' facilities, with three-fourths of them expressing such a preference, compared with less than two-thirds of those in other gerontographic groups.

The higher the value of an older person's tangible and collections assets, the more likely he or she is to prefer buying these services at vendors' facilities. And finally, older people who tend to patronize brokerage houses or mutual fund companies are less likely than any of the remaining groups to prefer purchasing financial services at vendors' facilities.

PATRONAGE PREFERENCES FOR CHECKING OR SAVINGS ACCOUNTS

Consumers were asked to indicate their preferences for various types of financial institutions in opening a checking or savings account. As expected, commercial banks are by far the most preferred financial institution, with 78.4 percent of those 55 and older expressing preference. One in ten (30.2%) indicated preference for savings and loan associations (S&Ls), while one in four older respondents (24.8%) preferred credit unions. Preferences for AARP, stock brokerage, and mutual fund companies were negligible.

While patronage preference for banks is strong not only among older but also among younger adults, the latter group is less likely to open a checking or savings account at a bank (78.1% vs. 71.7%). However, those under 55 are more likely than their older counterparts to patronize credit unions for savings and checking accounts (36.4% vs. 24.3%).

Baby Boomers vs. Seniors

Commercial banks are the most preferred financial-service providers for *savings/checking accounts*; they are preferred by seven in ten baby boomers and nearly eight in ten (78.8%) seniors. Nearly four in ten (38.3%) of the younger generation prefer to have savings/checking accounts at credit unions, compared with only half as many seniors (19.3%). Both groups equally prefer having such products at S&Ls, with about three in ten of them expressing preference.

Differences among Older Adults

Patronage preferences for financial institutions in opening a savings/ checking account show wide variability due to different social and demographic factors. Older persons' preferences tend to vary by factors such as age, socioeconomic status, sex, and location. Furthermore, different gerontographic segments tend to show different preferences for banks, credit unions, and AARP as places to have a savings or checking account. Also, older people prefer to open savings or checking accounts at different financial institutions depending on the amount of liquid assets they have. And financial patronage behavior with regard to checking and savings accounts shows variability across patronage clusters of older Americans. These differences are discussed in the sections that follow.

Commercial Banks. Preference for commercial banks as savings and checking account service providers is highest among the most educated older Americans. Eighty-five percent (85.4%) of northerners, in comparison with 71.6 percent of easterners, 72.7 percent of westerners, and 77.9 percent of older adults who live in the South, prefer having a savings or checking account at a commercial bank. A larger percentage of frail recluses than healthy indulgers (81.9% vs. 74.5%) prefers banks for these services. Commercial banks are more likely to be patronized by those who have liquid assets in excess of $5,000.

Bank patrons appear to have the stronger preference for receiving these services from commercial banks. However, almost four in five (79.0%) of older adults who receive most of their financial services from brokerage firms and mutual fund companies still prefer commercial banks as places to have their checking and savings accounts. Even a larger percentage (40.4%) of patrons of thrift institutions would go to a bank for checking and savings accounts. These findings suggest that the strongest loyalty toward financial institutions is among bank patrons, perhaps due to fewer services these older people may need.

Savings and Loans (S&Ls). The higher the older person's household income, the greater his or her preferences for S&Ls as a source of savings and checking account services. Mature adults who live in eastern and western states tend to favor S&Ls more than older residents of other geographic locations as places to have these accounts.

The more money the older person has, the more likely he or she is to patronize S&Ls. Also, older adults with high equities in real estate are more likely to favor these for savings and checking accounts than older adults who have smaller equities. Patrons of S&Ls are more likely to have assets in tangibles and collections valued between $5,000 and $50,000 than larger or smaller accounts.

Credit Unions. As people age in late life, preferences for credit unions and AARP tend to decline. The higher the older person's household income, the greater his or her preferences for this kind of organization as a savings and checking account service provider. Also, credit unions are favored more by those with some college education than by those older adults with higher or lower education. Older urban-dwelling people are more likely to patronize credit unions than their rural counterparts (26.5% vs. 19.6%). Credit unions are favored more by older adults residing in western states (30.3%) than by those who live in the East (18.7%), North (23.6%), or South (25.5%). In addition, a larger percentage of older males than older females (31.4% vs. 29.1%) prefers credit unions as places for having a savings or checking account. Older adults who live with others are twice as likely as those who live alone to express preference for dealing with a credit union when it comes to having a savings or checking account (29.2% vs. 14.3%). Healthy indulgers and frail recluses are more likely than healthy hermits (27.5% and 28.7% vs. 21.9%, respectively) to patronize credit unions for savings and checking accounts.

Credit unions are favored more by those with balances between $5,000 and $50,000 than by older adults with less than $5,000 or more than $50,000 in liquid assets. They are more likely to be patronized by those with securities valued between $5,000 and $50,000 than by older adults with smaller or larger investments in securities. Also, older adults who have $5,000 or more invested in tangibles and collections are more likely to patronize credit unions for savings and checking accounts than those with less invested in such assets. Finally, older people with other assets (business, insurance, etc.) valued between $5,000 and $50,000 are more likely than older adults with smaller or larger investments in other assets to prefer credit unions.

AARP. As mature Americans age in late life, patronage preferences for the AARP decline. The organization is preferred for savings and checking accounts among the least educated older adults. Also, ailing outgoers are more likely than healthy hermits (5.0% vs. 0.25%) to open a savings/checking account through AARP. The higher an older person's household income, the less likely he or she is to turn to AARP for these services.

Stock Brokerage Firms. The higher a mature American's household income, the higher the likelihood that he or she will look to stock brokerage companies for these account service needs. The more money in securities an older person has, the greater his or her likelihood to prefer these firms for savings and checking accounts. The higher the value of one's assets in this category the greater his or her likelihood to prefer stock brokerage companies for savings and checking accounts.

Mutual Fund Companies. Mature Americans with higher household incomes are more likely than their counterparts with relatively lower incomes to use mutual fund companies for their checking and savings account needs. The more money in securities an older person has the greater his or her likelihood to look to mutual fund companies for savings and checking account services. AARP as a place to open a savings or checking account is more likely to be preferred by older adults with small equities in real estate than by those with large equities.

The higher the value of one's assets in this category the greater his or her likelihood to prefer stock brokerage and mutual fund companies for savings and checking accounts. Also, of interest is the nearly half (49.8%) of multiple-institution patrons who would open/have a checking or savings account with AARP.

Multiple Institutions. Patrons of brokerage and mutual fund companies appear to prefer receiving different financial services from various types of financial institutions. Patrons of thrift institutions are probably the least loyal and would switch to other types of thrift institutions for basic financial services.

PATRONAGE PREFERENCES FOR CERTIFICATES OF DEPOSIT

When our respondents were asked to indicate the types of financial institutions they would prefer to patronize for certificates of deposit (CDs), the largest majority (63.9%) of older adults indicated commercial banks as the most preferred institutions. S&Ls were the second most preferred, with 35.7 percent of the older respondents expressing preference. Credit unions were the third most preferred (15.9%), followed by stock brokerage companies (8.4%). The percentage of older adults who prefer AARP and mutual fund companies was insignificant.

Commercial banks are not only a popular source of CDs among older adults but also among those under 55. While a larger percentage of younger than older adults is likely to prefer credit unions (23.1% vs. 15.6%) and mutual fund companies (4.2% vs. 2.0%) for CDs, older consumers are more likely than their younger counterparts to prefer S&Ls for this type of financial product (35.9% vs. 30.6%).

Baby Boomers vs. Seniors

While the percentage of baby boomers (59.1%) who would patronize a bank for CDs does not differ a great deal from that of seniors (63.7%), baby boomers are twice as likely as seniors to patronize a credit union

(22.0% vs. 11.9%). For CDs, baby boomers are less likely than older adults to patronize S&Ls, with 28.7 percent and 37.5 percent, respectively, expressing preference, but they are twice as likely to patronize a mutual fund company (7.3% vs. 3.4%).

Differences among Older Adults

Patronage preferences for financial institutions regarding the purchase of CDs differ according to the older person's sociodemographic characteristics, and several differences in patronage preferences for CDs can be noted among gerontographic groups. Also, an older person's propensity to patronize a financial-service provider for CDs varies with the type and amount of assets the person possesses. Patronage preferences for specific institutions were further analyzed among older adults (55+) by ownership or interest in safe investments.

The financial institutions older people patronize in general also affect where they go for their CD needs. Multiple-institution patrons would buy CDs at banks, credit unions, S&Ls, or AARP. For the remaining groups, preference for service provider reflects their present patronage habits. Thus, bank patrons prefer banks, and patrons of stock brokerage companies prefer having CDs at the same place they receive other financial services. It is interesting to note that those who would buy CDs at S&Ls are not only older adults who are patrons of thrift institutions (credit unions and S&Ls), but also many are likely to be patrons of brokerage and mutual fund companies.

Commercial Banks. When it comes to purchasing CDs, males are more likely than females to prefer commercial banks (69.2% vs. 59.6%). Older Americans' preferences for commercial banks for these certificates do not differ with income. Also, the best prospects for CDs at commercial banks are those elderly with high education. Older adults who live with others, in comparison to those who live alone, are more likely to prefer commercial banks (65.2% vs. 60.9%). Older adults who live in urban areas are more likely than their rural counterparts to prefer banks for CDs, with 70.3 percent and 62.7 percent, respectively, expressing willingness to do business with banks. When older adults contemplate purchasing a CD, two in three of them are likely to go to a commercial bank, unless they happen to live in western states. Only half of the latter group is likely to patronize a bank. A larger percentage of frail recluses (67.8%) than of ailing outgoers (59.7%) is likely to prefer getting a CD at a commercial bank.

The greater the value of the older person's assets in cash, CDs, checking, and saving accounts, the more likely he or she is to prefer commercial banks for this need. In the meantime, older adults with more money invested in securities are more likely than those with less money invested in these instruments to prefer purchasing CDs at such institutions. Also, older adults with higher real estate equities are also more likely than their lower-equity counterparts to patronize commercial banks for this particular product. The more money older people have in tangibles and collections, the more likely they to patronize banks for CDs. In the meantime, the percentage of older adults who express preference for commercial banks in purchasing CDs is higher among those whose other assets are valued in excess of $25,000 than among those with lower-valued assets. Older adults who presently have or would like to have safe investments, in comparison to those who do not have ownership or interest, would prefer a CD at a commercial bank, with 69.6 percent and 62.2 percent, respectively, expressing preference.

Credit Unions. Preference for credit unions as financial-service providers of CDs declines with age in late life. Older men are more likely than older women to prefer these organizations for their CD service needs (19.2% vs. 13.2%). Also, the greater the older person's household income, the greater his or her propensity to prefer credit unions as a source of CDs. Mature Americans who live with others are more likely than their counterparts who live alone to prefer credit unions (18.5% vs. 9.7%). Older adults who live in urban areas are almost as likely as those who live in rural areas to prefer this type of financial institution. Older adults who live in southern and western states are three times as likely as those who live in eastern states to prefer credit unions. These organizations are more likely to be preferred by frail recluses than by ailing outgoers, with 19.9 percent and 13.6 percent, respectively, expressing preference.

Also, older people with higher levels of liquid assets are more likely than those who do not have as much to prefer getting CDs at a credit union. Older adults who have less than $50,000 in securities are more likely to prefer these institutions for their CD needs, and older people who have between $5,000 and $50,000 in real estate tend to favor credit unions more than their counterparts who have higher or lower equity in real estate. Also, those who favor credit unions tend to have tangibles and collections valued between $5,000 and $25,000. These institutions are also likely to be preferred by one-fourth of older adults who have other assets valued between $5,000 and $25,000 than among those who have less (10.7%) or more (16.5%).

Savings and Loans (S&Ls). The higher a mature American's household income, the more likely he or she is to prefer S&Ls as a source of CDs. Older people with some college education are the best prospects for these organizations with respect to CDs. Older people who live with others are more likely than those who live alone to prefer S&Ls (37.9% vs. 30.7%). Older adults who live in urban areas are almost as likely as those who live in rural areas to prefer this type of financial institution. In the meantime, healthy indulgers are more likely to patronize S&Ls (44.0%), in comparison to healthy hermits (31.5%), ailing outgoers (35.4%), and frail recluses (36.1%).

The greater the value of the older person's assets in cash, CDs, checking, and saving accounts, the more likely he or she is to prefer S&Ls. Older adults with higher real estate equities are also more likely than their lower-equity counterparts to patronize S&Ls for CDs. Also, those who favor these financial organizations tend to have tangibles and collections valued between $5,000 and $25,000. A larger percentage of older people who have or would like to have safe investments (vs. those who do not) would go to S&Ls (41.3% vs. 23.2%).

AARP. As mature Americans age in late life, they become less likely to turn to the AARP for CD services. An older person's household income does not affect the likelihood that he or she will use this organization for CD service needs. However, low-education elderly prefer AARP. Older adults who live in urban areas are almost as likely as those who live in rural areas to prefer this institution for CD purchases and services. Although a relatively small percentage of older adults is likely to buy a CD through AARP, frail recluses are far more likely to do so than healthy hermits (4.9% vs. 1.3%).

Furthermore, older people with higher levels of liquid assets are more likely than those who do not have as much to prefer getting CDs through the AARP. The less money older people have in tangibles and collections, the more likely they are to patronize this organization for their CD needs.

Mutual Fund Companies. As people age in late life, their preference for mutual fund companies as CD service providers increases. Older persons' propensity to rely on such companies for their CD needs do not differ with income. Older adults who live in urban areas are almost as likely as those who live in rural areas to prefer this type of financial institution. Furthermore, relative to their counterparts with less money invested in securities, older Americans with more money invested in these instruments are more likely to prefer purchasing CDs at mutual fund companies.

Stock Brokerage Firms. Stock brokerage companies are favored more by older men than older women for CD-related needs (10.2% vs. 7.0%). Also, the greater an older person's annual household income, the greater his or her propensity to prefer these companies as a source of CDs. The best prospects for CDs at stock brokerage firms are those elderly with high education.

Stock brokerage companies are favored more by older people who live with other as places to open a CD account (10.0% vs. 4.8%) than those who live alone. Older adults who live in urban areas are almost as likely as those who live in rural areas to prefer this type of financial institution.

Those who live in the West are ten times as likely as older adults who live in the East to patronize stock brokerage companies (14.5% vs. 1.4%).

Furthermore, the best prospective buyers for CDs among stock brokerage companies are ailing outgoers, with 11.2 percent of them indicating preference, in comparison to healthy indulgers (5.5%) and frail recluses (6.6%).

Older adults with more money invested in securities are more likely than those with less money invested in these instruments to prefer purchasing CDs at stock brokerage companies. Older adults with higher real estate equities are also more likely than their lower-equity counterparts to patronize stock brokerage companies for CDs. Also, the more money older people have in tangibles and collections, the more likely they are to patronize stock brokerage companies for CDs. The higher the value of "other assets," the more likely the older person is to patronize stock brokerage companies for purchasing CDs.

Finally, a larger percentage of older people who have or would like to have safe investments (vs. those who do not) would turn to stock brokerage houses for CDs (10.1% vs. 4.8%).

PATRONAGE PREFERENCES FOR STOCKS

We also investigated consumer patronage preferences for stocks. While the majority of older adults (47.1%) prefer to buy stocks from stock brokerage companies, nearly one in five prefers commercial banks (18.9%) and mutual fund companies (18.7%). One-tenth of them (9.9%) would buy stocks from credit unions, and 13.7 percent would buy them through AARP. Only 6.4 percent indicated S&Ls as places to buy stocks.

When patronage preferences for stocks are compared between older and younger adults, several differences emerge. Older adults have stronger preferences for commercial banks (19.1% vs. 14.7%) and AARP (13.5% vs. 5.2%). On the other hand, older adults are less likely than their younger counterparts to prefer stock brokerage companies (46.5% vs. 58.2%) and mutual fund companies (18.5% vs. 23.5%) as places to buy stocks.

Baby Boomers vs. Seniors

Preferences for financial-service providers as places from which to purchase *stocks* vary widely. Nearly six in ten (58.0%) baby boomers, compared with 42 percent of older adults, prefer to patronize stock brokerage companies. Mutual fund companies are the second most preferred source, with 22.8 percent and 15.4 percent, respectively, expressing preference. While commercial banks are equally preferred by the two groups (16.0% vs. 15.7%), a larger percentage of baby boomers than senior citizens (12.2% vs. 7.1%) would go to a credit union for stocks. S&Ls are not popular places to buy stocks for either group (7.8% vs. 6.3%).

Differences among Older Adults

Patronage preferences for purchasing stocks vary by several demographic and socioeconomic characteristics of older adults. There are also differences across gerontographic groups. Furthermore, patronage preferences for financial-service providers regarding the purchase of stocks appear to be a matter of type and size of one's assets. Institutional-patronage preferences for stocks were also analyzed by ownership or interest in these financial assets.

Commercial Banks. Preferences for purchasing stocks at commercial banks declines with age in late life. In comparison to their female counterparts, older males are more likely to prefer banks for this purpose (21.1% vs. 16.9%). Older people who are likely to patronize commercial banks are more likely to have low than high levels of educational attainment. In comparison to those older adults who live alone, those who live with others are more likely to prefer commercial banks (20.8% vs. 14.5%). Commercial banks are favored more by those who live in rural areas than by those living in urban areas (25.8% vs. 17.2%). In the meantime, older adults living in western states are less likely to prefer buying stocks at these institutions, with 12.8 percent of them expressing such preferences, in comparison to those who live in southern and northern states (21.2% and 20.8%, respectively). Older adults in families where no person works are more likely to prefer purchasing stocks from banks, in comparison to those adults in families where at least one person works (23.9% vs. 16.8%). A larger percentage of frail recluses (22.7%) and ailing outgoers (22.5%) is likely to prefer commercial banks as places from which to purchase stocks, in comparison to healthy hermits (16.1%) and healthy indulgers (15.1%).

Older adults with liquid assets valued between $5,000 and $50,000 are more likely to prefer purchasing stocks at commercial banks than older adults with liquid assets valued at less than $5,000. In addition, the less money an older person has in securities, the less likely he or she is to use commercial banks as providers of stock services.

Credit Unions. Preferences for patronizing credit unions drops for stocks sharply at age 75 or later in life. Older adults who live in western states are better prospects for credit unions which sell stocks, with 13.5 percent of these older people expressing preference, in comparison to older adults who live in eastern states (5.0%). Southerners are also good prospects for stocks sold by these organizations, with 11.4 percent of them expressing preference.

The higher the value of the older person's liquid assets and securities, the lower his or her propensity to indicate preferences for credit unions for stock needs. Also, credit unions are less likely to be favored by older adults having real estate equity in excess of $50,000 than by those having equity under $50,000. In the meantime, older adults who have other assets valued at $5,000 to $25,000 are more likely to favor credit unions as places from which to buy stocks than their counterparts with lower or higher size of "other" assets. A larger percentage of older adults who said they either own or would like to own risky investments, in comparison to those who do not own or are not interested in risky investments, would prefer to buy stocks from commercial banks (25.2% vs. 18.1%).

Mutual Fund Companies. Patronage preferences for mutual fund companies as places from which to buy stocks declines with age in late life. In comparison to their female counterparts, older men are more likely to prefer these companies for their stock purchasing needs (22.6% vs. 15.6%). Also, the higher an older person's household income and level of education, the more likely he or she is to purchase stock through mutual fund companies. Older people who live with others are more likely than their counterparts who live alone to prefer buying stocks through mutual fund companies (21.5% vs. 12.1%). Those who live in urban areas are more likely than mature Americans in rural areas to prefer these firms (14.6% vs. 20.3%) when purchasing stocks. In the meantime, westerners are more likely than older adults who live in southern states to patronize mutual fund companies (22.8% vs. 17.1%). Healthy hermits are more likely than ailing outgoers to patronize mutual fund companies when they buy stocks (21.8% vs. 15.4%).

The higher the value of the older person's liquid assets, securities, and tangibles and collections, the greater his or her propensity to turn to mutual fund companies for stock needs. Also, the higher the older person's investment in real estate, the greater his or her propensity to prefer these companies as places from which to purchase stocks. Higher values of "other assets" are also associated with stronger preferences for mutual fund companies for stock needs. A larger percentage of older adults who said they either own or would like to own risky investments, in comparison to those who do not own or are not interested in risky investments, indicated that they would prefer mutual fund companies (29.9% vs. 17.2%).

Stock Brokerage Firms. Patronage preferences for stock brokerage firms as places from which to buy stocks declines with age in late life. Older men are more likely than their female counterparts to buy stocks from these kinds of companies (52.2% vs. 42.8%). The higher the older person's household income and the higher the level of education, the greater his or her propensity to report preferences for purchasing stocks through these firms. Relative to older adults who live alone, those who live with others are more likely to purchase stocks from stock brokerage companies (49.3% vs. 41.8%). Mature Americans who live in rural areas are less likely than their urban-dwelling counterparts to turn to stock brokerage companies (37.0% vs. 50.4%). Also, westerners are more likely than their northern counterparts to prefer buying stocks from stock brokerage firms (50.1% vs. 44.4%). Stock brokerage companies are favored more by healthy hermits (51.6%) and healthy indulgers (48.7%) than ailing outgoers (41.1%).

The higher the value of the older person's liquid assets, securities, and tangibles and collections, the greater his or her propensity to prefer stock brokerages for stock purchases. In addition, the higher the older person's investment in real estate, the greater his or her propensity to prefer such companies as places from which to purchase stocks. Higher values of "other assets" are associated with stronger preferences for stock brokerages. As expected, stock brokerage companies are the most preferred sources from which to purchase stocks among the majority of older respondents. Even bank patrons prefer these service providers, and this in part may reflect perceptions of the unavailability of stocks through other financial-service providers. A larger percentage of older adults who said they either own or would like to own risky investments, in comparison to those who do not own or are not interested in risky investments, indicated a preference for stock brokerage companies (67.6% vs. 44.3%).

Savings and Loans (S&Ls). Older adults who have children living within one hour's drive are more likely than those with no children nearby to prefer patronizing S&Ls for purchasing stocks (44.6% vs. 38.9%). Also, ailing outgoers are relatively more likely than frail recluses (8.8% vs. 4.8%) to patronize S&Ls. The higher the value of the older person's liquid assets, the greater his or her propensity to prefer S&Ls, which are also favored more by older adults with securities estimated at $5,000 to $50,000 than by those with more money in these assets.

AARP. Relative to older women, older men are more likely to buy stocks through the AARP (16.4% vs. 11.6%). Older people with higher incomes and levels of education are less likely than those with less education and relatively lower household income to prefer buying stocks through this organization. Ailing outgoers are more likely than the two former groups to prefer buying stocks through AARP (17.4% vs. 11.5% and 10.7%, respectively).

The higher the value of the older person's liquid assets, securities, and tangibles and collections, the lower his or her propensity to indicate preferences for the AARP as a provider of stocks. Similarly, the higher the value of the older person's "other" assets, the lower his or her propensity to turn to this organization for stock purchases. A larger percentage of older adults who said they either own or would like to own risky investments, in comparison to those who do not own or are not interested in risky investments, indicated a preference for buying stocks through the AARP (18.4% vs. 13.1%).

PATRONAGE PREFERENCES FOR GOVERNMENT
BONDS AND U.S. TREASURY BILLS

Patronage preferences for government bonds and U.S. Treasury bills were also investigated. When asked about the type(s) of institution older adults would prefer to purchase these financial services from, about half (49.3%) of older respondents indicated banks and a much smaller percentage would prefer stock brokerage firms (17.8%). One in ten of them indicated preference for S&Ls as outlets for purchasing government bonds and treasury bills. Credit unions are preferred by nearly 6 percent (5.9%) of the mature population, while AARP and mutual fund companies are the least preferred providers of these financial services (4.0%).

When patronage preferences for financial institutions concerning the purchase of government bonds and treasury bills are compared between younger and older adults, some interesting findings emerge. Preferences for commercial banks and stock brokerage companies are similar among the two groups, while preferences for the remaining institutions are stronger among the younger group. These findings suggest that institutional loyalty becomes concentrated in fewer types of institutions with age. Younger adults may patronize a larger variety of financial institutions for government bonds and treasury bills; with age they concentrate their patronage habits in fewer types of financial institutions—banks and stock brokerage houses.

Baby Boomers vs. Seniors

Commercial banks appear to be the most preferred place to buy *government bonds/U.S. Treasury bills*, with nearly half of the younger generation (48.4%), compared with 45.7 percent of seniors, expressing preference. While S&Ls are a distant second among the most preferred financial-service providers, such preferences are not shared by the elderly patrons who are twice less likely to prefer these service providers (17.9% vs. 8.8%). Stock brokerage firms are equally preferred by the two groups (15.9% vs. 16.9%, respectively), while twice as many baby boomers prefer buying U.S. Treasury bills from mutual fund companies (9.0% vs. 4.7%).

Differences among Older Adults

Patronage preferences for government bonds and treasury bills differ among groups of the older population based on several sociodemographic factors such as age, income, education, and location. Also, gerontographic segments favor different types of financial institutions for government bonds and treasury bills, while the amount of money the older person holds in various types of assets also says a lot about the types of financial institutions he/she prefers to patronize for purchasing government bonds and treasury bills. Following are details about these findings.

Commercial Banks. Preferences for commercial banks as sources of government bonds and treasury bills remain high among older adults but experience a slight decline after age 75. Commercial bank patrons for government bonds and treasury bills tend to have higher incomes. Also, older adults with children within one hour's drive are more likely than their counterparts whose children live farther away to prefer purchasing government bonds and treasury bills at a bank (51.0% vs. 38.9%). Also, older adults living in eastern and northern states are more likely to patronize banks for these financial products than older Americans in other regions. Commercial banks are more likely to be preferred by frail recluses than ailing outgoers, with 53.1 percent and 46.9 percent, respectively, expressing preference for these institutions.

The more money an older person has in liquid assets, the more likely he or she is to patronize commercial banks for government bonds and treasury bills. If one excludes older consumers who patronize several types of financial institutions, two-thirds (66.1%) of bank patrons prefer to purchase government bonds and treasury bills from their bank. Although a large percentage (61.4%) of older consumers who are patrons of brokerage and mutual fund companies would buy the same products from a stock brokerage firm, a larger percentage of them (27.7%) would consider banks and fewer (15.0%) would go to a mutual fund company.

Credit Unions. With age, preferences for credit unions show a constant decline in late life. Credit unions are more likely to be favored as a source of government bonds and treasury bills by older adults who live in southern states than by those living in the West (7.8% vs. 3.0%). The more money older investors have in securities, the lower their tendency to prefer credit unions. When it comes to government bonds and treasury bill purchases, these institutions tend to be mostly patronized by older adults with lower liquid assets.

Stock Brokerages. Older people with higher incomes and education levels tend to favor stock brokerage companies more so than their lower-income and lower-education counterparts. Older people who live in urban areas are twice as likely as those who live in rural areas to patronize such companies (20.2% vs. 10.3%). A larger proportion of healthy hermits (20.5%) than ailing outgoers (15.4%) are likely to patronize stock brokerage firms.

Furthermore, the more money an older person has in liquid assets, the more likely he or she is to patronize stock brokerage firms for government bonds and treasury bills. And the more money older investors have in securities, real estate, and tangibles and collections, the greater the likelihood they will purchase these products from stock brokerage companies. If one excludes older consumers who patronize several types of financial institutions, fewer (12.0%) would purchase government bonds and treasury bills from a stock brokerage house. Although a large percentage (61.4%) of older consumers who are patrons of brokerage and mutual fund companies would buy the same products from a stock brokerage firm, a larger percentage of them (27.7%) would consider banks and fewer (15.0%) would go to a mutual fund company.

Mutual Fund Companies. Older people with higher education tend to favor mutual fund companies more than those with lower education. Also, healthy indulgers and frail recluses are more likely than ailing outgoers to prefer mutual fund companies for these financial services. The more money older investors have in securities the greater the likelihood they will purchase these products from mutual fund companies. Although a large percentage (61.4%) of older consumers who are patrons of brokerage and mutual fund companies would buy the same products from a stock brokerage firm, a larger percentage of them (27.7%) would consider banks and fewer (15.0%) would go to a mutual fund company.

Savings and Loans (S&Ls). Older people who live with others tend to prefer S&Ls more than their counterparts who live alone (11.0% vs. 7.6%). Also, a significantly greater percentage of ailing outgoers (12.8%) and frail recluses (13.2%) than healthy hermits (7.2%) is likely to prefer these associations for these financial products.

AARP. As people age in late life, they show a constant decline in their preferences for the AARP as a source for government bonds and treasury bills. And while a small percentage of older adults is likely to prefer purchasing government bonds and treasury bills through AARP, a greater percentage of southerners than easterners prefers this outlet (5.0% vs. 1.3%). Healthy hermits are less likely than any of the remaining gerontographic groups to purchase government bonds and treasury bills from AARP. Older people with fewer tangible and collections assets have a stronger tendency to patronize AARP, in comparison to mature adults who have more assets in this category. This organizations tends to be mostly patronized by older adults with lower liquid assets who are buying government bonds and treasury bills.

PATRONAGE PREFERENCES FOR MONEY MARKET FUNDS

We also wanted to know where consumers go to open a money market account. Commercial banks are the most preferred type of financial institution for money market funds, with four in ten older adults likely to have or prefer having money market accounts at banks. Two in ten (19.5%) prefer stock brokerage companies, while 17.9 percent of those 55 and older prefer S&Ls. Mutual fund companies are lower on the list of preferred institutions for money market accounts, with 11.3 percent, while credit unions and AARP are on the bottom of the list with just 8.7 and 5.5 percent of older adults preferring them, respectively.

Preferences for service providers of mutual funds are not unique to older adults but also apply to adults under 55 years of age. However, younger adults are twice as likely as older customers to prefer credit unions for mutual funds (16.4% vs. 8.6%). Younger adults are also more likely to prefer mutual fund companies for this type of service (19.7% vs 11.1%).

Baby Boomers vs. Seniors

Baby boomers' preferences for financial institutions regarding *money market funds* vary widely, with commercial banks preferred by one-third (35.8%), and most of the remaining financial-service providers (credit unions, S&Ls, stock brokerage and mutual fund companies) by about one in five. These responses differed from those given by seniors for two service providers: credit unions (18.1% vs. 6.0%) and mutual fund companies (21.8% vs. 9.4%).

Differences among Older Adults

As we look at older Americans' preferences for money market sources, we can see differences across sociodemographic characteristics. Also, there are distinct patterns of patronage preferences for money market accounts among gerontographic groups.

Responses also varied according to the assets that they possessed or would like to possess and according to the financial institutions they currently patronized.

Commercial Banks. Preferences for commercial banks as places to get money market funds declines after age 65. Older people with less education are more likely than their more educated counterparts to set up money market accounts with these institutions.

Also, commercial banks are more popular among older adults living in rural areas than among those who live in urban areas, with 46.0 percent and 39.4 percent, respectively, preferring these institutions for money market accounts. A larger percentage of southerners (44.2%) and northerners (45.1%) is likely to prefer banks for money market accounts, in comparison to their counterparts who live in eastern (34.8%) or western (30.2%) states. In comparison to their female counterparts, a lot more older male respondents expressed preferences for these institutions (44.1% vs. 37.7%). Mature Americans who live within one hour's drive from their children's location are more likely than those who do not have children in close proximity to prefer commercial banks for these financial products (40.3% vs. 29.2%). In comparison to older adults who live alone, those who live with others are more likely to prefer these institutions for this purpose (42.9% vs. 35.5%). Ailing outgoers and frail recluses are prime prospects for money market accounts at commercial banks.

The more money an older person has in the form of cash, CDs, checking and savings accounts, the more likely he or she is to prefer commercial banks as places to have a money market account. Also, commercial banks are more likely to be favored by older adults who have assets in tangibles and collections valued between $5,000 and $25,000 than among those with a larger or smaller size of assets in this area.

Credit Unions. Older people age 65 and older are twice less likely than those age 55 to 64 to prefer credit unions for money market funds. Credit unions are not very popular places to have a money market account among older adults who live in the East (2.4%), while southerners are nearly five times more likely (11.6%) to go to credit unions for money market accounts. Older Americans who live with others are more likely than those who live alone to prefer these institutions (9.8% vs. 6.4%).

Mutual Fund Companies. Adults 65 and over are less likely than those age 55 to 64 to favor opening a money market account at a mutual fund company. Preferences for these companies as providers of money market accounts increase with increasing household income and education of older adults. Northerners are more likely than southerners to have money market accounts at mutual fund companies (15.9% vs. 7.6%). And compared to older women, older men are more likely to prefer using mutual fund companies for money market accounts (14.9% vs. 8.5%). Also, older adults from families where at least one person works are more likely than their counterparts from nonworking families to prefer mutual fund companies for money market accounts (13.3% vs. 6.9%). Mature Americans who live with others are more likely than those who live alone to favor mutual fund companies (12.8% vs. 8.1%) as places to have a money market fund account. Healthy hermits are most likely to patronize mutual fund companies for money market funds, with 16.2 percent of them expressing preferences, in comparison to ailing outgoers (6.3%).

The more money an older person has in securities, real estate, and tangibles and collections, the greater his or her tendency to prefer having a money market account at a mutual fund company. Also, such companies are likely to be favored by those who have more than $5,000 in "other assets" (business, insurance, etc.) than by those who have less.

Stock Brokerage Companies. Preferences for stock brokerage companies and mutual fund companies as providers of money market accounts increase with increasing household income of older adults, but preference for AARP for such services declines. Preferences for brokerage houses as providers of money market accounts increase with increasing household income and educational level of older adults. Older men are more likely than older women to prefer stock brokerage companies for money market accounts (22.1% vs. 17.4%). Older people who live with others are more likely than their counterparts who live alone to favor stock brokerage companies for this purpose (21.6% vs. 14.4%). A larger percentage of healthy hermits (22.6%) than frail recluses (15.8%) or ailing outgoers (17.0%) prefers such companies.

The more money an older person has in securities, real estate, and tangibles and collections, the greater his or her tendency to prefer having a money market account at a stock brokerage company. Similarly, the more "other assets" (business, insurance, etc.) a person has in this category, the stronger his or her preference for stock brokerage companies as providers of money market accounts.

Savings and Loans (S&Ls). S&Ls are more likely to be preferred by westerners than by easterners (22.4% vs. 14.4%). Also, frail recluses are twice as likely as healthy hermits (24.2% vs. 12.9%) to turn to S&Ls for these products.

The more money an older person has in the form of cash, CDs, checking, and savings accounts, the more likely he or she is to prefer S&Ls for their money market account needs. Those with real estate equities exceeding $50,000 are more likely than those with equities between $5,000 and $50,000 to prefer having money market accounts at these associations. Furthermore, those who have more than $25,000 in "other assets" (business, insurance, etc.) are more likely than their counterparts with fewer assets in this category to patronize S&Ls for money market funds.

AARP. The higher an older person's annual household income, the less likely he or she is to set up money market accounts through the AARP. Also, frail recluses are the best prospects for AARP, with nearly one-tenth of them indicating preference for a money market fund through this association.

Older people who have more money in liquid assets tend to be less likely to consider AARP for money market funds than their counterparts who have less money.

PATRONAGE PREFERENCES FOR IRA/KEOGH ACCOUNTS

Respondents were asked to indicate the types of financial institutions where they would prefer to have their IRA or Keogh accounts. More than one in three (36.9%) older adults indicated commercial banks as the most preferred alternative, followed by S&Ls (16.9%) and stock brokerage firms (14.4%). One in ten of older adults would prefer to have such accounts at a credit union, and only 7.5 percent and 3.3 percent would prefer mutual fund companies and AARP, respectively.

Patronage preferences for certain financial institutions concerning IRA or Keogh accounts are different for older than for younger adults. Older adults are less likely than their younger counterparts to prefer credit unions, stock brokerage companies, and mutual fund companies for IRA or Keogh services; and they are equally likely to prefer banks and AARP.

Baby Boomers vs. Seniors

Where do baby boomers prefer to have their *IRA/Keogh account*? Forty percent (19.7%) prefer banks, in comparison with 28.9 percent of their older counterparts. About one in five baby boomers prefers credit unions and mutual fund companies, while the figures for seniors are much smaller (7.6% and 3.5%, respectively). (The smaller figures for the latter group may reflect responses to less relevant services). Stock brokerage companies and S&Ls are next on the list, with 17.9 percent and 14.6 percent of baby boomers, respectively, expressing preferences.

Differences among Older Adults

Patronage preferences for IRA/Keogh plans show marked differences across sociodemographic characteristics of older adults. Differences also surface among gerontographic groups; type and value of the older person's assets are good predictors of his or her patronage preferences for financial institutions concerning IRA or Keogh services.

Commercial Banks. In comparison to their older female counterparts, males 55 and over tend to be more likely to prefer commercial banks (42.6% vs. 31.8%) to house their IRA/Keogh plans. A greater proportion of those who live with others, in comparison to those who live alone, tend to prefer banks for this purpose (41.1% vs. 27.1%). Older adults residing in western states are less likely than other older customers living in other parts of the country to prefer commercial banks. Nearly half (46.1%) of frail recluses would turn to a commercial bank, in comparison with just one-third of healthy hermits (32.1%), healthy indulgers (35.4%), and ailing outgoers (38.2%).

The best prospective clients for IRA/Keogh accounts in commercial banks are those older adults with liquid assets in the range of $5,000 to $50,000. Financial-institution patronage for IRAs or Keogh plans is high for commercial banks, but older adults with $50,000 or more invested in securities are as likely to prefer having retirement accounts at commercial banks as they do at stock brokerage houses (28.6% and 27.4%, respectively). The more money an older person has in real estate equity, the greater the chances he or she prefers to have or open an IRA/Keogh account at a commercial bank. Mature customers who patronize banks for such services are more likely to have "other assets" valued between $5,000 and $25,000 than either smaller or larger sizes of such assets. Finally, older people with more assets in other forms are also more likely to prefer having IRA/Keogh accounts with banks.

Savings and Loans (S&Ls). Men age 55 and older are more likely than their female counterparts to prefer S&Ls for their IRA/Keogh plan needs (19.5% vs. 14.9%). The higher the older person's household income, the stronger one's patronage preferences for S&Ls as places to have one's IRA/Keogh. Also, mature Americans who live with others are more likely than those who live alone to prefer these associations (20.0% vs. 9.7%). Easterners are more likely than northerners to patronize S&Ls (21.3% vs. 15.4%). One in five (20.9%) frail recluses would deal with S&Ls, in comparison with 15.4 percent of healthy hermits and 16.0 percent of ailing outgoers.

The greater the value of one's liquid assets, the greater the inclination to patronize S&Ls for IRA or Keogh plans. In the meantime, S&Ls are patronized by older adults with the same frequency regardless of the size of their security investments. The more money an older person has in real estate equity, the greater the chances he or she prefers to have or open an IRA/Keogh account at an S&L. Furthermore, older adults whose tangibles and collections are valued between $5,000 and $25,000 are less likely than those with fewer assets to patronize S&Ls (19.5% vs. 12.3%).

Mutual Fund Companies. Compared to women age 55 and older, men in this age group are more likely to turn to mutual fund companies for IRA/Keogh plans (11.2% vs. 4.6%). The higher the older person's household income and level of educational attainment, the stronger one's patronage preferences for mutual fund companies as places to have one's IRA/Keogh. Also, older people who live with others have a stronger tendency than their counterparts who live alone to prefer mutual fund companies for IRA/Keogh plans (9.2% vs. 3.7%). Older adults who live in the North are twice as likely as their southern counterparts to patronize such companies (10.4% vs. 4.9%). Furthermore, older adults who live in households where at least one person works are more likely than those in nonworking families to patronize mutual fund companies (8.8% vs. 4.6%). In addition, those with children living within one hour's drive are more likely than those who have no children in close proximity to patronize mutual fund companies for IRA and Keogh accounts (6.0% vs. 1.7%). Mutual fund companies are more popular among healthy indulgers (11.5%) than among ailing outgoers (3.7%) and frail recluses (6.9%), while healthy hermits are more likely than ailing outgoers (8.8% vs. 3.7%) to show such preferences for mutual fund companies for IRA/Keogh plans.

Mutual fund companies tend to be patronized more by those older adults with liquid assets in excess of $5,000. Similarly, patronage of these companies for IRA/Keogh plans increases with increasing size of investments in securities. The more money an older person has in real estate equity, tangibles and collections, and/or "other assets," the greater the chances he or she prefers to have or open an IRA/Keogh account with a mutual fund company.

Credit Unions. The higher the older person's household income, the more likely he or she is to prefer having an IRA/Keogh with a credit union. Older people who live with others are more likely than their counterparts who live alone to turn to these institutions for these needs (14.1% vs. 6.9%). Easterners are less likely to patronize credit unions than older adults residing in other parts of the country. Frail recluses are twice as likely as healthy indulgers (15.6% vs. 8.2%) to patronize credit unions for IRA or Keogh plans.

Older adults with liquid assets exceeding $50,000 are more likely than those with less such assets to patronize credit unions for IRA/Keogh accounts. These institutions are twice as likely to be patronized by older adults who have securities valued less than $50,000 than by those with more money invested. Also, credit unions are more likely to be preferred by those with real estate equities valued between $5,000 and $50,000 than by older adults having a smaller or larger size of real estate equity. In the meantime, older adults whose tangibles and collections are valued between $5,000 to $25,000 are more likely than those with more assets in this category to patronize credit unions (14.2% vs. 9.6%). Furthermore, older people with more assets in other forms are also more likely to prefer having an IRA/Keogh account at a credit union.

Stock Brokerage Companies. The higher the older person's household income and level of education, the more likely he or she is to have an IRA/Keogh with a stock brokerage company. Relative to those living alone, older Americans who live with others are more likely to use brokerage houses for these products (15.8% vs. 11.1%). Stock brokerage companies are more likely to be preferred as sources of IRA/Keogh accounts among those who live in urban than in rural areas (15.8% vs. 10.4%). Older adults who live in households where at least one person works are more likely than those in nonworking families to patronize these companies (15.8% vs. 11.1%). Frail recluses are less likely than mature consumers in other gerontographic segments to patronize stock brokerage companies.

Stock brokerage companies tend to be patronized more by those older adults with liquid assets in excess of $5,000. Financial-institution patronage for IRAs or Keogh plans is high for commercial banks, but older adults with $50,000 or more invested in securities are as likely to prefer having retirement accounts at commercial banks as they do at stock brokerage houses (28.6% and 27.4%, respectively). Also, patronage of bro-kerage houses for IRA/Keogh plans increases with increasing size of investments in securities. The more money an older person has in real estate equity, tangibles and collections, and/or "other assets," the greater the chances he or she prefers to have or open an IRA/Keogh account with a stock brokerage company.

AARP. Prospective customers for IRA/Keogh accounts through AARP are more likely to live in western than eastern states (4.7% vs 1.0%). Also, frail recluses are more likely than healthy hermits to seek IRA/Keogh plans through AARP (4.6% vs. 1.6%). When it comes to IRA/Keogh plan needs, the AARP is patronized by older adults with the same frequency regardless of size of their security investments. However, the higher the older person's assets in the form of tangibles and collections, the lower the propensity to get such services from this organization.

PATRONAGE PREFERENCES FOR ASSET-MANAGEMENT SERVICES

Patronage preferences were also examined with respect to asset-management services. Respondents in our study were asked to indicate whether they would patronize any of the following institutions for asset-management services: commercial banks, credit unions, S&Ls, stock bro-kerage companies, AARP, and mutual fund companies. The majority of older adults prefer commercial banks for asset-management services, with 38.7 percent of the respondents indicating preference. One in five (19.6%) prefers stock brokerage companies. S&Ls are lower on the list of preferred institutions, with 8.8 percent indicating preference, followed by mutual fund companies (6.7%), credit unions (6.4%), and AARP (3.6%).

In order to determine the extent to which these preferences are unique to older adults or apply to the entire U.S. population, responses given by older adults were compared to those given by adults under age 55. Commercial banks are more likely to be preferred by older than younger adults (39.0% vs. 32.6%), while credit unions are twice as likely to be preferred by the former than by the latter group (13.8% vs. 6.3%). Younger adults are more likely to seek asset-management services from a stock brokerage company than their older counterparts (26.6% vs. 19.3%), while younger adults are twice as likely as their older counter-parts to patronize mutual fund companies for such services (13.6% vs. 6.6%).

Baby Boomers vs. Seniors

A rather similar patronage-preferene pattern exists for asset-management services: banks (30.4% vs. 35.4%), stock brokerage companies (23.8% vs. 18.3%), mutual fund companies (15.03% vs. 4.4%), credit unions (13.9% vs. 5.5%), and S&Ls (11.3% vs. 8.8%).

Differences among Other Adults

A number of sociodemographic differences in responses were observed among the older respondents. Also, the older person's gerontographic characteristic is likely to predict patronage preferences for asset-management services. The amount and type of assets older adults have determine their likelihood of using asset-management services as well as their patronage preference for these services. Where older people get other financial services also has a bearing on where they turn for this kind of assistance.

Commercial Banks. As mature Americans age in late life, they become less likely to turn to banks for asset-management services. With respect to urbanity, nearly half (47.7%) of older adults living in rural areas, in comparison with 36.5 percent of those who live in urban areas, are likely to patronize commercial banks for asset-management services. Commercial banks are more likely to be patronized by older adults living in northern and southern states than those living in other regions of the country. Older males are more likely than older females to patronize these institutions for asset-management service needs (43.6% vs. 34.4%). Older people who live with others are more likely than those who live alone to prefer banks for these purposes (41.3% vs. 32.8%). Commercial banks are mostly favored more by frail recluses than any other gerontographic group. Healthy hermits are less likely to prefer banks than frail recluses and ailing outgoers.

The more money older persons have in securities, the lower their propensity to patronize banks for asset management. Also, commercial banks are more likely to be favored for asset-management services by older adults whose equity in real estate ranges between $5,000 and $50,000. Among older adults who are patrons of multiple types of institutions, banks are a preferred source, along with the AARP, of asset-management advice. Finally, bank patrons prefer receiving this type of service from banks.

Credit Unions. Preferences for patronizing credit unions show little change with increasing age. These institutions are unlikely to be patronized by older adults living in eastern states, but those who live in the South and West are far more likely to patronize them for asset-management services. The higher the value of an older person's liquid assets and securities, the lower his or her propensity to patronize credit unions for asset-management services. Also, credit unions are more likely to be patronized by those with real estate equities between $5,000 and $50,000 than by those with more equity. And they are most likely to be favored by older adults with "other assets" valued between $5,000 and $50,000.

Savings and Loans (S&Ls). Preferences for S&Ls for asset-management services show little change with increasing age. Also, ailing outgoers are more likely than any other gerontographic group to prefer these associations for such services.

The greater the size of older persons' liquid assets, the greater their likelihood of patronizing S&Ls. However, the more money older persons have in securities, the lower their propensity to patronize S&Ls for these services. S&Ls are more likely to be favored by those with tangible and collections assets between $5,000 and $50,000 than by those with assets in this area greater than $50,000 or less than $5,000.

Mutual Fund Companies. As mature Americans age in late life, they become less likely to use mutual fund companies for asset management. The higher mature Americans' annual household incomes, the more likely they are to choose these kinds of companies for these services. Also, older men are more likely than their female counterparts to prefer mutual fund companies (8.7% vs. 5.1%) for asset-management services. Mature Americans who live with others are also more likely than their counterparts who live alone to turn to these companies (8.1% vs. 3.5%). Healthy hermits and healthy indulgers are more likely than ailing outgoers to prefer mutual fund companies for asset-management services.

The more money older persons have in securities and tangibles and collections, the more likely they are to turn to mutual fund companies for asset-management services. Older individuals with sizable assets in real estate are more likely to favor mutual fund companies, in comparison to those with small equities. Also, these companies are likely to be patronized for asset-management services by those with "other asset" values greater than $50,000. Finally, mutual fund companies are preferred over other types of financial-service providers by older adults who patronize them for other financial services.

Stock Brokerage Companies. As people age in late life, they become less inclined to turn to stock brokerage companies for asset management. The higher the older person's income and level of education, the greater the propensity to patronize brokerage houses for these needs. Also, a greater percentage of older adults living in urban areas than those living in rural areas (21.2% vs. 15.4%) is likely to prefer stock brokerage companies for such services. Healthy hermits favor stock brokerage companies, with nearly one in four (23.7%) of them expressing preference, in comparison to healthy indulgers (17.2%), ailing outgoers (19.8%), and frail recluses (13.3%).

The more money older persons have in securities and tangibles and collections, the higher their likelihood to patronize stock brokerage firms for asset-management services. Older individuals with sizable assets in real estate are more likely to favor stock brokerage companies, in comparison to those with small equities. Also, the more money a person has in "other assets," the greater his or her propensity to patronize stock brokerage houses for asset-management services. Finally, brokerage houses are preferred over other types of financial-service providers by older adults who patronize them for other financial services.

AARP. Older Americans' preferences for the AARP as an asset-management services provider decline as they age in late life. Among older adults who are patrons of multiple types of institutions, this organization—along with commercial banks—is a preferred source of asset-management advice.

PATRONAGE PREFERENCES FOR FINANCIAL
PLANNING SERVICES

Older adults' patronage preferences for financial planning services vary widely. Nearly one-third (31.6%) prefer receiving such services at commercial banks. Stock brokerage companies are preferred by 22.9 percent, while one in ten of those age 55 would turn to AARP for financial planning services. S&Ls are favored by only 8.7 percent of the mature consumers, while mutual fund companies and credit unions are almost equally preferred by 7.0 percent and 6.6 percent, respectively.

Patronage preferences for commercial banks are equally high among younger (under 55) and older (55+) adults. The same appears to be the case with S&Ls and AARP. However, a higher percentage of younger adults, in comparison with their older counterparts, prefers credit unions, stock brokerage companies and mutual fund companies, for financial planning services.

Baby Boomers vs. Seniors

Commercial banks and stock brokerage companies are the most probable places both groups would turn to for advice about *financial planning*, with better than one in four baby boomers expressing preference (27.6% and 25.8%, respectively). These figures compare with 32.5 percent and 22.4 percent for the older group, respectively. In relation to seniors, baby boomers show a stronger preference for credit unions (14.5% vs. 5.5%), S&Ls (11.1% vs. 8.0%), and mutual fund companies (17.6% vs. 6.3%) as places to go for financial planning services.

Differences among Older Adults

Older persons' sociodemographic characteristics, as well as the gerontographic group to which they belong, do show some influence over their preferences for financial planning services. Also, the size and type of financial assets they hold can also provide information about patronage preferences for these services. Analysis of responses to this question was also done by present use or interest in using professional financial advice.

Commercial Banks. A larger proportion of older adults who live in northern and southern states (36.4% and 32.8%, respectively) are likely to turn to commercial banks for financial planning services than older adults who live in western states (22.1%). Healthy hermits are not as likely as older adults of other gerontographic characteristics to go to banks for financial planning services. And close to half (44.9%) of those older people who patronize banks for other services would choose these institutions to provide them with financial planning assistance.

Credit Unions. Compared to mature Americans in other geographic areas, those who live in eastern states prefer credit unions the least as sources of financial planning services. Also, frail recluses are more likely than healthy hermits (10.5% vs. 4.3%) to prefer credit unions for these services.

Older persons' propensities to seek financial planning services from credit unions decreases with increasing size of their liquid assets and securities. Older adults who prefer these institutions as sources of financial planning are more likely to have tangibles and collections less than $25,000. In the meantime, credit unions are more likely to be preferred by older adults with "other assets" (insurance, business assets, etc.) valued between $5,000 and $25,000 than by those with a greater size of such assets.

Savings and Loans (S&Ls). Westerners are more likely than northerners (11.2% vs. 6.1%) to turn to S&Ls for financial planning services. Older adults who live with others are more likely than those who live alone to patronize S&Ls for these services (9.8% vs. 6.0%). Also, older adults who have children that live within one hour's drive are more likely than those who do not have children in close proximity to patronize S&Ls (8.4 % vs. 3.1%). In terms of gerontographic group preferences, S & Ls are favored more by frail recluses (11.4%) and ailing outgoers (10.8%) than by healthy hermits (6.1%). Finally, preferences for "thrift" financial institutions, including S&Ls, decrease with increasing size of security assets.

Mutual Fund Companies. A slightly greater percent (10.0%) of those who live in rural areas, in comparison to those in urban areas (6.2%), prefer mutual fund companies for financial planning services. Westerners are more likely than southerners (9.5% vs. 5.3%) to patronize these companies for such services. Also, relative to their counterparts who live alone, mature Americans who live with others have a stronger preference for mutual fund companies as financial planning service providers (8.8% vs. 2.7%). A larger proportion of older people who do not have children living in close proximity are more likely than those who live close to their children to favor mutual fund companies (4.4% vs. 0.3%) as a sources of financial planning services.

The higher the value of a mature American's security assets, the higher his or her tendency to turn to mutual fund companies for financial planning services. Owners of real estate with equities greater than $50,000 are more likely than older adults with smaller equities to patronize these companies; they are less likely than older individuals who have equities worth between $5,000 and $50,000. Also, the more assets older people have in tangibles and collections, the more likely they are to patronize mutual fund companies for financial planning services. Finally, a relatively larger percentage (69.8%) of patrons of brokerage and mutual fund companies would seek such services from their primary service provider.

Stock Brokerage Companies. The higher an older person's household income and level of educational attainment, the stronger his or her preference for stock brokerage companies. Older adults who live in urban areas are more likely than those who live in rural areas to turn to these companies for financial planning needs, with 25.2 percent and 15.7 percent, respectively, expressing preference.

Preference for stock brokerage companies as sources of financial planning services increases with increasing size of liquid assets, securities, and real estate values. Similarly, the more assets older people have in tangibles and collections, the more likely they are to patronize these firms for such services, as are those who have more assets in the "other assets" category in the form of insurance, business assets, and so on. A relatively larger percentage (69.8%) of patrons of brokerage and mutual fund companies would seek such services from their primary service provider.

AARP. Older Americans' preferences for AARP decline as they age in late life. Older males are more likely than their female counterparts to prefer receiving financial planning services from this organization (13.2% vs. 8.1%). Also, a larger proportion of ailing outgoers (13.8%) than healthy indulgers (8.4%) and healthy hermits (8.2%) prefers receiving financial planning services from AARP.

The larger the value of an older persons' liquid assets, the less likely he or she is to seek financial planning services from the AARP. Preferences for "thrift" financial institutions, including this organization, decrease with increasing size of these assets. Finally, among patrons of multiple types of financial-service providers, AARP is preferred by three-fourths of this small group of patrons.

PATRONAGE PREFERENCES FOR TAX ADVICE

Preferences for financial institutions for tax advice were examined by asking respondents to indicate their favorite financial-service provider(s).

Although respondents had the option to indicate more than one service provider, some respondents indicated multiple sources while others indicated none. This was not surprising since the need for tax advice may vary considerably. Banks appear to be favored over other institutions for tax advice among people age 55 or older, with 27.7 percent of the older respondents expressing preference. AARP is favored among 17.1 percent of the respondents, or approximately one-third of those who are AARP members. Stock brokerage companies as sources for tax advice are preferred by 15.6 percent of older adults, followed by credit unions (6.7%), S&Ls (6.1%), and mutual fund companies (2.1%).

In order to examine the extent to which these figures apply to older adults only, comparisons in responses were made between older than 55 and those under 55 years of age. Banks are equally favored by both age groups, while the remaining financial institutions are more likely to be consulted for tax advice by younger than by older adults. As expected, older adults have stronger preferences for receiving advice from AARP, since most adults under 55 years of age do not qualify for membership.

Baby Boomers vs. Seniors

One in four of both younger and older groups (24.6% vs. 26.7%, respectively) would patronize commerical banks for *tax advice*; and while as many boomers would patronize stock brokerage companies, only half as many seniors would do the same for S&Ls, and eight times as many (11.0% vs. 1.4%) prefer getting tax advice from mutual fund companies. Credit unions are preferred by twice as many baby boomers as seniors (10.9% vs. 5.7%), and while AARP is preferred by a larger percentage of seniors (13.1%), fewer baby boomers (4.4%) would turn to this association for tax advice.

Differences among Older Adults

Patronage preferences for tax advice were analyzed by selected sociodemographic characteristics. The older person's gerontographic profile is likely to predict his or her preferences for receiving tax advice from various types of financial institutions. In addition, the type and amount of an older person's assets appear to be good predictors of his or her preferences for receiving tax advice from various types of financial institutions. Since the various patronage segments were formed on the basis of the responses older adults gave to questions regarding patronage preferences for various types of financial services, the analysis of preferences for any specific service by type of institutional patron segment is expected to reflect existing patronage patterns. Thus, bank patrons tend to prefer banks for tax advice, patrons of brokerage firms and mutual fund companies would look for advice at these institutions, and patrons of thrift institutions would turn to credit unions and AARP (but not to S&Ls) for tax advice.

Commercial Banks. Regardless of age, people 55 and older equally favor banks for tax advice. Also, older people in various income brackets tend to equally favor them for this kind of assistance. However, the higher an older person's level of education, the less likely he or she is to prefer commercial banks as places from which to obtain tax advice. Older adults who live with others are more likely than those who live alone to patronize commercial banks (29.4% vs. 23.7%) for help in this area. Compared to their peers who live in rural areas, older people who live in urban areas are less likely to prefer receiving tax advice from this source (33.1% vs. 26.5%). In the meantime, over one-third (36.8%) of older adults who live in northern states prefer commercial banks for tax advice, in comparison with those who live in the eastern or western states (20.0% and 16.6%, respectively), and with a little over one-fourth (27.8%) of those living in southern states. In terms of gerontographic groups, close to one-fourth (23.7%) of healthy indulgers, in comparison to higher percentages of ailing outgoers (30.5%) and frail recluses (31.5%), prefer receiving tax advice from commercial banks.

As a source of tax advice, commercial banks are more likely to be preferred by older adults with liquid assets valued at $5,000 or more than by those whose liquid assets that do not exceed $5,000. Preference for these institutions as sources of tax advice declines with increasing value of securities. In the meantime, older adults with personal and commercial real estate equities in the range of $5,000 to $50,000 are more likely than those with a smaller equity to prefer commercial banks for tax advice (30.0% vs. 24.1%).

Credit Unions. Older people 65 to 74 years of age were more likely than their older counterparts to prefer receiving tax advice from credit unions (8.5% vs. 4.2%). Older adults with household incomes between $20,000 and $50,000 are more likely than their higher-income counterparts to prefer these institutions for tax advice (8.3% vs. 4.7%). Easterners are less likely than older adults living in other parts of the country to seek tax advice from credit unions. Among gerontographic groups, frail recluses are twice as likely as healthy hermits to seek advice about taxes from credit unions.

Credit unions as sources of advice about taxes are more likely to be preferred by those with low values in liquid assets and securities than by those with higher values in these categories. These institutions are more likely to be favored by older Americans whose real estate equity is valued between $5,000 and $50,000 than by those with higher equities (8.5% vs. 3.9%).

Savings and Loans (S&Ls). As mature Americans age in late life, they become less likely to turn to S&Ls for tax advice. Older people who live with others are more likely than their counterparts who live alone to turn to these associations (7.5% vs. 2.8%) for this reason. Older easterners are more likely than mature consumers who live in western states to seek advice from S&Ls (9.2% vs. 3.9%). The higher the value of one's tangibles and collections, the greater his or her likelihood to prefer S&Ls and stock brokerage companies for tax advice.

Mutual Fund Companies. The older a mature American, the less likely he or she is to prefer getting tax advice from mutual fund companies. Relative to their peers who live alone, older people who live with others have a stronger tendency to get tax advice from these companies (2.7% vs. 5%).

Stock Brokerage Companies. Older Americans' preferences for stock brokerage firms as sources of tax advice decline as they get older. The more education an older person has, the more likely he or she is to prefer stock brokerage companies. Older adults who live in urban areas are more likely than their rural counterparts to prefer stock brokerage companies (17.0% vs. 12.0%). Also, those with children within one hour's driving distance are more likely to seek tax advice from a stock brokerage company than those with children living farther away (19.8% vs. 10.5%). Frail recluses are less likely to turn to stock brokerage companies for tax advice than older adults in other gerontographic groups.

In terms of assets, mature Americans' preferences for brokerage companies as providers of tax advice increase with increasing value of liquid assets and of assets in securities. Similarly, preference for stock brokerage companies for this information is the strongest among those with the largest real estate equity. The higher the value of one's tangibles and collections or "other assets" (insurance, business assets, etc.), the greater his or her likelihood to prefer stock brokerage companies.

AARP. Older people's preferences for the AARP as a provider of tax advice decreases with age. A larger percentage of older males (19.4%) than females (15.1%) reports preference for getting tax advice from this organization. Also, nonworking persons are somewhat more likely to prefer AARP (20.2%) in comparison to their counterparts from families where at least one person works (15.8%). Furthermore, healthy hermits are less likely than other gerontographic groups to prefer the AARP as a source of advice on taxes.

The lower the value of an older person's liquid assets, securities, and or tangibles and collections, the more likely he or she is to turn to the AARP for tax advice. Similarly, the greater the value of an older person's "other assets" (insurance, business assets, etc.), the less likely he or she is to prefer AARP as a source for tax advice.

PATRONAGE PREFERENCES FOR INSURANCE POLICIES

The present survey also assessed patronage preferences for nontraditional institutions regarding the purchase of insurance products. About two out of three older adults indicated willingness to purchase insurance policies from nontraditional institutions. AARP was preferred by 22.0 percent, followed by commercial banks (16.3%). Credit unions were preferred by 7.4 percent of those age 55 and older, while 6.1 percent indicated they would buy insurance policies from a mutual fund company. Stock brokerage companies and S&Ls were not favored as much as providers of insurance policies.

Younger people tend to have stronger preferences for nontraditional providers of insurance services than those age 55 and older. Younger adults are more likely to prefer credit unions, stock brokerage, and mutual fund companies. Since most respondents in the younger age group do not qualify for AARP membership, they are less likely than their older counterparts to prefer buying insurance from this source.

Baby Boomers vs. Seniors

For financial products such as insurance policies, a substantially larger percentage of baby boomers would purchase them from nontraditional institutions like a commercial bank (19.0% vs. 13.5%), mutual fund company (17.2% vs. 5.1%), or credit union (14.7% vs. 5.1%); one in ten baby boomers would turn to a stock brokerage company (10.3% vs. 2.9%), and 6 percent would buy from S&Ls (6.0% vs. 4.3%); and fewer baby boomers than seniors, as expected, would turn to AARP (5.8% vs. 17.8%)

Differences among Older Adults

Older persons' preferences for where they receive insurance services can be affected by their various sociodemographic characteristics, such as gender, urbanity, geography, education, and income. Patronage preferences for purchasing insurance services from nontraditional providers show variations across gerontographic groups. There are also differences in patronage choices according to the type and size of assets held by mature Americans. Where they receive other financial and related services can also indicate where they will be likely to go for insurance services. Specifically, older people who patronize a certain financial institution also have a greater likelihood of purchasing nontraditional services, such as insurance, from that institution.

Commercial Banks. Among those 55 and older, preferences for commercial banks as a source of insurance policies decline with age. Older adults with lower education, in comparison to those with higher education, are more likely to prefer banks as providers of insurance services. Also, those in rural areas are more likely than their urban counterparts to favor commercial banks (20.8% vs. 15.3%) for these services. In the meantime, nearly one in five older adults who live in northern and southern states (19.7% and 18.1%, respectively) would go to a bank for insurance services, in comparison with those who live in eastern states (12.8%) and western regions of this country (8.0%). And in comparison to older females, older males were found to have stronger preferences for obtaining insurance services from commercial banks (18.4% vs. 14.2%). Ailing outgoers (19.8%) and frail recluses (18.5%) are more likely than healthy hermits (13.2%) to prefer commercial banks for insurance services. Furthermore, the higher the value of the older person's securities, the lower his or her inclination to express preferences for commercial banks as sources of insurance products.

Credit Unions. As mature Americans age in late life, they are less likely to turn to credit unions for their insurance needs. In the meantime, older people with incomes between $20,000 and $50,000 are more likely than those with lower incomes to prefer receiving insurance services from these institutions (9.7% vs. 4.5%). Credit unions are more likely to be preferred by older adults living in western states (10.0%), northern states (8.4%), and southern states (7.3%) than by those living in eastern states (1.9%). In addition, older males are more likely than older females to prefer obtaining insurance services from credit unions (8.9% vs 6.2%). Frail recluses are more likely than other groups to favor credit unions for insurance policies.

The higher the value of the older person's liquid assets and/or securities, the less likely he or she is to prefer purchasing insurance policies from credit unions. These institutions are somewhat more likely to be preferred by those with equity valued between $5,000 and $50,000 (9.0%) than by those having higher equities (5.1%). Also, the smaller the size of the older person's "other assets," the greater the chance he or she prefers credit unions as providers of insurance products.

Savings and Loans (S&Ls). Older adults with lower education, in comparison to those with higher education, are more likely to turn to S&Ls for their insurance service needs. Relative to their peers who live alone, mature Americans who live with others are more likely to prefer these institutions to fulfill their insurance needs (4.5% vs. 2.0%). Easterners are more likely to favor S&Ls (7.4%) than their counterparts in northern states (2.5%). Frail recluses are more likely than healthy hermits and healthy indulgers to prefer S&Ls.

Mutual Fund Companies. As older people age in late life, they become less inclined to buy insurance policies from mutual fund companies. Older people who live with others are more likely than their counterparts who live alone to prefer receiving such services from these companies (7.5% vs. 2.8%). A larger percentage of easterners (9.2%) expressed interest in getting insurance services from mutual fund companies, in comparison with 3.9% of older adults who live in western states. Older adults with larger sizes of "other assets" are also more likely to prefer mutual fund companies as providers of insurance services.

Stock Brokerage Companies. Mature Americans in the middle-income range ($20,000–$50,000) are more likely to prefer stock brokerage companies for insurance services, in comparison to those having lower incomes (5.3% vs. 1.7%). Compared to their urban-dwelling counterparts, older people who live in rural areas are less likely to prefer brokerage houses for these needs (4.6% vs. 1.7%). A larger percentage of healthy hermits (6.0%) than frail recluses (1.3%) is likely to prefer stock brokerage firms as a nontraditional source from which to buy insurance services.

The smaller the size of the older person's liquid assets, the greater his or her likelihood to prefer purchasing insurance policies from stock brokerage houses. Stock brokerage companies are more likely to be preferred by mature Americans with relatively more money invested in securities.

AARP. Older persons' preferences for the AARP as a source of insurance policies decline with age, but not to the same degree as aforementioned institutions. Prime prospects for insurance services obtained through this association live in western and southern states, with nearly one-fourth of them (24.1%) expressing preference, in comparison to those living in the east (14.8%). A little more than 20 percent (21.7%) of northerners express preference for obtaining insurance policies through AARP. Ailing outgoers are more likely than healthy hermits (25.7% vs 19.9%) to prefer buying insurance through AARP.

The smaller the size of the older person's liquid assets, the greater his or her likelihood to prefer purchasing insurance policies from this organization. In the meantime, the higher the value of the older person's securities, the lower his or her inclination to express preferences for the AARP as a source of insurance products. In the meantime, the AARP is more likely to be preferred by those with equity valued between $5,000 and $50,000 than by those with smaller values of real estate equity.

REASONS FOR PATRONIZING FINANCIAL INSTITUTIONS

What are the main reasons older people patronize certain financial institutions? Respondents in our survey were presented with a list of reasons for patronizing financial institutions and they were asked to check those reasons which apply to their decision to start or continue to patronize a specific financial institution. Respondents could check more than one reason. Older adults' main reason for initiating and continuing their financial provider patronage behavior is found in the provider's staff or personnel's ability/willingness to explain various financial services, with 42.6 percent of the older respondents indicating this factor to be important. Convenience in reaching the service provider is also important, with 38.1 percent of the older respondents indicating this reason. Almost the same percent of mature people (38.0%) value the ease of doing business by phone or by mail, and a somewhat smaller percentage (36.4%) indicate that ease of getting related services at the same place is important. Three out of ten attribute their patronage decision to the financial institution's personnel or ability of its staff to assist them with filling out forms (30.1%), and to reasonable prices or fees (29.8%).

Personal influence appears to play a secondary role in the older person's patronage decision. A little over one in four considers referrals and endorsements by firms or professionals (22.3%) and advice of other people their age (21.1%) to be important. Age-based (senior) discounts are considered important by 17.9 percent of the older adults, while 16.5 percent of them think that billing or payment methods are important factors. Other factors mentioned to be important by at least one-tenth of mature people include advice of children or close relatives (14.3%), group/membership programs (12.3%), and proper age-stereotyping of older people in advertisements (11.6%).

In order to examine whether these responses apply only to older consumers or are common among older and younger adults, responses to the same questions given to mature people were compared to those of younger (under 55) adults. Only two factors, convenience in reaching the service provider and senior discounts, are valued more by older than by younger adults, although the latter reason is not relevant to the younger age group. Three other factors (ease of doing business by phone or mail, special deals or membership programs, and preference for spokespersons in ads) are of equal importance to both younger and older groups. However, a larger percentage of younger than older adults considers the remaining reasons to be important in their patronage decision concerning financial institutions.

Baby Boomers vs. Seniors

Two patronage motives appear to stand out: convenience in reaching the service provider and personnel/staff's ability or willingness to explain various services (see Table 9.2). Nearly half of baby boomers, compared with one-third of seniors, indicated these two reasons. About four in ten of the younger generation decide to patronize certain financial institutions because of their prices/fees (47.4%), ease of getting related services at the same place (40.8%), and ease of doing business by phone or by mail (41.8%); and a somewhat smaller percentage (about one-third) of the seniors indicated these factors are important. Also, of importance to the younger group is personnel/staff's assistance in filing out forms (36.8%), referrals/endorsements (32.7%), and advice of same-age peers

Table 9.2
Reasons for Patronizing Financial Institutions among Baby Boomers and
Seniors (65+) (Percent Who Feel Reason Is Applicable)

Reasons for Patronizing	Baby Boomers (%)	Seniors (%)
Reasonable prices or fees	49.45	26.84
Convenience in reaching the service provider	47.04	34.76
Ease of getting related services at the same place	40.86	30.86
Explanation of various services by staff/personnel	48.20	34.66
Personnel/staff assistance with filling out forms	36.79	24.81
Discounts to age groups (children, seniors)	10.13	15.66
Preference for billing/payment methods	21.48	13.57
You like the way their ads show people your age	9.92	11.44
Special deals through group or membership programs	10.15	9.64
Advice of children or close relatives	23.19	13.55
Advice of other people your age	30.09	17.96
Referrals/endorsements by firms or professionals	32.69	21.19
Ease of doing business by phone or by mail	41.77	32.27
Base:	(N = 589)	(N = 236)

(30.1%), while smaller percentages of seniors indicated the importance of these factors.

Differences among Older Adults

Reasons for patronizing financial institutions are likely to differ across older adults according to social and demographic factors. There are some generalities: for example, older men place more emphasis on the various factors than do older females, possibly reflecting women's lower involvement with financial decisions, traditionally dominated by males. And generally, most patronage reasons are considered more important by those who live with others than by those who live alone. Regardless of the older person's location, older adults who live in urban and rural areas perceive the patronage factors as of equal importance.

The older person's gerontographic profile appears to be a good indicator of his or her inclination to take certain factors into consideration in patronage decisions. Only the importance of billing methods, fees charged by financial institutions, and referrals are not likely to vary across gerontographic clusters. Furthermore, older adults' perceptions of the importance of various criteria in patronage decisions are likely to be conditioned by the type and size of their financial assets.

Also, older adults who favor certain type(s) of financial institutions for several services over other types of institutions tend to consider somewhat different reasons for patronizing them. For example, patrons of brokerage firms and mutual fund companies appear to be very sophisticated consumers. They consider a large number of factors in their decision to patronize certain financial institutions. Patrons of multiple types of institutions are also likely to consider multiple factors in their patronage decisions, while bank patrons are very similar to patrons of thrift institutions in the value they place on certain factors. The following differences were found on a factor-by-factor basis.

Staff/Personnel Service Explanations. The importance mature Americans place on this factor when making a decision about financial institution patronage declines as they age in late life. The higher an older person's annual household income, the more likely he or she is to place importance on this factor. Explanation of various services by staff/personnel is more important to older people with more education that it is to their peers with lower levels of education. With respect to geographic location, older adults who live in northern states tend to value this factor more than their counterparts who live in eastern and southern regions of the country. In terms of gerontographic groups, explanation of various services by staff or personnel is mostly valued by healthy indulgers (51.1%) and frail recluses (47.3%). Older adults who have security assets valued in excess of $50,000 are more likely than those who have fewer assets in securities to factor this element into their patronage decision. The larger the size of one's real estate equity and or the value of one's "other assets" (insurance, business assets, etc.), the more likely the older person is to consider personnel or staff's willingness/ability to explain various financial services. Those with assets in tangibles and collections valued at $5,000 or more are also more likely than those having less of these assets to consider this factor when assessing financial institutions.

Convenience in Reaching the Service Provider. The importance mature Americans place on this factor when making a decision about financial institution patronage declines as they age in late life. Older people with higher annual household incomes are more likely than their counterparts with relatively lower incomes to emphasize this convenience when deciding on a financial institution. Older people with higher levels of education are less likely than their less educated counterparts to consider convenience in reaching service providers. This service element is more important to older people who live with others than it is to their counterparts who live alone (41.2% vs. 30.7%). About half (49.0%) of healthy indulgers think that convenience in reaching the service provider is important in patronage decisions. This figure compares with 40.6 percent of frail recluses, 37.1 percent of healthy hermits, and just 30.6 percent of ailing outgoers. The higher the value of one's "other assets" (insurance, business assets, etc.), the more likely the older person is to take into consideration how convenient it is to reach the service provider.

Ease of Doing Business by Phone or by Mail. The importance mature Americans place on the ease of doing business via phone or mail when making a decision about financial institution patronage declines as they age in late life. The higher an older person's annual household income, the more likely he or she is to place importance on this factor. The ease of doing business by phone or by mail is more important to mature Americans with higher levels of education than it is to their counterparts with relatively lower levels of education. Older adults from families where at least one person still works are more likely than mature people from families where no person is in the labor force to consider this factor important. Healthy indulgers are more likely to value the convenience of doing business by phone or mail (44.5%) in comparison to healthy hermits (35.7%) and ailing outgoers (35.5%).

Older adults who have security assets valued in excess of $50,000 are more likely than those who have fewer assets in securities to consider the option of doing business by phone or by mail in their patronage decision. The higher the value of an older person's real estate equity and/or "other assets" (insurance, business assets, etc.), the more likely he or she is to consider this factor. Those with assets in tangibles and collections valued at $5,000 or more are also more likely than those having less of these assets to place importance on the ease with which they can do business with an institution by phone or by mail. Finally, patrons of multiple types of institutions are likely to value factors which relate to convenience.

Ease of Getting Related Services at the Same Place. The importance mature Americans place on this factor when making a decision about financial institution patronage declines as they age in late life. The higher an older person's annual household income, the more likely he or she is to consider the ease of getting related services at various financial institutions. In the meantime, mature Americans who live with others are more likely than those who live alone to be concerned with the ease of getting related services at the same place (39.5% vs. 29.1%). A larger percentage of older people who live with others, compared to the proportion of their counterparts who live alone, indicates that this factor is important to their decisions about financial institutions (39.9% vs. 33.4%). Ease of getting related services at the same place is of greater importance to healthy indulgers (45.2%) than to any other gerontographic group.

The larger the size of one's real estate equity and/or the value of "other assets" (insurance, business assets, etc.), the more likely the older person is to consider this factor. Those with assets in tangibles and col-lections valued at $5,000 or more are also more likely (than those with values under this figure) to consider the ease of getting related services at the same place. Finally, patrons of thrift institutions are more likely than bank patrons to evaluate financial-service providers on the basis of ease of getting related services from the same source.

Staff Assistance with Filling Out Forms. The importance mature Ameri-cans place on staff assistance with filling out forms when choosing a financial institution declines as they age in late life. The higher an older person's annual household income, the more likely he or she is to place importance on this factor. Among gerontographic groups, frail recluses are more likely than healthy hermits to need assistance with filling out forms (35.2% vs. 25.4%).

The higher the value of one's "other assets" (insurance, business as-sets, etc.), the more likely the older person is to take into consideration the availability and willingness of personnel/staff to help fill out forms. Also, patrons of multiple types of institutions are likely to value factors such as this one which relate to personnel assistance.

Prices/Fees. The importance of prices remains relatively unchanged in late life. However, the higher an older person's annual household income and level of educational attainment, the more likely he or she is to place importance on prices when considering various financial institutions. A larger percentage of older adults who live with others are more likely than those who live alone to attach importance to prices or fees charged (32.3% vs. 23.9%).

Older adults who have security assets valued in excess of $50,000 are more likely than those who have fewer assets in securities to consider prices and fees in their patronage decision. The larger the size of an older person's real estate equity or of "other assets" (insurance, business as-sets, etc.), the more likely he or she is to consider fees charged by finan-cial institutions when seeking a service provider.

Referrals. The importance of referrals remains relatively unchanged in late life. The higher an older person's annual household income, the more likely he or she is to indicate that referrals from professionals are important in making decisions about financial institutions. Compared to their counterparts with less education, older people with relatively higher levels of education are more likely to emphasize referrals or en-dorsements when making these patronage decisions. The advice of other professionals also is more important to older people who live with others than to those who live alone (24.3% vs. 17.6%).

The more liquid assets older persons have, the more likely they are to mention they patronize financial institutions because the staff/personnel explain various services and as a result of referrals or endorsements by other firms or professionals. The larger the size of their securities assets, real estate equity, and/or their "other assets" (insurance, business assets, etc.), the more older adults tend to rely on referrals or endorsements by other firms or professionals in choosing a financial institution. Also, older adults who have security assets valued in excess of $50,000 are more likely than those who have fewer assets in securities to consider refer-rals/endorsements by firms or professionals when considering patron-age options. The higher the value of a mature American's tangibles and collection assets, the more likely he or she is to consider this factor.

Finally, patrons of brokerage firms and mutual fund companies are more likely than those who rely on other types of institutions for finan-cial services in general to take into consideration referrals and endorse-ments by firms or professionals. In the meantime, bank patrons are more likely than thrift institution patrons to consider this element when de-ciding on a financial institution.

Peer Influences. The importance mature Americans place on this factor when making a decision about financial institution patronage declines as they age in late life. And when considering different financial institu-tions, men and women place about the same emphasis on advice from other people their age. Mature Americans living with others have a stronger tendency than those who live alone to place importance on the advice of people of similar age (23.5% vs. 15.2%) when making these decisions. Advice of other people of similar age is more important among older adults with incomes between $20,000 and $50,000 than among those with lower incomes (24.5% vs. 16.0%). It is more valuable to north-erners than to southerners (24.3% vs. 17.6%). In looking at geronto-graphic groups, we see that ailing outgoers place more emphasis on word-of-mouth communication from peers of similar age than do frail recluses (25.8% vs. 17.9%).

The larger the size of one's real estate equity, the more likely the older person is to consider the advice of other people of the same age when assessing financial institutions. Also, this input is more important to older adults with "other assets" (insurance, business assets, etc.) exceed-ing $5,000 than to those with fewer assets in this category.

Senior Discounts. The importance of senior discounts remains relatively unchanged in late life. Preference for senior discounts as an attribute in patronage decisions is not sensitive to the older person's household in-come. Frail recluses and healthy hermits are likely to differ with respect to the importance they place on senior discounts, with a larger percent-age of the former group (24.2%) than of the latter group (13.4%) citing this reason. Senior discounts are more likely to be considered as a pa-tronage reason by those who have liquid assets between $5,000 and $50,000 than by those older adults with a smaller size of liquid assets (21.4% vs. 10.3%).

Payment/Billing Options. The importance mature Americans place on this factor when making a decision about financial institution patronage declines as they age in late life. Billing/payment preferences were shown not to be sensitive to the older person's household income. A larger percentage of older people who live with others, compared to the portion of those who live alone, places importance on billing or payment methods (18.7% vs. 11.1%) when considering financial institutions.

The importance of billing or payment methods and age-stereotypes in ads declines with increasing size of the older person's securities. In addition, older adults with real estate valued between $5,000 and $50,000 are more likely than their counterparts with less or no equity (18.3% vs. 11.9%) to choose a financial institution because they like its billing/payment policy.

Age-Based Discounts. The importance mature Americans place on this factor when making a decision about financial institution patronage declines as they age in late life. The higher an older person's annual household income, the more likely he or she is to place importance on age-based discounts when considering different financial institutions.

Finally, patrons of multiple types of institutions are likely to value senior discounts when making a decision about what financial institutions they will patronize.

Family Advice. The importance of advice of relatives remains relatively unchanged in late life. Also, both older males and older females equally consider the advice of relatives when deciding on financial institutions. The higher an older person's annual household income, the more likely he or she is to place importance on this factor. Older adults who live alone and have children in close proximity are more likely to contact them for advice, in comparison to those who have no immediate access to their children (23.5% vs. 7.6%). Advice of family members on patronage decisions concerning financial institutions has a stronger influence on ailing outgoers than frail recluses (17.9% vs. 12.4%).

Club/Membership Programs. The importance mature Americans place on this factor when making a decision about financial institution patronage declines as they age in late life. Preference for senior membership programs as an attribute in patronage decisions is a factor not sensitive to the older person's household income. Also, ailing outgoers are more receptive to special deals through these programs than are healthy hermits (15.0% vs. 9.7%).

Age-Stereotypes. The importance of age-stereotypes in ads remains relatively unchanged in late life. Older males and females place importance on the way ads portray older people in their decision to patronize financial institutions at about the same rate. Also, the higher the older person's household income, the higher the likelihood the individual wants ads to properly portray people of his or her age. While only a small percentage of older Americans consider the way older people are portrayed in ads, a larger percentage of ailing outgoers (14.7%) than healthy hermits (9.5%) or frail recluses (8.6%) cites this reason to be an important patronage motive.

USE OF CREDIT CARDS

Respondents in our study were asked to indicate the credit cards they frequently use; they were presented with a list of credit cards and asked to indicate those cards they had used in the previous six months. Three-fourths (75.3%) of older adults had used a department store card in the previous six months, and two-thirds (65.2%) of them had used Visa. Less than half (46.6%) had used MasterCard, and 42.9 percent said they had used gasoline cards. One in five (21.8%) had used Discover and 11.8 percent used American Express. Diners Club or Carte Blanche had been used by a substantially smaller percentage of older adults (2.3%). With respect to the number of credit cards used, nearly two-thirds of the older adults used one to three cards in the previous six months; 22.3 percent used four or more.

A comparison between younger and older adults with regard to use of credit cards provides interesting insights. The reader should be reminded, however, that this analysis does not take into account (1) the opportunities for using one's credit cards and (2) the respondent's ability to recall accurately the cards used in the previous six months. Given that older people tend to shop less frequently and have a greater difficulty in remembering and recalling information than their younger counterparts, the numbers may underestimate credit card use of older adults. Both age groups were found to use department store cards, gasoline cards, and Diners Club or Carte Blanche equally the same. However, younger adults are more likely than older adults to use the remaining credit cards; and they are more likely to use a larger number of credit cards as well.

Baby Boomers vs. Seniors

Another objective of this research was to examine the number and types of credit cards used by baby boomers and elderly. Respondents were asked to indicate the credit card they had used in the previous six months from the following list: Visa, Discover, MasterCard, American Express, Diners Club or Carte Blanche, department store card, and gasoline card. The number of credit cards used was grouped into three categories: none, 1–3, and 4 or more (see Table 9.3).

Baby boomers appear to use a larger number of credit cards than their senior counterparts. While the number of credit cards reportedly used is higher for baby boomers, the data should not be interpreted as frequency

Table 9.3
Use of Credit Cards by Baby Boomers and Seniors (65+)

	Baby Boomers (%)	Seniors (%)
Used in Past Six Months		
Visa	73.62	59.37
Discover	28.03	15.75
MasterCard	51.57	41.45
American Express	23.75	7.84
Department store card	71.35	76.56
Diners Club or Carte Blanche	1.66	1.43
Gasoline card	47.01	42.00
Number of Credit Cards		
0	13.24	10.43
1–3	59.38	70.26
4 or more	30.19	16.50
Base:	(N = 596)	(N = 248)

of credit used by the two groups. Department store cards are the credit cards used least frequently by baby boomers with 71.3 percent of them reporting usage in the previous six months (compared with 76.6% of seniors). Both groups collectively use department store cards more than other cards. Visa is also popular among baby boomers, with 73.6 percent of them reporting usage (compared with 59.4 percent of seniors), while MasterCard is used by 51.6 percent and 41.4 percent of the two groups, respectively. Baby boomers are three times as likely as seniors to report use of American Express (23.7% vs. 7.8%) and nearly twice as likely to use Discover (28.0% vs. 15.7%). Finally, use of gasoline cards by the two groups is rather high, with 47 and 42 percent, respectively, indicating use. Use of other premium cards (Diners and Carte Blanche) is negligible.

Profile of Older Users

Users of credit cards can be profiled on the basis of several demographic, socioeconomic, gerontographic, and financial-asset characteristics. The four financial-institution patron groups (banks, broker/mutual fund, thrifts, and multiple) who also make different use of certain types of credit cards are included.

Generally speaking, the number of credit cards used by mature Americans declines with age in late life. Older males tend to use a larger number of cards than their female counterparts. With increasing income and levels of educational attainment, older adults use a larger number of credit cards. Furthermore, compared to mature Americans from non-working families, those from families in which someone works are more likely to use a larger number of credit cards. Older people who live with others and/or who live in urban areas tend to use a larger number of credit cards than those who live alone and/or live in rural areas.

The more liquid assets, securities, and/or tangibles and collections assets an older person has, the greater his or her likelihood to use a large number of credit cards. Also, mature people who have larger real estate equities are more likely than their counterparts with smaller values in real estate to use a large number of cards to pay for products and services they buy. Similarly, the higher an older person's "other assets" (insurance, business assets, etc.), the more cards he or she is likely to use. Patrons of brokerage firms and mutual fund companies tend to use a larger number of credit cards in general.

Department Store Cards. Use of department store cards remains fairly constant in late life, showing little variation across the three age groups of older adults (55–64, 65–74, 75+). However, older females are more likely than their male counterparts to use these cards. Use of department store cards within the six-month period surveyed was not sensitive to the older person's household income. Also, the higher his or her annual household income, the more likely an older American is to use these cards. Department store cards are used with the same frequency by older people of all education levels. The use of these cards is higher among those older adults from families without a working member than it is among those in families where at least one person works. In terms of gerontographic groups, frail recluses are more likely than healthy hermits (78.1% vs. 72.6%) to use department store cards.

Department store cards are more likely to be used by those who have either sizeable ($50,000 or more) or few (under $5,000) assets invested in real estate. Patrons of brokerage firms and mutual fund companies are more likely than patrons of banks and thrifts to use department store cards.

Gasoline. Use of gasoline cards remains fairly constant in late life, showing little variation across the three age groups of older adults (55–64, 65–74, 75+). Older males are more likely than older females to use this kind of credit card. Also, older people with higher household incomes and education levels are more likely than their less educated counterparts with relatively lower incomes to use it. Mature people living with others are more likely than their counterparts living alone to use this kind of card. Southerners are twice as likely as their eastern counterparts (54.3% vs. 27.5%) to use gasoline cards. In looking at gerontographic groups, we see that frail recluses are more likely than healthy hermits to use gasoline cards (48.6% vs. 39.9%).

In terms of assets, gasoline cards are more likely to be used by older adults who have $50,000 or more in real estate equity than by those whose equity is valued between $5,000 and $50,000. The higher the value of their tangibles and collections and/or their "other assets" (insurance, business assets, etc.), the greater older people's propensity to use them.

Diners Club or Carte Blanche. Use of Diners Club or Carte Blanche cards remains fairly constant in late life, showing little variation across the three age groups of older adults (55–64, 65–74, 75+). Older males are more likely than older females to use these cards. The higher a mature American's household income, the more likely he or she is to use them. Older people's use of Diners Club or Carte Blanche is the same across various education backgrounds. Those from families where only one person works are more likely than those from nonworking families to use Diners Club or Carte Blanche. Mature people living with others are more likely than their counterparts living alone to use these cards.

Visa. As mature Americans get older, they tend to use Visa cards less frequently. Both male and female adults are equally likely to use this card. However, the higher an older person's annual household income and level of educational attainment, the more likely he or she is to use Visa. And Visa users live predominantly in urban areas.

Older adults with liquid assets in excess of $5,000 are more likely than those with liquid assets less than $5,000 to use Visa. Those with more assets in securities are also more likely than their counterparts with lesser amounts in this category to use this card. It is more likely to be used by older adults who have larger commercial and personal real estate equities than by those with smaller equities. The higher the value of their tangibles and collections and/or of their "other assets" (insurance, business assets, etc.), the greater older people's propensity to use Visa. Finally, Visa is used more by broker/mutual fund and multiple institutional patrons than by those older adults who patronize banks and thrift institutions.

MasterCard. Older Americans' use of MasterCard declines as they age in late life. Relative to their female counterparts, older males have a stronger tendency to use this particular card. Compared to their counterparts with relatively lower household incomes and levels of education, mature Americans with higher incomes and more education are more likely to pull out a MasterCard. Older adults from families where only one person works are more likely than those from nonworking families to use MasterCard. Also, mature people living with others are more likely than their counterparts living alone to use this card.

A larger percentage of MasterCard users (50.2%) has liquid assets between $5,000 and $50,000, than of either those with less (41.8%) or more

(44.1%) liquid assets. The higher the value of their tangibles and collections, the greater the older people's propensity to use this card.

American Express. The American Express card is used less by older people as they age in late life. Older males are more likely than older females to use it, as are older people with higher household incomes when compared to those with relatively lower incomes. Similarly, mature Americans with more education are more likely than their relatively less educated counterparts to use an American Express. Older adults from families where only one person works are more likely to use American Express than those from nonworking families. In addition, mature people living with others are more likely than their counterparts living alone to use this card. Older adults who have children in close proximity are more likely to use American Express than those who have no children within one hour's drive (15.3% vs. 2.4%). Furthermore, this particular card's most frequent users appear to live in southern states, while those who live in northern states use it less frequently (17.1% vs. 6.7%).

Older people with more assets in securities are more likely than those with relatively lower values in this category to use American Express. It is more likely to be used by older adults who have larger commercial and personal real estate equities than by those with smaller equities. The higher the value of their tangibles and collections and of their "other assets" (insurance, business assets, etc.), the stronger older people's tendency to use American Express. American Express is more likely to be used by older adults who tend to patronize brokers and mutual fund companies for a variety of financial services than by any other patron group.

Discover. Older people's use of the Discover card declines as they age. Older men and women tend to use this card at about the same rate. The higher a mature American's annual household income, the more likely he or she is to use a Discover card. However, older people's educational level was shown to have no bearing on the frequency with which they use it. Mature people living with others are more likely than their counterparts living alone to use Discover. Older adults who have children in close proximity are less likely to use it (12.2% vs. 24.7%).

Users of Discover are more likely to have liquid assets valued less than $50,000. Discover is used more by broker/mutual fund and multiple institutional patrons than by those older adults who patronize banks and thrift institutions.

Needs/Concerns of Users of Specific Cards

Users of specific cards were profiled with regard to their main needs and concerns in day-to-day life. Ten concerns/needs were used to profile the users/nonusers of seven different credit cards.

Visa. Users of Visa differ from users of other credit cards with respect to a number of needs/concerns. A larger percentage of them, in comparison to Discover users, is: concerned with improving or maintaining their health condition through exercise and diet (65.0% vs. 59.4%); and being able to make significant contributions to charities (15.3% vs. 12.3%). Visa users, in comparison to American Express users, are more concerned with having to depend on others for routine daily tasks (34.0% vs. 21.6%), and taking time to enjoy simple things in life (34.5% vs. 28.5%).

Discover. Users of Discover differ from users of other credit cards with respect to a number of needs/concerns. A larger percentage of them, in comparison to Visa users, is concerned with being able to work after retirement (16.9% vs. 13.6%). In comparison to American Express users, a larger percentage of them is concerned with having to depend on others for routine daily tasks (37.6% vs. 21.6%), with maintaining the respect of others in late life (39.5% vs. 22.5%), and with taking time to enjoy simple pleasures in life (35.7% vs. 28.5%).

MasterCard. Users of MasterCard differ from those of other credit cards in a number of ways. In comparison to users of American Express, MasterCard users are concerned with having to depend on others for routine daily tasks (37.1% vs. 21.6%) and with maintaining the respect of others in late life (37.0% vs. 22.5%).

American Express. Users of American Express are the least concerned credit card users in the ten areas examined.

Department Store Cards. Users of department store cards differ from users of other credit cards. In comparison to users of Discover, a larger percentage of them is concerned with making significant contributions to charities (17.2% vs. 12.3%). In comparison to users of American Express, users of department store cards are more concerned with having to depend on others for routine daily tasks (34.6% vs. 21.6%), making significant contributions to charities (17.2% vs. 11.5%), enjoying simple pleasures in life (36.2% vs. 28.5%), and with maintaining the respect of others in late life (39.9% vs. 22.5%).

Diners Club/Carte Blanche. While there appear to be significant differences between the percentages of those who use these cards and users of the remaining cards, these percentages should be interpreted with caution because of the small sample size of respondent users of these two cards.

Gasoline Cards. Users of gasoline cards differ from users of other cards in a number of ways. In comparison to users of Discover, a larger percentage of them is concerned with making significant contributions to charities (16.4% vs. 12.3%). In comparison to users of American Express, a larger percentage of them is concerned with being able to take care of themselves when they get older (58.0% vs. 52.9%), having to depend on others for routine daily tasks (37.6% vs. 21.6%), being able to make significant contributions to charities (16.4% vs.11.5%), and maintaining the respect of others in late life (38.1% vs.22.5%). However, it should be noted that these comparisons assume that older adults used only one credit card in the previous six months, suggesting caution with these figures.

ASSET OWNERSHIP AND COMPOSITION

The study also sought to determine the asset composition of Americans. Respondents were asked to indicate the approximate value of their household assets in the following areas: (1) cash, CDs, checking and savings accounts; (2) stocks, bonds, or mutual funds; (3) tangibles and collections (jewelry, cars, artwork, etc.); (4) real estate equity (personal and commercial); and (5) other assets (business owned, insurance value, etc.). Response categories were: less than $5,000, $5,000–$24,999, $25,000–$49,999, $50,000–$99,999, and $100,000 or more.

Nearly one in three (32.4%) older Americans has liquid assets in excess of $50,000, and half of them (47.8%) estimate such assets between $5,000 and $50,000. However, half of them (49.4%) have less than $5,000 in securities and one-fourth have stocks, bonds, or mutual funds valued between $5,000 and $50,000. Nearly one in four (18.4%) has less than $5,000 in real estate equity, with another half of them estimating the value of their equities between $5,000 and $50,000.

About one in three (30.8%) estimates his or her value of tangibles and collections in excess of $25,000; and one-fourth (24.0%) of older Americans value such assets at less than $5,000. The distribution of other assets is skewed, with nearly half of them (46.7%) reporting values under $5,000 and three in ten (30.8%) estimating such assets in excess of 30.8 percent.

Asset composition of older Americans was also compared to that of their younger counterparts. Asset composition of the two groups differs in several ways. Older adults have a larger portion of assets in liquid form, securities, and real estate.

Baby Boomers vs. Seniors

The percentage of baby boomers who own more than $50,000 of liquid assets is four times lower than that of their senior counterparts (10.2% vs. 39.3%) (see Table 9.4). Baby boomers also own fewer securities valued at $5,000 or more (34.3% vs. 47.9%) and real estate valued at $50,000 or more (43.7% vs. 60.0%). On the other hand, the younger generation has more money invested in tangibles and collections than the older generation, with 70.4 percent and 65.2 percent, respectively, indicating amounts in excess of $5,000; and they have more in "other assets," with

Table 9.4
Asset Composition among Baby Boomers and Seniors (65+)

	Baby Boomers (%)	Seniors (%)
Cash, CDs, checking and savings accounts ($50,000 or more)	10.22	39.33
Stocks and bonds/mutual funds ($5,000 or more)	34.27	47.92
Tangibles and collections ($5,000 or more)	70.43	65.16
Real estate equity ($50,000 or more)	43.73	60.05
Other assets ($5,000 or more)	49.16	38.04
Base:	(N = 597)	(N = 249)

49.2 percent and 38.0 percent, respectively, reporting more than $5,000 in such investments.

Profiles of Older Asset Holders

The older person's assets in the five main categories vary by selected demographics, gerontographic characteristics of older Americans, and by the different types of financial institutions they patronize for the majority of their financial-services needs. There are a few differences regarding the general concerns of different asset-holding groups (health, independence, etc.) and in their preferred information sources. As the following profiles reflect, asset composition was also analyzed by payment-system groups: cash/check only, credit card/senior membership discounts or programs, and user multiple methods.

Liquid. As a group, as people age they keep more of their assets in liquid accounts. A larger percentage of males, in comparison to the proportion of females, has liquid assets in excess of $50,000 (29.2% vs. 22.8%). The older person's propensity to report higher values of these assets increases with income and education. Compared to those from nonworking families, older Americans from homes where at least one person works report higher liquid values. In comparison to those who live farther than one hour's drive from their children, those who live closer to their children are more likely to have assets in this category in excess of $50,000 (62.0% vs. 27.5%). Older people who live in urban areas are more likely than their rural counterparts to have liquid assets in excess of $50,000 (26.7% vs. 20.8%). A larger percentage of healthy hermits (28.1%) than frail recluses (23.6%) and healthy indulgers (21.1%) reports liquid assets in excess of $50,000. A larger percentage of bank patrons (37.2%), in comparison to no more than one-fourth of aged consumers of the remaining patronage groups, reports liquid assets in excess of $50,000. The more liquid assets older persons have, the more they are preoccupied with improving or maintaining their health condition through exercise and diet, as well as with finding ways to enjoy themselves. In the meantime, older people who have fewer liquid assets are more concerned with maintaining their social and economic independence by means of working after retirement or making better investments.

Finally, users of credit cards and membership programs have larger investments ($50,000+) in liquid accounts (38.5%) than users of multiple payment systems (28.9%) and cash /check only users (31.8%).

Securities. The percentage of older Americans that has more than $5,000 in securities and tangibles and collections does not change much with age in late life. A larger percentage of males, in comparison to the proportion of females, has securities over $5,000 (52.0% vs. 40.3%). The older person's propensity to report higher values of these assets increases with income and education. Older adults who live with others, in comparison to those who live alone, report higher incidence of security assets in excess of $5,000 (46.7% vs. 40.2%). Compared to those who live farther than one hour's drive from their children, fewer of those who live closer to their children have assets in this category valued at $5,000 or more (35.3% vs. 46.7%). And relative to their rural counterparts, urban-dwelling older people are more likely to have securities valued at over $5,000 (49.1% vs. 35.5%). About half of healthy hermits (51.9%) and ailing outgoers (49.2%), in comparison with frail recluses (39.6%) and healthy indulgers (37.8%), report investments in excess of $5,000 in securities. Also, a larger percentage of bank patrons (71.6%), in comparison with patrons of brokerage and mutual fund companies (51.0%) and thrift institutions (57.4%), has $5,000 or more invested in securities. The more securities older persons have, the more they are preoccupied with improving or maintaining their health condition through exercise and diet, as well as with finding ways to enjoy themselves. At the same time, older adults who have lower amounts invested in securities are more concerned with maintaining their social and economic independence by means of working after retirement or making better investments. A larger percentage of those who have security investments in excess of $5,000 prefers to hear news from an agent (71.6%) and TV or print ads (69.9%) than to receive information in the mail (65.1%) or learn in group meetings (65.4%). Nearly three-fourths (73.9%) of older Americans who have securities in excess of $5,000 use credit and senior discounts/programs to pay for a variety of goods and services they buy, in comparison with 59.2 percent of multiple-method payment users and 67.2 percent of cash/check only users.

Tangibles and Collections. The older person's propensity to report higher tangible and collections assets increases with income and education. A larger percentage of older adults who live with others, compared to the proportion of those who live alone, possesses assets in this category valued at over $5,000 (80.1% vs. 63.3%). A larger percentage of urban-dwelling older people, relative to the proportion of those in rural areas, reported having tangibles and collections in excess of $5,000 (77.8% vs. 66.2%). In addition, a larger percentage of westerners (79.6%) and southerners (77.2%) than northerners has assets in this category worth $5,000 or more. In terms of gerontographic groups, tangible assets are widely held by ailing outgoers, with nearly nine in ten (89.5%) expressing values in such assets in excess of $5,000, in comparison with three-fourths of frail recluses.

Real Estate. As mature Americans age in late life, they have fewer assets in real estate. A larger percentage of males, in comparison to the proportion of females, has real estate equity in excess of $50,000 (73.3% vs. 55.3%). The older person's propensity to report higher values of these assets increases with income and education. Compared to those who are in families where nobody works, older Americans from homes where at least one person works report higher real estate equities. In addition, compared to their peers who live alone, mature Americans who live with others are more likely to have real estate equity valued at more than $50,000 (69.5% vs. 46.4%). Mature Americans who live in urban areas are more likely than those in rural areas to report equities in excess of $50,000 (66.5% vs. 53.6%). Furthermore, a larger percentage of easterners (69.6%) reports $50,000 or more invested in real estate equity than their counterparts in the North (59.4%) and South (62.6%). When we look at gerontographic group responses, we see that seven in ten (71.1%) of ailing outgoers, in comparison with 56.4 percent of frail recluses and 63.9 percent of healthy hermits, report real estate equities in excess of $50,000. Real estate investments are larger among bank patrons than among patrons of brokerage firms and mutual fund companies. In terms of the concerns that characterize different asset-holding groups, becoming physically, socially, and financially dependent on others is of greater concern to those older Americans who have smaller real estate equities than to those with larger equities. Finally, three-fourths (75.8%) of credit/senior membership users have real estate equities in excess of $50,000, in comparison to those who use multiple methods (62.4%) and check/cash only (65.3%).

"Other" (Insurance, Business Assets, Etc.). As mature Americans age in late life, they have fewer assets in this "other" category. A larger percentage of males, in comparison to the proportion of females, has "other assets" in excess of $5,000 (66.1% vs. 42.9%). The older person's propensity to report higher values of these assets increases with income and education. And compared to those from nonworking families, older Americans from homes where at least one person works report higher

values of these assets. Older adults who live with others, in comparison
to those who live alone, report higher incidence of "other assets" valued
at $5,000 or more (62.1% vs. 32.8%). More older people who live in urban
areas, compared to the proportion of their counterparts who live in rural
areas, have assets in this category worth $5,000 or more (55.0% vs.
46.1%). In terms of gerontographic groups, frail recluses own the least
in "other" assets. And as far as preferred information sources go, an
agent is the best information source for older people who have assets
invested in the "other" category.

PREFERENCES FOR USING IRA/KEOGH OR PENSION TO PAY POST-RETIREMENT EXPENSES

Respondents were presented with a list of expenses usually incurred
after retirement, and were asked to indicate the best way they think
people should pay for them—that is, the type of assets they should use.
One source was IRA/Keogh or pension. We found that older adults feel
that investments for retirement are likely to be used to pay for a variety
of expenses. About one in three indicated that IRA/Keogh and pension
are the investments that should be used to pay for leisure/travel and
major purchases such as cars and furniture. Also, a significant percentage
of older adults feels that such savings should go into personal and business investments (27.2%). Nearly one-fourth (23.9%) of those 55 and
older feel that these funds should be used to pay for emergency medical
bills, and nearly as many think they should be used for home improvements (23.1%) and to pay for gifts to relatives and charities (23.0%). One
in five (20.5%) feels that money from retirement savings should be set
aside to pay for nursing home or long-term care expenses.

Older adults' plans and preferences for spending retirement income
are not the same as those of younger people. When responses to the
same question are compared between the two groups, several differences
emerge. While both younger and older adults hold similar views on the
use of retirement savings to pay for unexpected medical bills and for
home improvements, they differ on the remaining expenditure categories
examined.

Nearly half (48.0%) of those 55 and older, in comparison to their
younger counterparts (31.9%), think that these assets should be spent on
leisure/travel. Thirty percent of the older respondents, in comparison
with 20 percent of the younger adults, feel that such funds should be
used to pay for nursing home or long-term care expenses. Fairly similar
results emerge with respect to the use of retirement assets to pay for gifts
to relatives and charities (30.9% vs. 22.5%). Finally, older adults are more
likely than their younger counterparts to see these assets properly used

to pay for major purchases (44.2% vs. 31.8%) as well as personal and business investments (40.3% vs. 26.6%).

Baby Boomers vs. Seniors

Half of baby boomers would use IRA/Keogh investments to travel and buy major durable items such as cars and furniture, a figure twice as large as that for seniors. Baby boomers are also twice as likely as older adults to use these funds for personal and business investments, with 41.5 percent and 21.5 percent, respectively, reporting preference. Nearly one-third of baby boomers would use these funds to pay for nursing home or long-term cared (32.4%) and gifts to relatives (32.7%), compared with 18.4 percent and 15.3 percent of seniors, respectively, for these two expense categories. About one in five baby boomers (23.3%) and seniors (18.4%) would use IRA/Keogh investments to pay for home improvements, and the same proportion of the two groups would set these funds aside to pay for any large, unexpected medical bills.

Differences among Older Adults

The way the older person prefers to use his or her retirement savings depends a lot on certain background characteristics such as age, sex, socioeconomics, and other factors. Also, the older person's gerontographic profile provides a good indication of his or her preferences for using IRA/Keogh or pension to pay for various post-retirement expenses.

With increasing age, there is a decline in preferences for paying post-retirement expenses out of one's savings for retirement. Both older males and older females equally prefer to use these savings to pay for large, unexpected medical bills. However, for the remaining expenses, older males were more likely than their female counterparts to prefer using savings for retirement to pay for these expenses. With increasing income, older adults prefer to use IRA/Keogh and pensions to pay for the various expenses in late life. Also, the same is true with respect to education, with the more educated preferring to use more retirement assets to pay for all expenses examined, except medical expenditures. Older adults prefer to use savings for retirement to pay large, unexpected medical bills, regardless of level of education. Older adults who live with others are more likely than those who live alone to prefer paying for the various post-retirement expenses using retirement savings.

Older adults from households with nonworking members are no more likely than those from households where at least one member works to prefer paying for the various expense items using IRA/Keogh or pension funds.

In addition to these general findings, some specific differences surfaced among various groups with different characteristics across expense categories.

Nursing Home/Long-Term Care. Westerners are more likely than those who live in eastern and northern states to prefer using retirement savings to pay for nursing home or long-term care expenses. Older people who have children living within one hour's driving distance are more likely than those who have no children in close proximity to use these assets to pay for nursing homes or long-term care expenses (20.9% vs. 13.0%). Healthy indulgers and frail recluses are also more likely than their older counterparts in other gerontographic groups to use these savings for nursing home or long-term care.

Medical Bills. With age, older Americans increasingly feel that their retirement savings should be used to pay for medical bills. Healthy indulgers and frail recluses are more likely than healthy hermits to favor the use of IRA/Keogh or pension funds to pay for large medical bills.

Gifts/Donations. A larger percentage of westerners (28.0%) than easterners (18.4%) and southerners (20.6%) is likely to use these assets to buy gifts for relatives and make donations to charities. Also, healthy indulgers and frail recluses are more likely than their older counterparts in other gerontographic groups to use these savings for gifts.

Major Purchases. Older adults who live in the South are less likely than older adults who live in other parts of the country to spend their retirement savings to purchase major items. Those who have children living within one hour's driving distance are more likely than those who have no children in close proximity to use these assets to pay for major purchases (29.2% vs. 16.9%). Healthy indulgers and frail recluses are also more likely than their older counterparts in other gerontographic groups to use these savings for major purchases.

Investments. Healthy indulgers and frail recluses are also more likely than their older counterparts in other gerontographic groups to use these savings for personal and business investments.

PREFERENCES FOR USING OTHER INVESTMENTS TO PAY POST-RETIREMENT EXPENSES

Respondents were also asked to indicate whether they would use other investments to pay for various post-retirement expenses commonly incurred in late life. Such investments include all assets *except* IRA/Keogh, pension, home-equity, and long-term care insurance. Approximately two-thirds of the older adults surveyed feel that such investments should be used to pay for major purchases, such as cars and furniture (67.8%) and vacation/travel (65.6%). More than half think that these assets should be used to pay for home improvements (55.8%), gifts to relatives and charities (53.7%), and personal and business expenses (52.7%). However, only one in three thinks that these investments should be used to pay for large, unexpected medical bills (34.6%) and nursing home or long-term care bills (31.4%).

Older people differ from younger adults with respect to their views on reasons for other investments. A smaller percentage of older adults (55 and older) than younger adults (under 55) use these investments to pay large, unexpected medical bills (28.5% vs. 34.7%) and for home improvements (47.6% vs. 55.5%). On the other hand, older adults are more likely than their younger counterparts to think that these assets should be spent on vacations (72.7% vs. 65.1%), gifts to relatives and charities (67.8% vs. 53.0%), major purchases (71.8% vs. 67.7%), or on other personal and business investments (64.2% vs. 52.3%).

Baby Boomers vs. Seniors

Both age groups would more freely spend funds from Aother investments (except IRA/Keogh, home equity, and supplemental long-term care insurance). Such Adiscretionary long-term investments baby boomers prefer to spend on gifts (76.5%), vacations (75.8%), major purchases (73.9%), and for personal or business investments (70.1%), while a substantially smaller percentage of them would pay for home improvements (47.8%), large, unexpected medical bills (32.2%), and nursing home or long-term care (31.1%). These figures are generally higher than those of seniors with the exception of two expense items where a large percentage of seniors would use Aother investments to pay for them: large, unexpected medical bills (38.0%) and home improvements (56.9%).

Differences among Older Adults

Older adults' perceptions of how assets in other investments should be spent differ on the basis of several demographic and socioeconomic factors. The older person's gerontographic profile is also a rather good indicator of his or her opinion on how older people should spend "other" investments. Generally, older adults' propensity to prefer using other investment assets to pay for the various expense items increases with income and education levels. The higher the income and education the more likely older adults are to prefer spending other investment assets on various expense items. Older adults who live in urban areas do not differ significantly from those who live in rural areas in their views on whether assets from other investments should be used to pay for commonly incurred post-retirement outlays. Furthermore, the presence of children in close proximity does not affect the older adults' views on how these assets should be used. In general, adults from nonworking families are similar to those from families where at least one person works with respect to how they think these assets should be spent on various expense categories.

Medical Bills. With increasing age, older adults tend to believe that other investments should be used to pay large, unexpected medical bills. Older males are more likely than their female counterparts to prefer using them to pay these expenses (38.1% vs. 31.5%). In the meantime, older adults who live with others are no more or less likely to favor using their investments to pay for larger, unexpected medical bills. Older adults who live with others are more likely than their counterparts who live alone to use their investments to pay for these post-retirement expenses. Also, those who live in western states are more likely than older adults who live in northern states (37.7% vs. 31.4%) to favor spending these assets on unexpected medical bills. Older adults in families where no person works are more likely than their counterparts in families where at least one person works to think these assets should be used to pay for large, unexpected medical bills. In terms of gerontographic groups, frail recluses are more likely than older adults in other groups to favor spending these assets on large, unexpected medical bills.

Investments. Those age 55 to 64 are more likely than their older counterparts to think that these assets should be used for other personal and business investments. Older males are more likely than their female counterparts to prefer using such investments this way (59.2% vs. 47.1%). Older adults who live with others are more likely than their counterparts who live alone to use their investments to pay for these post-retirement expenses. Furthermore, westerners are more likely than any other geographic group to invest these assets in other business ventures. Frail recluses and healthy indulgers are more likely than healthy hermits and ailing outgoers to put these resources in other types of personal and business investments.

Vacation/Travel. Older males are more likely than their female counterparts to prefer using such investments to pay for vacation/travel (68.6% vs. 63.2%). Older adults who live with others are more likely than their counterparts who live alone to use their investments to pay for these post-retirement expenses. Also, westerners are more likely than any other geographic group to spend these assets on vacation/travel. Wide variations in preferences for spending on vacation/travel also exist, with a relatively larger percentage of healthy indulgers (78.8%) than ailing outgoers (64.8%) and healthy hermits (55.2%) expressing preferences for spending on leisure.

Gifts/Donations. Older males are more likely than their female counterparts to prefer using such investments for gifts to relatives and donations to charities (57.5% vs. 50.7%). Those who live in urban areas are more likely than those who live in rural areas (55.2% vs. 48.9%) to use these assets only to pay for these expenses. Older adults who live with others are more likely than their counterparts who live alone to use their investments to pay for these post-retirement expenses. In addition, easterners are more likely than westerners to use these assets to buy gifts for relatives or make donations to charities (56.7% vs. 50.4%). When we look at gerontographic groups, we see that healthy indulgers are more likely than any other group to prefer spending these assets on gifts and donations to charities.

Major Purchases. Older males are more likely than their female counterparts to prefer using such investments to pay for major purchases (70.5% vs. 65.7%). Older adults who live with others are more likely than their counterparts who live alone to use their investments to pay for these post-retirement expenses. Frail recluses and healthy indulgers are more likely than healthy hermits and ailing outgoers to prefer spending these assets on major purchases, such as cars and furniture.

Home Improvements. Older adults who live with others are no more or less likely to favor using their investments to pay for home improvements. Westerners are more likely than any other geographic group to spend these assets on such expenses. In terms of gerontographic groups, relatively larger numbers of healthy indulgers (60.2%) and frail recluses (59.1%) than healthy hermits (52.0%) are likely to favor spending investment assets on home improvements.

Nursing Home/Long-Term Care. A relatively larger percentage of older westerners (38.3%) and southerners (36.3%), in comparison to older adults who live in eastern states (21.0%), thinks that these assets should pay for nursing home or long-term care expenses. A larger percentage of frail recluses (42.0%) than any other gerontographic segment is likely to feel the need for spending these assets on nursing home or long-term care.

PREFERENCES FOR METHODS OF GETTING CASH FROM HOME EQUITY

There are several ways one can get cash out of home equity. When respondents were asked to respond to six major methods, they were inclined to prefer a variety of methods. The most popular or best received method is the traditional one which involves sale of one's home and purchase of a less expensive home. Nearly half (47.6%) of older respondents indicated intentions to use this method. About one in four (26.4%) indicated preference for renting, rather than buying another home, keeping all the cash. Responses to more innovative methods were not as affirmative. A little over one in five (20.7%) of older adults prefers receiving all the cash now and making monthly payments to the lender. Nearly as many (17.3%) prefer receiving cash up front and letting the lender get their home when they move or die. About one in eight (12.6%) would rather receive monthly cash payments from the lender and let the lender get their home when they move or die. The least preferred alternative was preferred by just under 10 percent (9.8%) of older Americans. Relatively few mature home owners would prefer to sell their home, but continue to live there and receive small monthly payments from the new owner.

Preferences for the six methods of receiving cash from home equity were analyzed among younger versus older adults. Younger adults show a stronger preference for getting all the home equity in cash and making monthly payments to the lender, with 40.3 percent of them indicating preference, compared with 20.3 percent for older adults. Older adults, on the other hand, would rather sell their present home and rent another one, keeping all the cash, with about one in four (26.4%) showing preference for this option vis-à-vis 17.5 percent of younger adults. Preferences for the remaining methods of getting cash from home equity did not differ between the two groups.

Baby Boomers vs. Seniors

What are baby boomers' attitudes toward home-equity use? How do they feel about using a reverse mortgage? Both age groups feel that the best use of home equity is to sell their existing home, buy a less expensive one, and keep the cash difference (see Table 9.5). Nearly half (47.8%) of baby boomers and four in ten (41.1%) seniors reported preference for this option. While receiving all the cash from equity and paying the lender back over time is preferred by 40 percent of baby boomers, only 16.2 percent of seniors prefer this option. About one in six (17.7%) of baby boomers (compared with one-fourth of seniors) prefers selling their present home, renting another one, and keeping the cash difference. The remaining methods are less attractive to both groups. Selling one's home, but continuing to live there and receiving small monthly payments from the new owner is the least attractive option, with only 4.8 percent of baby boomers favoring it, compared with nearly twice as many seniors (8.7%).

Older Americans' preferences for these various methods of tapping into their home equity shows some variations across sociodemographic groups. And while preferences for the majority of methods for tapping one's home equity do not differ across gerontographic segments, two methods show significant differences. This information is reflected in the following profiles.

Receive All Cash Now/Make Monthly Payments to the Lender. With age, older adults are less likely to prefer receiving all the cash now and making monthly payments to the lender. Male older adults are more likely

Table 9.5
Preferences for Methods of Getting Cash from Home Equity among Baby
Boomers and Seniors (65+) (Percent Who Would Use)

	Baby Boomers (%)	Seniors (%)
Receive all the cash now and you make monthly payments to the lender	40.24	16.21
Sell your home, but continue to live there and receive small monthly payments from the new owner	4.76	8.74
Sell your present home, rent another home, and keep all the cash	17.66	25.02
Sell your present home, buy a less expensive home, and keep the cash difference	47.77	41.08
Receive all the cash now and the lender gets your home when you move or die	12.40	14.00
Receive monthly cash payments and the lender gets your home when you move or die	10.12	9.86
Base:	(N = 828)	(N = 324)

than their female counterparts to prefer this option with more than one
in four (26.6%) of them compared with 16.2 percent of the older females
preferring this method. The higher the older person's annual household
income and level of education, the greater his or her preference for getting cash from home equity by receiving all cash now and making
monthly payments to the lender. Also, compared to older adults from
families where no person works, older Americans from families with at
least one working person are more likely to prefer getting cash out of
their homes this way (22.2% vs. 17.2%). Older adults who live with others tend to prefer getting cash from home equity by receiving all the cash
up front and making monthly payments to the lender, in comparison
with those who live alone (22.5% vs. 16.5%). A larger percentage of frail
recluses (26.6%) and healthy indulgers (24.8%) than healthy hermits
(16.5%) is likely to prefer receiving all the cash now and making monthly
payments to the lender.

Sell Present Home/Rent Another Home. As mature Americans age in late
life, their preference for selling their present home, renting another
home, and keeping all the cash as a way of tapping into their home's
equity declines. Older males are more likely than older women to prefer
this option (29.3% vs. 24.0%). Older Americans with higher education
are more likely to prefer selling their present home and renting another,
keeping all the cash.

Sell Present Home/Buy a Less Expensive Home. As older people age, they become less likely to favor selling their present home, buying a less expensive home, and keeping the cash difference as a way of accessing the equity they have accumulated in their homes. More than half (56.4%) of older male Americans prefer this method, in comparison with 41.5 percent of older females. The higher the older person's annual household income and level of education, the greater his or her preference for selling the home and buying a less expensive one. About half (50.3%) of those who live alone, in comparison with 42.4 percent of those who live with others, favor this means of getting cash from the equity of their homes. Those who have no children in close proximity are more likely to prefer the same method, with 48.4 percent of them preferring selling their present home and buying a less expensive one, in comparison with 38.3 percent of those who have children in close proximity. Frail recluses and healthy indulgers are the most likely and healthy hermits are the least likely to prefer getting money out of their home equity by selling their present home and buying a less expensive one (54.9 percent, 56.2 percent, and 38.3 percent, respectively).

Receiving Monthly Cash Payments/Lender Keeps Home When They Move or Die. Receiving monthly cash payments and letting the lender get their home when they move or die as a way of getting cash from one's home equity loses its appeal among older Americans as they age in late life. A little over one in five older males prefers this alternative, in comparison with 13.9 percent of older females. In comparison to older adults from families where no person works, older Americans from families with at least one working person are more likely to prefer receiving monthly cash payments and letting the lender keep their home when they move or die (14.4% vs. 8.5%). Older adults who live in the East were somewhat more likely than their counterparts in the North (15.5% vs. 10.4%) to prefer this method of getting cash from the equity they have in their homes.

Receiving All Cash Now/Letting Lender Have Their Home When They Move or Die. In comparison to older adults from families where no person works, older Americans from families with at least one working person are more likely to prefer receiving all the cash now and letting the lender have their home when they move or die (18.6% vs. 14.1%).

USE OF HOME EQUITY TO PAY FOR POST-RETIREMENT EXPENSES

Respondents were also asked to indicate whether using home equity was the best way to pay various expenses which may occur after retirement. These expenses varied in scope from large, unexpected medical bills, to long-term care and personal business expenses. Older Americans also feel that the use of home equity is the best way (among other sources) to pay for such expenses. One in four of those age 55 and over feels that people should use their home equity to pay for home improvements. However, for the remaining expense categories, the percentage of older Americans who feel that people should use their home equity to pay for them is very small. For example, only 7 percent (6.9%) feel that they should use their home equity to pay for large, unexpected medical bills and nursing home or long-term care.

More than half (54.6%) of the younger group, or twice as many older adults, feel that home equity should be used by older adults to pay for home improvements after retirement. Also, three times as many younger adults think that after retirement people should use the equity of their home to finance major purchases and for personal and business investments. Furthermore, younger adults, in comparison to their older counterparts, favor use of home equity to pay for: vacation/travel; large, unexpected bills; and even to buy gifts and give to charities, although the percentage of those who have such an opinion is very small.

Baby Boomers vs. Seniors

What are baby boomers' attitudes toward home-equity use? How are they compared to those of seniors? Our data showed that both age groups feel that the best use of home equity is to sell their existing home, buy a less expensive one, and keep the cash difference. Nearly half (47.8%) of baby boomers and four in ten (41.1%) seniors reported preference for this option. While receiving all the cash from equity and paying the lender back over time is preferred by 40 percent of baby boomers, only 16.2 percent of seniors prefer this option. About one in six (17.7%) of baby boomers (compared with one-fourth of seniors) prefers selling their present home, renting another one, and keeping the cash difference.

The remaining methods are less attractive to both groups. Selling one's home, but continuing to live there and receiving small monthly payments from the new owner is the least attractive option, with only 4.8 percent of baby boomers favoring it, compared with nearly twice as many seniors (8.7%).

Differences among Older Adults

The way older people feel one's home equity should be used depends a lot on certain sociodemographic characteristics. We notice variation in responses by factors such as age, sex, socioeconomics, and living arrangements. Also, the older person's gerontographic characteristics are good predictors of his or her attitudes toward use of home equity to pay for several expenses after retirement. With age, older Americans tend to become decreasingly likely to suggest that after retirement people should use their home equity to pay for the seven major expense categories studied. Only for nursing home or long-term care is the decline not as steep with age in late life.

Home Improvements. With age, older Americans tend to become decreasingly likely to suggest that after retirement people should use their home equity to pay for home improvements. Male Americans age 55 and over are more likely than females over the same age to think that after retirement people should use their home equity to pay for home improvements (29.8% vs. 19.6%). Also, the higher the older person's household income and level of education, the more likely he or she is to favor this use of home equity. In comparison to those who live alone, a larger percentage of older adults who live with others is likely to favor use of home equity to pay for home improvements (27.5% vs. 16.1%). A larger percentage (8.3%) of easterners age 55-plus, in comparison to their southerner counterparts (3.1%), as well as to older adults who live in the North (3.7%), is likely to favor use of home equity by retirees for these purposes. Older adults who live in the West are more likely than older Americans who live in the North to favor use of home equity for home improvements after retirement, with 9.0 percent and 4.6 percent, respectively, favoring this option.

Older adults in households where at least one member works are more likely than older adults from households without working members to favor use of home equity for home improvements after retirement, with 26.6 percent and 18.7 percent, respectively, expressing this opinion. A larger percentage of healthy indulgers (29.6%) and frail recluses (28.1%) than healthy hermits (21.4%) and ailing outgoers (21.9%) favors use of home equity for home improvements after retirement.

Major Purchases. With age, older Americans tend to become decreasingly likely to suggest that after retirement people should use their home equity to pay for major purchases. Men age 55 and over are more likely than females in the same age bracket to think that people should use their home equity after retirement to pay for major purchases (such as cars and furniture) (6.6% vs. 3.1%). The higher the older person's household income, the more likely he or she is to favor using home equity this way. In comparison to those who live alone, a larger percentage of older adults who live with others is likely to favor use of home equity to pay for such major purchases (5.7% vs. 2.4%). Older adults in households where at least one member works are more likely than older adults from households without working members to use home equity this way (5.5% vs. 2.9%).

Medical Bills. With age, older Americans tend to become decreasingly likely to suggest that after retirement people should use their home equity to pay for these kinds of expenses. A larger percentage of older Americans (8.5%) who have no children living in close proximity, in comparison to older adults who have children living close by (1.7%), would use home equity for large, unexpected medical bills.

Nursing Home/Long-Term Care. With age, older Americans tend to become decreasingly likely to favor using their home equity to pay for these care needs, though this decline is not as great as it is for other expense categories. Male Americans age 55 and over are more likely than females over the same age to think that people should use their home equity after retirement to pay for nursing home or long-term care expenses (8.6% vs. 5.4%). In comparison to those who live alone, a larger percentage of older adults who live with others is likely to favor use of home equity to pay for nursing home or long-term care (7.9% vs. 4.3%). Twice as many frail recluses as ailing outgoers and healthy indulgers (10.8% vs. 4.7% and 5.8%, respectively) favor use of home equity to pay for nursing home or long-term care expenses after retirement.

Vacation/Travel. With age, older Americans tend to become decreasingly likely to suggest that after retirement people should use their home equity to pay for leisure expenses. Men age 55 and over are more likely than females over the same age to think that people should use their home equity to pay vacation/travel expenses after retirement (3.2% vs. 1.5%). In comparison to those who live alone, a larger percentage of older adults who live with others is likely to favor use of home equity for vacation and travel expenses (2.8% vs. 1.0%).

While relatively few older adults favor use of home equity to pay for vacation and travel expenses, older adults who live in the West and East are more likely than older adults who live in the South to favor use of home equity for this purpose, with 3.7 and 3.5 percent versus 0.8 percent of the respondents from these regions, respectively, expressing this opinion. A larger percentage of frail recluses (4.7%) than healthy indulgers (1.1%) recommends use of home equity by retirees to pay for vacation and travel expenses.

Investments. With age, older Americans tend to become decreasingly likely to suggest that after retirement people should use their home equity to pay for other investments. In comparison to those who live alone, a larger percentage of older adults who live with others is likely to favor use of home equity to pay for personal and business investments (5.7% vs. 2.8%). Twice as many ailing outgoers as healthy hermits (7.1% vs. 3.1%) think that home equity should be used for personal and business investments.

Gifts/Donations. With age, older Americans tend to become decreasingly likely to suggest that after retirement people should use their home equity for gifts and donations to charities.

10

Insurance

Our research interests were also in examining how consumers respond to various types of insurance services. Our studies examined preferences for insurance services, reasons for patronizing specific insurance companies, and preferences for methods of purchasing insurance services, including reasons for deciding to buy or not to buy insurance by phone or mail. Special focus was on long-term care insurance (LTC), where we examined consumers' willingness to buy this product for themselves, their spouses, and their parents. We also examined attitudes and motivations for buying LTC insurance, patronage preferences for nontraditional insurance service providers, as well as the characteristics of older Americans willing to buy specific LTC policies.

PREFERENCES FOR INSURANCE SERVICES

Consumers in our study were asked to indicate their preferences for insurance services. Specifically, they were asked to indicate whether they presently have or would like to have the following types of insurance: long-term care, "medigap," car, and home-health care insurance.

In order to determine whether such preferences are unique to the older population or apply to the adult population in general, responses given by adults age 55 or older were compared to those given by younger adults. Actual use/ownership and desire for each service were combined into one "preference" category. A larger percentage of older adults than younger adults (77.7% vs. 47.0%) reported preferences for "medigap." However, a larger percentage of younger adults than older adults (95.9% vs. 89.8%) expressed preference for car insurance.

Baby Boomers vs. Seniors

While nearly all baby boomers (98.4%) have (or would like to have) car insurance, fewer (87.9%) seniors expressed similar preferences. Nearly as many baby boomers as seniors have or would like to have long-term care insurance (74.9% vs. 70.4%) and home-health care insurance (58.6% vs. 61.0%), while 43 percent of the younger group (compared with 87.9% of seniors) prefer "medigap" insurance.

Differences among Older Adults

One-third of those age 55 and over said they have long-term care insurance, with another 41 percent expressing preferences for this product. More than half (51.8%) have "medigap," and another 28.8 percent said they would like to have this type of insurance. About nine in ten adults age 55 and over have car insurance, with only 3 percent presently expressing interest in being covered. Finally, approximately one-third of the older adults in America said they have home-health care insurance, while another third would like to have it.

Preferences for certain types of insurance services are not uniform across older adults. Rather, there are significant variations in preferences by factors such as age, sex, and other demographic and lifestyle characteristics. There are also differences across gerontographic groups, with healthy hermits being least likely to prefer various insurance products, except car insurance. These differences further vary by type of insurance.

Long-Term Care. Preferences for long-term care insurance do not change much with age in late life. More older men than older women consider this coverage important (75.2% vs. 69.6%). Additionally, the higher an older person's income and level of educational attainment, the greater his or her preference for such long-term care insurance. In terms of geography, a larger percentage of southerners than northerners (75.1% vs. 69.5%) prefers long-term care insurance.

"Medigap." Preference for "medigap" jumps by more than 10 percent after age 65. Older adults who live in rural areas are more likely than those who live in urban areas to prefer this kind of insurance (82.6% vs. 76.8%). Also, health insurance that supplements medicare is more likely to be preferred by older adults who come from nonworking than from working households (81.7% vs. 75.9%). Finally, ailing outgoers are more likely than frail recluses to have or express desire for "medigap" (83.5% vs. 78.2%).

Car. As mature Americans age in late life, their preference for car insurance gradually declines. Mature males are are more likely than older females to favor car insurance coverage (94.0% vs. 86.5%). In addition, older people with higher income and education levels are more likely than their less educated and lower-income counterparts to prefer car insurance. Elderly who live with others are more likely than those who live alone to have or prefer such coverage (91.2% vs. 86.8%).

Home-Health Care Insurance. As older people age, their preferences for home-health care insurance generally remain unchanged. Older male adults are more likely than their female counterparts to favor this type of insurance (66.6% vs. 59.5%). In the meantime, more southerners than older adults who live in the West are likely to indicate preferences for home-health care coverage (66.5% vs. 58.7%). Also, mature Americans who live with others are more likely than their counterparts who live alone to have or prefer home-health care insurance (65.4% vs. 56.9%).

PREFERENCES FOR SOURCES OF INFORMATION REGARDING NEW INSURANCE SERVICES

Consumers prefer to hear about new insurance products and services via a number of different sources of information. Respondents in our research were asked to tell us how they prefer to find out about new insurance services. They were presented with five different types of information sources (TV or print ads, agents, direct mail, phone, and group meetings or seminars) and were asked to indicate their most preferred alternative.

Preferences for sources of information vary across groups of consumers. Receiving news in the mail appears to be the most preferred method of finding out about new insurance services among older adults, with 35.5 percent of these respondents in our sample expressing preference for this vehicle. Agents are the second most preferred mode, with 28.5 percent of older Americans expressing preference for this method. Advertisements are third on the list (16.5%), followed by group meetings or seminars (6.8%), and phone contact (3.9%).

Older adults' preferences for information sources do not differ from those of younger adults, with the exception of preference for TV or print ads. The latter method is more preferred by those under 55 than by those 55 and older (22.0% vs. 16.3%).

Baby Boomers vs. Seniors

How do baby boomers prefer to find out about new insurance services? Respondents were asked to indicate the most preferred sources of information from which they like to hear about new insurance products. While baby boomers and seniors did not differ with respect to their preferences for TV or print ads and telephone solicitation, a larger percentage (41.8%) of baby boomers than seniors (34.4%) prefers to receive news in the mail. On the other hand, a smaller percentage of baby boomers than seniors (26.5% vs. 32.9%) prefers to hear about new insurance products from agents on a person-to-person basis; and they are less likely to prefer to hear about such products in group meetings (5.0% vs. 8.1%).

Differences among Older Adults

As the following profiles illustrate, older adults do not have similar preferences for information sources regarding new insurance services. Rather, their preferences can be predicted by certain demographic and social characteristics. For example, there are wide geographic variations in preferences for information sources. Gerontographic characteristics of older adults can also predict preferences for two types of information sources regarding new insurance products.

TV/Print Advertising. Older males are more likely than their female counterparts to prefer finding out about new insurance services from TV or print ads (19.2% vs. 14.4%). A larger percentage of southerners (21.6%) and westerners (20.8%) than either northerners (11.6%) or easterners (10.8%) would prefer getting insurance service information via these media.

Group Meetings or Seminars. Older females are more likely than their male counterparts to prefer learning about new insurance products in group meetings or seminars (8.3% vs. 4.9%). Mature adults who live in urban areas are more likely than their rural counterparts to prefer hearing about new insurance products this way (7.4% vs. 3.7%). Additionally, older adults who live alone are more likely than those who live with others (9.9% vs. 5.4%) to express preference for learning about new insurance services in these types of settings.

Agents. Older adults who live in rural areas are more likely than their urban counterparts to prefer to be visited by an agent and be told about new insurance services available on the market (33.5% vs. 27.3%, respectively). Also, easterners and northerners also have similar preferences for agents as sources of new product information, with 30.4 percent and 36.5 percent, respectively, expressing preference for this method. These figures are relatively higher than the percentage of southerners (24%) and westerners (21.4%) who prefer this information source. Finally, those who prefer to hear about new insurance products from sales agents are more likely to be healthy indulgers than either frail recluses or ailing outgoers (34.2% vs. 25.6% and 25.5%, respectively).

Direct Mail. Preference for receiving news in the mail declines with age.

Telephone. Mature Americans' preference for receiving news by phone increases with age in late life. Southerners are less likely than their counterparts who live in other regions of this country to prefer telephone contact as a source of new product information. Also, older adults with

(32.0% vs. 16.7%). Advice of children or close relatives is twice as important to baby boomers as it is to older adults (27.5% vs. 12.5%). Age-based discounts are of equal importance to both age groups, while age-stereotyping in ads is less important to baby boomers than to seniors, with 11.5 percent and 18.5 percent, respectively, indicating the importance of this factor. Special deals through group or membership programs are not important in the patronage decision of either age group (4.4% vs. 7.3%).

Differences among Older Adults

The various patronage reasons are not of equal importance among older adults. Rather, they tend to vary by sociodemographic characteristics. For example, the older the person, the fewer the factors considered. In the meantime, older adults who live with others place a greater emphasis on all thirteen factors before making patronage decisions than older adults who live alone. The gerontographic profiles of older Americans are also very good predictors of the type of factors they would consider before choosing providers to buy various types of insurance services. By examining characteristics of older adults who tend to value various patronage reasons, a profile of those who pay attention to certain reasons can be developed.

Price. When evaluating insurance companies, price is more of a concern to men than it is to women. This factor is most likely to be considered by ailing outgoers than any other gerontographic group.

Ease of Doing Business Via Telephone or Mail. Older males tend to give a greater consideration to how easy it is to do business with a company over the telephone or through the mail. Older adults with higher incomes place a greater emphasis on this factor. Also, ailing outgoers are more likely than frail recluses to emphasize how easy or difficult it is to do business with an insurance company this way (49.7% vs. 42.0%).

Assistance with Filling Out Forms. Relative to their counterparts with more education, older people with lower education are more likely to put importance on assistance provided by staff in filling out forms when evaluating insurance companies. Older men and women consider this factor at the same rate. This factor is more important to ailing outgoers than it is to healthy hermits (42.5% vs. 31.5%). In the meantime, personnel/staff assistance with filling out forms is more important to ailing outgoers than it is to frail recluses (42.5% vs. 35.0%) and is more valuable to healthy indulgers than it is to health hermits (37.6% vs. 31.5%).

Staff Explanations. Staff explanations of various services is of more importance to older men than it is to older women. It is more important to older Americans in rural areas than it is to those who live in urban areas (43.3% vs. 34.2%).

Billing/Payment Methods. Mature males are more likely than older women to be concerned with companies' billing and payment policies. Also, older adults with lower incomes and lower levels of education are more likely than their higher-income counterparts to evaluate insurance companies on this basis. Ailing outgoers are more likely than healthy hermits to consider this factor (36.8% vs. 29.8%).

Convenience of Reaching Service Provider. Older men tend to think this factor is more important than do older women. Older people who live in rural areas are more likely than their urban-dwelling counterparts to consider convenience in reaching the service provider (32.9% vs. 27.1%). Also, ailing outgoers are more likely than healthy hermits to consider this element to be of importance, with 30.4 percent and 25.3 percent of the two groups, respectively, indicating this patronage reason.

Membership Programs. Mature men and women generally place equal value on this factor. In the meantime, older adults who have children within one hour's driving time are more likely than those with children who live farther away to patronize insurance companies on the basis of special deals available through group membership programs (26.9% vs. 16.9%). Southerners are nearly twice as likely as their eastern counterparts (32.5% vs. 17.8%) to patronize insurance companies because of membership programs. Finally, special deals through group or special programs are of more importance to ailing outgoers than they are to healthy hermits (36.5% vs. 24.4%). Also, when evaluating insurance companies, ailing outgoers are more likely than frail recluses to emphasize special deals through group or membership programs (36.4% vs. 26.5%).

Age-Based Discounts. Age-based discounts are of equal importance to older men and older women. In the meantime, mature adults who live in the West are more likely than their counterparts who live in the North (30.8% vs. 22.4%) to respond to age-based discounts. Relative to healthy hermits, ailing outgoers are more concerned with these kinds of deals (33.0% vs. 21.2%) when evaluating insurance companies. Also, ailing outgoers put more importance on age-based discounts than frail recluses (33.0% vs. 25.0%).

Availability of Related Services. The availability of related services at the same place is more important to older males than it is to older females. Older people with lower education are more likely than their higher-educated counterparts to consider this element and it is more important to older people who live in rural areas than it is to their counterparts who live in urban areas (26.1% vs. 19.0%).

Finally, ailing outgoers place more importance than healthy hermits on the ease of getting related services at the same place (25.5% vs. 17.9%). Also, ailing outgoers are more likely than frail recluses to emphasize this factor when making a decision about insurance company patronage (25.5% vs. 17.8%).

Referrals and Endorsements. Older men are more likely than older women to consider endorsements and referrals when making a decision about insurance company patronage. Older adults with higher incomes place a greater emphasis on this factor. Similarly, the higher the older person's education, the greater the likelihood he or she would rely on the word of other firms or professionals. Also, referrals or endorsements by firms or professionals are more important to ailing outgoers than they are to healthy hermits (25.6% vs. 17.2%). Also, ailing outgoers are more likely than frail recluses to emphasize this factor when making a decision about insurance companies (25.6% vs. 16.3%).

Age-Stereotypes in Advertising. Sensitivity to age-stereotypes in ads and advice from relatives do not decline with increasing age in late life. However, older females are more likely than older males to consider insurance ads' portrayal of people their age (20.2% vs. 15.6%). The greater preoccupation of older male adults with the many factors may reflect the males' inclination to be the decision makers for insurance products. Older adults with lower incomes and levels of education are more likely than their higher-income counterparts to evaluate insurance companies on the basis of their portrayal of older persons in ads. Finally, ailing outgoers are more likely than healthy hermits to put importance on this factor when making a decision about insurance company patronage (26.3% vs. 11.7%). In the meantime, this is of more concern to ailing outgoers than it is to frail recluses (26.3% vs. 17.3%) and is also of more importance to healthy indulgers than it is to healthy hermits.

Advice of Peers. Men and women generally put the same emphasis on peer advice when evaluating insurance companies. However, the advice of others their age is more important to older adults who have children who live within an hour's drive than it is to their counterparts with children who live farther away (21.7% vs. 3.8%).

Advice of Relatives. The advice of family members is no more or less important to older men than it is to older women when choosing an insurance company. However, this input is more important to older people with lower education than it is to their more educated counterparts. Additionally, ailing outgoers are more concerned than healthy hermits with the advice of family members (18.6% vs. 11.1%). In the meantime, this input is more important to ailing outgoers than it is to frail recluses (18.6% vs. 12.1%).

PATRONAGE PREFERENCES FOR NONTRADITIONAL INSURANCE-SERVICE PROVIDERS

Americans buy insurance policies from a wide variety of distribution outlets. Besides the traditional sources (insurance companies or their agents) our research sought to determine the nontraditional sources from which people prefer to buy such policies.

AARP is the most preferred nontraditional insurance-service provider among those age 55 and older, with 22 percent of older Americans expressing preference for purchasing insurance services from this source. Commercial banks are second on the list, with one in eight (16.3%) older Americans indicating willingness to purchase insurance policies from a bank. Credit unions and mutual fund companies are almost equally preferred, with 7.4 percent and 6.1 percent, respectively, indicating preference. Similarly, S&Ls and stock brokerage companies are preferred by nearly 4 percent of the older Americans.

Patronage preferences of older Americans tend to differ from those of their younger counterparts. Credit unions and mutual fund companies are more likely to be preferred for insurance products by younger than by older adults. As expected, AARP is a preferred source among those age 55 and older but not among younger age groups. Commercial banks and S&Ls are almost equally preferred by younger and older adults.

Differences among Older Adults

Patronage preferences of older adults show wide variations by background characteristics. For example, preferences for nontraditional providers of insurance products show decline for certain providers but no significant change for other insurance providers. These help us develop useful profiles of those most likely to patronize the specific providers of insurance products.

AARP. The appeal of buying insurance services from the AARP falls as people get older, though overall preference for this alternative does not decline as rapidly as it does for commercial banks, credit unions, and mutual fund companies. Easterners are less likely than older adults living in other areas to prefer buying insurance products through AARP. Finally, ailing outgoers are more likely than healthy hermits to prefer getting insurance products from this organization (25.7% vs. 19.9%).

Commercial Banks. As mature Americans age in late life, their preferences for buying insurance services at commercial banks shows a steady decline. These institutions are more likely to be patronized by older adults with lower education than by those with higher education. In the meantime, older adults who live in rural areas are more likely than those who live in urban locations to show interest in patronizing commercial banks for insurance services. Older adults who live in northern and southern states are more likely than their counterparts who live in other geographic areas to turn to a commercial bank for insurance services. Mature males are more likely than older females to patronize commercial banks (18.5% vs. 14.2%). Finally, these banks are most likely to be preferred by ailing outgoers and frail recluses.

Credit Unions. As people age in late life, their preference for buying insurance services at credit unions shows a steady decline. The higher the older person's household income the greater his or her likelihood to patronize these kinds of institutions. Westerners are more likely to patronize a credit union than easterners (10.0% vs. 1.9%). Finally, credit unions are preferred mostly by frail recluses; they are also more likely to be patronized by ailing outgoers than by healthy hermits and healthy indulgers.

Mutual Fund Companies. As mature Americans age, the appeal of buying insurance services from mutual fund companies shows a steady decline. Mature Americans who live with others are more likely than their counterparts who live alone to prefer buying insurance products from such companies (7.5% vs. 2.8%).

Stock Brokerages. As mature people get older, they become less inclined to buy insurance services from stock brokerage firms. The decline in preference with age, however, is not as drastic as it is for aforementioned alternatives. The higher the older person's household income the greater his or her likelihood to patronize stock brokerage companies. Older adults who live in urban areas are more likely than those who live in rural areas to express interest in patronizing such companies for insurance products. Finally, stock brokerage companies are more likely to be patronized by healthy hermits than by frail recluses (6.0% vs. 1.3%).

Savings and Loans (S&Ls). There are no changes in preferences for S&Ls with age, suggesting that older adults remain loyal patrons to these institutions. S&Ls are more likely to be patronized by older adults with lower education than by those with higher education. Also, easterners are more likely than northerners to patronize S&Ls, with 7.4 percent and 2.5 percent, respectively, expressing preference. Older adults who live with others are more likely than those who live alone to prefer buying insurance products from these associations (4.5% vs. 2.0%).

PREFERENCES FOR METHODS OF PURCHASING INSURANCE SERVICES

We asked respondents to tell us the ways they prefer to buy insurance policies, whether they prefer to buy them at their home or office, through the mail, by phone, or at vendors' facilities. (Respondents could indicate more than one preferred method.)

We found that buying insurance services at vendors' facilities is the most preferred method, since nearly four in ten (39.2%) expressed such a preference. Three out of ten adults age 55 and over prefer buying insurance by phone, and nearly as many (27.8%) from door-to-door salespeople. Buying through the mail is the least preferred method, with only 8.6 percent of our older respondents expressing preference for this distribution mode.

Our interest also was in examining whether older adult buyers prefer buying insurance policies from different outlets in comparison to their younger counterparts. By comparing responses given by those age 55 and older to those under 55, it was found that the two groups differ in two significant ways. First, a larger percentage of younger adults (45.5%), in comparison to older adults (38.7%), prefers buying insurance policies at vendors' facilities. However, older adults were more likely than their younger counterparts to report preferences for buying through the mail (8.9% vs. 6.3%).

Baby Boomers vs. Seniors

We also compared responses given by baby boomers to those given by seniors. Purchasing insurance at vendors' facilities is the most preferred way of acquiring such products, with 45.3 percent of baby boomers (compared with 35.0% of seniors) indicating preference. Purchasing insurance policies by phone and door-to-door were equally preferred by the two age groups, with 32.3 percent and 30.3 percent, respectively, reporting preference. Only 6.7 percent of the younger group indicated preference for buying through the mail. Responses for the last three methods given by boomers were fairly similar to those given by the older group.

Differences among Older Adults

Certain demographic and social characteristics of the older person are likely to predict his or her greater (or lower) inclination to prefer various methods of distribution for insurance policies. Preferences for methods of buying insurance policies are also likely to differ among older adults in various gerontographic groups. Following are the differences for the different purchasing methods.

Vendors' Facilities. Preference for buying them at vendors' facilities declines with age. Males are more likely than females to prefer buying insurance policies at vendors' facilities, with 45.2 percent and 34.6 percent, respectively, reporting preference for this method. Preference for purchasing insurance policies at vendors' facilities as well as by phone increases with increasing income and education. Older adults who live with others are more likely than those who live alone to prefer buying insurance services at vendors' facilities (42.7% vs. 31.1%). A larger percentage of westerners (44.2%) than easterners (31.9%) expressed preference for buying insurance policies via this distribution channel. Finally, frail recluses prefer purchasing these services at vendors' facilities more than any other group (47.3%), while ailing outgoers is the group least likely to prefer this mode of distribution (34.8%).

Telephone. Among older adults who live alone, those whose children live within one hour's driving distance are more likely to buy by phone than their counterparts who do not have children in close proximity (36.2% vs. 26.1%). In the meantime, mature Americans who live in urban areas are more likely than their rural counterparts to prefer buying insurance over the phone, with 31.8 percent and 25.3 percent, respectively, expressing preference for this distribution mode. Finally, of the gerontographic groups, healthy indulgers are those least likely to prefer phone as a method of buying insurance.

Home or Office. About one-third of older adults who live in rural areas, in comparison with one-fourth of their urban counterparts, are likely to express preference for buying insurance from salespeople at their home or office.

Door-to-Door. Although preferences for buying door-to-door do not differ among older adults living in most geographic regions, twice as many respondents who live in eastern states as their counterparts from western states (33.8% vs. 16.7%) expressed preference for this method. One-third of healthy indulgers, compared with 26.8 percent of healthy hermits and 23.6 percent of frail recluses prefer buying insurance policies from salespeople door-to-door.

Mail. Ailing outgoers are more likely than healthy indulgers (10.9% vs. 6.8%) to prefer buying through the mail.

REASONS FOR BUYING OR NOT BUYING INSURANCE BY PHONE OR MAIL

In considering whether or not to buy various types of insurance by phone or by mail, many people go through a decision process during which a number of factors are likely to be taken into account. Respondents in our sample were presented with a list of eight reasons for buying or not buying direct, and they were asked to indicate the reasons they would consider before buying various types of insurance by phone or through the mail.

Two out of five older adults who think of buying various types of insurance direct are likely to want to know whether the company has a toll-free (800) number. About one in three (32.7%) considers the price of the service, while one in four is likely to consider cancellation and refund policies. Convenience, in comparison to other ways of buying the same services, is also nearly as important, with 23.8 percent of older adults mentioning this factor. Twenty-one percent consider availability of alternate insurance plans, and 18.3 percent consider waiting time. One in ten

Table 10.2
Reasons Considered before Buying Various Types of Insurance by Phone or through the Mail among Baby Boomers and Seniors (65+)

Reasons Considered	Baby Boomers (%)	Seniors (%)
Price	41.44	25.85
Type of credit card accepted	12.94	6.65
Cancellation and refund policy	35.94	19.17
Convenience, in comparison to other ways of buying the same product/service	32.40	15.62
Free pick-up service	8.46	3.76
Availability of toll-free (800) number	49.67	36.55
Selection of products or services	30.22	12.75
Days to wait before receiving	24.93	13.74
Base:	(N = 555)	(N = 214)

considers type of credit accepted for payment, and a much smaller percentage considers the availability of free pick-up service (for policies and claims).

Older adults differ markedly from their younger counterparts with respect to the reasons they consider before deciding to buy (or do not buy) various types of insurance direct. Younger adults are more likely than their older counterparts to consider price, cancellation and refund policy, convenience, availability of a toll-free number, and selection of coverage options. However, the two age groups do not differ in the importance they place on the remaining factors.

Baby Boomers vs. Seniors

What makes people in different generations buy insurance policies direct from service providers? About half (49.7%) of baby boomers, compared with 36.5 percent of seniors, consider the availability of a toll-free (800) number (see Table 10.2). Four in ten (41.4%) baby boomers consider price, compared with one in four (25.8%) older adults. Convenience, in comparison to other ways of buying the same product/service, is twice more important to baby boomers than to seniors, with 32.4 percent and 15.6 percent, respectively, indicating the importance of this factor. Similarly, twice as many boomers consider cancellation and refund policy when they decide whether to buy insurance policies direct (35.9% vs. 19.2%). Three in ten (30.2%) of the former group, compared with only

12.7 percent of the latter, are influenced by the availability of insurance products. Types of credit card accepted and free pick-up service (for forms) are not as important to seniors. One in four baby boomers (24.9%) and half as many seniors (13.7%) consider the number of days they must wait before they start receiving insurance coverage.

Differences among Older Adults

Older adults' perceptions of the importance of various reasons for buying insurance directly from the supplier differ by selected demographic and social factors. However, all eight factors do appear to be considered less with increasing age in late life.

Gerontographic groups also differ in the way they respond to a number of factors related to direct buying. Following are differences by each specific factor.

Toll-Free Number. The availability of a toll-free number is likely to be considered equally the same by all older adults age 55 and over, regardless of age. This element is more important to mature Americans who live with others than it is to their counterparts who live alone (23.0% vs. 15.9%). Finally, nearly half (48.3%) of frail recluses indicated they would consider the availability of a toll-free phone number, in comparison with 35.9 percent of healthy indulgers and 37.6 percent of healthy hermits.

Price. A larger percentage of older males is more likely than their female counterparts to consider price (38.9% vs. 27.8%) before buying direct. Mature Americans with higher household incomes are more likely than those with relatively lower incomes to place importance on price when considering direct purchasing. In the meantime, older people who live with others are more likely than those who live alone to consider this factor (36.2% vs. 23.9%). Price is considered to be an important factor by about one-third of older adults living in various parts of the country, except eastern states where a smaller percentage (23.6%) considers this factor. Finally, ailing outgoers and frail recluses pay more attention to price than healthy hermits and healthy indulgers.

Convenience. When considering buying direct, older men are more likely than their female counterparts to consider convenience (26.6% vs. 21.7%). The higher an older person's household income, the more likely he or she is to be concerned with this factor. In the meantime, convenience is more important to mature Americans who live with others than it is to those who live alone (26.6% vs. 16.9%). A larger percentage of northerners (24.4%) and southerners (26.9%) than easterners (17.8%) considers this element before deciding whether to buy direct.

Selection of Services. Selection of services is more important to mature males than it is to their female counterparts in deciding whether to buy direct (25.4% vs. 17.6%). Older people with higher income are more concerned with service selection than are their lower-income counterparts. Just over one-fourth of southerners—26.6 percent—are concerned with this factor, compared to 21.5 percent of northerners and 12.9 percent of easterners.

Pick-Up Service. The higher an older person's annual household income, the more likely he or she is to place importance on free pick-up for policies and claims when contemplating direct purchasing.

Cancellation and Refund Policies. With increasing education older adults are less likely to consider cancellation and refund policies of insurance companies, suggesting that this factor is more important among the lower than the higher educated. These policies are more important to mature Americans who live with others than they are to those who live alone (28.5% vs. 18.7%). Finally, ailing outgoers are more likely than the remaining gerontographic groups to consider cancellation and refund policies.

Waiting Period. Older people who live with others are more likely than those who live alone to emphasize waiting periods when making a decision about buying direct (20.4% vs. 13.1%). Older adults who live in rural areas are more concerned with waiting time than older adults who live in urban areas, with 22.6 percent and 17.1 percent, respectively, expressing such a concern.

Credit Card Acceptance. Ailing outgoers are twice as likely as frail recluses (12.4% vs. 6.4%) to consider the type(s) of credit card(s) accepted.

MEDIA USE PROFILES OF THOSE LIKELY TO BUY LTC INSURANCE

Older adults who indicated willingness to buy long-term care insurance for themselves, to cover nine areas they might need assistance with, were profiled using media consumption habits. Specifically, those who indicated willingness to pay for each benefit were analyzed by seven types of media and several specific and general types of magazines.

Types of Media Used

Older adults who indicated it would be worth paying for long-term care insurance that would give one the *freedom to choose the place and type of care* appear to have a unique mass media use profile. In relation to those who are unwilling to pay, a larger percentage of those who would pay watches premium TV cable channels at least once a week, with 37.3 percent and 29.3 percent, respectively, indicating cable viewing habits. A larger percentage of older Americans who are willing to pay for LTC insurance, in comparison to those who are not (63.7% vs. 58.7%), listens to the radio every day. Six in ten (60.7%) of those who indicate they would pay to have freedom to choose the place and type of care, in comparison with about half (50.6%) of those who did not think it is worth paying for this future benefit, watch TV adventure and drama shows several times a week. Similarly, a larger percentage of the former group (34.8%), in comparison to those unwilling to pay for this type of long-term care insurance benefit (24.3%) indicated they use a VCR to record or play movies at least once a week.

Premium TV cable channels are also watched more frequently by those who think it is worth paying for coverage concerning *housekeeping and chores*, with 39.6 percent of them viewing, in comparison with 33.9 percent of those who do not find this type of coverage worth paying for. The former group is also more likely than the latter to listen to the radio on a daily basis (66.0% vs. 61.0%), and more likely to watch TV adventure and drama shows several times a week (62.5% vs. 56.5%).

Older adults who are willing to buy long-term care insurance for *home-health and personal-care* coverage are more likely to watch TV comedy and variety shows several times a week, with 59.5 percent, in comparison with 54.0 percent, of those who watch these programs, reporting willingness to pay for such a coverage. The same pattern also exists with respect to preference for TV adventure and drama shows (61.4% vs. 54.5%).

A larger percentage (39.4%) of older Americans who feel it is worth paying for insurance to cover *companion or monitoring services* watches premium TV cable channels at least once a week, in comparison to those unwilling to pay (34.8%). Similarly, those interested in paying for coverage are more likely than those who do not to watch TV comedy and variety shows several times a week, with 60.6 percent and 56.7 percent, respectively, indicating viewership. Viewership of TV adventure and drama shows was also higher among those in the former group (66.0% vs. 56.2%).

The media use habits of older adults willing to pay for long-term care insurance to receive *nutrition and preventive health-care* information differ from those unwilling to pay for such programs. A larger percentage of the former group watches premium TV cable channels (40.8% vs. 33.3%), TV comedy and variety shows (63.1% vs. 54.6%), TV adventure and drama shows (66.1% vs. 77.3%), TV news and documentaries (82.5% vs. 77.3%), and uses a VCR to record or play movies at least once a week (36.2% vs. 31.8%).

With respect to willingness to pay for long-term care insurance to cover *legal and tax advice* older people might need in the future, mature Americans who think it is worth paying for such a coverage also have heavier media use habits than those who do not. Specifically, a larger percentage of the former group, in comparison to the latter, watches premium TV cable channels (41.2% vs. 31.9%), TV comedy and variety shows several times a week (62.4% vs. 54.2%), TV adventure and drama shows (65.0% vs. 54.6%), and TV news and documentaries (82.2% vs. 76.9%). They are also more likely to use a VCR to record or play movies once or more a week (46.9% vs. 42.2%).

Older Americans who think it is worth paying for insurance that covers *adult day care* watch TV comedy and variety shows more frequently, with 63.1 percent of them reporting viewership, in comparison with 55.6 percent of those who do not feel it is worth paying for this type of coverage. Also a larger percentage (66.2%) of the first group (in comparison with 56.4% of the latter group) watches TV adventure and drama shows several times a week. Those willing to pay for *transportation or escort services* also watch more TV comedy and variety shows (63.6% vs. 55.1%) and TV adventure and drama shows (67.4% vs. 55.5%).

Paying for long-term care insurance to cover future assistance with *money management and bill payment* is more appealing to older adults who are heavy users of television. A larger percentage (43.7%) of the older Americans who are of the opinion it is worth paying for covering these services, in comparison to those who are not willing to pay (33.7%), watches TV premium channels once or more a week; a larger percentage of them watches TV comedy and variety shows (63.8% vs. 56.1%), TV adventure and drama shows (68.0% vs. 56.7%), and TV news and documentaries (84.6% vs. 77.7%); and they are more likely than those not willing to pay (for covering money management and bill payment) to use a VCR to record or play movies once or more a week (38.4% vs. 31.9%).

Magazine Readership. Responses given to the nine types of long-term care insurance coverage were analyzed by specific and general types of magazines respondents indicated they read on a regular basis. The purpose of this analysis was to develop a profile of older Americans willing to pay to cover themselves for each specific service. Based on this analysis a profile of those who feel it is worth paying for each of nine services (vs. those who do not) can be developed for each type of coverage, based on statistically significant differences in magazine readership.

The following are magazine readership profiles of those who think it is worth paying now to cover specific services or benefits they might use in the future versus those who do not:

Freedom to Choose Place and Type of Care

- *Family Circle* (11.8% vs. 7.6%)
- *Good Housekeeping* (13.2% vs. 9.7%)
- *Reader's Digest* (6.6% vs. 3.6%)
- Sports/athletics (spectator) magazines (40.0% vs. 1.4%)

Housekeeping and Chores

- *Good Housekeeping* (11.8% vs. 7.6%)
- *Modern Maturity* (13.2% vs. 9.7%)
- *People* (6.6% vs. 3.6%)
- *Reader's Digest* (39.9% vs. 32.4%)
- Health/nutrition magazines (6.6% vs. 3.8%)
- General interest magazines (for women) (12.7% vs. 8.1%)
- Religious magazines (6.5% vs. 3.1%)

Home-Health Care and Personal Care

- *Reader's Digest* (37.3% vs. 31.0%)
- Homes/decorating magazines (11.2% vs. 7.0%)

Companion or Monitoring Services

- *McCall's* (7.9% vs. 3.4%)

Nutrition and Preventive Health-Care Programs

- *Better Homes and Gardens* (11.3% vs. 8.0%)
- *Ladies' Home Journal* (7.7% vs. 4.5%)
- *McCall's* (6.7% vs. 3.7%)
- *Modern Maturity* (13.4% vs. 9.5%)
- *People* (6.8% vs. 3.5%)
- *Reader's Digest* (41.2% vs. 31.9%)
- *Woman's Day* (4.3% vs. 2.3%)

Legal and Tax Services

- *Family Circle* (7.4% vs. 3.4%)
- *People* (6.6% vs. 3.3%)
- Other magazines for the aged (9.3% vs. 6.5%)
- General interest magazines (18.5% vs. 14.9%)

Adult Day Care

- Homes/decorating magazines (12.5% vs. 8.9%)
- Wildlife/nature/outdoors magazines (6.6% vs. 3.5%)

Transportation or Escort Services

- *Family Circle* (7.3% vs. 4.4%)
- *Good Housekeeping* (12.5% vs. 7.8%)
- *People* (6.7% vs. 3.9%)
- *Reader's Digest* (39.9% vs. 33.4%)

Money Management and Bill Payment

- *Family Circle* (7.4% vs. 4.7%)
- *People* (8.7% vs. 3.6%)
- *Woman's Day* (6.1% vs. 2.1%)
- Health/nutrition magazines (7.9% vs. 4.0%)

11

Summary and Implications for Marketing Strategy

The research presented in this section shows major differences in the way older consumers respond to various marketing offerings. The responses of older Americans do not only differ from those of their younger counterparts; they also vary widely by demographic and psychographic characteristics. Furthermore, in examining variations in such responses across mature consumers by selected characteristics, it was noted that the person's gerontographic profile *in general* was a better predictor of his or her responses to marketing offerings than other demographic factors. Therefore, the following recommendations for strategy development focus on specific gerontographic profiles rather than on other demographic characteristics; implications for target marketing are suggested to the extent consumers in a given gerontographic group represent a viable segment for the marketer's offerings. However, other characteristics such as age and income can be used to develop marketing strategies for specific demographic groups.

FOOD AND BEVERAGES, FOOD STORES, AND RESTAURANTS

The results of the two studies presented have implications for manufacturers of food products and beverages, food stores, and restaurants. These implications can be outlined in the context of a strategic marketing framework, which includes market segmentation, product or store positioning, and marketing mix decisions.

Food and beverage manufacturers should consider two viable segments of the mature market: healthy indulgers and ailing outgoers. In positioning food and beverages for healthy hermits, emphasis should be placed on the product's nutritional value and its aroma. Special promotions involving price reductions and advertising that stimulate word-of-mouth communication should be used for healthy indulgers. Ailing outgoers, on the other hand, are more demanding. Specifically, food manufacturers should position products for this segment based on taste. Products should be developed to appeal to their physical or health requirements such as developing packaging and containers which are easy to open, with clear labeling and instructions. Pricing strategies should include rebate programs whenever possible, and couponing should be part of the marketer's sales promotion strategy. When advertising is used, older adults should be properly stereotyped, and group conformity in product or brand use should be emphasized. Finally, food manufacturers who target this segment should benefit if they allocate funds to programs that would educate retail personnel about their products. Such information is likely to be communicated from sales clerks to ailing outgoers, who are sensitive to product ingredients.

Food stores serve all older customers, but ailing outgoers is the group most responsive to various offerings of food stores and supermarkets. In order to win the loyalty of this important segment, food stores and supermarkets should carry well-known brands and products, and items suitable to the older person's health needs (e.g., low sodium, low fat). Food stores should use frequent price-reduction promotions, and offer these older customers several options of paying for their groceries (check, credit) by accepting more credit cards and making it easier for an older person to pay by check. Using senior discounts and making sales clerks aware of older people's special needs should result in more sales to ailing outgoers. Because of their physical or health requirements and needs, food stores should pay particular attention to location and layout. These retail facilities should be located near other retail facilities older consumers tend to patronize (e.g., pharmacies, drug stores, cleaners). Store layout and environment in general should be designed to offer comfort, convenience, and opportunities for socialization among older shoppers. Food stores should use directional signs to help these shoppers locate items, and should have an adequate number of check-out registers so that the standing and waiting time is short.

APPAREL AND FOOTWEAR

There appear to be two viable gerontographic segments for apparel and footwear products: healthy indulgers and ailing outgoers. Each of these groups is likely to respond differently to marketing strategies of manufacturers and retailers. In buying apparel and footwear, healthy indulgers are sensitive to social norms and opinions held by their peers, so these products should be positioned on social acceptance in order to appeal to this group. In targeting healthy indulgers, marketing mix decisions should focus on the channel of distribution. Specifically, healthy indulgers place a great deal of emphasis on product assortment and, as a result, they do not perceive mail order to be a viable channel (due to limited assortment), preferring to purchase apparel and footwear products from retail outlets. Department stores should be used as distribution channels. These stores could attract healthy indulgers by carrying well-known brand names of apparel and footwear products; they should offer special-assistance services (e.g., alterations), and offer assistance in locating merchandise suitable to the older person's needs. The data presented in the previous section also suggest that advertising to healthy indulgers should be done through television and radio. The major themes of these ads should be emphasis on brand names and group conformity or acceptance.

Targeting ailing outgoers requires a somewhat different marketing strategy. First, product positioning for this group should focus on product functionality or performance and social acceptance. Second, product design should focus on attributes which are likely to meet this groups physical needs, such as sizes that fit and special features (e.g., velcro fasteners instead of zippers, straps instead of shoe laces). Third, pricing strategies should include several discount programs such as senior discounts, "sales," rebates, and coupons. Fourth, promotion should include direct mail; and informal fashion shows could be used to inform ailing outgoers about new apparel products. Advertising appeals should emphasize group conformity and social acceptance. Finally, distribution strategies are likely to vary in effectiveness, depending on whether ailing outgoers buy apparel and footwear products from a store or through mail order catalogs. Retail outlets, especially department stores, distributing apparel and footwear products should emphasize the following: ease of finding merchandise suitable to one's needs, "special" sales, special-assistance services (e.g., alterations), wide assortments consisting of well-known brands, social acceptance (popular or prestigious outlets), and convenience in doing business with the retailer (e.g., hassle-free returns). Direct marketers of apparel and footwear products, on the other hand, should emphasize brand names, selection (variety of sizes, style, features, etc.), prompt delivery, and free pick-up service for returns.

PHARMACEUTICAL PRODUCTS

Ailing outgoers are by far the segment that uses the largest number of prescription drugs and personal-care products. Therefore, strategies of pharmaceutical manufacturers and retailers should focus mainly on this relatively large segment of the mature consumer market. First, with respect to product positioning, pharmaceutical products can be positioned on several domains, since ailing outgoers are likely to perceive a variety of reasons to be relevant to the purchase and consumption of these products. Some of the main domains or themes suggested by our studies include: ease of product use, including ease of reading information on labels and brochures; special "deals" such as sales, coupons, and rebates; and social acceptance/approval of those who use the product or brand.

In order to effectively reach ailing outgoers the marketing mix should be designed in a way that contains the elements or stimuli this group is most likely to find attractive. Specifically, in developing product strategy, emphasis should be placed on easy-to-use features (e.g., easy-to-open packages, easy-to-read and understand information/directions). Because ailing outgoers use a wide variety of pharmaceutical products, these consumers are likely to demand wide product assortments. In pricing pharmaceutical products likely to be demanded by ailing outgoers, marketers and retailers should use a variety of price-saving incentives such as rebates and coupons. Ailing outgoers are also receptive to a wide variety of promotional tools available to marketers. Emphasis should be placed on advertising, but ads should properly depict older users of pharmaceutical products. Some promotional expenditures should be used to educate pharmacists and sales representatives of personal-care products. Finally, ailing outgoers are receptive to a variety of distribution methods. Drug stores and pharmacies should carry well-known brands of pharmaceutical products; they should use price-saving incentives such as special "sales" and senior discounts. Pharmacists should be located in convenient areas for easy access; and pharmacists and their salespeople should be sensitized to the needs of the older consumer. Finally, direct marketers of pharmaceutical products should implement several marketing tactics: accept several types of credit cards, emphasize prompt product delivery, convenience and savings by ordering direct; they should try to reduce purchase risk by offering reasonable order-cancellation and return policies, provide free pick-up service for returns, and make an 800 (toll-free) number available to their customers.

HOUSING

The research findings suggest four different sets of strategies for marketing housing, each focusing on specific types of housing: single-family houses; apartments, townhomes or condominiums; retirement communities; and nursing homes.

The best market for *single-family houses* appears to be the frail recluses. Older adults in this segment are not only more likely than people in other segments to occupy a single-family house, but also plan to live in such a house (most likely in the same house) in the foreseeable future. Single-family houses marketed to this segment should be positioned on the basis of their accessibility to medical, personal- and home-care services. While our studies do not provide information on every variable of the marketing mix or this market's receptivity to home-modification services, they do suggest important implications for builders who wish to appeal to frail recluses: locate single-family housing projects near hospitals and medical centers; promote accessibility of the housing project to personal- health- and home-care services; offer as part of the association fee, or on an "a la carte" basis, several types of personal- and home-care services that promote independent living; and emphasize personal selling.

Healthy indulgers appear to be the most viable market segment for *apartments, townhouses*, or *condominiums*. These housing projects should be positioned to healthy indulgers on the basis of their locational convenience and security. Developers of apartments, townhouses, or condominiums should build such projects near shopping centers. These structures should include home-security systems, and offer access to home-care services either as part of the association fee or on an "a la cart" basis. Promotion of these housing projects should emphasize proximity to various types of retail facilities and services, access to various types of personal- and home-care services, and security. Personal selling should be included in the developer's marketing mix.

The most viable segment of the market for *retirement communities* is ailing outgoers. In order to appeal to ailing outgoers marketers should position retirement communities as facilities that promote independence and as viable housing alternatives to increasing costs of maintaining a single-family house. Developers of retirement communities should build such facilities at places that have access to public transportation, and personal- and home-care services. They should promote both accessibility to such services as well as personal and home security. Ailing outgoers find seminars very useful channels for receiving information about various housing options.

Two viable segments for *nursing homes* were identified: ailing outgoers and healthy indulgers. There appears to be no rationale for developing a different strategy for marketing nursing homes to ailing outgoers, since they were found to respond to various housing attributes the same way as other gerontographic groups. In order to appeal to healthy indulgers, nursing homes should position themselves as facilities that provide continuous health-care services, as an alternative to a hospital. When designing nursing homes and amenities to appeal to healthy indulgers, emphasis should be placed on the availability of (accessibility to) health-care services, and to a lesser extent upon the provision of planned social activities. The marketing mix should also include personal selling.

TECHNOLOGY PRODUCTS AND
TELECOMMUNICATION SERVICES

The viable segments for high-tech products and telecommunication services are different for different types of products and services. Healthy indulgers are a viable segment for home-security systems, telephone answering machines, appliances, automobiles, and telecommunication services ranging from operator-assisted to discount "package" long-distance plans. Frail recluses are a good market for home-security services, energy-saving appliances or installed devices, and telecommunication services. Ailing outgoers are also a good market for telecommunication services.

Marketers who wish to target the healthy indulgers and ailing outgoers should promote new products and services through organized groups when possible. Direct channels of distribution should also be used, and the convenience in buying direct should be emphasized. Senior or member discounts should be offered to ailing outgoers. To effectively reach frail recluses, marketers should advertise on TV and print media. Personal selling and senior discounts should be part of the firm's promotional mix. Marketers of high-tech products should make multiple payment systems available to them; and when marketing electronic products direct, marketers should emphasize not only acceptance of a variety of credit cards but also make a toll-free number available to prospective buyers.

HEALTH CARE

Because health-care products and services can be of various types relating to preventive, acute, and long-term care, these offerings are of appeal to different gerontographic groups. Ailing outgoers appear to be the group most likely to be the heaviest users of health-care products and services. They are more likely than the average mature person to use description drugs, dietary meals, and health clubs; and they prefer using health-membership programs. Frail recluses, on the other hand, prefer to use exercise equipment at home (rather than going to the health club). They are also heavy users of self-diagnostic equipment at home. Frail recluses are positively oriented toward health-membership programs, and they are the heaviest potential users of home-health care services. Finally, healthy indulgers prefer to receive paid at-home assistance with their chores, and they are likely to have a health-club membership.

Because many health-care products related to acute care and long-term care are addressed under other topics (e.g., housing and long-term care, food), the focus of this research was on health-care services provided by hospitals and surgeons (i.e., "acute health care"). Specifically, health-care professionals and hospitals who wish to attract ailing outgoers should position their services on "reasonable prices/fees." Senior discounts and membership programs are effective sales promotion tools for reaching ailing outgoers. When advertising is used, age-stereotypes should be avoided. Direct mail and telephone or personal contact are preferred to other forms of communication. Finally, because ailing outgoers prefer personal attention, health-care professionals should enhance their direct contact systems for appointments, feedback, and health-monitoring services.

When marketing to healthy indulgers, health-care professionals and hospitals should position their services on reputation. Use of TV or print ads and testimonials seem to work well with this segment. Because healthy indulgers are not very price sensitive, prices and fees should be set to reflect the value of health-care services. Finally, this group is attracted to special assortments of health-care services offered, so hospitals should promote "packages" of services that one can receive when visiting health-care providers.

Finally, health-care providers targeting frail recluses should position their services on "convenience"; they should offer locational convenience (e.g., health clinics, accessibility to hospitals). In order to appeal to frail recluses, group-membership programs should be used and advertising should avoid age-stereotyping. In communicating with this group, emphasis should be placed on direct mail. Finally, several methods of payment for services should be made available to this segment.

TRAVEL AND LEISURE

The research presented suggested two viable segments for travel and leisure services: healthy indulgers are a viable segment for airlines and cruise lines, while ailing outgoers are a prime segment for hospitality services. When targeting healthy indulgers, airlines and cruise lines should position themselves on price and convenience. Their product lines should include a wide range of travel-related services. Pricing strategies should include special price offerings to groups through membership programs. Senior discounts should be included in the marketer's promotional mix, as well as advertising that uses testimonials and properly stereotypes older people. Finally, direct marketing channels (phone or mail) should be used as ways of enabling the older person to purchase travel-related services.

On the other hand, hotel and motel marketers should target ailing outgoers, positioning their facilities on "value." These service providers should try to develop alliances with other providers of travel and leisure services to enhance the assortment of their offerings. Special prices should be offered to membership groups, and senior discounts should be included in the promotional mix of these service providers. Advertisements (when used) should properly stereotype older customers. Staff should be trained to assist older guests with filling out registration and other forms. Hoteliers should adopt "no-hassle" check-approval policies, and they should sponsor seminars where they will have opportunities to promote their offerings. Finally, hotels and motels should develop clientele mailing lists for promotions, and train representatives to effectively deal with customers over the phone.

FINANCIAL SERVICES

Although older adults in different gerontographic groups have different preferences for financial services, they are not necessarily equally viable for the various types of financial-service providers. Thus, a group may prefer to receive certain types of financial services only from a selected group of financial-service providers. Thus, the findings suggest not only general implications for financial-service providers, but also institution-specific marketing strategies—that is, the types of services on which various institutions should focus when trying to reach older customers in the four groups.

For *commercial banks*, frail recluses appear to be the viable segment for financial services, including financial planning, money market funds, stocks, bonds, treasury bills, CDs, insurance policies, savings and checking accounts, asset-management services, and tax advice. Ailing outgoers also prefer commercial banks for money market funds, stocks, insurance policies, and tax advice, while healthy indulgers are a primary market for financial-planning services. Frail recluses are also the primary segment of interest to *credit unions*, with consumers in this segment likely to prefer these institutions for financial-planning services, savings and checking accounts, CDs, IRA/Keogh plans, tax advice, and insurance policies. When ailing outgoers consider patronizing credit unions, chances are they will prefer receiving financial-planning services, while healthy indulgers are likely to prefer having savings and checking accounts at these institutions rather than receiving other types of services.

Savings and loan associations (S&Ls) appear to have multiple-target clientele. Frail recluses are more likely to patronize these institutions than the average mature consumer for financial planning, money market funds, U.S. government bonds and treasury bills, IRA/Keogh investments, and insurance policies. Healthy indulgers are good prospects for CDs and stocks, while ailing outgoers are attracted to S&Ls for financial-planning services, U.S. government bonds and treasury bills.

Healthy hermits are the primary market for *brokerage companies*. These individuals prefer receiving a number of financial products from these institutions, including money market funds, government bonds and treasury bills, IRA/Keogh investments, stocks, tax advice, insurance policies, and asset-management services. Ailing outgoers would patronize brokerage companies for savings and checking accounts, IRA/Keogh plans, CDs, and tax advice. Finally, healthy indulgers will patronize these service providers for IRAs/Keoghs, stocks, and tax advice. *Mutual fund companies* also have multiple targets for their services. Healthy hermits prefer buying money market funds, stocks, and IRA/Keogh services, while healthy indulgers would patronize these service providers for IRA/Keogh accounts, government bonds and treasury bills, and asset-management services. Finally, frail recluses are a viable segment for government bonds and treasury bills.

AARP is also preferred by older adults in various gerontographic groups, especially frail recluses. Frail recluses prefer receiving a variety of financial products and services through AARP, including money market funds, government bonds and treasury bills, CDs, IRA/Keogh accounts, and tax advice. Ailing outgoers would prefer receiving through AARP government bonds and treasury bills, financial-planning services, and tax advice. Finally, healthy indulgers would prefer to go to AARP for government bonds and treasury bills and for tax advice. Healthy hermits do not prefer receiving any service from AARP.

These differences in preferences for institutions regarding specific financial services notwithstanding, two groups appear to be the most viable segments for a wide variety of financial services: healthy indulgers and frail recluses. Financial-service providers who are likely to be patronized by healthy indulgers should position their services on the basis of convenience and personal relationship. Long-term investments should be positioned as vehicles that would enable customers in this segment to pay for post-retirement expenses such as home improvements. Besides the specific types of services healthy indulgers prefer receiving from different types of institutions, this group of people is most receptive to financial advice (for a fee) and would respond to free financial services for keeping large balances; they prefer doing business with a financial-service provider who can offer them overdraft protection or personal line of credit, as well as a wide variety of moderate- and low-risk investments. Financial institutions can effectively reach healthy indulgers through personal selling, either person-to-person (e.g., private banking) or over the phone (telemarketing). The sales representatives should be knowledgeable to answer a wide variety of questions these customers might have. Convenience should be a main theme of advertisements.

Frail recluses appear to be the next best market for financial services. They would open an IRA/Keogh account at any financial institution. This group also values overdraft privilege or personal line of credit, and is particularly interested in reverse-mortgage plans. Frail recluses are receptive to senior discounts and welcome assistance from bank personnel, who should offer to help them fill out forms and help them understand the various types of financial services.

INSURANCE

Three gerontographic segments are viable for insurance services, depending on the type of insurance. Healthy indulgers are a viable segment for long-term care and car insurance; ailing outgoers are a good market for long-term care, "medigap," and home-health care insurance; and frail recluses prefer long-term care insurance. Ailing outgoers appear to be the most viable gerontographic group; they are those most sensitive to various offerings of insurance-service providers. "Convenience" is one important dimension on which insurance companies can effectively position their services. In developing products for ailing outgoers, companies should develop a wide variety of offerings ranging from insurance policies to investment instruments. Insurance companies could provide assistance with filling out forms as a complimentary service, offer liberal cancellation and refund policies and make policy coverage effective as quickly as possible. In developing long-term care policies, the following benefits should be included in order to effectively appeal to ailing outgoers: home care and personal care; companion or monitoring services; nutrition and preventive health-care programs; legal and tax advice; adult day care, transportation and escort services; and money management and bill payment services.

Pricing or insurance products should be competitive for comparable policies, and a wide variety of payment systems or plans should be made available. Special discounts should be offered to those who belong to certain groups (e.g., AARP) or are members of special promotional programs. This can be facilitated by developing partnerships with nontraditional service providers such as brokerage firms. Finally, in order to effectively promote insurance products to ailing outgoers, companies should sponsor events where there is opportunity to explain products to groups of potential customers. Incentives should be offered to the sales force for cross-selling related products, as well as to existing customers and other institutions selling related products (e.g., banks and brokerage firms) to recommend the company's products to prospective customers. Senior discounts should also be used, and efficient telemarketing systems should be developed. Finally, convenience in dealing with the service provider directly should be emphasized in ads and sales presentations.

Selected Bibliography

Bartos, Rena. (1980). "Over 49: The Invisible Consumer Market." *Harvard Business Review*, Vol. 58 (January–February): 140–148.

Dychtwald, Ken, and Joe Flower. (1989). *Age Wave*. Englewood Cliffs, NJ: Jeremy P. Tarcher.

Menchin, Robert S. (1991). *The Mature Market: A Gold Mine of Ideas for Tapping the 50+ Market*. Chicago: Probus Publishing Co.

Moschis, George P. (1996). *Gerontographics*. Westport, CT: Quorum Books.

Moschis, George P. (1994). *Marketing Strategies for the Mature Market*. Westport, CT: Quorum Books.

Moschis, George P. (1993). "How They Are Acting Their Age." *Marketing Management*, Vol. 2, No. 2: 39–50.

Moschis, George P. (1992). *Marketing to Older Consumers*. Westport, CT: Quorum Books.

Moschis, George P. (1991). "Marketing to Older Adults." *Journal of Consumer Marketing*, Vol. 8, No. 4 (Fall): 33–41.

Moschis, George P. (1987). *Consumer Socialization: A Life-Cycle Perspective*. Boston: Lexington Books.

Novak, Thomas P., and Bruce MacEvoy. (1990). "On Comparing Alternative Segmentation Schemes: The List of Values (LOV) and Values and Lifestyles (VALS)." *Journal of Consumer Research*, Vol. 7 (June): 105–109.

Ostroff, Jeff. (1989). *Successful Marketing to the 50+ Consumer*. New York: Prentice-Hall.

Schewe, Charles, and Anne L. Balazs. (1992). "Role Transitions in Older Adults." *Psychology and Marketing*, Vol. 9 (March–April): 85–99.

Wolfe, David B. (1990). *"Serving the Ageless Market": Strategies for Selling to the Fifty-Plus Market*. New York: McGraw-Hill.

Index

About the Authors

GEORGE P. MOSCHIS is Professor of Marketing and Director of the Center for Mature Consumer Studies at Georgia State University, Atlanta. Also a member of the university's gerontology program, he has consulted for leading corporations and government agencies worldwide and lectures frequently. Among his many publications are three books published by Quorum: *Marketing to Older Consumers* (1992), *Marketing Strategies for the Mature Market* (1994), and *Gerontographics* (1996).

EUEHUN LEE is Assistant Professor of Marketing at Sejong University in Seoul, Korea. He is an affiliate member of the Center for Mature Consumer Studies at Georgia State University. Dr. Lee has worked as a consultant and as a marketing researcher for several firms and government agencies in Korea and the United States. His research interests include the effects of life events on consumer behaviors over one's life span.

ANIL MATHUR is Associate Dean for Faculty Development and Associate Professor of Marketing at the Frank G. Zarb School of Business, Hofstra University. He has published over 30 articles in journals and conference proceedings. His research interest is in the areas of consumer behavior, services marketing, marketing research, and research methodology. Dr. Mathur has consulted with numerous corporations on a multitude of marketing problems.

JENNIFER STRAUTMAN is an Atlanta-based freelance writer and editor. She earned her Master of Science degree in marketing from Georgia State University. Earlier in her career, she worked for the Associated Press as a newswriter and for the State Taxation Institute in Atlanta as a reporter for several publications for attorneys, CPAs, and other professionals in the tax arena. Most recently, Ms. Strautman worked in public affairs and communications as an associate with an Atlanta consulting firm.

ISBN 1-56720-344-2

EAN

9 781567 203448

90000>

HARDCOVER BAR CODE